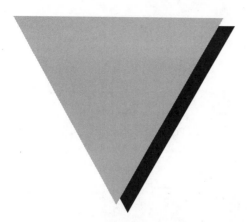

Transcultural Children's Literature

Linda Pratt
Elmira College

Janice J. Beaty
Professor Emerita
Elmira College

Merrill,
an imprint of Prentice Hall
Upper Saddle River, New Jersey   Columbus, Ohio

Library of Congress Cataloging-in-Publication Data

Pratt, Linda
    Transcultural children's literature/Linda Pratt, Janice J. Beaty.
        p.   cm.
    Includes bibliographical references and index.
    ISBN 0-13-432816-7
    1. Children's literature—History and criticism. 2. Foreign countries in literature.
I. Beaty, Janice J. II. Title.
    PN1009.5.F68P73   1999
    809'.89282—dc21

98-27483
CIP

Cover art: © Nenad Jakesevic
Editor: Bradley J. Potthoff
Production Editor: Mary M. Irvin
Design Coordinator: Diane C. Lorenzo
Text Designer: Pagination
Cover Designer: Ceri Fitzgerald
Production Manager: Pamela D. Bennett
Electronic Text Management: Marilyn Wilson Phelps, Karen L. Bretz, Tracey Ward
Director of Marketing: Kevin Flanagan
Marketing Coordinator: Krista Groshong
Marketing Manager: Suzanne Stanton

This book was set in Novarese by Prentice Hall Publishing Co., and was printed and bound by R. R. Donnelley & Sons Company. The cover was printed by Phoenix Color Corp.

© 1999 by Prentice-Hall, Inc.
Simon & Schuster/A Viacom Company
Upper Saddle River, New Jersey 07458

Photo Credits: All photos by Janice J. Beaty

Printed in the United States of America

10 9 8 7 6 5 4 3 2 1

ISBN: 0-13-432816-7

Prentice-Hall International (UK) Limited, *London*
Prentice-Hall of Australia Pty. Limited, *Sydney*
Prentice-Hall of Canada, Inc., *Toronto*
Prentice-Hall Hispanoamericana, S. A., *Mexico*
Prentice-Hall of India Private Limited, *New Delhi*
Prentice-Hall of Japan, Inc., *Tokyo*
Simon & Schuster Asia Pte. Ltd., *Singapore*
Editora Prentice-Hall do Brasil, Ltda., *Rio de Janeiro*

*To all children
who are the heart and soul of our world*

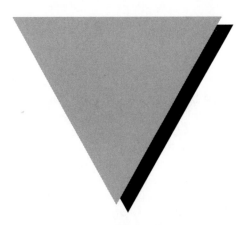

Preface

In *Transcultural Children's Literature*, we survey a world of picture books that beckons children to begin personal odysseys of learning about different cultures and peoples. Extending the foundation built by multicultural children's literature, transcultural children's literature embraces books about peoples, cultures, and geographic regions outside the country in which the reader lives. Preschool, kindergarten, elementary, and prospective teachers will discover that transcultural children's books provide countless interesting places for children to visit and things for children to see. Reading these books will encourage and help children broaden and deepen their understanding and appreciation of peoples, cultures, and places outside the United States.

We develop and present a rationale for, and theoretical basis of, transcultural children's literature in the introductory chapter. This first chapter also describes the relationships between multicultural education, book bonding, and scaffolding and the experiences children have reading transcultural books. In addition, we propose a cultural paradigm for assessing and comparing transcultural children's books in terms of their geographic, social, economic, and political elements. Finally, we include guidelines and criteria to help teachers in selecting transcultural books that provide children with itineraries of exploration rather than mere "sightseeing."

In each of the next nine chapters, we focus on children's books set in specific countries throughout the world's major geographic regions. We include a summary of each book and suggest classroom activities that reinforce key aspects of that book or that help students relate to another place, culture, or people. In the final chapter, we identify potential areas of research and pose specific questions intended to stimulate further study of transcultural children's literature and its use in the classroom. The appendices provide lists of topics from reviewed books, supplemental media resources, and book publishers to assist teachers in designing their own activities or in integrating transcultural children's books with science, geography, social studies, and other content areas.

As the world changes and draws us ever closer to one another, we envision transcultural children's literature enabling children to embark on around-the-world odysseys toward global citizenship.

ACKNOWLEDGMENTS

Creating *Transcultural Children's Literature* was like building another world—a world founded on the support and encouragement of others. To everyone involved, we extend our sincerest appreciation. In particular, we owe a special thanks to Ms. Linda Scharp McElhiney from Prentice Hall for supporting the idea of the text; Dr. Thomas K. Meier, President of Elmira College, and Dr. Bryan D. Reddick, Academic Vice President, for their ongoing support; Dr. J. Michael Pratt, Assistant Professor of Computer Information Systems, for his technical assistance; Dr. Mark J. Tierno, Academic Dean at the University of Wisconsin, for his contribution to the cultural paradigm in Chapter 1; Ms. Joanna Wheatly, Ms. Rebecca Blunt, Ms. Angela Povoish, Mr. Joseph Fahs, Jr., and other Elmira College students for their research assistance; Ms. Kathleen Galvin and Ms. Elizabeth Walve, Elmira College librarians, for their reference work; Dr. Margaret C. Locke, Professor Emerita, for her continued words of encouragement; and to friends and family in the United States and the Bahamas for always being there.

We would also like to thank the reviewers of our manuscript for their comments and insights: John D. Beach, University of Nebraska at Omaha; Dana L. Fox, University of Arizona; Alis Headlam, College of St. Joseph; Kara Keeling, Christopher Newport University; Hollis Lowery-Moore, Sam Houston State University; Harold Nelson, Minot State University; Jeff Oliver, University of Colorado; Lynn S. Orlando, Holy Family College; and Richard A. White, Eastern Illinois University.

Our final expressions of appreciation go to our editor at Prentice Hall, Mr. Brad Potthoff, and to Ms. Mary Evangelista, editorial assistant; Ms. Mary Irvin, production editor; Ms. Linda Poderski, copy editor; and Ceri Fitzgerald, cover designer, for their assistance and ongoing support.

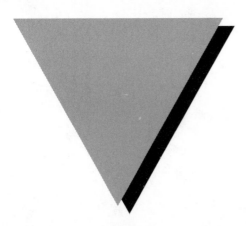

Contents

CHAPTER 1
**The Changing World of Children's Literature in a
Changing World   1**

Background of Transcultural Children's Literature   2
Definition of Transcultural Children's Literature   2
Multicultural Education   2
Multicultural Children's Literature   3
Transcultural Children's Literature   3
    Basic Beliefs   3
    Rationale   4
    Areas of Future Research   5
Connecting the World With Children's Literature   6
    A Cultural Paradigm: An Introduction   6
    Geography   7
    Economic System   8
    Social System   10
    Political System   11
Connecting Children's Literature to the World   12
    Selecting Transcultural Children's Literature   12
    Representative Transcultural Children's Literature From Cultural and Geographic
        Regions   16
Summary   17

CHAPTER 2
Children's Books About Africa   21

Examining the Cultural Region of Africa and the Patterns of Children's Books   22

Countries and Children's Books Reviewed   22
    Benin   22
    Cameroon   24
    Egypt   27
    Ethiopia   29
    Gambia   30
    Ghana   31
    Kenya   33
    Lesotho   36
    Madagascar   37
    Morocco   38
    Nigeria   39
    South Africa   43
    Sudan   49
    Tanzania   50
    Zimbabwe   51
    Africa: General   51
Summary   57

CHAPTER 3
Children's Books About Asia   63

Examining the Cultural Region of Asia and the Patterns of Children's Books   64
Countries and Children's Books Reviewed   64
    Cambodia   64
    China (People's Republic of)   65
    India   77
    Japan   84
    Korea   92
    Nepal   96
    Thailand   96
    Tibet   98
    Vietnam   100
Summary   102

CHAPTER 4
Children's Books About Canada   109

Examining the Cultural Region of Canada and the Patterns of Children's Books   110
Children's Books Reviewed   110
Summary   129

CHAPTER 5
Children's Books About the Caribbean   133

Examining the Cultural Region of the Caribbean and the Patterns of Children's
   Books   134
Countries and Children's Books Reviewed   134
     Antilles (Lesser)   134
     Bahamas   136
     Dominican Republic   137
     Haiti   138
     Jamaica   141
     Martinique   144
     Puerto Rico   146
     St. Lucia   152
     Trinidad and Tobago   153
     U.S. Virgin Islands   158
     Caribbean: General   159
Summary   162

CHAPTER 6
Children's Books About Central America, Mexico, and South America   167

Examining the Cultural Region of Central America, Mexico, and South America and the
   Patterns of Children's Books   168
Countries and Children's Books Reviewed   169
     Central America: El Salvador   169
     Central America: Guatemala   170
     Central America: Nicaragua   174
     Central America: Panama   176
     Mexico   178
     South America: Argentina   188
     South America: Bolivia   189
     South America: Brazil   190
     South America: Colombia   193
     South America: Peru   194
     South America: Venezuela   195
Summary   197

CHAPTER 7
Children's Books About Eastern Europe   201

Examining the Cultural Region of Eastern Europe and the Patterns of Children's
   Books   202

Countries and Children's Books Reviewed   202
    Czech Republic   202
    Poland   206
    Romania   208
    Russian Federation (formerly part of the Soviet Union)   213
    Ukraine   233
    Yugoslavia (former)   234
Summary   235

CHAPTER 8
Children's Books About Western Europe   241

Examining the Cultural Region of Western Europe and the Patterns of Children's
    Books   242
Countries and Children's Books Reviewed   242
    Austria   242
    Denmark   245
    England   246
    France   251
    Germany   256
    Greece   260
    Iceland   264
    Ireland   265
    Italy   268
    Netherlands   270
    Norway   271
    Spain   272
    Sweden   273
    Switzerland   274
Summary   275

CHAPTER 9
Children's Books About the Middle East   281

Examining the Cultural Region of the Middle East and the Patterns of Children's
    Books   282
Countries and Children's Books Reviewed   282
    Iran   282
    Iraq   287
    Israel   289
    Lebanon   292
    Saudi Arabia   293
    Syria   295

West Bank   298
Summary   300

CHAPTER 10
Children's Books About the Pacific, Australia, and Antarctica   305

Examining the Cultural Region of the Pacific, Australia, and Antarctica and the Patterns
of Children's Books   306
Countries and Children's Books Reviewed   307
Antarctica   307
Australia   309
Borneo   321
New Zealand   322
Philippines   324
Polynesian Islands   325
Summary   326

CHAPTER 11
Transcultural Children's Literature in the Changing Classroom   331

Conclusions About Transcultural Children's Literature   331
Distribution of Books Over Time   331
Distribution of Books by Grade Level   332
Numbers of Books About Specific Countries   333
Genres of Transcultural Books   335
Story Elements in Transcultural Books   335
Cultural Paradigms in Transcultural Books   337
General Conclusions   338
Assessing Children's Transcultural Awareness and Responses to Their Readings   338
Assessing Prior Knowledge   339
Assessing Awareness of a Cultural Region   339
Our World and Our Future   341

APPENDIX A: TOPICAL CHILDREN'S BOOK INDEX   343

APPENDIX B: VIDEO, CD-ROM, AUDIOBOOK, AND INTERNET RESOURCES   362

APPENDIX C: PUBLISHERS' ADDRESS LIST   374

APPENDIX D: ACTIVITIES FOR PRE-SERVICE AND IN-SERVICE EDUCATORS   377

AUTHOR/TITLE/ILLUSTRATOR INDEX   383

SUBJECT INDEX   389

1

The Changing World of Children's Literature in a Changing World

The nightly news, the Internet, and growing international travel are all constant reminders that the world is continuing to shrink. As it does so, the global community continues to expand. Implied by this growth is an emerging awareness that citizenship is extending beyond the traditional borders of individual countries to the global community. With this evolving notion of citizenship comes a changing view of education. Supporting children in this process of becoming global citizens is a distinct body of children's literature that draws on the many peoples and cultures around the world for inspiration and subject matter. We call this assemblage of children's picture story books **transcultural children's literature.**

What is the origin and meaning of transcultural children's literature? How is this body of children's literature related to multicultural education and multicultural children's literature? What beliefs and rationale underlie the pedagogical use of transcultural children's books with children in the classroom? What paradigm is available for characterizing and evaluating transcultural books? What guidelines are available for selecting transcultural children's literature? These questions and others have primarily shaped the view of transcultural children's literature that we present and explore in this book.

BACKGROUND OF TRANSCULTURAL CHILDREN'S LITERATURE

Our journey to a transcultural awareness began when we systematically perused children's books that we identified initially as multicultural. Although we had seen many of these books before individually, a pattern emerged when we compared them with each other. In particular, we noted that each book seemed to belong to one of two distinct categories: (a) those books that were geographically and culturally centered in the United States and (b) those that were not.

When attempting to discern what key factors distinguished the books in the first group from those in the second, we realized that the geographic region (e.g., country) and cultural milieu of the reader were crucial. Thus, a book about Native Americans read by a child whose home is in the United States we regarded as **multicultural,** whereas a book about China read by that same child we designated as **transcultural.** With this distinction in mind, we surveyed many hundreds more children's books to determine whether they also could be sorted into the two groups identified as either multicultural or transcultural. By the end of this process, we concluded that the distinction between multicultural and transcultural was real—a distinction that is relative to the reader's cultural and geographic "home."

DEFINITION OF TRANSCULTURAL CHILDREN'S LITERATURE

We define transcultural children's literature as *children's books that portray peoples, cultures, and geographic regions of the world that exist outside the reader's own country. Thus, which books are deemed to be transcultural is relative to the reader's own home culture and geographic region.*

MULTICULTURAL EDUCATION

Our view of transcultural children's literature can be further elucidated within the context of multicultural education and multicultural children's literature. To begin, our notion of multicultural education is essentially the same as that defined by Grant (1994):

> Multicultural education is a philosophical concept and an educational process. It is a concept built upon the philosophical ideals of freedom, justice, equality, equity, and human dignity that are contained in United States documents such as the Constitution and the Declaration of Independence. It recognizes, however, that equality and equity are not the same thing: equal access does not necessarily guarantee fairness. (p. 4)

Like Grant (1994) and Banks (1996), we consider multicultural education much more than an adjustment to the elementary school curriculum in the United States. Rather, multicultural education entails a major shift in how education is perceived and how it is practiced. Essential to successfully implementing a multicultural education curriculum is multicultural children's literature, which can act as a key change agent for translating multicultural educational ideals into pedagogy.

MULTICULTURAL CHILDREN'S LITERATURE

Although there is as yet no consensus about a single definition of multicultural children's literature (Harris, 1997), its potential as an agent of positive change is implied by its various definitions. Bishop (1997) states that "multicultural literature should include books that reflect the racial, ethnic, and social diversity that is characteristic of our pluralistic society and of the world" (p. 3). Although we agree with the portion of Bishop's definition that multicultural literature should "reflect the racial, ethnic, and social diversity that is characteristic of our pluralistic society," we apply the last phrase of her definition ("of the world") to our concept of transcultural children's literature. We do this primarily because we believe that children's books about peoples and cultures existing outside the reader's culture and geographic location constitute a body of children's literature different from multicultural children's literature.

This distinction between multicultural and transcultural children's literature notwithstanding, we strongly believe that if multicultural children's books "reflect the racial, ethnic, and social diversity" in the United States, then children who read such books have both the choice and the right to decide whether they will bond with those books and in what specific ways. For example, a child reading the book *Abuela* (Dorros, 1991) may choose to bond with the book by emulating Rosalba or by taking an imaginary trip to New York City with Rosalba's grandmother. Book bonding is fundamentally a personal process ultimately controlled by the child. But children will encounter meaningful book-bonding opportunities and choices only when the books they read, to quote Bishop (1997), "reflect the racial, ethnic, and social diversity . . . of our pluralistic society" (p. 3).

Linking our concept of book bonding with Grant's (1994) definition of multicultural education leads to a significant implication. Limiting book-bonding opportunities and decisions to monocultural literature (books about a perceived mainstream culture of a society) is counterproductive. More specifically, if educators fail to include multicultural literature in the elementary school curriculum, then children are apt to believe that the "philosophical ideals of freedom, justice, equality, equity, and human dignity" clearly apply to a particular segment of American society rather than to all citizens (Grant, 1994).

TRANSCULTURAL CHILDREN'S LITERATURE

Basic Beliefs

Although we agree that multicultural children's literature must remain the most significant component in the elementary school literacy curriculum, we also believe that transcultural children's literature should be a major complementing element. Underly-

ing transcultural children's literature is a set of basic beliefs concerning the pedagogical use of books about peoples and cultures outside the United States:

1. Transcultural children's literature can positively assist children in shaping their own beliefs about people from other cultural regions.

2. All children have the capacity to learn about and understand peoples and cultures in geographic regions outside their own. The breadth and depth of their understanding depend on the background experiences they bring to the reading experience and on the extent to which they are motivated to devote time and effort to learn about peoples, cultures, and places outside their cultural and geographic "homes."

3. Teachers play an important role in helping children cultivate their personal views of peoples from other cultural regions by

   a. the quality and diversity of transcultural children's literature they select and make available to children for book bonding

   b. the extent to which they immerse their students in transcultural children's literature by providing meaningful activities that reinforce what children read about and integrate with other parts of the curriculum

   c. the types and quality of interactions they create for their students to experience while reading and responding to transcultural children's literature

   d. the contextual scaffolding they provide (e.g., to clarify or illustrate lifestyles) by either direct or indirect instruction

   e. the degree of understanding, receptivity, and interest they model toward a given culture and cultural region

Rationale

Whereas multicultural children's literature helps children establish a sense of belonging and self-worth (Bishop, 1997) in the cultural region in which they live, transcultural
children's literature serves a similar yet distinctly different and broader purpose. We
believe that one major purpose of transcultural children's literature is to act as a key
agent of change by providing children with book-bonding choices and experiences
related to peoples, cultures, and geographic regions elsewhere in the world.

> There is no one right way to think and feel, and no society can claim to have all of the
> right answers; we can each gain perspective and insight into our world by examining the
> perspective of other societies and cultures. (Lo & Leahy, 1997, p. 222)

An underlying goal here is to help children acquire an awareness of a more inclusive
world—a global community—shared by many peoples. This transcultural view builds
on and extends the multicultural view that many children in the United States internal-
ize. In other words, one reason for accepting transcultural children's literature is that

it can assist children in extending their views on how they relate to the world beyond the borders of the United States and how that wider world relates to them.

The second reason for recognizing transcultural children's literature stems from the realization that ancestral heritage alone does not necessarily lead to a cultural understanding of the geographic regions from whence one's ancestors originally came. The natural tendency is to believe that an understanding of the cultures of one's ancestors is inherited. A difference exists, though, between having a strong affinity for ancestral homelands and possessing a genuine understanding of them. A good example of this distinction is apparent in the book *Gregory Cool* (Binch, 1994). Gregory, who is from the United States, visits his grandparents and cousin living on the Caribbean island of Tobago. Although Gregory is a member of the family, he is quite unfamiliar and uncomfortable with the island culture. With firsthand experience and assistance from his relatives, Gregory gradually learns about the island culture of Tobago. This children's book illustrates the important role that transcultural children's literature can play in helping children develop broader and deeper cultural understandings.

The third reason for differentiating transcultural children's literature is to establish it as a distinct body of children's books and potential area of research and classroom use. Some journals, such as *Book Links* and *The Reading Teacher*, have been helpful in bringing attention to the increasing number of what we designate as transcultural children's books. Others, such as *Bookbird*, have also contributed by identifying authors of transcultural children's books and publishing critiques. Additionally, other journals—for example, *The New Advocate*—have published articles relating to what can be considered transcultural topics but generally under the title "multicultural children's literature."

Historically, what we identify as transcultural children's literature has been either labeled "international children's literature" or subsumed under the title "multicultural children's literature." Consequently, transcultural children's literature has been largely overlooked as a subject of research for its own sake and as a tool for teaching and learning. Additionally, what research has been done on international children's literature appears sparse and out of date, given the substantial increase in the number and quality of transcultural children's books published during the 1990s. Research on transcultural children's books published prior to 1990 also may have limited applicability to currently available transcultural children's books. Similarly, children's literature anthologies and textbooks seem to have relegated their treatment of international children's books primarily to folktales from around the world. Thus, a recognizable need for thorough study of transcultural children's literature continues.

Areas of Future Research

Examples of areas of transcultural children's literature that deserve to be researched further include the following: (a) the nature of transcultural children's books as elucidated by language, themes, cultural milieu, illustrations, quality, and authenticity of writing; (b) the relationship between children and transcultural children's literature as it pertains to book bonding, changes in cultural understanding, and extrapolation of such understanding to the wider global community; and (c) the roles teachers have in scaffolding, promoting book bonding, and modeling cultural understandings.

Thus, researching transcultural children's literature and promoting its classroom use help form a worldview that transcends national boundaries and recognizes an emerging global community of distinct cultural regions or "neighborhoods." As Bieger (1995/1996) states, "Each time we read a good piece of literature, we are changed by the experience; we see the world in a new way. For these reasons, literature can be a powerful vehicle for understanding cultures and experiences different from our own" (p. 311).

CONNECTING THE WORLD WITH CHILDREN'S LITERATURE

A Cultural Paradigm: An Introduction

When teachers provide children with books about the lives of people in other countries and cultures, they need to obtain a representative body of literature. Children's ready access to such a collection of books is important for two interrelated reasons. The first involves **book bonding**, a term we have coined that is exemplified by Dudley-Marling's (1997) classroom observation: "Making available texts in which my students could find a range of cultural stories, customs, and traditions enabled my students to make their own decisions about their relationship to the stories and characters in those texts" (p. 132). The second reason, and the one we emphasize, is to ensure the authentic portrayal of cultures (Harris, 1996) and countries. Thus, given the importance of book bonding, it is paramount that readers bond with authentic depictions of peoples and their cultural regions. To gauge the degree to which a particular book accurately reflects a culture, one can begin by asking (a) What elements do cultures have in common, (b) How can these common elements be organized into a conceptual framework or paradigm, and (c) How can one determine whether particular books reflect people and their cultural regions authentically?

To answer these questions, we devised a **paradigm** consisting of four elements that are inherent in virtually every culture: (a) geographic location, (b) economic system, (c) social system, and (d) political system (shown in Figure 1.1).

Figure 1.1
Cultural paradigm.

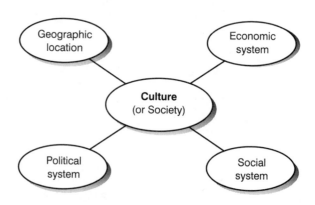

Figure 1.2
Interrelationships among cultural elements.

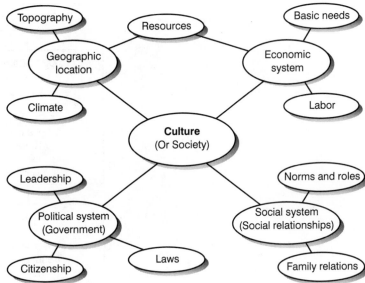

Although all societies seem to contain these four elements, the cultural patterns resulting when they are woven together are often complex, sometimes subtle, and typically unpredictable. Further, the detailed nature of one society may differ markedly from that of another even though the four elements appear to be very similar in each. For example, two desert societies that appear to be similar because of their comparable geographic setting may be vastly different socially, economically, and politically. Similarly, even though all four elements are comparable in two or more societies, their complex interplay (see Figure 1.2) can yield distinct cultural differences. Such has occurred in the Caribbean region, where many similar yet distinct island cultures exist. To ascertain the relevance of these four cultural elements, detailed characterizations of geographic location, economic system, social system, and political system are necessary.

Geography

Geography encompasses a country's or region's topography, climate, and natural resources (Figure 1.3). **Topography** includes mountain ranges, volcanoes, valleys, plains, deserts, rivers, lakes, oceans, and the like. **Climate** can be classified in many ways, including tropical, subtropical, temperate, arctic, and arid. Last, **natural resources** comprise such things as water, soil, plants, animals, minerals, and fossil fuels.

Geography or physical location significantly influences every society or culture. Topography, climate, and natural resources generally set broad limits to how a society structures itself and functions. Natural resources in particular dictate the options available to a people confronted with meeting basic needs such as food, water, and shelter. How members of a society meet these needs largely determines, in turn, on what economic systems they depend. Take, for instance, two books with stories that

Figure 1.3
Geographic location.

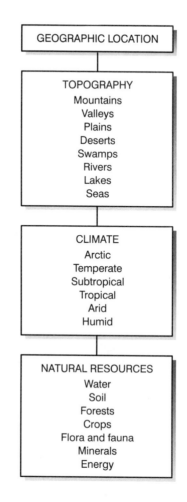

occur in geographic locations in or near a desert—Ali: *Child of the Desert* (London, 1997), which takes place in rural Morocco, and *The Day of Ahmed's Secret* (Heide & Gilliland, 1990), which is set in Cairo, Egypt. Although both settings are in arid locations, the social and economic influences have created two distinct ways of life.

To help organize the chapters in this text, we divided the world into nine geographic regions: *Africa* (Chapter 2), *Asia* (Chapter 3), *Canada* (Chapter 4), *the Caribbean* (Chapter 5), *Central America, Mexico, and South America* (Chapter 6), *Eastern Europe* (Chapter 7), *Western Europe* (Chapter 8), *the Middle East* (Chapter 9), and *the South Pacific, Australia, New Zealand, and Antarctica* (Chapter 10).

Economic System

The means by which people of a given geographic location, country, or region obtain what they need constitute the **economic system** (see Figure 1.4). The economy of any society is directly affected by available resources, how they are used, and how they are developed. Inherent in any society's economic system are processes or systems of production, consumption, transportation, communication, and technology. The first priority of any economic activity, however, is to meet the fundamental needs of life: food, water, clothing, and shelter. Once the basics are provided, an economy can then satisfy demands for various goods and services (e.g., tools, health care, education, vehicles).

Exposing readers to economic systems can lead to a heightened awareness and broader understanding of the economic differences among countries. For example, *The Streets Are Free* (Kurusa, 1995) informs the reader that economic issues can even affect where children play. Based on actual events in Caracas, Venezuela, the book describes how children who had only streets to play in were instrumental in getting a community playground built. To illustrate a different perspective on economics, the lighthearted

Figure 1.4
Economic system.

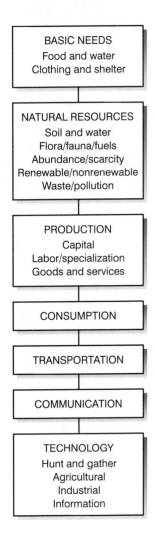

West African fable *The Market Lady and the Mango Tree* (Watson, 1994) not only teaches a basic lesson in economics (e.g., what is free, what can be sold) but also introduces the dynamics of a local market in a rural community. Although this market is set in Africa, similar ones are common in many rural and urban communities around the world.

Social System

The **social system** of virtually every society is organized around a few central concepts and associated subsidiary concepts as indicated in Figure 1.5. Social norms define a culture's values, ethics, and morals, as well as the standards by which members of the culture interact with one another. These standards also establish the rules for social and gender roles; for interactions among adults and between adults and children; for courtship, marriage, and divorce; and for various relationships among members of a family.

Figure 1.5
Social system.

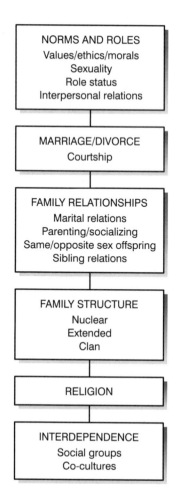

Societies also establish normative family structures, such as nuclear or extended families, and some societies consist of more than one form of familial structure. Additional key elements of a social system include the importance and influence of religion, history, and intergroup relationships. In multicultural societies, such as those of Canada, Russia, and the West Indies, intergroup relationships are particularly significant.

References to social norms, roles, and interpersonal relations are especially meaningful and prevalent in the literature of any culture. Consequently, knowledge concerning a culture's expectations of normal interpersonal behavior underlies a meaningful understanding of the literature about that culture. A good illustration of the importance of interpersonal behavior occurs in the book *Hue Boy* (Mitchell, 1993), which shows that many people in an island community offer parental-like advice to ease a young boy's worry about his perceived problem. The various concepts outlined in Figure 1.5 provide a useful perspective from which teachers can better prepare themselves to inform students of other societies through transcultural children's literature.

Political System

The **political system** of a society plays a vital role in determining how and in what forms the geographic, economic, and social systems manifest themselves. The political system is an important determiner of historical and ethical characteristics of a society (Figure 1.6). Membership in a society and the rights, privileges, and responsibilities that come with that membership define the key concept of *citizenship*. Leadership in most political systems is organized around the discharge of executive, legislative, and judicial duties. Elections are often employed to determine who undertakes leadership responsibilities, although elections take many forms and vary in importance from culture to culture. An increasing number of societies today also employ some form of representative governance, determined through popular elections, to formulate policies and make laws that are then applied by a judicial branch of government. These political and legal activities are those generally practiced by democratic governments that strive to balance the sometimes conflicting demands of their people. Democracies may be parliamentary or republican, federated or confederated, or even embody vestiges of a monarchy (e.g., United Kingdom, Sweden, Japan). In contrast, dictatorships and totalitarian systems typically impose and practice antidemocratic forms of government.

Occasionally, children's books deal explicitly with the impact of a political system on a society, but many deal with political issues either implicitly or not at all. For example, the long, difficult struggle of Black South Africans to vote in popular, nationwide elections is the focus of the book *The Day Gogo Went to Vote* (Sisulu, 1996). In contrast, the book *Let the Celebrations Begin!* (Wild, 1991) tells about children living in a concentration camp during World War II but only alludes to the Holocaust and says nothing explicitly about the political system that planned and perpetrated it. Being aware of how the political system is reflected, either directly or indirectly, can help teachers scaffold themes, plots, characters, and events in some transcultural stories.

The four elements of the cultural paradigm (geographic location, economic system, social system, and political system) assist teachers in understanding societies

Figure 1.6
Political system.

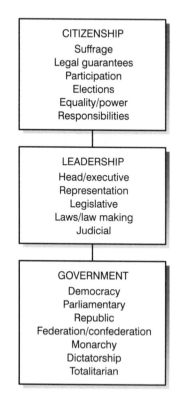

other than their own. The ways people adapt to local geography and climate and use natural resources affect how they organize their economic, social, and political systems into the many societies found around the world. An awareness of these fundamental forces of cultural development is important to understanding and effectively using transcultural children's literature in the classroom.

CONNECTING CHILDREN'S LITERATURE TO THE WORLD

Selecting Transcultural Children's Literature

Because transcultural children's literature can shape, to varying degrees, students' perceptions of other countries, peoples, and cultures, it is important to assess potential transcultural books individually and collectively in terms of their geographic, economic, social, and political attributes. Guidelines for selecting transcultural literature as presented in Figure 1.7 can assist in revealing transcultural patterns. These guidelines are most effective when used as a supplement to professional judgment, rather than as an isolated, definitive checklist.

After reviewing several possible transcultural books by using the guidelines, we typically see patterns emerge. For example, the books may have stories set in rural

A children's book is transcultural if . . .	YES	NO	Can't tell or N/A
1. most readers are from one society and cultural region and the book is about a different society and cultural region.			
2. the setting of the book takes place in a society and cultural region that differs from the reader's.			
3. the major characters in the book are from a society and cultural region that differs from the reader's.			
4. the plot and theme provide insights into another society and its culture.			
5. the author seems well versed in the society and cultural region portrayed in the book.			

The book's setting imparts a transcultural quality if the author . . .	YES	NO	Can't tell or N/A
1. portrays the physical aspects of a society and cultural region in ways that avoid value judgments.			
2. describes the society and cultural region on the basis of the experiences of someone from that region, rather than of a casual, naive visitor.			
3. describes the society and cultural region realistically, rather than sensationally or stereotypically.			
4. shows the kinds of dwellings, workplaces, and outdoor scenes typical of a society and cultural region.			
5. uses illustrations to convey visually accurate and typical scenes of a society and cultural region.			

The author's physical portrayals of people convey a transcultural quality if . . .	YES	NO	Can't tell or N/A
1. their stature, skin color, and facial features seem realistic and typical for a society and cultural region.			
2. the main characters and those in supporting roles are distinct individuals, rather than cloned, stereotyped caricatures.			
3. the main characters and those in supporting roles are described in non-pejorative terms.			

Figure 1.7
Guidelines for selecting transcultural children's literature.

The author's depictions of a people's social roles and activities express a transcultural quality if . . .	YES	NO	Can't tell or N/A
1. they reveal a diverse and authentic repertoire of social relationships, structures, and situations.			
2. they include the typical variety of economic representations found in a society and economic region.			
3. they distinguish among and fairly represent the social and behavioral activities of co-cultures and neighboring societies and cultural regions.			
4. they provide positive role models.			
The author's narration of what people think and do enhances a book's transcultural quality if . . .	**YES**	**NO**	**Can't tell or N/A**
1. people's thoughts and actions seem genuine and are believable.			
2. people are shown deriving personal satisfaction and enjoyment from what they think and do.			
The book's plot exhibits a transcultural quality if . . .	**YES**	**NO**	**Can't tell or N/A**
1. it avoids stereotyping the cultural region, society, co-cultures, or characters.			
2. the characters solve problems, make decisions, and act successfully without the paternalistic help of someone from another culture or society.			
The book's theme or moral expresses a transcultural sense when . . .	**YES**	**NO**	**Can't tell or N/A**
1. it does not exploit stereotypes of a cultural region, society, or people.			
2. the reader does not have to be from the culture or society in question to understand or appreciate the theme.			
The book's illustrations convey a transcultural quality if . . .	**YES**	**NO**	**Can't tell or N/A**
1. they show people as distinct individuals who live, work, and play in a variety of settings and engage in many different activities.			
2. they are drawn in a style(s) characteristic of the society and cultural region.			
3. the artist is from the cultural region in question, rather than from the reader's.			
4. they accurately reflect past or present-day scenes typical of the cultural region.			

Figure 1.7, *continued*

The book's language communicates a transcultural sense if . . .	YES	NO	Can't tell or N/A
1. the author uses words that people from the cultural region commonly use. 2. words foreign to the reader are defined or inferred from their context. 3. words foreign to the reader are accompanied by their pronunciations.			
The author's perspective	YES	NO	Can't tell or N/A
1. Is the author a member of the society or from the cultural region written about in the book? 2. Does the author represent a particular segment of the society or cultural region? 3. Does the author's perspective represent the society or cultural region as a whole?			
The student's perspective	YES	NO	Can't tell or N/A
1. Does a student need prior knowledge about a given country to benefit from reading transcultural children's literature? 2. After reading transcultural children's literature, can the student make generalizations about the country and culture?			
Comparison with other books	YES	NO	Can't tell or N/A
1. Is the book similar to most other books about the same society or cultural region? 2. Do the "types of books" fall into discernible categories? For example, folktales—Africa. 3. Do the majority of other books stereotype a society or cultural region? 4. Has the book been reviewed by others?			

Figure 1.7, *continued*

areas inhabited by characters who all dress alike and live in similar dwellings. Realizing this, then, we should offset the imbalance in these books by finding other books that offer alternative images of the culture and cultural region so that children will have a more nearly authentic portrayal of that culture. As Dudley-Marling points out (1997), "[I]t was unreasonable for me to have assumed that *a* [single] piece of literature could speak to the culture and experience of *all* people from a particular continent, region, or country" (p. 127). In other words, one transcultural children's book by itself cannot provide a comprehensive and authentic view of a cultural region.

In addition to the guidelines in Figure 1.7 for assessing transcultural children's literature, there are complementary techniques for selecting transcultural books. One entails covering the words in a book and looking only at the illustrations. One then can ask what message or messages the illustrations convey about the country, the people, and the culture referred to in the book. This strategy can be reversed by covering the pictures and reading the text. From the text, one can ask what vision emerges about the culture. After assessing the pictures and words in isolation from one another, one can consider further the underlying themes and plots of the book. With practice, this three-step technique can enable an individual to develop a more discerning sense of how well a book's illustrations and text support and reinforce one another and how a society is being represented. Bishop (1991) describes another strategy that involves carefully selecting a children's book as a "perfect" example or model. This book can serve as a "benchmark" for assessing other children's books. These strategies can be used by both students and teachers.

Representative Transcultural Children's Literature From Cultural and Geographic Regions

This chapter has defined transcultural children's literature, offered a paradigm for examining cultures, and suggested guidelines for choosing books. Chapters 2 to 10 review representative transcultural books published in the 1990s from each of nine geographic regions (see Appendix C for a list of publishers of transcultural children's literature). Because there is no definitive way to categorize the cultural regions of the world, we opted for commonly recognized geographic boundaries. Each region is introduced with a brief description of its general geographic location, followed by a list of its constituent countries. We then present one or more book summaries for some, but not all, of the countries in that region.

Each book summary consists of a brief citation followed by a synopsis of the book's plot. Each citation has key information about the book, consisting of author, title, illustrator, publisher, copyright date, ISBN, and suggested age ranges (P = preschool—ages 3 to 4; E = early elementary—ages 5 to 7; M = middle elementary—ages 8 to 9; and L = later elementary—ages 10 to 11). The book summaries, ranging in length from one to several paragraphs, are arranged within each country alphabetically by titles. The number of book summaries varies considerably among countries and regions because of the uneven availability of books. This variability may affect the distribution of books among genres in some cases.

Each book synopsis is prefaced by a story review chart that indicates with "bullets" (•) which aspects of the story (setting, plot/events, characters, and theme) are most important or well developed, like this:

Story Review Chart

Setting	Plot/Events	Characters	Theme
•	•	•	•

(Refer to Appendix A for a comprehensive index of topics appearing in the books reviewed.) A cultural paradigm chart follows by identifying the story's featured transcultural elements, like this:

Cultural Paradigm Reference Classification Chart

Geographic Location	Economic System	Social System	Political System
•	•	•	•

A brief critique of the book's illustrations and a few suggested classroom activities end each synopsis. (Refer to Appendix B for technological resources supporting classroom activities.)

The criteria for deciding which transcultural books to review included (a) published in 1990 or later, (b) designated as a picture book, (c) written in or translated into English, (d) readily available in the United States, (e) appealing to preschool through elementary school readers, (f) of acceptable literary and artistic quality, and (g) reflects a transcultural understanding.

SUMMARY

With the rationale and set of beliefs underpinning transcultural children's literature, one can now apply our cultural paradigm and guidelines as a framework for examining books about peoples, cultures, and geographic regions around the world. In Chapters 2 through 10, we provide information about nine geographic regions and several of their corresponding constituent cultures. Many of these books can be used to enhance any collection of transcultural children's literature. By using these books, children can better chart their personal odyssey to the global community.

REFERENCES CITED

▼▼

Banks, J. A. (1996). Multicultural education and curriculum transformation. *Journal of Negro Education*, 64(4), 390-400.

Bieger, E. M. (1995, December/1996, January) Promoting multicultural education through a literature-based approach. *Reading Teacher*, 49(4), 308-312.

Bishop, R. S. (1991). *The multicolored mirror: Cultural substance in literature for children and young adults.* Fort Atkinson, WI: Highsmith Press.

Bishop, R. S. (1997). Selecting literature for a multicultural curriculum. In V. J. Harris (Ed.), *Using multicultural literature in the K-8 classroom.* Norwood, MA: Christopher-Gordon.

Dudley-Marling, C. (1997). "I'm not from Pakistan": Multicultural literature and the problem of representation. *New Advocate*, 10(2), 123-134.

Grant, C. A. (1994, Winter). Challenging the myths about multicultural education. *Multicultural Education*, 4-9.

Harris, V. J. (1996). Continuing dilemmas, debates, and delights in multicultural literature. *New Advocate*, 9(2), 107-122.

Harris, V. J. (Ed.). (1997). *Using multicultural literature in the K-8 classroom.* Norwood, MA: Christopher-Gordon.

Lo, D. E., & Leahy, A. (1997). Exploring multiculturalism through children's literature: The Batchelder Award winners. *New Advocate*, 10(3), 215-228.

Suggested References
▼▼▼

Au, K. H. (1993). *Literacy instruction in multicultural settings*. Orlando: Harcourt Brace Jovanovich.

Bishop, R. S. (Ed.). (1994). *Kaleidoscope: A multicultural booklist for grades K-8*. Urbana, IL: National Council of Teachers of English.

Diamond, B. J., & Moore, M. A. (1995). *Multicultural literacy: Mirroring the reality of the classroom*. New York: Longman.

Harris, V. J. (1993). *Teaching multicultural literature in grades K-8*. Norwood, MA: Christopher-Gordon.

Hilliard, L. L. (1995). Defining the "multi-" in "multicultural" through children's literature. *Reading Teacher*, 48(8), 728-729.

Lindgren, M. V. (Ed.). (1991). *The multicolored mirror: Cultural substance in literature for children and young adults*. Fort Atkinson, WI: Highsmith Press.

Madigan, D. (1993). The politics of multicultural literature for children and adolescents: Combining perspectives and conversations. *Language Arts*, 70, 168-176.

Rudman, M. K. (1995). *Children's literature: An issues approach*. New York: Longman.

Taxel, J. (1994). Political correctness, cultural politics, and writing for young people. *New Advocate*, 7(2), 93-108.

Walmsley, S. (1994). *Children exploring their world: Theme teaching in elementary school*. Portsmouth, NH: Heinemann.

Children's Books Cited
▼▼▼

Binch, C. (1994). *Gregory cool*. New York: Dial Books for Young Readers. (Tobago)

Dorros, A. C. (1991). *Abuela*. New York: E. P. Dutton. (Puerto Rico)

Heide, F. P., & Gilliland, J. H. (1990). *The day of Ahmed's secret*. New York: Lothrop, Lee & Shepard Books. (Egypt)

Kurusa. (1995). *The streets are free*. Toronto: Annick Press. (Venezuela)

London, J. (1997). *Ali: Child of the desert*. New York: Lothrop, Lee & Shepard Books. (Morocco)

Mitchell, R. P. (1993). *Hue boy*. New York: Dial Books. (Caribbean)

Sisulu, E. B. (1996). *The day Gogo went to vote*. Boston: Little, Brown. (South Africa)

Watson, P. (1994). *The market lady and the mango tree*. New York: Tambourine Books. (Benin)

Wild, M. (1991). *Let the celebrations begin!* New York: Orchard Books. (Poland)

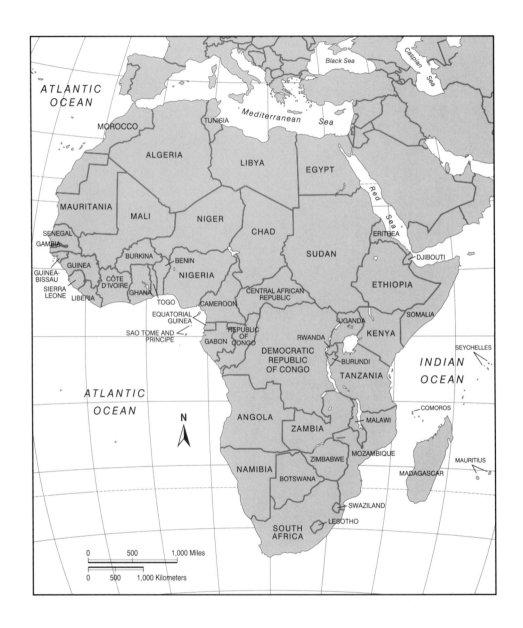

2

Children's Books About Africa

AFRICA

The continental land mass of Africa is located south of Europe. It is bordered on the north by the Mediterranean Sea, on the west by the Atlantic Ocean, and on the east by the Red Sea and the Indian Ocean.

Countries

Algeria, Angola, Benin, Botswana, Burkina Faso, Burundi, Cameroon, Central African Republic, Chad, Comoros, Côte D'Ivoire, Democratic Republic of Congo (formerly Zaire), Djibouti, Egypt, Equatorial Guinea, Eritrea, Ethiopia, Gabon, Gambia, Ghana, Guinea, Guinea-Bissau, Kenya, Lesotho, Liberia, Libya, Madagascar, Malawi, Mali, Mauritania, Mauritius, Morocco, Mozambique, Namibia, Niger, Nigeria, Republic of Congo (formerly Congo), Rwanda, São Tomé & Príncipe, Senegal, Seychelles, Sierra Leone, Somalia, South Africa, Sudan, Swaziland, Tanzania, Togo, Tunisia, Uganda, Western Sahara, Zambia, Zimbabwe

EXAMINING THE CULTURAL REGION OF AFRICA AND THE PATTERNS OF CHILDREN'S BOOKS

Africa consists of more than 50 countries ranging greatly in size, population, and geography. Africa can be divided into two large subregions—North Africa and sub-Saharan Africa. One major attribute of Africa as a whole is its geography—whether one scans the endless horizon of the vast Sahara or is immersed in the lush, humid tropical forests of west central Africa or is roaming the immense savannas of East Africa, the land and wildlife of Africa are unforgettable. Similarly, the diversity of the African peoples and cultures leaves its imprint on any memories of this part of the world.

Children's literature in the first half of the 20th century tended to be highly Europeanized. This inclination has given way to a literacy based on African characters acting according to indigenous traditions, experiences, values, and realities. Since the early 1980s, themes appearing in African children's literature have been rooted primarily in stories of local life, adventure, and historical fiction (Osa, 1985). Children's books about Africa available in the United States have yet to tap deeply into the literary traditions of Africa. When selecting transcultural children's books about Africa, we discover that a significant proportion of them overlook Africa's tremendous geographic, climatic, economic, cultural, or political diversity (Henderson & Elleman, 1996). Most children's books with African themes, for example, take place in rural settings. Consequently, children in the United States still tend to view Africa as a single country with one people who speak one language and have one culture. Exposure to a variety of more recently published books will broaden children's views of this diverse cultural region.

COUNTRIES AND CHILDREN'S BOOKS REVIEWED

Benin

Benin is located in western Africa, with the Atlantic Ocean to the south, Togo to the west, Burkina and Niger to the north, and Nigeria to the east.

 Cowen-Fletcher, Jane. It *Takes a Village.* Scholastic, 1994. 32 pp. (ISBN 0-590-46573-2). Contemporary Fiction, P-M.[1]

Story Review Chart			
Setting	Plot/Events	Characters	Theme
•	•	•	•

---

[1]A = all ages, P = preschool, E = early elementary, M = middle elementary, L = late elementary

Cultural Paradigm Reference Classification Chart			
Geographic Location	Economic System	Social System	Political System
•	•	•	

Expecting a hectic day selling mangos at the market, Yemi's mother asks her to take care of her younger brother, Kokou. Yemi is proud of this responsibility and tells her mother and, later, other vendors at the market that she will be caring for her brother by herself. The seasoned caretakers smile at Yemi and watch her discover the real meaning of child rearing.

Once alone with her brother, Yemi stops for a moment to buy him some peanuts. Kokou wanders off, and Yemi frantically searches for him. Although Yemi at first worries about her brother's well-being, she soon discovers that all of Kokou's needs are met by those around him. Yemi thanks everyone and returns to her mother, who in turn tells her the African proverb, "It takes a village to raise a child."

Colored pencil and watercolor illustrations depict the fresh fruits, colorful clothing, and vendor specialties found on market day in one rural African community.

Classroom Applications

This book is an excellent backdrop for supporting such classroom topics as communities, extended families, markets and the various specialties of the vendors, family responsibility, learning through experience, and the meanings of proverbs. Other activities include asking students to compare their experience of caring for someone else with Yemi's and discussing what events took place and what it felt like to assume responsibility for someone else. Another application is for students to define a proverb and to discuss the meaning of "It takes a village to raise a child." Can this same proverb be applied to child rearing in the United States as well?

 Watson, Pete. *The Market Lady and the Mango Tree*. illustrated by Mary Watson. Tambourine Books, 1994. 32 pp. (ISBN 0-688-12970-6). Contemporary Fiction, P-M.

Story Review Chart			
Setting	Plot/Events	Characters	Theme
•	•	•	•

Cultural Paradigm Reference Classification Chart			
Geographic Location	Economic System	Social System	Political System
•	•	•	

After observing African village children gathering and eating fallen fruit under a mango tree, a market vendor devises a scheme for cornering the market on this free fruit. Market Lady, as she is called, nets the mango tree boughs and funnels the falling fruit directly to her lap, thereby making herself the sole vendor of the mango tree fruit. As her sudden wealth increases, so does her greed, eventually making her fruit affordable only to the wealthy. All is well until Market Lady experiences an ill-fated dream about her mango enterprise. When she awakens, she realizes it is wrong to sell something that is free and makes haste to remedy the situation. The story ends with Market Lady dismantling her business and giving her fruit to the children.

Illustrations at the beginning of the book display the vivid colors of the market, village homes, a factory island, and a country road along a river.

Classroom Applications

Through the market scenario, American students are introduced to the concept of an *outdoor market*. They can sample the foods and goods displayed and sold in a way that is different from what they commonly experience but that is familiar to children in other parts of the world. Teacher and students can turn their classroom into a 1-day market and invite students from other classes, administrators, and family members to participate. Mangoes, of course, are one fruit that everyone has to sample. Basic to the market scene is setting up a business. If students could sell something that is now free, what would it be? How would they sell it? They can also discuss whether they *should* sell something that is free.

Cameroon

Cameroon is located in western Africa and borders the North Atlantic Ocean between Nigeria and Equatorial Guinea.

 Alexander, Lloyd. *The Fortune-Tellers*. illustrated by Trina Schart Hyman. Dutton Children's Books, 1992. 32 pp. (ISBN 0-525-44849-7). Folktale, E–M.

Story Review Chart			
Setting	Plot/Events	Characters	Theme
	•	•	

Cultural Paradigm Reference Classification Chart			
Geographic Location	Economic System	Social System	Political System
	•	•	

Not satisfied with his life, a young carpenter goes to another town to have his fortune told. When the carpenter finds the fortune teller, he asks questions about his future wealth, fame, marital status, and happiness. The fortune teller responds with positive but obvious answers, such as, when you become well known, you'll become famous. Pleased to hear about his bright future, the carpenter returns home. Halfway home, however, he remembers other questions, so he returns to the fortune teller. When he

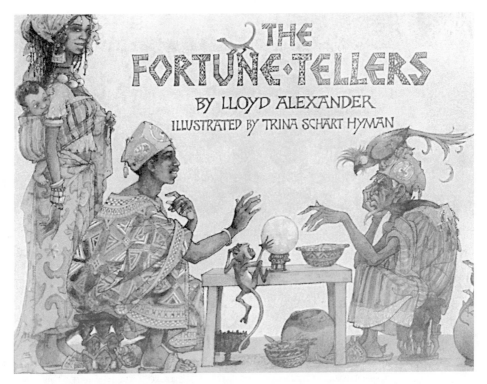

Cover of THE FORTUNE-TELLERS by Lloyd Alexander, illustrated by Trina Schart Hyman. Copyright © 1992 by Lloyd Alexander, text. © 1992 by Trina Schart Hymen, illustrations. Used by permission of Dutton Children's Books, a division of Penguin Books USA Inc.

arrives, the fortune teller is gone. At that moment, the landlady enters the room and believes that the carpenter is the fortune teller, who has used his powers to become young. The landlady offers him free rent to tell fortunes. Unable to convince the landlady that he is not the old fortune teller, the carpenter tells her fortune. From this comical beginning, the carpenter ultimately becomes a successful fortune teller who is rich, famous, married, and happy. The original fortune teller, who never actually saw the future, ironically suffers terrible mishaps and is never seen again. The story ends with the new fortune teller attributing his good fortune to the original fortune teller's ability to see into the future.

The full-color detailed illustrations are done in acrylic, ink, and crayon. They capture the charm of rural Africa and highlight the beautiful designs and colors of traditional African clothing. Although stylized, the people are physically attractive and vary in size and build. The settings, whether depicting a town or a savanna, reveal intricate detail associated with African life. For example, in the occasional background illustration, nurturing adult-child interactions can be seen.

Classroom Applications

The idea of predicting the future is intriguing in any culture. This story is a good springboard for comparing how different people around the world view looking into the future. For example, teachers can begin by having students read horoscopes in U.S. daily newspapers and then discuss "psychic" television shows. Students then can research how soothsayers in other countries foretell the future. What they learn can lead to discussion about whether anyone anywhere can actually accomplish this feat.

 Mollel, Tolowa, M. *The King and the Tortoise*. illustrated by Kathy Blankley. Clarion Books, 1993. 32 pp. (ISBN 0-395-64480-1). Folktale, E–M.

Story Review Chart

Setting	Plot/Events	Characters	Theme
	•	•	•

Cultural Paradigm Reference Classification Chart

Geographic Location	Economic System	Social System	Political System
		•	•

Believing that he is the cleverest man in the world, a king challenges his subjects to prove otherwise by fashioning a robe of smoke. First to accept this challenge is a nimble hare. After the hare fails to make a robe of smoke, a sly fox tries but also fails. Next to face the challenge is a powerful leopard who believes that he surely will succeed, but he too is defeated by the smoke. An elephant claiming his strength to be a sign of cleverness attempts the difficult task but also meets with defeat. A tortoise comes forth to make the final attempt even though he does not possess the other contenders' notable attributes. Before beginning, he asks the king for a week's time and a promise to provide him with whatever he should need to accomplish the task. Laughingly, the king agrees. When the tortoise returns in a week, he asks for thread. The king, humoring himself and those around him, gives the tortoise all the thread that is available. The tortoise then announces to the king that he needs a thread of fire to make a robe of smoke. To save face, the king says that he no longer needs the silly robe and proclaims that he and the tortoise are the cleverest in the kingdom.

Illustrations depict a group of villagers of different ages in ancient, rural Cameroon. The people and the animals appear animated and quickly escort the reader through the text. The vibrant multicolored border that trims one side of each page contrasts well with the overall sepia tones that dominate the text.

Classroom Applications

Students can take turns reading the story aloud while others in the class dramatize the characters' actions. *The King and the Tortoise* can also lead to a discussion about the lesson that mental acuity, and not physical prowess, leads to success. This book can initiate a study of the different types of royal regalia that African rulers wore. How did the colors and styles differ from country to country? Also, how did the climate influence the types of traditional royal garments worn?

Egypt

Egypt is located in the northeast corner of Africa. The Mediterranean Sea is to the north, the Red Sea to the east, Israel on its northeast border, Libya on the west, and Sudan on the south.

 Heide, Florence Parry, and Gilliland, Judith Heide. *The Day of Ahmed's Secret.* illustrated by Ted Lewin. Lothrop, Lee & Shepard Books, 1990. 32 pp. (ISBN 0-688-08894-5). Contemporary Fiction, P-L.

Story Review Chart

Setting	Plot/Events	Characters	Theme
•	•	•	•

Cultural Paradigm Reference Classification Chart

Geographic Location	Economic System	Social System	Political System
•	•	•	

Ahmed begins his day of work by sharing with the reader that he has a secret he will reveal to his family that night. This Egyptian boy delivers fuel canisters to Cairo residents who have gas stoves. Going through the streets of Cairo on a cart pulled by a donkey, Ahmed explains how the people of Cairo are connected with one another through sounds, colors, work, beliefs, families, ancestry, and location. For example, when delivering a fuel canister to an old woman, Ahmed tells how proud he is that he now has the strength to do this work for his family. At lunch, Ahmed shares thoughts on the antiquity of the city, the importance of quiet time, and the relationship he has to the surrounding environment. During the afternoon, Ahmed explains how time and place connect people. At the end of the day, Ahmed finally reveals his secret to his family by showing that he can write his name, and he reminds the reader that written language outlasts spoken language.

This book offers the reader several things to ponder. For example, the idea that every sound an individual makes (e.g., shouting someone's name, blowing a whistle) is as much a part of the life of a community as is each person. The book also effectively communicates the importance of values and beliefs, such as pride, dignity of work, and value of family, without being overly judgmental.

Equally intriguing are the book's illustrations. The watercolors link past and present, young and old, and modern life and old traditions. Illustrations clearly support the narrative and offer wonderful details of urban people, their various roles, their

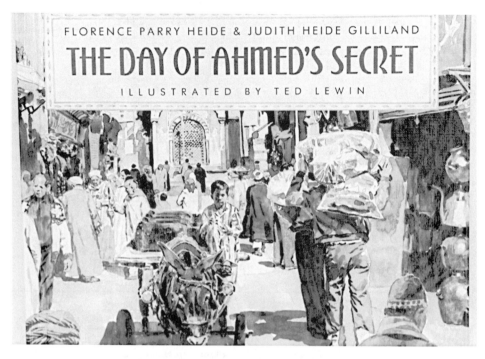

Cover of The Day of Ahmed's Secret *by Florence Parry Heide and Judith Heide Gilliland, illustrated by Ted Lewin, 1990. New York: Lothrop, Lee & Shepard Books, a division of William Morrow & Co., Inc. Printed with permission from William Morrow & Co., Inc.*

facial expressions, and how they interact. For example, the reader can observe Ahmed's respect for adults by seeing how he responds to his father, Hassan.

Classroom Applications

Several classroom lessons based on *The Day of Ahmed's Secret* can be taught. One suggestion is to have students compare different alphabets used around the world. For example, Arabic, Cyrillic, Chinese, and Greek alphabets differ greatly from the English alphabet. Another activity is to have students talk about secrets they wish to share. Further, ask each student to think of a sound that best represents her- or himself and, when signaled by the teacher, to make their sounds. A classroom discussion can link these "signature" sounds with the everyday sounds associated with schools in general. Students can also discuss how a school in Cairo might compare with a school in the United States. This book can also be used to initiate discussions about families and communities and how each individual's contribution to the immediate family and community can enhance the overall well-being of the world.

▼ David, Rosalie. *Growing Up in Ancient Egypt.* illustrated by Angus McBride. Troll, 1994. 32 pp. (ISBN 0-8167-2717-1). Historical Nonfiction, M-L.

Story Review Chart

Setting	Plot/Events	Characters	Theme
•	•	•	•

Cultural Paradigm Reference Classification Chart

Geographic Location	Economic System	Social System	Political System
•	•	•	•

Growing Up in Ancient Egypt provides a collection of facts about the people and places of the distant past. Information is provided about where ancient Egypt was located, where the people lived, how they lived, who some of the rulers were, and how the people were ruled. Basic facts about mummification and the pyramids appear at the end of the book. Much of the information is interesting and holds the reader's attention. Realistic illustrations help the reader visualize much of the information in the text.

Classroom Applications

Students can use this book to compare life in ancient and present-day Egypt in terms of the geographic, economic, social, and political aspects of the cultural paradigm. As a follow-up, students can compare America's "young past" with America's present and discuss similarities and differences between America and Egypt. Students can further discuss why people around the world are so fascinated with ancient Egypt.

Ethiopia

Ethiopia is located in northeastern Africa, bordering Sudan, Somalia, and the Red Sea.

 Kurtz, Jane. *Pulling the Lion's Tail*. illustrated by Floyd Cooper. Simon & Schuster Books for Young Readers, 1995. 32 pp. (ISBN 0-689-80324-9). Folktale, E-L.

Story Review Chart

Setting	Plot/Events	Characters	Theme
	•	•	•

Cultural Paradigm Reference Classification Chart

Geographic Location	Economic System	Social System	Political System
		•	

This book recounts the poignant experiences of a young Ethiopian girl living with her recently widowed father who has just remarried. As she tries to adjust to the new situation at home, the young girl is perplexed by her stepmother's shyness, aloofness, and apparent lack of love for her. She goes to her grandfather for advice on how to win her stepmother's love. The grandfather agrees to tell her how but only after she pulls a strand of hair from the tail of a lion. Such a difficult feat can only be accomplished with great patience so that the lion and the young girl can become used to each other gradually. By the time she manages to pull a hair from a lion's tail, the young girl and her stepmother have likewise become more accustomed to each other so that they can talk and do things together as mother and daughter.

Illustrations not only realistically depict the physical appearance, dress, and customs of some Ethiopians but also capture the emotional tension between the young girl and her stepmother and the story's happy ending.

Classroom Applications

Pulling the Lion's Tail is a useful device for helping children discuss the difficulties they—whether in the United States, in Africa, or in other parts of the world—face when their families change as a result of death or divorce. As this story tells us, patience can often be an effective strategy for coping with such changes. In addition to changes in families, students can talk about other changes that take place during their lives, such as physical and intellectual changes. How have they changed as students and as friends? Do students in other countries experience these same types of changes? Which aspects of the cultural paradigm influence some changes that the students have identified?

Gambia

Gambia is located in western Africa and borders the Atlantic Ocean between Senegal and Guinea-Bissau.

 Da Volls, Linda. *Tano and Binti: Two Chimpanzees Return to the Wild.* illustrated by Andy Da Volls. Clarion Books, 1994. 32 pp. (ISBN 0-395-68701-2). Contemporary Fiction, E-M.

Story Review Chart

Setting	Plot/Events	Characters	Theme
•		•	

Cultural Paradigm Reference Classification Chart

Geographic Location	Economic System	Social System	Political System
•		•	

Two chimpanzees, Tano and Binti, are transported from the London Zoo to a forest preserve in Gambia where Amber, an older female chimpanzee, teaches them how to survive on their own. Once Tano and Binti are able to fend for themselves in their new forest home, Amber leaves them. After a year passes, she brings her infant and the adult male troop leader to meet Tano and Binti. By the end of the story, Tano and Binti are living with Amber and the other chimpanzees in the Gambian forest.

The authenticity of the information about chimpanzees and the realistic pastel illustrations clearly indicate that both the author and the illustrator are intimately familiar with these animals and their way of life.

Classroom Applications

What is the difference between animals living in captivity and in the wild? Why would people want to help chimpanzees make the transition from living in a zoo or laboratory to living in a natural environment? Do other animals make this type of transition? Students can use this book as a basis for discussing these questions and for studying mammals, zoos, wildlife conservation, and primate behavior in general.

Ghana

Ghana is in western Africa and borders the North Atlantic Ocean between Togo and the Côte D'Ivorie.

 Dupré, Rick. *Agassu: Legend of the Leopard King.* Carolrhoda Books, 1993. 40 pp. (ISBN 0-87614-764-3). Folktale, E-M.

Story Review Chart

Setting	Plot/Events	Characters	Theme
•	•	•	•

Cultural Paradigm Reference Classification Chart

Geographic Location	Economic System	Social System	Political System
•	•	•	•

This story of life as a West African slave chained to a fishing boat reminds the reader of a harsh reality of the past. Agassu, a young slave whose name means "leopard," learns from the gods that he is the chosen heir of the Adja tribe. The gods melt Agassu's chains with firebolts and send him to his people on the crest of a wave. Once back with his people, Agassu as king passes judgment on the former ruler and his sons for the cruelties they inflicted on his people. Agassu forgives rather than punishes them. He tells them to use the gifts of power, strength, and goodness, which guided his judgment of them, to help them become better people.

Oil and acrylic illustrations painted on a collage base create varied color combinations and compositions that express the unique beauty of rural African folklore. Hidden within the illustrations are portraits of African American civil rights leaders. A glossary indicates on which page most of these leaders can be found.

Classroom Applications

This book describes a political system traditionally practiced in much of Africa—namely, one in which a respected tribal king is expected to govern justly and wisely and to teach others to do the same. Students can express their views on why everyone should treat other people justly and wisely. The political dimension of the story provides opportunities for students to compare democratic and autocratic systems of government and to weigh the pros and cons of kingship and its inheritance. This book can also serve as a springboard for discussing contemporary world leaders, such as Nelson Mandela. Finally, teachers and students can use this book as a basis for discussing the harmful impacts slavery had on both America and Africa.

 Medearis, Angela Shelf. *Too Much Talk.* illustrated by Stefano Vitale. Candlewick Press, 1995. 32 pp. (ISBN 1-56402-323-0). Folktale, P-L.

Story Review Chart			
Setting	Plot/Events	Characters	Theme
	•	•	•

Cultural Paradigm Reference Classification Chart			
Geographic Location	Economic System	Social System	Political System
		•	

This simply written whimsical tale tells of a farmer and how he and others meet and react to various animals, plants, and inanimate objects that talk. When the farmer and others converse with these talking characters, they frantically run away to tell someone else about their strange experience. The person who is told one of the fantastic stories predictably asserts the impossibility of talking animals and plants. Then that person later meets an animal or some other object that actually speaks. The story ends with the people telling the king all about the talking animals and plants. He dismisses their claims as being "too much talk" and sends them away. When talking aloud about how ludicrous the peoples' stories are, the king's throne talks and agrees with him. The king runs away in fright and is not seen again.

Illustrations entail bold designs painted in oil on wood. Each two-page spread has a differently designed border that highlights the illustration. All the illustrations are highly stylized and effectively frame the dialogue and actions in the text.

Classroom Applications

Too Much Talk invites students to follow along with, act out, or tell the story. The dialogue engages readers with its repetitive lyrical narrative that playfully shows the humorous actions of the various characters. The theme of not believing something until it is personally experienced can be developed into an enjoyable literature-response activity. Students can create their own whole-class or small-group big book based on their personal experiences of not believing something until they actually see or hear it for themselves. This book is especially suitable for young emergent readers.

Kenya

Kenya is located in eastern Africa and borders the Indian Ocean between Tanzania and Somalia.

 Aardema, Verna, retold by. *How the Ostrich Got Its Long Neck*. illustrated by Marcia Brown. Scholastic, 1995. 32 pp. (ISBN 0-590-48367-6). Folktale, E-M.

Story Review Chart

Setting	Plot/Events	Characters	Theme
•	•	•	•

Cultural Paradigm Reference Classification Chart

Geographic Location	Economic System	Social System	Political System
•		•	

According to a pourquoi tale of the Akamba people, who live in Kenya, the first ostrich had long legs but a very short neck. Consequently, the ostrich found it difficult to catch insects on the ground, reach berries on tall bushes, and drink water. One day, a crocodile tearfully pleads with various animals to remove his painful tooth, but only the ostrich is willing to help. While the ostrich tries to pull out the bad tooth with its beak, the crocodile's hunger takes over, and the crocodile closes its mouth tightly around the ostrich's head. A heated tug of war ensues. Eventually, the ostrich escapes but with a much longer neck. With its longer neck, the ostrich now can easily reach insects on the ground, berries in the tops of bushes, and water. This delights the ostrich as it struts about with its head held high but far from the rivers where crocodiles live.

Numerous stylized illustrations depict key events in the story in a whimsical way that brings humor to a story that otherwise might seem unpleasant.

Classroom Applications

This story is essentially social in nature because it embodies a society's need to explain strange or puzzling aspects of the natural world in ways that are based on every day experiences, familiar observations, and common sense. Teachers can choose an animal indigenous to their particular part of the United States and ask students to write individual or group stories explaining the origin of an animal's salient attributes, such as a squirrel's large bushy tail. Students can also write a similar story about an animal that lives in another part of the United States. Their stories then can lead to reading other pourquoi stories from around the world.

Sayre, April Pulley. *If You Should Hear a Honey Guide.* illustrated by S. D. Schindler. Houghton Mifflin, 1995. 32 pp. (ISBN 0-395-71545-8). Informational, E-M.

Story Review Chart

Setting	Plot/Events	Characters	Theme
•		•	•

Cultural Paradigm Reference Classification Chart

Geographic Location	Economic System	Social System	Political System
•		•	

The distinctive call of the honey guide, a bird that lives in East Africa, beckons the reader to follow it through the wild bush on a hunt for one of its favorite foods. While vicariously following the honey guide, the reader encounters a rich variety of animals, including a honey badger, elephants, zebras, a snake, a lion, and crocodiles, that inhabit the forests, hills, rivers, and savanna of Kenya. The honey guide finally reaches its destination, a beehive deep inside a hollow tree. By leading a honey badger or human to a hard-to-get-at hive, the honey guide can eat the honeycomb wax left on the ground after its partner tears apart the hive to get the sweet honey inside.

Muted watercolor illustrations effectively complement events of the story by depicting the terrain, vegetation, and animals of the East African bush in a series of realistic and informative scenes.

Classroom Applications

If You Should Hear a Honey Guide can be used to initiate discussion on the interdependency of humans, animals, and plants. Students can examine books from other countries and find additional examples of living things depending on one another to live. Are there different types of honey bees? What are the many ways that people use honey? Students can research information and develop a poster display that would answer these and other student-initiated questions.

 Kroll, Virginia. *Masai and I.* illustrated by Nancy Carpenter. Four Winds Press, 1992. 32 pp. (ISBN 0-02-751165-0). Contemporary Fiction, E.

Story Review Chart

Setting	Plot/Events	Characters	Theme
•	•	•	•

Cultural Paradigm Reference Classification Chart

Geographic Location	Economic System	Social System	Political System
•		•	

In studying about and feeling kinship with the Masai of Africa, an American child named Linda compares what her life is like with what it would be like if she were Masai. She begins by comparing the daily events of her life as an American with what it would be like to be a Masai girl. She thinks about what her parents and siblings would do each day, her bedtime and morning rituals, her pets, her clothing, mealtime ordeals, and behaving properly at special events.

Illustrations in this book are in oil and color pencil. The artist insightfully compares American and Masai cultures. For example, Linda is shown making her bed with sheets on a mattress on one page and rolling up a cowhide bedroll as a Masai child on the facing page. Overall, the illustrations effectively support the intent of the text.

Classroom Applications

From this book, readers learn what parents, siblings, and others typically do in the Masai culture. By reading additional books about family life in other parts of Africa, other cultural regions, and different regions in America, students can acquire a basis for comparing how families in different cultures function. They can do this by first asking themselves about the many similarities they share with other children from Africa, America, and around the world. Then they can use a Venn diagram to compare systematically the similarities of their families and families in different cultural regions.

 Jacaranda Designs. *Mcheshi Goes to the Game Park*. Highsmith Press, 1992. 28 pp. (ISBN 9966-884-48-3). Contemporary Fiction, P–E.

Story Review Chart

Setting	Plot/Events	Characters	Theme
•		•	

Cultural Paradigm Reference Classification Chart

Geographic Location	Economic System	Social System	Political System
•		•	

Mcheshi and her younger brother venture through a wildlife reserve with their uncle, a game park ranger, who teachers them the importance of protecting endangered animals. During their brief safari, the children learn about safety on a game preserve and to identify the animals living there. The book is written in both English and Kiswahili and is illustrated by several artists living in Kenya. The inside front cover provides a map of the game park, and the last pages offer activities related to the story.

Classroom Applications

The most appealing feature of this book is that it helps dispel the misperception that wild animals roam freely throughout Africa. The story is seen through the eyes of African children, and the reader quickly realizes that visiting a wildlife refuge is as new an experience for some Kenyan children as it would be for the American reader. This would be a good book for American teachers to use in conjunction with a book about how to prepare for a visit to an American zoo or an animal preserve or to explore thematic units on endangered species. Students can also discuss the misperception that animals abound freely in other cultural regions. For example, do kangaroos hop down the sidewalks of Sydney, Australia? Do bison roam the streets of Bozeman, Montana, or the students' hometown?

Lesotho

Lesotho is a landlocked country in southern Africa.

 Mennen, Ingrid. *One Round Moon and a Star for Me.* illustrated by Niki Daly. Orchard Books, 1994. 32 pp. (ISBN 0-531-06804-8). Contemporary Fiction, P-E.

Story Review Chart			
Setting	Plot/Events	Characters	Theme
•	•	•	•

Cultural Paradigm Reference Classification Chart			
Geographic Location	Economic System	Social System	Political System
•		•	

The story opens with a young child who initially relishes his surrounding environment—the stars, moon, sun, and the people all around him. He becomes insecure about his place in the world, however, after his father comments on how much his new sibling resembles both parents. The young child asks his father whether he truly is his father. The father reassures his son that he is and confirms his son's valued place in the family by pointing out to him the location of his own star in the night sky.

The sensitively rendered watercolor and pencil illustrations depict the young child's close relationship to the world around him. These pictures show how a young child's feelings of insecurity are put to rest by the family's understanding, love, and support.

Classroom Applications

This is an excellent book for teachers wanting to discuss family relationships and related questions that children raise about their place in their families and in the universe. This is especially true after new siblings arrive and the older children need to reconfirm their status in the family. Another activity is for students to examine star constellations on astronomy charts and to select individually their favorite constellation. If students are grouped according to choices, they then can discuss their individual reasons for selecting their constellation and identify their favorite star or stars within the constellation. As a group, students can jointly write a fictitious story about their individual star's importance to the total constellation and share it with their classmates.

Madagascar

Madagascar is an island in the Indian Ocean off the east coast of Mozambique in southern Africa.

 Rappaport, Doreen. *The New King*: A *Madagascan Legend*. illustrated by E. B. Lewis. Dial Books for Young Readers, 1995. 32 pp. (ISBN 0-8037-1460-2). Historical Fiction, E-L.

Story Review Chart			
Setting	Plot/Events	Characters	Theme
	•	•	•

Cultural Paradigm Reference Classification Chart			
Geographic Location	Economic System	Social System	Political System
		•	•

Young Prince Rakoto is told that his father was tragically killed in a hunting accident and that he is now king. Unable to accept his father's death, Rakoto commands the Royal Doctor to bring his father back to life. After the doctor is unable to obey his command, he visits the Royal Wizard, who sympathetically tells the new king that neither can he restore life to his father. Rakoto then seeks out the High Counselor, who explains to the young king that neither the doctor nor the wizard is a criminal for being unable to do what is impossible. The young king finally goes to the Wise Woman. She tells Rakoto of the first man and woman, who decided that passing life on like a banana tree was preferable to living forever like the moon. This, she explained, is why people only live one life. The Wise Woman then tells the young king what his father had passed on to him. The story ends with Rakoto, as an adult, passing on the lessons he learned from his father to his own children.

Illustrations are in watercolors and movingly portray the different emotions experienced by the young king. Additionally, illustrations show a majestic array of colorful and authentic-looking clothing worn by the royal family and other characters in the story.

Classroom Applications

The New King: A *Madagascan Legend* poignantly tells of a child's struggle to cope with his father's death and with his new responsibilities as king. The idea that life itself cannot be obtained with money and power serves as a thought-provoking introduction to a science lesson on the cycle of life. To lead a nation at a young age poses certain difficulties. Students can identify potential problems and devise solutions for them. If students were president of the United States today, how would they govern the country? What problems would they address, and what solutions would they offer?

Morocco

Morocco is located in northern Africa; it is bordered on the east by Algeria and on the south by Western Sahara.

 London, Jonathan. *Ali: Child of the Desert*. illustrated by Ted Lewin. Lothrop, Lee & Shepard Books, 1997. 32 pp. (ISBN 0-688-12560-3). Contemporary Fiction, E-M.

Story Review Chart			
Setting	Plot/Events	Characters	Theme
•	•	•	•

Cultural Paradigm Reference Classification Chart			
Geographic Location	Economic System	Social System	Political System
•	•	•	

Now old enough to go with his father on a long journey to sell camels in the Moroccan market town of Rissani, Ali rides atop Jabad, a camel at the rear of the herd plodding its way across the Sahara. When a sandstorm suddenly strikes, Ali and his father become separated. Ali and Jabad continue west toward their destination. At nightfall, Ali follows the sound of bells to an oasis, where he finds a goatherd, an old Berber named Abdul, and his grandson, Youssef. Abdul invites Ali to stay and share a meal with them. He then tells the two boys a story about the warrior-tribesmen of the Berber. The next morning, Ali decides to stay at the oasis rather than go with Abdul, in hopes that his father will come by on the way to Rissani. Abdul gives Ali a rifle and tells him to shoot it every hour to signal his father. Nearly out of food, firewood, and ammunition, Ali finally hears his father riding toward the oasis.

The social and geographic systems predominate in this story of the rite of passage from childhood to manhood. Host-guest customs, the father-son relationship, and the relationship between Berbers and the desert are highlighted.

The wonderfully painted watercolors capture the stark beauty and solitude of the Sahara. Also, the accurate depictions of camels, goats, clothing, and facial expressions create memorable images of desert life.

Classroom Applications

Students can find and mark the Sahara on a large wall map and then list what they would take with them if they were traveling by camel through the desert. What would

Cover of Ali: Child of the Desert *by Jonathan London, illustrated by Ted Lewin, 1997. New York: Lothrop, Lee & Shepard Books, a division of William Morrow & Co., Inc. Printed with permission from William Morrow & Co., Inc.*

they do if they got lost? They can also talk about difficult situations they have over-come and how they felt about the decisions they made.

Nigeria

Nigeria is located in western Africa and borders on the North Atlantic Ocean between Cameroon and Benin.

 Olaleye, Isaac. *Bitter Bananas*. illustrated by Ed Young. Boyds Mills Press, 1994. 32 pp. (ISBN 1-56397-039-2). Contemporary Fiction, P-M.

Story Review Chart			
Setting	Plot/Events	Characters	Theme
•	•	•	

Cultural Paradigm Reference Classification Chart

Geographic Location	Economic System	Social System	Political System
•	•	•	

Yusuf lives in a tropical rain forest in Africa. He tends a palm tree that produces sweet sap he loves to drink, and he sells any extra at the market. One day, Yusuf discovers that baboons are stealing his precious palm sap. He devises various clever schemes to scare off the baboons, but they always come back. Finally, Yusuf adds bitter wormwood juice to ripe bananas and to bowls of palm sap. With the help of his family, Yusuf carries the terrible-tasting concoctions into the forest. When the baboons eat the bananas and drink the sap, they are so disgusted by the bitter taste that they leave for good.

Brightly colored cut-paper illustrations capture the lush, verdant qualities of a tropical rain forest and entice young readers to look carefully at the pictures.

Classroom Applications

Bitter Bananas is one story that teachers might want to include in their shared book collections, especially for younger emergent readers. The repetitive language of the text beckons young readers to participate in the story reading. They can also sample pieces of bananas and talk about how they taste. Are they sweet or bitter? What other foods are sweet? What other foods are bitter? Older students can use the illustrations in *Bitter Bananas* to talk about how rain forests differ from forests in the United States. They can also create their own cut-paper illustration of a nearby forest or wooded area, such as a park.

 Onyefulu, Obi. *Chinye: A West African Folk Tale*. illustrated by Evie Safarewicz. Viking, 1994. 32 pp. (ISBN 0-670-85115-9). Folktale, E-L.

Story Review Chart

Setting	Plot/Events	Characters	Theme
	•	•	•

Cultural Paradigm Reference Classification Chart

Geographic Location	Economic System	Social System	Political System
		•	

Reminiscent of the Cinderella motif, this story tells of Chinye, a quiet, obedient girl who works hard to please her stepmother, Nkecki; and stepdaughter, Adanma. One night, Nkecki tells Chinye to fetch water for Adanma's bath. To reach the water, Chinye has to walk through a dark forest filled with wild animals. Along the way, Chinye meets an antelope and a hyena that help her. She then meets an old woman who tells her to go to a hut full of gourds and to pick the smallest and quietest one. Chinye does so and returns home. The next morning, she breaks open the gourd, which contains a treasure. When Chinye tells her stepmother how she got the magic gourd, the stepmother sends Adanma to get water the next time. Adanma meets the old woman but ignores her advice about which gourd to choose. When Nkecki and Adanma open the largest and loudest gourd, it releases a whirlwind that gathers up all their belongings and blows them away. Too proud to ask others in the village for help, Nkecki and Adanma leave, but Chinye stays to share her new wealth with the village.

Very colorful illustrations and bold geometric patterns grab the reader's attention and help the events in the story unfold.

Classroom Applications

Chinye: A West African Folk Tale tells a moral: Good things happen to those who are good. This moral also tells which forms of social conduct and personal attributes one West African culture values. Students can use this story in conjunction with other similar stories to compare Cinderella stories from around the world. The outcome of this comparison, along with the books, can be displayed in the school library.

 Olaleye, Isaac. *The Distant Talking Drum.* illustrated by Frané Lessac. Boyds Mills Press, 1995. 32 pp. (ISBN 1-56397-095-3). Poetry, P-E.

Story Review Chart

Setting	Plot/Events	Characters	Theme
•	•	•	

Cultural Paradigm Reference Classification Chart

Geographic Location	Economic System	Social System	Political System
•		•	

This movingly written collection of poems provides the reader with rich insights into Nigerian village life. The poems vividly depict village life through everyday activities such as growing, harvesting, and marketing food; spending a rainy day at school; playing games; and listening to stories told by adults.

To enhance the meaning of the words in the poems, the illustrator creates brightly colored pictures rendered as stylized folk art. Each illustration portrays people actively engaged in their daily lives.

Classroom Applications

After listening to some selected poems, such as those related to school, students can write or dictate to teachers or other students their own poems on what it is like to spend a rainy day at school and what kinds of games they like to play. Students can also illustrate their poems with stylized American or African folk art.

Mollel, Tolowa M., retold by. *The Flying Tortoise: An Igbo Tale.* illustrated by Barbara Spurll. Clarion Books, 1994. 32 pp. (ISBN 0-395-68845-0). Folktale, E-L.

Story Review Chart

Setting	Plot/Events	Characters	Theme
•	•	•	

Cultural Paradigm Reference Classification Chart

Geographic Location	Economic System	Social System	Political System
•		•	

The birds tell Mbeku, an unpleasant tortoise with a shiny, impressive shell, that the Skylands have invited the Earthdwellers to a feast. Stating that he is an Earthdweller, Mbeku contrives a way to go to the feast. He convinces the birds to give him feathers and asks his only friend, who is a lizard, to make him wings so that he can fly. At the feast, Mbeku pronounces himself king of the Earthdwellers and states that his name is "All of you." He asks for whom the food has been prepared; the king of the Skylands says, "For all of you." Playing off this trickery, Mbeku explains to his bird counterparts that because the food was for him, he ate all of it. Upset with Mbeku's selfish behavior, the birds take back their feathers so that he can't fly home. Mbeku cries out apologetic pleas until the birds agree to help him. At first, the birds want to ask the lizard to make a soft pile for Mbeku to land on. At the last minute, the birds discover that Mbeku is really not sorry for his past trickery, so they tell the lizard to make the pile hard. Mbeku's landing is so hard that his shell breaks. The lizard tries to repair it, but the result is a mottled, mosaic shell, which tortoises carry with them to this day.

Each page is filled with illustrations that humorously show the emotions of the various characters. The tortoise's facial expressions, for example, are as diverse as slyness and sobbing remorse. Plants and the other animals are painted in brilliant hues and add extra charm to this fun-filled tale.

Classroom Applications

A retold Igbo Nigerian tale, *The Flying Tortoise* is part of the West African oral tradition. Students can practice their own storytelling by reciting the story to one another or by acting it out. Making imaginative props and costumes such as a large tortoise shell and wings covered with feathers can generate excitement and fun. Teachers can also use this book as an example of either a pourquoi story or a trickster tale. Additionally, American children might find it fascinating to compare the characteristics of the tortoise in *Tortoise and the Hare* (Lang, 1993) with the tortoise Mbeku. Another comparison can be made between how tortoises are viewed and treated within the American and African cultures.

 Gershator, Phyllis, retold by. *The Iroko-Man: A Yoruba Folktale.* illustrated by Holly C. Kim. Orchard Books, 1994. 32 pp. (ISBN 0-531-06810-2). Folktale, P-E.

Story Review Chart

Setting	Plot/Events	Characters	Theme
	•	•	•

Cultural Paradigm Reference Classification Chart

Geographic Location	Economic System	Social System	Political System
		•	

This story is a retelling of a Yoruba folktale similar to the story *Rumplestiltskin* (Grimm & Grimm, 1993). According to legend, the Earth Goddess, at the time of creation, plants the Iroko tree before all other trees. A man-spirit with magical powers for good as well as evil inhabits one of the larger and older Iroko trees from which he ventures out and causes all those who gaze on him face-to-face to go mad and die. After no children are born in a Nigerian village for many years, the young women plead with Iroko-Man for children. Iroko-Man asks what they are willing to pay him to have children. The wives of farmers can pay in food, but Oluronbi, the wife of a woodcutter, can only offer her first-born child. After their child is born, Oluronbi and her husband are unwilling to give it to Iroko-Man because they fear the baby would go mad and die if it looked at him. When Iroko-Man does not get the child promised to him, he captures Oluronbi walking through the forest and transforms her into a small bird. When Oluronbi's husband searches for her, he hears a bird sing out sadly and knows what Iroko-Man has done. So he cleverly decides to carve a wooden child, dress it, and take it to Iroko-Man. Having now been paid in full, Iroko-Man changes the bird back into the man's wife. The story ends with Iroko-Man being very pleased with his wooden Iroko-Child.

Highly stylized illustrations are fashioned from cut papers painted in bright colors and bold patterns. They convey a sense of long-ago Nigerian village life, including dress, rituals, and homes.

Classroom Applications

Like many folktales, the story of Iroko-Man tells about the beliefs of a society. Teachers may have students compare *The Iroko-Man: A Yoruba Folktale* with *Rumplestiltskin* (Grimm & Grimm, 1993) by discussing what beliefs, moral lessons, and personal challenges each of these books reveals. Students can also try their hand at folk art by creating their own version of Iroko-Man and Iroko-Child, which can be displayed along with the book and some information on folk art.

South Africa

South Africa lies at the southern end of Africa, where the Atlantic and Indian Oceans meet.

 Isadora, Rachel. *At the Crossroads*. Mulberry Books, 1991. 32 pp. (ISBN 0-688-13103-4). Contemporary Fiction, P-L.

Story Review Chart

Setting	Plot/Events	Characters	Theme
•	•	•	•

Cultural Paradigm Reference Classification Chart

Geographic Location	Economic System	Social System	Political System
•	•	•	•

After a 10-month absence while working in the mines, the fathers of several children in South Africa are anxiously awaited by their families at home. This picture book movingly portrays the excitement and anticipation of children during an otherwise typical day. Washing, dressing, and attending school takes on new importance with the knowledge of their fathers' impending return. After school, the children go directly to the crossroads to wait. Play turns into a hopeful vigil as they wait all night. With the dawn, they are rewarded when their fathers finally arrive.

This outstanding story is brought to life through its captivating watercolor illustrations that reveal the hardships imposed by apartheid on Black South Africans. Several illustrations include significant detail of children and landscapes that are worthy of attention and discussion.

Classroom Applications

Relationships between the economic and social systems are clearly reflected in the activities and circumstances experienced by these children and their families. The 10-month absence of their fathers was an economic and political reality that exacted a substantial social price. Teachers may want to use this story to stimulate discussions about political change in South Africa. Students can also share the feelings they personally experienced when they, too, had to wait to see someone they cared for in their own lives.

 Sisulu, Elinor Batezat. *The Day Gogo Went to Vote*. illustrated by Sharon Wilson. Little, Brown, 1996. 32 pp. (ISBN 0-316-70267-6). Contemporary Fiction, E-M.

Story Review Chart

Setting	Plot/Events	Characters	Theme
•	•	•	•

Cultural Paradigm Reference Classification Chart

Geographic Location	Economic System	Social System	Political System
•	•	•	•

A young girl named Thembi, who lives in South Africa, tells about the time her beloved Gogo (great-grandmother) went to vote for the first time in 1994. Until that time, no Black South African had been allowed to vote in a national election. Because so many

Cover of At the Crossroads *by Rachel Isadora, illustrated by Rachel Isadora, 1991. New York: Mulberry Books, a division of William Morrow & Co., Inc. Printed with permission from William Morrow & Co., Inc.*

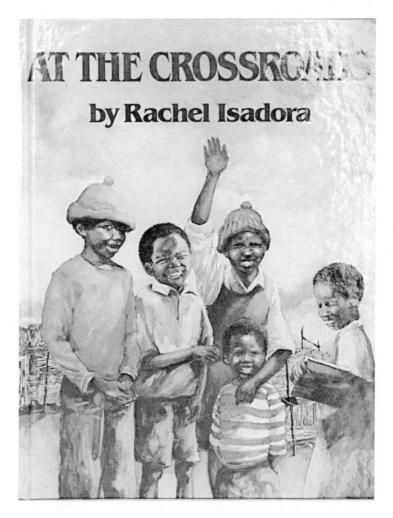

Black people in South Africa had struggled for the right to vote, Gogo tells her family it was her duty to vote for the leaders of a new government. Also, at her age, she may never have another chance to do so. On the day of the election, Gogo is driven by car to the polls to vote, and Thembi goes along to carry Gogo's blue bag. Gogo enters the voting booth and soon emerges to drop her paper ballot into a large box. Photographers take pictures of Thembi's great-grandmother, and others applaud because she is the oldest person from the township to vote. On returning home, family members and neighbors have a party to celebrate the first free election in South Africa. The next day, Thembi and Gogo see their pictures in the newspaper and listen to Thembi's cousins read the story about the election.

The political and social dimensions of the transcultural paradigm dominate this story of history unfolding. The exceptional book communicates a powerful message about participatory democracy while at the same time showing the importance of strong family and community ties.

Wilson's half- and full-page pastels beautifully enrich the story. Thembi's and Gogo's love and respect for each other comes through movingly in nearly every scene. Drawings also show Gogo's dignity and determination as she teaches her great-grand-daughter the responsibilities of a citizen of the new South Africa.

Classroom Applications

Students can discuss why it is important to vote and what they would feel or do if, when they were old enough to vote, their government prevented them from voting. Additionally, they can ask their families or friends whether they vote and, if so, what they remember about voting for the first time. Another participatory activity is for students to go to a polling site before or after an election or to ask an election official to come to class and explain how one votes and possibly help conduct a mock election. Last, students can find out who their representatives in Congress are and send them letters/e-mail messages about issues of concern to the class.

 Cooper, Floyd. *Mandela: From the Life of the South African Statesman.* Philomel, 1996. unpaginated. (ISBN 0-399-22942-6). Contemporary Biography, E-L.

Story Review Chart			
Setting	Plot/Events	Characters	Theme
•	•	•	•

Cultural Paradigm Reference Classification Chart			
Geographic Location	Economic System	Social System	Political System
•	•	•	•

The life and times of Nelson Mandela, from his boyhood to being the president of South Africa, fill this book with inspiration and hope. From his father, a tribal chief of a small rural village in South Africa, Nelson learns the importance of always holding firm to one's sense of what is right and just. When he is 7 years old, his father sends him to school, which he likes very much because there he can learn many new things that interest him. After his father's death, Nelson attends increasingly larger and better schools, until he receives his law degree from the University of Johannesburg. While living in Johannesburg, Nelson Mandela becomes painfully aware of the poverty, injustice, indignities, and denial of opportunities that are imposed on Blacks and other peoples of color living in South Africa. After receiving his law degree and setting up a law practice, he stubbornly but peacefully protests apartheid, the system of government that forces non-White South Africans into an existence apart from that of the ruling White South Africans. Soon, Mandela becomes a strong leader of the African National Congress, which works to give all South Africans the opportunity to vote. Because of his leadership and his actions against apartheid, he is arrested, unjustly convicted of trying to overthrow the government, and sentenced to life in prison. After being in prison for 27 years, Nelson Mandela is released in 1990. He then helps write a new constitution that guarantees justice and fair treatment for all South Africans. In 1994, he is elected the first Black president of South Africa.

Those aspects of the transcultural paradigm emphasized in this superb book are clearly social and political. The social dimension reveals how Mandela's parents, heritage, and experiences helped him know what was right and wrong and just and when to hold steadfastly on to those views. Similarly, the political issues raised remind the reader of what can happen when the rights of people are unjustly denied by others and what one person of goodwill, wisdom, and resolve can accomplish.

Cooper's evocative color illustrations help trace the emergence of Nelson Mandela as a great political leader from his roots in a small farming village to becoming the first democratically elected Black president of South Africa.

Classroom Applications

Students can discuss what they would feel, think, and do if someone controlled their lives—told them where they could live and go to school, what they could do, whom they could talk to—just because of their skin color, who their parents were, or what they believed. Further, they can talk about why going to school was so important to Nelson Mandela and why they think school is important to them. Last, students can discuss what would have happen if Mandela had not stood up for what he knew was right and why it is important to learn and decide what is right, wrong, and just and then to stand up for those ideals.

 Isadora, Rachel. *Over the Green Hills*. Greenwillow Books, 1992. 32 pp. (ISBN 0-688-10509-2). Contemporary Fiction, P-L.

Story Review Chart

Setting	Plot/Events	Characters	Theme
•	•	•	•

Cultural Paradigm Reference Classification Chart

Geographic Location	Economic System	Social System	Political System
•	•	•	

A young boy named Zolandi accompanies his mother on a journey to visit his grandmother and bring her food and firewood. Through his adventure, the reader learns about foods, animals, geography, climate, homes, and people. What distinguishes this book are the genuine personal interactions between Zolandi and his mother, the people they meet on their journey, and the grandmother. For example, when some friends discover their destination, they give food and a book for Zolandi's grandmother. Zolandi, in turn, helps others.

Watercolor pictures capture the vibrant colors of the South African landscapes. The blues, greens, and terra cotta hues accentuate the ocean, sky, flora, and earth that serve as a backdrop to Zolandi's adventure. Zolandi's carefully rendered facial expressions show his ability to focus on tasks, his sense of humor, and his love for his grandmother.

Classroom Applications

Teachers and students can discuss the nature and role of the extended family and thereby gain an understanding of the social system commonly practiced in Africa generally. The African extended family can also be compared with the types of extended families existing in several cultural groups in the United States. Another application is for students to recount the events of visiting someone they know. Were there any similarities to Zolandi's visit? Did they see their grandmother? Did they stay overnight? Did they help anyone along the way?

 Mennen, Ingrid, and Daly, Niki. *Somewhere in Africa*. illustrated by Nicolaas Maritz. Dutton Children's Books, 1992. 32 pp. (ISBN 0-525-44848-9). Contemporary Fiction, P-M.

Story Review Chart

Setting	Plot/Events	Characters	Theme
•	•	•	•

Cultural Paradigm Reference Classification Chart

Geographic Location	Economic System	Social System	Political System
•		•	

Ashraf, who lives in Cape Town, South Africa, tells of his connection with the rest of Africa through his favorite library book. The story opens with the reader discovering that Ashraf lives in a city, rather than in a rural part of Africa. On his way to and from the library, Ashraf communicates his positive view of the city through his thoughts and actions. He notices the sights, sounds, and delights in everything he does, from jumping over sidewalk cracks to listening to the fruitman's songs. Once he reaches the library, Ashraf pretends to browse the bookshelves, but he is really interested in his favorite book on African wildlife, which he renews. At the end of the book, Ashraf links the animal life in rural Africa and himself with the sun that shines on all of them.

The beauty and uniqueness of this story emerge from the urban setting. So many children's stories about Africa take place in rural settings that one may have the impression that Africa has no cities. The story also dispels the misperception that all African children live surrounded by elephants, lions, and zebras. *Somewhere in Africa* offers children another perspective of Africa.

Bold designs and colors characterize the pictures in this book. Whether looking at a detailed close-up of a pair of feet or an aerial view of the city, the illustrations mesh Ashraf's cheerful fondness of city life with his inquisitive interest in rural Africa.

Classroom Applications

Ashraf's actual trip to the library and his mental junket to the savanna provide students with broad views of the lands and people of Africa. Teachers and students can compare city life with country living in Africa, as well as in the United States. Students can also pick a country in Africa and discuss, in addition to being connected by the sun, other ways they are connected with that particular country. Last, students can compare their favorite books with Ashraf's.

Sudan

Sudan is located in northeastern Africa and borders the Red Sea between Eritrea and Egypt.

 Kessler, Cristina. *One Night: A Story From the Desert.* illustrated by Ian Schoenherr. Philomel, 1995. 32 pp. (ISBN 0-399-22726-1). Contemporary Fiction, P-M.

Story Review Chart

Setting	Plot/Events	Characters	Theme
•	•	•	•

Cultural Paradigm Reference Classification Chart

Geographic Location	Economic System	Social System	Political System
•		•	

Muhamad lives with his family in the desert of North Africa. His grandmother teaches him how to survive in the harsh desert and to appreciate its beauty. His father recounts the tests of manhood and sets before Muhamad the task of tending goats for several days without losing any. One night, Muhamad must remain in the desert until a goat gives birth to her kid. When he returns home the next day with all the goats plus the new one, his father beckons Muhamad to sit beside him as a man worthy of a blue turban worn by Tuareg men.

Vivid earth tone illustrations depict the key scenes in the story and capture the beauty of the desert. Illustrations also show important aspects of the way of life and customs of Muhamad's people, the Tuareg.

Classroom Applications

This book can serve as a centerpiece for discussing the passage from childhood to adulthood and the different ways that different cultures view this transition. Additionally, younger readers can recall others who have positively influenced them or discuss what life is like in the deserts in Africa and in the United States. The importance of animals to people can also be examined.

Tanzania

Tanzania is located in eastern Africa and borders the Indian Ocean between Mozambique and Kenya.

 Mollol, Tolowa M. *Big Boy.* illustrated by E. B. Lewis. Clarion Books, 1995. 32 pp. (ISBN 0-395-67403-4). Contemporary Fiction, P-E.

Story Review Chart			
Setting	Plot/Events	Characters	Theme
•	•	•	•

Cultural Paradigm Reference Classification Chart			
Geographic Location	Economic System	Social System	Political System
•		•	

Big Boy tells of a young boy who wishes he were big enough to go bird hunting with his older brother. His mother insists that he finish his lunch and take a nap. The young boy, however, sneaks out of the house with his slingshot to hunt by himself. He spots a bird and stalks it but soon becomes tired and falls asleep. While dreaming, he discovers that the bird he stalked has magical powers to grant wishes. The boy tells the bird that he wants to be bigger and stronger. After the bird grants his wish, he at first dreams of the advantages of someone who towers above other people and even elephants. He then dreams about unexpected disadvantages of being large. When his family finds him asleep, the boy awakes in his mother's arms and realizes that being small also has its advantages.

Watercolor illustrations subtly capture the boy's frustration of being small and his wonderfully fantastic adventures as a "big boy." The carefully rendered scenes in and around his home in a Tanzanian town seamlessly merge the boy's real world into the one he imagines in his dreams. The illustrations effectively highlight the key events throughout the story.

Classroom Applications

Using this story as a model, students can write their own stories about the advantages and disadvantages of being older or younger in America. After finishing their stories, students can discuss whether these advantages and disadvantages might be the same for children living in Africa. The author of this story has written several books about Africa, and students may want to conduct an author study. They can research T. M. Mollel's life and read his books, such as *The Flying Tortoise: An Igbo Tale, The King and the Tortoise, The Orphan Boy,* and *Rhinos for Lunch and Elephants for Supper!* to discover the hows and whys of his works. In what ways is the author's writing similar to the students'?

Zimbabwe

Zimbabwe is located in southern Africa. It is landlocked by Mozambique, South Africa, Botswana, and Zambia.

 Stock, Catherine. *Where Are You Going, Manyoni?* Morrow Junior Books, 1993. 48 pp. (ISBN 0-688-10352-9). Contemporary Fiction, E-M.

Story Review Chart

Setting	Plot/Events	Characters	Theme
•	•	•	•

Cultural Paradigm Reference Classification Chart

Geographic Location	Economic System	Social System	Political System
•		•	

This story depicts the daily walk to school of a young elementary school student. Although her walk is lengthy, Manyoni experiences the beauty of rural Zimbabwe. She passes the baobab, wild fig, and acacia trees and sees bushpigs, baboons, and impalas, among other animals. The breathtaking landscapes that Manyoni comes upon include the Limpopo riverbed, the Tobwani Dam, and expansive grasslands. The story ends with Manyoni reaching her school, where she discovers that she still has time to play with her friends before school begins. The author includes end pages listing unfamiliar words along with their definitions and spellings. Pictures with the names of the wildlife found in the story are also referenced.

Classroom Applications

This on-the-way-to-school story contains a universal theme that most children can understand even though the actual sites that Manyoni visits are unfamiliar to American children. Class discussion of the flora, fauna, and landscapes that Manyoni sees on her way to school would help American children learn about the geography of another cultural region. Teachers can also ask students to describe what they see on their way to school and to compare these places with those Manyoni sees when going to school.

Africa: General

 Kroll, Virginia. *African Brothers and Sisters.* illustrated by Vanessa French. Four Winds Press, 1993. 32 pp. (ISBN 0-02-751166-9). Contemporary Fiction, P-E.

Story Review Chart

Setting	Plot/Events	Characters	Theme
•		•	•

Cultural Paradigm Reference Classification Chart

Geographic Location	Economic System	Social System	Political System
•	•	•	

Jesse and his father play their favorite question-and-answer game about Africa and its many peoples. Jesse's father begins by telling him that some of his African "siblings" are teachers, engineers, and businessmen like his uncle. Jesse, in turn, recalls interesting facts about various African groups, such as the Ibo and the Ashanti, and their lives as farmers and weavers. Jesse then asks his father about the cultural traditions of other groups. The book concludes with Jesse and his father comparing themselves with African storytellers whose tales bring people back again and again to hear more favorite stories.

Watercolor and pencil illustrations realistically portray the various peoples, scenes, and cultures described by Jesse and his father.

Classroom Applications

African Brothers and Sisters provides an informative but brief description of the numerous economic and social systems of Africa. A guide to pronouncing the names of the cultural groups Jesse and his father talk about appears at the end of the book, as does a map of Africa. Students can play the same question-and-answer game in the story to discover more about the cultures in the United States and in many other cultures around the globe.

 Hadithi, Mwenye. *Baby Baboon*. illustrated by Adrienne Kennaway. Little, Brown, 1993. 32 pp. (ISBN 0-316-33729-3). Folktale, P-M.

Story Review Chart

Setting	Plot/Events	Characters	Theme
•	•	•	

Cultural Paradigm Reference Classification Chart

Geographic Location	Economic System	Social System	Political System
•		•	

Thirsty after chasing a hare into a hole and tired of waiting for the hare to come out, Leopard calls Baby Baboon and Baboon, who are playing and laughing in a tree, for assistance. Leopard, who wants to go to the river for water, offers them some hare for dinner if they prevent the hare from escaping. After agreeing to the Leopard's offer,

Baboon guards the hole, but the hare runs out another one. Angry that the hare escaped, Leopard changes his dinner menu and chases Baby Baboon and Baboon. He catches Baby Baboon, but before he eats him, clever Vervet Monkey, who is high in a tree with Baboon, tells Leopard to toss Baby Baboon into the air to make him tender to eat. Leopard throws Baby Baboon into the air and Baboon grabs him. Angry at his loss, Leopard again chases after Baboon and Baby Baboon. The story ends with Leopard stalking Baboon and Baby Baboon, who laugh at Leopard.

Vibrant watercolor illustrations charmingly personify the animal characters in the story and closely parallel the simple but exciting story.

Classroom Applications

The story playfully introduces readers to some animal and plant life found in parts of Africa. Emergent readers can make simple props and masks and act out this story while the teacher reads it to them. To extend the story, students can act out what they would do if Leopard caught Vervet Monkey. How could Baboon and Baby Baboon help Vervet Monkey get away? Students can also talk about the differences between monkeys and baboons.

 Kennaway, Adrienne. *Little Elephant's Walk*. HarperCollins, 1992. 32 pp. (ISBN 0-06-020377-3). Fictionalized Travelogue, P-E.

Story Review Chart

Setting	Plot/Events	Characters	Theme
•		•	

Cultural Paradigm Reference Classification Chart

Geographic Location	Economic System	Social System	Political System
•		•	

Little Elephant, protected by his mother, roams the savanna and forests of Africa. During their odyssey, they encounter lions, zebras, impalas, lizards, hyenas, and many other kinds of animals. Little Elephant sees firsthand how these animals behave and survive in the beautiful but often dangerous African landscape.

Illustrations closely parallel the events in the text and realistically capture the habitats, physical characteristics, and behaviors of both familiar and not so familiar African animals.

Classroom Applications

This book emphasizes the geographic features and animal life of, presumably, East Africa. Teachers and students can select a rural setting in the United States and identify an animal's experiences on a walk through that part of the country. A comparison can then be made with Little Elephant's trek.

Silver, Donald, M. *One Small Square: African Savanna*. illustrated by Patricia J. Wynne and Dianne Ettl. Scientific American Books for Young Readers, 1995. 48 pp. (ISBN 0-7167-6516-0). Informational, P-M.

Story Review Chart

Setting	Plot/Events	Characters	Theme
•		•	•

Cultural Paradigm Reference Classification Chart

Geographic Location	Economic System	Social System	Political System
•		•	

More a reference book than a story, *One Small Square: African Savanna* describes in some detail the life inhabiting a small plot of African savanna. The book emphasizes the seasonal changes in the land and in the vegetation and animals as they struggle to survive. Also highlighted are numerous important interactions between plants and animals and between various animals (predators and prey). Hands-on activities illustrate and reinforce many concepts presented in the text. The living things inhabiting the savanna are assigned to major groups. A comprehensive index helps the reader find information about specific plants and animals.

Many vivid and colorful illustrations support the book's central themes and concepts, as well as accurately depict the physical and behavioral characteristics of the animals and plants of the African savanna.

Classroom Applications

This book deals exclusively with the natural history of a major ecosystem in Africa. Teachers and children can discuss the concept of *ecosystem* and identify the various kinds of ecosystems existing all around the world. Following the discussion, teacher and students can go outdoors to the playground, to a nearby park, or to a grassy area. Each student can select a 1- to 3-ft square piece of land and carefully record or draw what she or he sees. After students return to their classroom, they can compare notes on what they found and construct a hall mural detailing the results of their study.

 Mollel, Tolowa M. *The Orphan Boy*. illustrated by Paul Morin. Clarion Books, 1990. 32 pp. (ISBN 0-89919-985-2). Contemporary Fiction, E-M.

Story Review Chart

Setting	Plot/Events	Characters	Theme
•	•	•	•

Cultural Paradigm Reference Classification Chart

Geographic Location	Economic System	Social System	Political System
•		•	

The Orphan Boy tells why the planet Venus is known to the Masai as Kileken. According to the legend recounted in this story, as an old man searches for a star missing from the night sky, a young boy suddenly appears in his camp. The boy, calling himself Kileken, says he's an orphan searching for a home. The old man invites the boy to stay with him. Kileken, without being asked, does seemingly impossible chores every morning and returns each night to the old man's camp. Although the old man is puzzled by this behavior, he refrains from asking questions about Kileken's remarkable ability and treats him as the son he never had. Eventually giving in to his growing curiosity, the old man asks the boy how he is able to do what seems impossible. Kileken explains that his father gave him special powers that he must keep secret; otherwise, all the old man's good fortune will end. The old man's curiosity grows so strong, however, that he follows the boy's herd of cattle one morning. After miraculously creating a lush pasture with abundant water in the midst of severe drought, Kileken discovers the old man watching him. At that moment, sorrow replaces the trust they shared, and Kileken becomes a bright star that ascends into the morning sky. The old man recognizes this star as the one that originally had disappeared from the sky—a star that appears at dawn and reappears at night.

Beautifully drawn illustrations accentuate the sensitive relationship between the old man and the young boy, as well as the sense of mystery and sorrow in this legend.

Classroom Applications

The Orphan Boy provides a memorable portrait of the homeland of the Masai and their relationship with it. Children can write about the betrayal of trust, theirs or someone else's, or about an experience that was mysterious and inexplicable. After discussing the Masai legend of Venus, students can locate stories from other cultural regions about Venus. What are the similarities? What scientific information is also available on the Internet and in books about Venus? Can any relationships be drawn between scientific facts and legends about Venus?

 Mollel, Tolowa M. *Rhinos for Lunch and Elephants for Supper!* illustrated by Barbara Spurll. Clarion Books, 1991. 32 pp. (ISBN 0-395-60734-5). Folktale, P-E.

Story Review Chart

Setting	Plot/Events	Characters	Theme
•	•	•	•

Cultural Paradigm Reference Classification Chart

Geographic Location	Economic System	Social System	Political System
•		•	

Rhinos for Lunch and Elephants for Supper! is a Masai tale (East Africa) of mistaken identity. The story begins when a rabbit is frightened away from its den by the threatening voice of a monster inside. The rabbit tells a fox about the monster. The fox confidently offers to get rid of the monster and approaches the rabbit's den. The monster's loud, menacing voice scares off both the fox and the rabbit. A leopard, a rhino, and finally an elephant also agree to rid the den of the monster, but they, too, are all frightened by its fearsome voice. Awakened by the commotion of the fleeing animals, a frog boldly volunteers to remove the supposedly fearsome monster. Shouting menacingly into the den, the frog finally flushes out the monster, which turns out to be a small, sleepy caterpillar whose voice had been made loud as it echoed from the den. The story ends when the animals look at each other sheepishly in disbelief and then laugh boisterously.

Brightly colored illustrations create a lush tropical African setting. Animals are rendered so as to accentuate their anthropomorphic nature.

Classroom Applications

The folktale nature of *Rhinos for Lunch and Elephants for Supper!* provides students with a lesson on fear. Teachers and students can share an example of when they overcame something they feared by simply learning more about what frightened them. They can also discuss how, in retrospect, some commonly held fears can now be viewed as humorous as the one presented in the story.

 McDermott, Gerald, retold by. *Zomo the Rabbit: A Trickster Tale From West Africa*. Harcourt Brace Juvenile Books, 1992. 32 pp. (ISBN 0-15-299967-1). Folktale, P-E.

Story Review Chart

Setting	Plot/Events	Characters	Theme
•	•	•	•

Cultural Paradigm Reference Classification Chart

Geographic Location	Economic System	Social System	Political System
•		•	

Zomo the Rabbit is one of several animal tricksters common in the tales of West Africa. Although Zomo is very clever, he also wants to be wise. So, he asks Sky God to grant his wish. But Sky God tells Zomo that he must earn wisdom by doing three "impossible" tasks: bring to Sky God the scales of Big Fish, the milk of Wild Cow, and the tooth of Leopard. Through various ruses, tricks, and knowledge of his "victims'" behavior, Zomo is able to complete all three tasks successfully. Sky God bestows Zomo with wisdom by telling him that three things are worth having: courage, good sense, and caution. Told that he has very little caution, Zomo must escape his irate victims by being fleet afoot.

Bold geometric patterns, bright colors, and stylized images of the characters wonderfully express the book's whimsical qualities that spring from the lighthearted pranks of Zomo.

Classroom Applications

After brainstorming about what it means to be wise, students can map out how they plan to acquire wisdom. What must they do? How long will it take? Can anyone acquire wisdom? Can they help others become wise? What wisdom would they pass on to Zomo? Students can also write and illustrate their own animal tales and compare them with American trickster tales and with *Zomo the Rabbit: A Trickster Tale From West Africa*. When illustrating their stories, students can experiment with the illustrator's artistic style of using bold geometric designs and bright color schemes.

SUMMARY

Although Africa comprises more than 50 countries, only 15 are represented by 30 books reviewed for this chapter. Another 7 books are about sub-Saharan Africa in general, rather than with any particular country. Availability of books was the major reason for this disproportion. Books about a few countries, such as Kenya, Nigeria, and South Africa, were readily available, whereas books about many other African countries are difficult to obtain or simply nonexistent. This underrepresentation of many African countries notwithstanding, the diversity of settings, characters, plots, and illustrations in the books available attest to a continent of geographic and cultural richness. Whether the reader travels back to the time of the pharaohs, accompanies a South African going to a voting booth for the first time, or explores the incredible savanna in Kenya, children's books about Africa provide a wide range of experiences from which a child will gain both enjoyment and understanding.

The 37 reviewed books fall into eight literary genres. The dominant ones are contemporary fiction (18) and folklore (12). One or 2 books belong to each of the following six categories: informational, historical nonfiction, historical fiction, poetry, fictional travelogue, and contemporary biography. This distribution of books among genres offers children many choices of what to learn about Africa, its peoples, and numerous cultures. Typically, children have been introduced to Africa primarily through its folklore or stories written by non-African authors. The strong showing of contemporary fiction will help balance the extensive African folktale tradition. We hope the next step is an ongoing increase in the availability of children's books written by African authors and illustrated by African artists.

Analysis of the content of the reviewed books indicates that the characters are consequential in all 37, the setting and plot/events are important in 30, and a theme is obvious in 29. Similarly, the social component of the transcultural paradigm is evident in all books reviewed; the geographic element, in 30; the economic, in 13; and the political, in just 7.

References Cited

▼▼

Henderson, D., & Elleman, B. (1996). Reading the world: Africa. *Book Links*, 5(3), 42-48.

Osa, O. (1985). The rise of African children's literature. *Reading Teacher*, 38(8), 750-754.

Suggested References

▼▼

Berry, J. (1991). *West African folk tales*. Evanston, IL: Northwestern University Press. (West Africa)

Bischof, P. B. (1991). Publishing and the book trade in sub-Saharan Africa: Trends and issues and their implications for American libraries. *Journal of Academic Librarianship*, 16, 340-347. (General)

Broderick, K. (1995). Reading the world: Africa. *Book Links*, 5(3), 42-48. (General)

Diakiw, J. (1990). Children's literature and global education: Understanding the developing world. *Reading Teacher*, 44(4), 296-300.

Eiseman, T. O. (1986). Primary school literature and folktale in Kenya: What makes a children's story African? *Comparative Education Review*, 30, 232-246. (Kenya)

Emenyonu, E. N., & Nnolim, C. E. (Eds.). (1994). Current trends in literature and language studies in West Africa. In *Studies in West African literatures and languages*. Ibadan: Kraft Books. (Nigeria)

Fayose, P. O. E. (1995). *A guide to children's literature for African teachers, librarians, and parents*. Ibadan: AENL Educational. (Nigeria)

Frew, A. W. (1997). Book strategies: David Macaulay's pyramid. *Booklinks*, 7(2), 20–23. (Egypt)

Garrett, J. (1997). Islam and other belief systems in West African children's books. *Bookbird*, 35(3), 21–25. (West Africa)

Hamidou, A. (1997). Bringing books to Algeria—slowly but surely. *Bookbird*, 35(4), 46–49. (Algeria)

Heale, J. (1997). *The best of Bookchat*. Grabouw: Bookchat. (South Africa)

Joseph, M. (1997). Frames and pictures. *Bookbird*, 35(1), 18–21. (General)

Labbo, L. D. (1995). Safari sojourns: Exploring South Africa with the new geography standards. *Social Studies and the Young Learner*, 8, 8-12. (South Africa)

Labbo, L. D., & Field, S. L. (1998). Visiting South Africa through children's literature: Is it worth the trip? South African educators provide the answer. *Reading Teacher*, 51(6), 464-475. (South Africa)

Matchet, M., et al. (1996). Other worlds, other lives: Children's literature experiences. Proceedings of the International Conference on Children's Literature, 4-6 April. Pretoria: Unisa (University of South Africa) *Bookbird*, 35(2). (South Africa)

McGillis, R. (1996). In South Africa. *Bookbird*, 34(1), 62–64. (South Africa)

Nyariki, L. M. (1996). Reading opportunities for the young in Kenya. *Bookbird*, 34(4), 31-32. (Kenya)

Osa, O. (1995). *African children's and youth literature*. New York: Twayne. (General)

U.S. Department of State, Office of Public Communication, Bureau of Public Affairs. (1996). *Background notes*. Washington, DC: Author.

Wiseman, C. (1992). African tales on stage. *Booklinks*, 1, 24-26. (General)

Children's Books Cited

▼▼

Aardema, V. (1995). *How the ostrich got its long neck*. New York: Scholastic. (Kenya)

Alexander, L. (1992). *The fortune-tellers*. New York: Dutton Children's Books. (Cameroon)

Cooper, F. (1996). *Mandela: From the life of the South African statesman*. New York: Philomel. (South Africa)

Cowen-Fletcher, J. (1994). *It takes a village*. New York: Scholastic. (Benin)

David, R. (1994). *Growing up in Ancient Egypt*. New York: Troll. (Egypt)

Da Volls, L. (1994). *Tano and Binti: Two chimpanzees return to the wild*. New York: Clarion Books. (Gambia)

Dupré, R. (1993). *Agassu: Legend of the leopard king*. Minneapolis, MN: Carolrhoda Books. (Ghana)

Gershator, P. (1994). *The Iroko-Man: A Yoruba folktale*. New York: Orchard Books. (Nigeria)

Grimm, J., & Grimm, K. (1993). *Rumplestiltskin: A fairy tale*. New York: North-South Books.

Haddithi, M. (1993). *Baby baboon*. Boston: Little, Brown. (General)

Heide, F., & Gilliland, J. H. (1990). *The day of Ahmed's secret*. New York: Lothrop, Lee & Shepard Books. (Egypt)

Isadora, R. (1991). *At the crossroads*. New York: Mulberry Books. (South Africa)

Isadora, R. (1992). *Over the green hills*. New York: Greenwillow Books. (South Africa)

Jacaranda Designs. (1992). *Mchesi goes to the game park*. Fort Atkinson, WI: Highsmith Press. (Kenya)

Kennaway, A. (1992). *Little elephant's walk*. New York: HarperCollins. (General)

Kessler, C. (1995). *One night: A story from the desert*. New York: Philomel. (Sudan)

Kroll, V. (1992). *Masai and I*. New York: Four Winds Press. (Kenya)

Kroll, V. (1993). *African brothers and sisters*. New York: Four Winds Press. (General)

Kurtz, J. (1995). *Pulling the lion's tail*. New York: Simon & Schuster Books for Young Readers. (Ethiopia)

Lang, J. (1993). *Tortoise and the hare*. Racine, WI: Western.

London, J. (1997). *Ali: Child of the desert*. New York: Lothrop, Lee & Shepard Books. (Morocco)

McDermott, G. (1992). *Zomo the rabbit: A trickster tale from West Africa*. New York: Harcourt Brace Juvenile Books. (Nigeria)

Medearis, A. S. (1995). *Too much talk*. Cambridge, MA: Candlewick Press. (Ghana)

Mennen, I. (1994). *One round moon and a star for me*. New York: Orchard Books. (Lesotho)

Mennen, I., & Daly, N. (1992). *Somewhere in Africa*. New York: Dutton Children's Books. (South Africa)

Mollel, T. M. (1990). *The orphan boy*. New York: Clarion Books. (General)

Mollel, T. M. (1991). *Rhinos for lunch and elephants for supper!* New York: Clarion Books. (General)

Mollel, T. M. (1993). *The king and the tortoise*. New York: Clarion Books. (Cameroon)

Mollel, T. M. (1994). *The flying tortoise: An Igbo tale*. New York: Clarion Books. (Nigeria)

Mollel, T. M. (1995). *Big boy*. New York: Clarion Books. (Tanzania)

Olaleye, I. (1994). *Bitter bananas*. New York: Boyds Mills Press. (Nigeria)

Olaleye, I. (1995). *The distant talking drum*. New York: Boyds Mills Press. (Nigeria)

Onyefulu, O. (1994). *Chinye: A West African folktale*. New York: Viking. (Nigeria)

Rappaport, D. (1995). *The new king: A Madagascan legend*. New York: Dial Books for Young Readers. (Madagascar)

Sayre, A. P. (1995). *If you should hear a honey guide*. Boston: Houghton Mifflin. (Kenya)

Silver, D. M. (1995). *One small square: African savanna*. New York: Scientific American Books for Young Readers. (General)

Sisulu, E. B. (1996). *The day Gogo went to vote*. Boston: Little, Brown. (South Africa)

Stock, C. (1993). *Where are you going, Manyoni?* New York: Morrow Junior Books. (Zimbabwe)

Watson, P. (1994). *The market lady and the mango tree*. New York: Tambourine Books. (Benin)

SUGGESTED CHILDREN'S BOOKS
▼▼

Aardema, V. (1993). *Bringing the rain to Kapiti Plain: A Nandi tale*. New York: Puffin Books. (Kenya)

Aardema, V. (1993). *Sebgugugu the glutton: A Bantu tale from Rwanda, Africa*. Lawrenceville, NJ: Africa World Press. (Rwanda)

Aardema, V. (1994). *Misoso: Once upon a time tales from Africa*. New York: Knopf. (General)

Aardema, V. (1994). *Traveling to Tondo: A tale of the Nkundo of Zaire*. New York: Knopf. (Democratic Republic of Congo, formerly Zaire)

Aardema, V. (1997). *Anansi does the impossible*. New York: Atheneum. (General)

Angelou, M. (1996). *Kofi and his magic*. New York: Crown. (General)

Banks, K. (1997). *Baboon*. New York: Farrar, Straus & Giroux. (General)

Bunting, E. (1997). *I am the mummy Heb Nefert*. San Diego: Harcourt Brace. (Egypt)

Chase, A. (1997). *Jomo and Mata*. Kansas City, MO: MarshMedia. (East Africa)

Chocolate, D. (1992). *Talk, talk: An Ashanti legend*. New York: Troll. (Ghana, Côte D'Ivorie)

Climo, S. (1992). *The Egyptian Cinderella*. New York: HarperCollins. (Egypt)

Feelings, M. (1994). *Moja means one: A Swahili counting book*. New York: Puffin Books. (Kenya)

Franklin, K. (1992). *Old, old man and the very little boy*. New York: Atheneum/Macmillan. (General)

Geraghty, P. (1994). *The hunter*. New York: Crown. (General)

Gray, N. (1991). *A country far away*. New York: Orchard Books. (General)

Grimsdell, J. (1993). *Kalinzu: A story from Africa*. New York: Kingfisher LKC. (General)

Haskins, J., & Benson, K. (1998). *African beginnings*. New York: Lothrop, Lee & Shepard Books. (General)

Hoffman, M. (1995). *Boundless grace*. New York: Dial Books for Young Readers. (General)

Kimmel, E. (1994). *Anansi and the talking melon*. New York: Holiday House. (General)

Knutson, B. (1990). *How the guinea fowl got her spots: A Swahili tale of friendship*. Minneapolis, MN: Carolrhoda Books. (General)

Kroll, V. (1998). *Faraway drums*. Boston: Little, Brown. (General)

Kurtz, J. (1997). *Trouble*. San Diego: Harcourt Brace. (Eritrea/Ethiopia)

Le Tord, B. (1993). *Elephant moon*. Garden City, NY: Doubleday. (General)

Martin, F. (1994). *The honey hunters*. Cambridge, MA: Candlewick Press. (General)

Mollel, T. (1992). *The princess who lost her hair: An Akamba legend*. New York: Troll. (General)

Mollel, T. M. (1997). *Kele's secret*. New York: Lodestar Books. (Kenya)

Onyefulu, I. (1997). *Chidi only likes blue: An African book of colors*. New York: Cobblehill. (Nigeria)

Onyefulu, I. (1996). *Ogbo: Sharing life in an African village*. San Diego: Harcourt Brace. (General)

Seeger, P. (1994). *Abiyoyo*. New York: Simon & Schuster Books for Young Readers. (South Africa)

Souhami, J. (1995). *The leopard's dream*. Boston: Little, Brown. (West Africa)

Walsh, J. P. (1994). *Pepi and the secret names*. New York: Lothrop, Lee & Shepard Books. (Egypt)

Williams, K. L. (1993). *Galimoto*. Columbus, OH: Varsity Read Servs. (Malawi)

Williams, K. L. (1994). *When Africa was home*. New York: Orchard Books. (General)

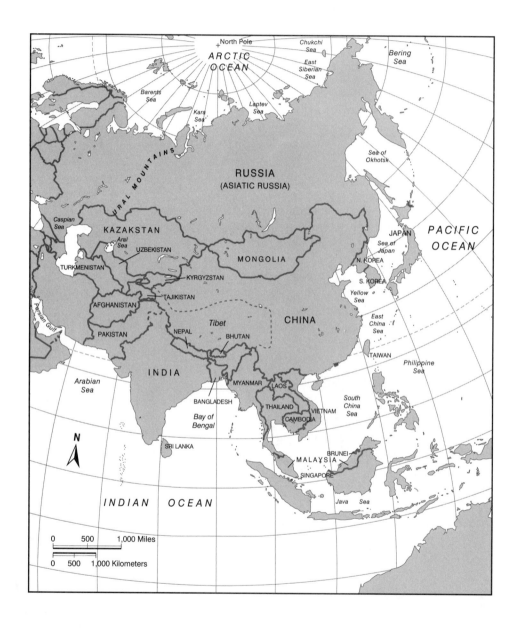

3

Children's Books About Asia

ASIA

Asia consists of two major regions: North Asia and South Asia. North Asia extends from the Caspian Sea and Ural Mountains in the west to the Pacific Ocean in the east and from the Arctic Ocean in the north to the Himalayas and South China Sea in the south. South Asia extends from India in the west through Southeast Asia, which extends into the southwestern Pacific Ocean.

Countries

Afghanistan, Bangladesh, Bhutan, Cambodia, India, Japan, Kazakstan, Kyrgyzstan, Laos, Malaysia, Mongolia, Myanmar (formerly Burma), Nepal, North Korea, Pakistan, People's Republic of China, Russian Federation (Asiatic Russia), Singapore, South Korea, Taiwan, Tajikistan, Thailand, Tibet, Turkmenistan, Uzbekistan, Vietnam

EXAMINING THE CULTURAL REGION OF ASIA AND THE PATTERNS OF CHILDREN'S BOOKS

Asia is a remarkably diverse region by most any standard. The Arctic tundra in Asiatic Russian (Siberia), steamy tropical forests in Southeast Asia, thousands of miles of coastline, the world's highest mountain peaks, countless small islands, and a massive continental area all attest to a broad range of geographic and climatic conditions. The numerous nations making up this region have a wide spectrum of political and economic systems. The cultures of Asia are likewise highly diverse. Moreover, Asian cultures have roots that extend back thousands of years. Given all these circumstances, then, the array of transcultural children's books about Asia is quite extensive, and the number and variety of books are growing steadily.

Traditionally, children's literature about China, India, Japan, Vietnam, and other Asian countries has focused on ancient myths, legends, fables, and folktales (Louie, 1996; Marchetti, 1993; Pike, 1991). Such genres arise naturally from the ancient and honored cultural traditions of Asian peoples and the importance of passing on belief systems, moral principles, and customs from one generation to the next. Recently, however, more children's books about Asia are modern fiction and nonfiction. Children's literature, both traditional and contemporary, can play an important role in helping American children acquire a greater awareness, appreciation, and understanding of the peoples and cultures of Asia (Chi, 1993; Dowd, 1992).

COUNTRIES AND CHILDREN'S BOOKS REVIEWED

Cambodia

Cambodia is located in Southeast Asia and is bordered by the Gulf of Thailand on the southwest, Thailand on the west and north, Laos on the north, and Vietnam on the east.

 Spagnoli, Cathy. *Judge Rabbit and the Tree Sprit: A Folktale From Cambodia.* told by Lina Mao Wall, adapted by Cathy Spagnoli, and illustrated by Nancy Hom. Children's Book Press, 1991. 32 pp. (ISBN 0-89239-071-9). Folktale, P-M.[1]

Story Review Chart

Setting	Plot/Events	Characters	Theme
	•	•	•

---

[1]A = all ages, P = preschool, E = early elementary, M = middle elementary, L = late elementary

Cultural Paradigm Reference Classification Chart

Geographic Location	Economic System	Social System	Political System
		•	•

A husband and wife live happily together until one day the king calls the husband to war. The wife pleads with her husband to stay, but he reluctantly goes off to battle. On his way, the husband's anguish compels him to cry out his desire to return to his beloved wife. A tree spirit overhears the husband's heartfelt lament. While the husband continues his journey, the tree spirit goes to the husband's house to see what would make him want to return. On reaching the house, the tree spirit sees the wife and decides to transform himself into the form of her husband. The tree spirit believes that his living with the wife will make both her and himself happy.

All goes well for several months, until the real husband returns. The wife sees that she now has two husbands whom she cannot tell apart. Confused, she insists they all see a judge. Because the wife is unable to identify her real husband, the judge tells all three to live together. Refusing to abide with the judge's decision, the real husband seeks advice from someone else. He finds Judge Rabbit, who, after listening to the husband's plight, claims he can solve the problem. The two of them quickly return to the village. Judge Rabbit proclaims that only the real husband can fit into a bottle. The tree spirit jumps at this chance to prove that he is the real husband, so he enters a bottle, and Judge Rabbit quickly seals it tightly with a cork. Judge Rabbit then tells the husband and wife to throw the bottle into the woods, which they do. Thereafter, the husband and wife live without being troubled anymore by the tree spirit.

Wisdom overcoming supernatural powers is a central message of this book. The reader learns that the characters revere wisdom and seek the advice of those who are wise. Other virtues portrayed in this story are respect for one another, love between husband and wife, and duty to one's ruler.

Illustrations are done in silkscreen, colored pencils, and watercolors. The pages are boldly framed, and the compositions contain bright color scenes engulfed in lush tropical flora.

Classroom Applications

Have you ever sought advice on solving a problem? Ask students to talk about those individuals whose advice they seek and why. What does it mean to transform oneself from one form to another? Students can create a web of good deeds they would do if they were able to transform themselves into other things or other people. What other stories have characters that undergo transformations? Help students locate these books and describe the changes the characters undergo. Another activity is to look at the role of the rabbit in the story and to compare it with how rabbits are portrayed in other folktales around the world.

China (People's Republic of)

China is located in central Asia and borders many countries on the south (Vietnam, Laos, Myanmar, India, Bhutan, and Nepal), west (India, Pakistan, Tajikistan,

Kyrgyzstan, and Kazakstan), and north (Mongolia and Russian Federation). Its eastern coastline extends from the Sea of Japan in the north to the South China Sea in the south.

 Hong, Lily Toy. *The Empress and the Silkworm.* Albert Whitman, 1995. 32 pp. (ISBN 0-8075-20009-9). Historical Fiction, E-L.

Story Review Chart

Setting	Plot/Events	Characters	Theme
•	•	•	

Cultural Paradigm Reference Classification Chart

Geographic Location	Economic System	Social System	Political System
•	•	•	•

This book recounts the legend of how silk was discovered in ancient China. The story opens when Si Ling-Chi, young wife of the Yellow Emperor, Huang-Ti, finds a cocoon that falls from a mulberry tree into her cup of hot tea. She then discovers that the threads of the cocoon not only unwind in the hot tea but also are transformed into very delicate, silvery filaments that seem to have descended from heaven.

Later, Si Ling-Chi dreams about her husband wearing an elaborately woven yellow robe that can be fashioned only from the exquisite gift of the mulberry worm. The next day, she shows the thread to her husband and explains from where it came. She tells her husband about her dream in which he wears a beautiful robe woven from the shiny thread.

Si Ling-Chi and her servants spend months feeding mulberry leaves to the worms, unwinding their cocoons, and weaving the lustrous fabric. Eventually, they finish the radiant yellow robe, and the emperor wears it to the Autumn Moon Festival. Because the cloth made from the mulberry cocoon is more beautiful than any other, the emperor orders that his wife's remarkable discovery be kept secret. Thus, for 2,700 years, only the Chinese knew how to make silk.

The Empress and the Silkworm provides the reader with glimpses of ancient Chinese customs, social organization, history, economics, and clothing. It also portrays a decisive and active woman who occupies a regal social position. Although Si Ling-Chi assumes a respectful position when she presents her discovery of silk to her husband and his court, it is she who recognizes the potentials of silk, designs a practical use for it, and oversees its production.

Enchanting, softly colored illustrations done in gouache and airbrush acrylics highlight pivotal events in the story, as well as demonstrate aspects of life in a royal Chinese court.

Classroom Applications

To tie this story to the classroom, students can discuss the concept of *discovery* and share what everyday discoveries they have made. Students can also write about how their discoveries could be produced and marketed in today's world. Students also can offer reasons for why the empress, rather than someone else, such as the emperor or one of his wise men, discovers silk. Another suggestion is to write or talk about how something as small and seemingly insignificant as a silkworm cocoon could have such a tremendous impact on human life. How is silk fabric made? Students can locate information about silk on the Internet or in reference books. What other fabrics are made from animals? From plants? Students can share the outcome of their work in a class poster board session.

 Demi. *The Empty Pot*. Henry Holt, 1990. 32 pp. (ISBN 0-8050-17-6). Folktale, E-M.

Story Review Chart

Setting	Plot/Events	Characters	Theme
	•	•	•

Cultural Paradigm Reference Classification Chart

Geographic Location	Economic System	Social System	Political System
	•	•	•

Ping, a boy living long ago in China, loves flowers so much that everything he plants produces a profusion of sweet-smelling blossoms. The old emperor of China also loves flowers, which he plans to use in choosing his successor.

So one day, the emperor gives special seeds to all the children in his kingdom and tells them that the one who shows him the best effort will become the new emperor. Ping tries tirelessly to grow a flower from his seed but nothing sprouts. Because the other children seem to have grown beautiful flowers, Ping feels ashamed of his empty pot. Ping's father, however, consoles him by reminding him that he did his best, which is all the emperor really asked for.

When the day of judging the flowers finally arrives, the emperor looks scowlingly at the flowers of all the children. When he comes to Ping, he asks why he brought an empty pot. Ping replies that he was unable to get the seed to grow despite everything he did. The emperor immediately proclaims Ping to have put forth the best effort. The emperor then explains that all the seeds had been boiled, so nothing could have grown from them. Admiring Ping's effort, courage, and honesty, the emperor rewards him by making him the new emperor.

This simply written story communicates a moral message about being true to oneself and always trying to do one's best. It shows that many will sacrifice what is right for what is perceived to be a greater material gain.

Colorful, delicate illustrations on each page weave a serene tapestry of scenes that wonderfully complement the moral theme of this folktale. The pictures, framed within a circle and full of details, are in pen, ink, and watercolors. The surrounding circular frame is what appears to be soft pastel green rice paper, which creates a sense of traditional Chinese art.

Classroom Applications

Sharing personal stories about honesty and dishonesty and about telling the truth and lying can lead to engaging discussions. *The Empty Pot* reminds students that remaining true to one's values and being honest with others is, in the end, the best policy. Students can refer to some of the feelings mentioned in the book, such as excitement, happiness, hope, disappointment, and shame, and discuss the circumstances in which they, too, experienced these same feelings. Another activity is to ask students how they think plants grow. After webbing their ideas, the teacher can provide each student with some seeds and small cups of soil. Students can plant their seeds, place them on the classroom windowsills, and record any growth in daily observation logs. What factors influenced the plants' growth? How did the students feel about their plants' growth? Another activity is to have students use pen and ink (or fine-tipped felt pens) and watercolors to illustrate their grown plants on rice paper.

 San Souci, Robert D., retold by. *The Enchanted Tapestry.* illustrated by László Gál. Dial Books for Young Readers, 1990. 32 pp. (ISBN 0-8037-0862-9). Folktale, P-M.

Story Review Chart

Setting	Plot/Events	Characters	Theme
•	•	•	•

Cultural Paradigm Reference Classification Chart

Geographic Location	Economic System	Social System	Political System
•	•	•	

A widow lives in a humble house near a forest in long-ago China. There she weaves tapestries like her grandmother and mother before her. By selling her beautiful tapestries, she is able to provide for her three sons, Li Mo, Li Tu, and Li Ju.

One day, she begins weaving a tapestry containing pictures of a fine house, flowers, gardens, and serene fields. After the work goes on for months, the two older impatient sons, Li Mo and Li Tu, tell their mother to stop working on the tapestry so that they can sell it to buy more food. The youngest son, Li Ju, works hard as a woodcutter to earn enough to feed all four. But unlike his older brothers, Li Ju tells his mother never to sell the tapestry because he sees in it her lovingly woven dreams.

When a harsh argument over the tapestry finally ensues, a wind blows it far away. Soon afterward, the mother becomes deathly ill, and she pleads with her two older sons to find and return the tapestry because otherwise she will die. As each of the two older sons searches in turn for the tapestry, an old woman offers each of them gold if they would rather end their dangerous journey. Both Li Mo and then Li Tu take the gold to the city, rather than return home.

When his brothers fail to return, Li Ju asks his mother to let him find her tapestry. She does not want him to because her two older sons have vanished. But Li Ju's persistence finally convinces her to let him go. When Li Ju meets the old woman, he rejects the offer of gold and continues the arduous search. Eventually, he finds a golden palace and beautiful fairies, one of which falls in love with him. This fairy weaves herself into the lost tapestry and gives it to Li Ju, who returns home just in time to save his mother.

When they hang the tapestry, it magically becomes the very place it depicts. Li Ju and his mother enter the enchanted scene, where they find the lovely fairy, whom Li Ju marries, and together all three live happily. One day, the two older brothers come to the gates of their magnificent house as beggars, but they are carried off by a gust of wind to a strange place where they find themselves holding pieces of tapestry and hearing mocking laughter.

A son's unconditional love for his mother enables him to overcome dangers and make her dream come true. This story is imbued with important social lessons: Those who deserve good fortune receive it; self-sacrifice; and duty to family and parents. This book also examines the social structure within ancient Chinese folklore and alludes to the economic conditions of ancient China.

Watercolor, colored pencil, and gouache illustrations marvelously capture the various moods in this story. The muted color scheme also enhances the ethereal quality of the magical parts of *The Enchanted Tapestry*.

Classroom Applications

What is a tapestry? Students can discuss what a tapestry is and find out whether tapestries are found in other cultural regions in the world. Another activity is to involve students in drawing, in tapestry-like form, what they perceive as their perfect dream and to write or discuss what they need to do to make their dreams reality. Students can search for other folktales from around the world that also emphasize the lessons in this book, such as greed and lack of compassion, and compare them with those taught in this book.

 Teague, Ken. *Growing Up in Ancient China*. illustrated by Richard Hook. Troll, 1994. 32 pp. (ISBN 0-8167-2716-3). Historical Nonfiction, E-L.

Story Review Chart

Setting	Plot/Events	Characters	Theme
•		•	

Cultural Paradigm Reference Classification Chart

Geographic Location	Economic System	Social System	Political System
•	•	•	•

A fascinating and informative introduction to Chinese history and culture, *Growing Up in Ancient China* describes various aspects of life in ancient China, including early Chinese history, customs associated with marriage and childbirth; how children were raised, clothed, and educated; everyday life in cities and the countryside; and festivals and religious ceremonies.

Although all elements of the transcultural paradigm appear in this book, the social one is paramount as it begins to explain how the Chinese people lived together and created an enduring and magnificent civilization.

This book is richly illustrated with carefully rendered color drawings that provide the reader with accurate slices of life in China's past. The illustrations show how people of ancient China lived, dressed, interacted, played, and worked.

Classroom Applications

Students can use this book as a basis for comparing China, a country of traditions and history that go back thousands of years, with a country that has much younger roots, such as the United States of America. For example, students might find it interesting to compare the foods of China with those typically consumed in earliest America. Other comparisons could involve clothing, modes of transportation, religious beliefs, and art.

 Hong, Lily Toy. *How the Ox Star Fell From Heaven.* Albert Whitman, 1991. 28 pp. (ISBN 0-8075-3428-5). Folktale, E-M.

Story Review Chart

Setting	Plot/Events	Characters	Theme
•	•	•	•

Cultural Paradigm Reference Classification Chart

Geographic Location	Economic System	Social System	Political System
•	•	•	•

Ox Star lives a leisurely life with other oxen in the royal palace of the Emperor of "All the Heavens." In contrast with the oxen's and emperor's regal lifestyle, the people of the lowly Earth live a subsistence existence. Each day, the Earth People laboriously toil for mere morsels of food. At times, they eat only once every 3 to 5 days.

Concerned for his subjects, the emperor decrees that the Earth People will eat one meal every 3 days. The emperor sends his entrusted messenger, Ox Star, to Earth to convey this proclamation to the Earth People. Ox Star, however, inaccurately communicates the emperor's message. Instead of saying the people are to eat one meal every 3 days, Ox Star proclaims they will have one meal 3 times a day.

The people hail this decree, but the emperor becomes so infuriated that he banishes Ox Star and the other oxen from heaven and sends them to Earth, where they become beasts of burden. Although Ox Star's mistake ends the oxen's life of leisure, it initiates the beginning of a less burdensome existence for the Earth People. The story ends with the insight that one's misfortune may lead to someone else's good fortune.

Through color and style, illustrations effortlessly transform Ox Star's lofty life as a privileged courtier to one of Earth's beast of burden.

Classroom Applications

The meanings of messages are often altered, intentionally or otherwise. Have the class sit in a large circle. Give one student a brief message to whisper to another. Each student in turn whispers the message to the next student. When the message finally returns to the student who first sent it, compare it with the original one. Can the students explain why the message changed? What do they now think about the veracity of rumors and helping pass them on? Similarly, messages that are not accurately communicated from one person to another can lead to misunderstandings and unintended consequences. Have students share their anecdotal experiences with saying or hearing something that was miscommunicated. Their anecdotes can be dictated or written, organized by type (e.g., instructive, humorous, frightening), and listed in a class book. Another class book that students can create is one in which they write down sayings (e.g., "One's misfortune may lead to someone else's good fortune") and figures of speech ("beast of burden") they find in books they read about other countries and cultures. After organizing these sayings by country and book, a task that can serve as an introduction to the why and how of citing sources, students record their interpretations of the sayings in their class book. Also, students can select sayings that are relevant to their everyday lives and experiences and explain why. These class books can also become a basis for cross-cultural comparisons of folktales, legends, and stories containing traditional themes from other lands.

 Steele, Philip. *Journey Through China.* illustrated by Martin Camm, Mike Roffe, and Ian Thompson. Troll, 1991. 32 pp. (ISBN 0-8167-2113-0). Informational, E-L.

Story Review Chart

Setting	Plot/Events	Characters	Theme
•		•	

Cultural Paradigm Reference Classification Chart

Geographic Location	Economic System	Social System	Political System
•	•	•	•

Modern China is the focus of this informative, comprehensive book. China's capital city, the country's influence on other parts of the world, and modern urban life are just a sampling of the many themes discussed. Numerous scenes of everyday life in various parts of China highlight the geographic diversity of this region and the cultural variation of its many peoples. Considerable factual information appears throughout the book, adding to its authoritativeness and informative value.

All components of the transcultural paradigm—geographic, economic, social, and political—appear in this book. The text is richly complemented with numerous captioned color photographs and drawings that focus on people as they work, play, travel, and otherwise engage in everyday life.

Classroom Applications

Before reading the book, students can generate their own questions about what they want to find out about China. After reading *Journey Through China*, students can share their answers in discussion groups. Where would the students like to visit in China, and what would they like to do? Students can plan a travel itinerary to include everyone's interest for a pretend visit to China. Groups can then share their itineraries with other groups in the class. What are the students' favorite places to visit? Students can tabulate these results and present them to another class.

 Yep, Laurence. *The Junior Thunder Lord*. illustrated by Robert Van Nutt. BridgeWater Books, 1994. 32 pp. (ISBN 0-8167-3455-0). Folktale, E-M.

Story Review Chart

Setting	Plot/Events	Characters	Theme
•	•	•	•

Cultural Paradigm Reference Classification Chart

Geographic Location	Economic System	Social System	Political System
•	•	•	

As a young boy, Yue has difficulty learning his lessons until one day the smartest boy helps him because he believes that people who are well off should help those who are less so. Yue remembers these words, and when he grows up and becomes a merchant, he helps out his neighbors.

During a severe drought, the crops fail, leaving little for people to trade with. Because his customers are unable to buy his goods, Yue has to leave his family to find new customers. Yue's search brings him to Thunder Country, where people honor the thunder lords who make thunder and help dragons bring rain. Yue goes to an inn and orders a meal. While waiting for his food, a huge, wild-looking man named Bear Face enters the inn. The innkeeper scorns Bear Face for his oafishness, but Yue buys him a large meal. Bear Face repays Yue's kindness by becoming his protector and later saving his life.

Yue and Bear Face become best friends, and together they travel to Yue's village. When Bear Face sees the devastating effects of the drought, he shouts angrily at the sky, causing dark clouds to appear. He then suddenly changes into a junior thunder lord, pounds on drums, and brings thunder to the village. Bear Face carries Yue up into the storm clouds, where Yue squeezes rain from the clouds onto his parched village far below. After saying good-bye to each other, Bear Face lowers Yue back to Earth. From that time on, Yue's village always has enough rain.

Richly colored dramatic illustrations help create a playful, imaginative adventure. Scenes of traditional Chinese life intermix fantasy and realism.

Classroom Applications

Discuss with the class why some people have believed that thunder lords or some other supernatural forces cause rain, lightning, and thunder. Have students then offer their own explanations for why it rains, thunders, and lightnings. Finally, divide the class into three groups, with one group investigating a scientific explanation for rain, another for thunder, and the third for lightning. Finally, these groups can share with the entire class what they learned about these natural phenomena. Another class activity entails students talking about kindness and respect. Questions raised might include the following: Why should a person be kind and respectful? Who benefits from kindness and respect and why? How does a person learn to be kind and respectful? What are some ways to show kindness and respect?

 Goldstein, Peggy. *Lóng Is a Dragon: Chinese Writing for Children.* China Books and Periodicals, 1991. 30 pp. (ISBN 0-8351-2375-8). Informational, M-L.

Story Review Chart

Setting	Plot/Events	Characters	Theme
		•	•

Cultural Paradigm Reference Classification Chart

Geographic Location	Economic System	Social System	Political System
		•	

The fascination and excitement of first learning to write can be revisited with the help of Goldstein's book on Chinese script. The book begins by briefly introducing the development of Chinese characters, from their earliest forms to those used today. Next, students learn the names of the actual strokes and their directions needed to form Chinese characters. Accompanying written Chinese characters are their phonetic pronunciations, which enable students to begin speaking this language. The Chinese characters representing the numbers from 1 to 12 are then shown, along with their pronunciations. Other characters and strategies for combining words into phrases complete these beginning lessons on the Chinese language. The book ends with a description of Chinese calligraphy and a final sentence for the reader to try translating for fun.

The text in English, the illustrations, and the Chinese characters work together to create an interesting first look at the Chinese language. The black and red color combinations of ink on each page provide simple models for even the youngest scribe to follow and understand.

Classroom Applications

The most obvious classroom application is using this book as a guide for helping children learn to write in a language different from their own. Teachers and students can include this book as part of an overall study of China or as part of a lesson on writing and speaking in different languages. Students can experience an exercise in calligraphy by writing Chinese characters with ink and brushes on rice paper.

 Hillman, Elizabeth. *Min-Yo and the Moon Dragon*. illustrated by John Wallner. Harcourt Brace, 1992. 32 pp. (ISBN 0-15-200985-X). Folktale, E-M.

Story Review Chart

Setting	Plot/Events	Characters	Theme
•	•	•	•

Cultural Paradigm Reference Classification Chart

Geographic Location	Economic System	Social System	Political System
•		•	•

The unlikely hero is the core theme of *Min-Yo and the Moon Dragon*, which takes place long ago in China before stars appeared in the sky. The story begins when seven wise men go to the emperor to tell him the moon is slowly falling to Earth. None of the emperor's aides knows why this is happening or how to stop it. The emperor sends word throughout his kingdom for every wise man, magician, and wizard to think of a way to keep the moon from eventually crashing into Earth.

One old wise man goes to the emperor and tells him about a cobweb staircase in the mountains that people had long ago climbed to visit the dragon who lives on the moon. The wise man further says that someone could climb this staircase and ask the moon dragon to stop the moon from falling to Earth. Unfortunately, the staircase is invisible during the day and very fragile. Consequently, whoever attempts to traverse the staircase must complete the journey in one evening and weigh very little.

Hearing all this, the emperor sends messengers throughout his realm to find the person who weights the least. Afraid of the dangerous journey to the moon, all the people who weigh very little hide from the messengers except for a young girl named Min-Yo. She lives with her parents, who eke out a living by weaving rope from silk. When told of the falling moon, the cobweb staircase, the moon dragon, and the emperor's reward, Min-Yo is eager for the adventure and agrees to go to the moon. She leaves her mother and father and goes to the emperor's palace. There, Min-Yo prepares for the trip: She is measured for specially tailored clothes, learns about the delicate cobweb staircase from the wise old man, and wonders what the moon dragon eats.

On the day of departure, Min-Yo puts on her special clothes to keep warm and packs vegetables in a silk bag, hoping the dragon will find them tasty. She then stuffs her pockets with food and a large diamond given to her by the emperor. At sunset, she steps onto the wispy, sagging staircase and carefully inches her way toward the moon. On reaching her destination, Min-Yo jumps from the staircase into the midst of countless moon flowers. She soon spots a cave and enters. There she finds the moon dragon. Bowing respectfully to this translucent-skinned creature, Min-Yo asks the dragon whether he can stop the moon from crashing into Earth. He admits that he does not know how but that he believes if they put their minds together they might think of a way. Each solution they come up with, however, has a flaw.

Tired from all their thinking, Min-Yo and the dragon rest and have a delicious meal together. Then Min-Yo offers the dragon the diamond as a gift from the emperor. The dragon shows Min-Yo where he keeps all the jewels that visitors had brought in the past. Min-Yo tells the dragon he would tip over if he tried to wear them all, just as she almost fell off the staircase when she carried the large diamond in her pocket. Suddenly, the dragon realizes why the moon is falling: All the gemstones inside the cave have made the moon tip over and fall.

Having no real need to keep his diamonds and other jewels, the moon dragon and Min-Yo toss them all into the night sky. When they are finished, the sky sparkles with countless points of beautiful bright light, and the moon begins to drift away from Earth. With dawn approaching, Min-Yo has to return home. She promises the dragon her family will weave silk rope to strengthen the cobweb staircase so that people can once again safely visit the moon and bring him tasty foods to eat. The prospect of not feeling lonely again greatly pleases the dragon. Finally, Min-Yo bows to the dragon and steps onto the staircase as she and the dragon say good-bye.

Softly colored illustrations augment the enchantment of this story. They create ethereal, serene landscapes that resemble those found in traditional Chinese paintings. Also adding to the authenticity of the scenes are depictions of the clothing, architecture, and customs of an ancient royal Chinese court. Similarly, moon flowers, the moon dragon, his cave, and the diamond-speckled night sky combine to create a world of beauty and magic.

Classroom Applications

Students can compare creation myths of the stars, learn about current scientific explanations, and create star maps that identify constellations. Further, they can compare the dragon myths of China and Europe and find out how spider webs, cobwebs, silk, and diamonds are made.

 Chang, Cindy, retold by. *The Seventh Sister: A Chinese Legend.* illustrated by Charles Reasoner. Troll, 1994. 32 pp. (ISBN 0-8167-3411-9). Legend, E-L.

Story Review Chart

Setting	Plot/Events	Characters	Theme
•	•	•	•

Cultural Paradigm Reference Classification Chart

Geographic Location	Economic System	Social System	Political System
•		•	

The Seventh Sister tells about seven beautiful sisters who, according to legend, dwell in the heavens, where they weave the tapestry of the starry night sky. Magpies then spread this wondrous tapestry over Earth each night, only to have the sun's rays melt it each morning.

One of the seven sisters is named Mei, and she is sad and lonely. A cowherd named Chang, who lives in fertile lowland China, is also living a lonely life. Wanting to learn the source of his loneliness, he consults the stars. One night, he dreams of a magpie telling him of a beautiful maiden who will remain with him if he hides her magical robe, which she must have to return to her heavenly abode. The next morning, Chang meets Mei and hides her robe as the dream foretold. Unable to return to her sisters now, Mei becomes morose and tearful. To end her tears, Chang sings to her. Mei, in turn, sings to him of her unhappiness. The two then fall in love.

The next day, the sun rises earlier than usual and does not set. Mei tells Chang the sun is angry with her because her sisters are unable to finish the tapestry of the night sky without her. Unable to rest, the sun becomes tired and angry. Mei realizes she must rejoin her sisters. Chang agrees and gives the magical robe to Mei so that she can help her sisters weave the starry night sky. Greatly saddened by having to leave behind her beloved Chang, Mei sobs, and her tears become the Milky Way.

After dreaming of being with Mei again, Chang finds a magpie feather that magically takes him to be with Mei. But the Milky Way separates the two of them except for one night each year when a flock of magpies forms a bridge that unites the two lovers. Chang and Mei can still be seen in the evening sky as two bright stars on each side of the Milky Way.

Classroom Applications

The legend of the seventh sister is the basis of a festival celebrated in China on the seventh day of the seventh month each year. Colorful and imaginative illustrations intensify the sense of longing, love, loss, and eventual reunion in this story. Students can compare this Chinese Festival of the Milky Way with Valentine's Day in the United States. How are they alike and different? Also, they can find out more about the Milky Way: What is it, where is it located, and why is it called the Milky Way? Compare this story with others about the Milky Way (Lee, 1990) or stars in general (Hillman, 1992; Hong, 1991). Do other stories from other cultures include the Milky Way? Also, do other stories have the characters leave Earth and live elsewhere for a period of time each year? Students can also compare good luck symbols, such as the magpie in China and the lucky charm or rabbit's foot in the United States. What are other past or present good luck symbols found in other places around the world?

 Zhensun, Zheng, and Low, Alice. A *Young Painter: The Life and Paintings of Wang Yani—China's Extraordinary Young Artist.* photographs by Zheng Zhensun. Scholastic, 1991. 80 pp. (ISBN 0-590-44906-0). Contemporary Biography, E–L.

Story Review Chart

Setting	Plot/Events	Characters	Theme
•		•	

Cultural Paradigm Reference Classification Chart

Geographic Location	Economic System	Social System	Political System
•		•	

This fascinating book is about Wang Yani, a highly talented child artist from China. A *Young Painter* traces the emergence of her artistic talents and successes from a child prodigy at the age of 3 until she becomes a teenager with many interests in addition to painting.

Much of the book recounts in her own words how and why she paints, what she paints, and how the world has reacted to her remarkable talent and achievements. Woven into her story are numerous insights into China's culture and its people. The importance of the family in particular stands out. Yani tells how her parents' support and love have helped her become not only an artist but also a sensitive and thoughtful person.

At the end of the book is a fascinating look at the traditional tools, styles, and techniques Chinese artists have used for centuries to create some of the world's most beautiful and appreciated art.

The book contains many color photographs of Yani at different ages, her parents, and many of her paintings, including a few foldouts. Of particular interest are the photographs that show how she paints and those that trace how her work has changed as she has gotten older.

Classroom Applications

Painting their favorite animals on rice paper will enable students to experience first-hand what Yani enjoys doing and also gives them a deeper understanding and appreciation of her artistry. Students can also share their special talents or interests with one another and find books about their individual interests and talents. Students can then write or dictate how they developed their special interests or talents, who or what influenced their interests and talents, and how they plan to continue pursuing them.

India

India is a subcontinental region located south of the Himalayas. It is bordered on the northwest by Pakistan; on the north by China, Nepal, and Bhutan; on the east by Bangladesh; and on the south by the Indian Ocean.

 Bond, Ruskin. *The Cherry Tree*. illustrated by Allan Eitzen. Boyds Mills Press, 1991. 32 pp. (ISBN 1-56397-621-8). Contemporary Fiction, P-M.

Story Review Chart

Setting	Plot/Events	Characters	Theme
•	•	•	•

Cultural Paradigm Reference Classification Chart

Geographic Location	Economic System	Social System	Political System
•		•	

Six-year-old Rakhi returns home from a bazaar, eating some cherries. She offers her grandfather, whom she calls Dada, one of the cherries and quickly devours the rest. Rakhi looks at the cherry seed in her hand and asks Dada whether it is lucky. Dada says that it is if she makes it work for her. So Rakhi plants it.

Soon, winter and then spring arrive in the Himalayan foothills of northern India. When Rakhi discovers that her cherry seed has sprouted, she waters and watches it. As the tree grows, a few mishaps almost destroy it. Despite these near disasters, the cherry tree grows large enough to produce cherries.

As the tree grows, Rakhi becomes a young woman. Dada explains to her that both she and the cherry tree each resulted from one small seed that grew and changed over time. The story ends with Rakhi telling Dada that one day she will tell her children how her cherry tree came to be.

This intergenerational story shows the universal themes of growth and maturity. Just as Rakhi raises her cherry tree from a seed, so does her grandfather help guide her through her early years. The reader is left thinking that one day Rakhi will continue where her grandfather left off and guide her own children through their formative years.

Illustrations beautifully portray the parallel growth of a child and her tree. The faces of both the child and her grandfather convey the emotions elicited by nurturing something. Whether the two are celebrating how much her tree has grown or being concerned with almost losing it, Rakhi and Dada's facial expressions help tell this endearing story.

Classroom Applications

Planting seeds and recording their growth can introduce students to the scientific method of inquiry and discovery. Students can also use a Venn diagram to compare the similarities and differences of the life cycles of plants and humans. What are the similarities and differences of nurturing them? Students can additionally discuss personal experiences in watching over a younger sibling, interacting with grandparents, or caring for a pet or plant. Another activity is for students to locate the Himalayas and compare this range with a mountain range in the United States.

 Das, Prodeepta. *I Is for India*. Silver Press, 1997. 26 pp. (ISBN 0-382-39278-7). Alphabet Book, P-L.

Story Review Chart

Setting	Plot/Events	Characters	Theme
•		•	

Cultural Paradigm Reference Classification Chart

Geographic Location	Economic System	Social System	Political System
•	•	•	

The alphabet book I Is *for India* provides an abundance of information about the Indian culture. The topics are numerous, diverse, and include animals, entertainment, festivals, clothing, markets, foods, dances, and religions. Each letter of the alphabet begins the name of something appearing in a photograph and being described in the accompanying caption.

Can taking a tour of India be as simple as learning one's ABC's? Although this is not the case, this book does get the reader started in becoming more aware of this remarkable country by providing an assemblage of fascinating and varied information.

Brightly colored photographs framed within dotted borders include information about people from all ages and walks of life in India. Some pages also have photographs of animals and a few landscapes.

Classroom Applications

The class can develop its own alphabet book for which each student picks one or two letters to illustrate. Alternatively, students can find photographs that "spell" their names and then make up stories based on those photographs. Older students might choose one photograph and study its given topic in greater depth—for example, Odissi, the ancient traditional Indian dance.

 Demi. *One Grain of Rice*: A *Mathematical Folktale*. Scholastic, 1997. 34 pp. (ISBN 0-590-93998-X). Folktale, E-M.

Story Review Chart

Setting	Plot/Events	Characters	Theme
	•	•	•

Cultural Paradigm Reference Classification Chart

Geographic Location	Economic System	Social System	Political System
•	•	•	•

The opening scene in this folktale shows the raja ordering his rice farmers to give him most of their harvest for safekeeping. He promises that, in time of famine, all the people will have food to eat.

All is well for a few years until a famine comes. Although his people are desperate for food, the raja refuses to give them any. Even as their hunger mounts, the raja plans a grand feast for himself because he thinks that, as raja, he deserves one.

Critical of the raja's attitude and actions, a village girl name Rani devises a clever scheme to earn a most generous reward from the raja. She catches some rice falling from a basket and returns it to the raja. Impressed by her honesty, he asks her to name her reward. She replies by only asking for a single grain of rice that would be doubled each day for 30 days. Thinking this is truly a meager reward, the raja agrees and begins his payments. After 27 days, however, the raja ends up giving Rani over a billion grains of rice, with which she can feed all the hungry people. Her simple lesson in mathematics teaches the raja not only how to be a good and generous leader but also the concept of *the power of doubling*.

Superb miniature illustrations are suggestive of 16th- and 17th-century Indian art. Several pages of bright colors painted on a gold background bordered with red and gold contribute to an aura of far away and long ago. Two pages unfold to indicate just how many elephants it would take to transport the raja's reward to Rani.

Classroom Applications

Rice is a major food staple for many cultural regions around the world. Students can determine where and how it grows and how it is prepared. They can also get recipes from home or from a cookbook and develop a rice cookbook. What is the power of doubling? Students can use rice to discover firsthand how quickly one grain leads to a large number of grains through doubling.

 Tagore, Rabindranath. *Paper Boats*. illustrated by Grayce Bochak. Caroline House, 1992. 32 pp. (ISBN 1-878093-12-6). Poetry, P–M.

Story Review Chart

Setting	Plot/Events	Characters	Theme
•		•	•

Cultural Paradigm Reference Classification Chart

Geographic Location	Economic System	Social System	Political System
•		•	

In an attempt to feel more connected with the surrounding world he has never seen, a young village boy sails paper boats downstream. He writes his name and where he lives on the boats and fills them with gifts of shiuli flowers for whoever finds them. Nature assists the young boy in his adventure by offering clouds as sails and gusts of wind to carry his boats to distant destinations. In his dreams, "fairies of sleep" sail his ships to unknown ports of call.

Cover illustration from Paper Boats *copyright © 1992 by Grayce Bochak. Published by Boyds Mills Press, Inc. Reprinted by permission.*

This seemingly simple poem sends the fundamental message that children, like adults, want to connect with the world around them. The young boy's ingenious solution for reaching faraway places is through his paper boats.

Delicately crafted cut-paper illustrations in soft colors enhance the contemplative and serene mood of the poem. They also embody the seriousness of the young boy's play and subtly connect his dreams with longed-for experiences in other places that may be out of sight but not out of his imaginative mind.

Classroom Applications

Have students experience the fun of devising ways to connect themselves with the rest of the world and then trying them out. Using a shortwave radio or e-mail via the Internet to send and receive messages allows students to extend their electronic presence around the world. Watching global news broadcasts enables them to see dreamed-of places and the people who live there. After discussing the pros and cons of these methods, students can mark on a map those places they have visited in person or electronically.

Barry, David, adapted by. *The Rajah's Rice: A Mathematical Folktale From India*. illustrated by Donna Perrone. Scientific American Books for Young Readers, 1994. 32 pp. (ISBN 0-7167-6568-30). Folktale, E-M.

Story Review Chart

Setting	Plot/Events	Characters	Theme
	•	•	•

Cultural Paradigm Reference Classification Chart

Geographic Location	Economic System	Social System	Political System
•	•	•	•

Chandra, a village girl living in ancient India, loves to think about numbers and to count things. So begins another story (see Demi's *One Grain of Rice: A Mathematical Folktale*, 1997) about the amazing power of doubling. She also enjoys washing the elephants that belong to the rich and powerful rajah.

The rajah is a harsh ruler because, at harvest time, he collects so much rice from the people who farm his land that they never have enough to feed themselves. This angers Chandra, but she can do nothing about it until one day all the rajah's prized elephants become seriously sick. Doctors from all over the rajah's domain try to cure the elephants, but the animals only become sicker. Chandra tells the rajah that she can help the elephants. After examining them carefully, she sees that they are suffering from painful ear infections. She then goes about curing the elephants of their painful affliction.

The rajah is so grateful that he offers Chandra any reward she desires. Rejecting offers of precious jewels, Chandra instead puts her counting skills to work. She tells the rajah that all she wants is rice but that it must be given to her in the following way: two rice grains placed on the 1st square of a chessboard, four on the 2nd, eight on the 3rd, and so on until all 64 squares have their proper allotment.

Thinking that her demand for rice will cost him very little, the rajah readily accedes to her request. Having to double the amount of rice for each square on a chessboard, however, eventually takes rice the rajah has in his storehouses. Realizing that Chandra's reward cannot be fulfilled, he asks her what he could do instead. Bargaining from a position of strength now, she tells the rajah to give his people the land they farm and to only take as much rice from them as he truly needs. The rajah accepts her offer, and the people of the village celebrate.

The social, economic, and political elements of the transcultural paradigm are all evident in this story.

Brightly colored illustrations depict scenes of a village market, Indian clothing, an ornate palace, and elephants.

Classroom Applications

Re-creating Chandra's scheme with a chessboard is an engaging way for students to learn about the mathematical concept of *the power of doubling*. Provide students with grains of rice (or some other small item in plentiful supply) and have them divide up into groups. Ask each group to be responsible for part of the chessboard. Students can allocate rice grains to the first few squares by simply counting them out. Thereafter, have them use the strategy described in the story: Weigh out 500 grains of rice and then use that weight as a basis for estimating the amount of rice to put on other squares. Students can also discuss how this story on the power of doubling compares with Demi's (1997) *One Grain of Rice: A Mathematical Folktale*.

 Schmidt, Jeremy. *In the Village of the Elephants*. photographs by Ted Wood. Walker, 1994. 32 pp. (ISBN 0-8027-8226-4). Informational, E-L.

Story Review Chart

Setting	Plot/Events	Characters	Theme
•		•	

Cultural Paradigm Reference Classification Chart

Geographic Location	Economic System	Social System	Political System
•	•	•	

The story *In the Village of the Elephants* begins when Bomman is awakened early by his father's elephant, Mudumalai, who tosses sticks against the wall of the house. So begins each day in a small village in the Nilgiri Hills of southern India, where the people and elephants log the forests together and have done so for centuries. To help his father, Bomman rides Mudumalai to the river, where he bathes and scrubs him. Later, he helps feed his giant companion, and that's no easy task.

Nearly ruined by too much logging in the recent past, the forests in the Nilgiri Hills are now a wildlife sanctuary. Bomman's father and Mudumalai patrol the forest to help protect it and the animals living there. Bomman hopes someday to follow in his father's footsteps and work in the forest with the people and elephants he loves.

A collection of photographs vividly reveals everyday village life in southern India. Photographs of people and elephants living and working together show a way of life rooted in tradition yet adapting to change.

Classroom Applications

Given that Bomman does not attend a formal school, have students suggest what lessons Bomman learns by working in the forest with his father and Mudumalai. Students then can apply the notion of "learning from life" to their own lives by thinking about what they can and do learn from everyday activities, such as going to the store and the bank. The often conflicting demands of resource conservation and economic development are evident in this book. Students can research a controversy over whether to develop or conserve a local resource such as a lake shoreline or farmland.

Japan

Japan is a group of islands lying east of Korea and the Russian Federation. It is bordered on the west by the Sea of Japan and on the east by the Pacific Ocean.

Wells, Ruth. A *to Zen: A Book of Japanese Culture*. illustrated by Yoshi. Simon & Schuster Books for Young Readers, 1992. 25 pp. (ISBN 0-88708-175-4). Alphabet Book, E-L.

Story Review Chart

Setting	Plot/Events	Characters	Theme
•		•	

Cultural Paradigm Reference Classification Chart

Geographic Location	Economic System	Social System	Political System
•	•	•	•

A *to Zen* uses the Roman alphabet as an itinerary for the reader to follow on an engaging exploration of Japanese culture. From A for "Akido" to Z for "Zen," the reader learns Japanese words for many views of life in Japan. Martial arts, puppet theater, a formal tea ceremony, clothing, and money are but a few of the stops along this pleasurable journey.

Each page in A *to Zen* is highlighted by a colorful painting that shows a commonplace object, custom, activity, or scene characterizing everyday life in Japan.

Classroom Applications

The organization of this book lends itself to having students, individually or in groups, pick one page to investigate in greater detail, perhaps by comparing it with something similar in the United States that begins with the same letter. Students can compile the outcome of their group work into an ABC book of information.

Biddle, Steve, and Biddle, Megumi, retold by. *The Crane's Gift*. illustrated by Megumi Biddle. Barefoot Books, 1994. 28 pp. (ISBN 1-56957-932-6). Folktale, E-L.

Story Review Chart

Setting	Plot/Events	Characters	Theme
•	•	•	•

Cultural Paradigm Reference Classification Chart

Geographic Location	Economic System	Social System	Political System
•		•	

An elderly married couple live alone in the mountains of northern Japan. They are poor and childless. The man gathers wood from the surrounding forests to make charcoal, which he sells in a nearby village.

One cold winter night, the man finds a beautiful white crane caught in a hunter's trap. He gently releases the magnificent bird, and it flies off, looking back thankfully. Warmed by his good deed, the old man returns home. Later that night, a beautiful young lady knocks at their door and asks for a place to stay the night. The couple invite her in and tell her she may stay for as long as she wants. Days later, the young woman explains that she had lost her parents and would like to stay with the couple as their daughter. The old couple happily accept her offer.

The young woman spends her days and nights weaving beautiful fabric, which the old man sells in the village. The young woman makes her new parents promise never to open the door to the workroom while she is weaving. She continues to make more exquisite cloth day after day, but the work appears to exhaust her. Consumed with concern and curiosity, the old man and woman peek into their adopted daughter's workroom. There they discover that she is a beautiful white crane that pulls out its feathers to make into yarn. The next day, the young woman asks the old man and his wife to accept the most beautiful cloth she has yet made as a token of her deep love and respect. She also tells the man that she is the crane he set free last winter and that, to repay his kindness, she changed herself into a young woman and wove the cloth. But because they broke their promise to her, she must leave them and return to her home before another winter arrives.

Wonderfully painted illustrations of the mountain landscapes in northern Japan communicate a sense of peaceful beauty, as well as the timeless passing of the seasons.

Classroom Applications

The social values of kindness and respect for living things are reflected in the story. Students can talk about how they have demonstrated these values toward others. Weaving is a skill that has been practiced in many places around the world. Students might like to try weaving if a loom is available or to try learning more about where and how weaving is done. An additional activity is to examine the magnificent white cranes of Japan. What does the crane symbolize? Is any bird revered in the United States? If yes, what does it symbolize? Students can look further into which nations revere which birds and what the birds symbolize.

 Demi, selected and illustrated by. *In the Eyes of the Cat: Japanese Poetry for All Seasons.* translated by Tze-si Huang. Henry Holt, 1992. 80 pp. (ISBN 0-8050-3383-1). Poetry, E-L.

Story Review Chart

Setting	Plot/Events	Characters	Theme
•			•

Cultural Paradigm Reference Classification Chart

Geographic Location	Economic System	Social System	Political System
•		•	

This wonderful anthology of Japanese poetry sensitively distills the essence of many scenes from nature. Although the poems are each only a few lines long, they nonetheless charm the mind as well as the heart. Images created by these simple yet ethereal poems encompass the seasons and their passage, weather (snow, rain, mist, fog, dew), time (dawn, day, night), habitats (Earth as a whole, ponds, streams, forests, fields), and celestial objects (sun, moon, stars). The poems also describe salient aspects of many kinds of animals. One poem invites the reader to imagine insects; another, snails. A veritable menagerie of creatures seemingly comes alive for an all too brief moment. One theme common to these poems is the implicit interrelationship all living things have with one another and with the world.

Every poem is complemented by an evocative illustration that shows an animal living in its distinctive way in its nurturing habitat.

Classroom Applications

Most animals described in collections of poems are fairly familiar to students in the United States. Students can select a picture of their favorite illustration and write their own poems about personal or vicarious experiences with the animal portrayed. These poems could be sung to some of the students' favorite tunes or, alternatively, recited with the accompaniment of traditional Japanese music.

 Williams, Laura E. *The Long Silk Strand: A Grandmother's Legacy to Her Granddaughter.* illustrated by Grayce Bochak. Boyds Mills Press, 1995. 32 pp. (ISBN 1-56397-236-0). Contemporary Fiction, P-L.

Story Review Chart

Setting	Plot/Events	Characters	Theme
•	•	•	•

Cultural Paradigm Reference Classification Chart

Geographic Location	Economic System	Social System	Political System
		•	

The Long Silk Strand is a moving story set in Japan about a young girl named Yasuyo and her father, mother, younger brother, and grandmother, who all live together. One night after dinner, Grandmother empties a bag filled with short pieces of silk threads onto the table. She then ties these short threads together into one long strand, which she winds into a ball. Grandmother explains to Yasuyo that each thread represents a fond memory, beginning with when she visited her grandmother above the clouds.

The next morning, Yasuyo's mother tells her that Grandmother has died. While looking for the large ball of thread as a fond reminder of her beloved grandmother, Yasuyo instead finds in the garden a long silk strand dangling from the sky. She climbs the silken strand to the top of the clouds, where she finds Grandmother waiting for her. Yasuyo tells Grandmother that she will remain with her always, but when she looks down on her family to say good-bye to them, she realizes that they will miss her very much. Grandmother patiently convinces Yasuyo to return home and gives her a thread to remind her of the last time they were together. When Yasuyo reaches her home, she imagines telling her grandchild of the time she visited her grandmother above the clouds.

Cut-paper illustrations in soft tones closely parallel key events of the story. They present touching scenes of a young girl coming to terms with her grandmother's passing.

The strong intergenerational relationships typical of a close family are central to this story of love and loss. Respect for, and devotion of, the elderly in particular emphasize the importance attached to traditions that bind the family together through time.

Classroom Applications

Students may want to talk or write about what they do to remember people, places, and events important to them. Perhaps some may have personal photograph albums or scrapbooks they would like to bring to class. Students can also ask their grandparents or family friends to reminisce about their lives. Students then can write down some of these recollections and bring them to class for sharing. Another activity involves making paper cutouts of special times spent with their family or friends. Students can also develop a special moment class book in which, once a month, each class member can add a note about something special that happened to him or her during the month.

 Namioka, Lensey, retold by. *The Loyal Cat*. illustrated by Aki Sogabe. Harcourt Brace, 1995. 40 pp. (ISBN 0-15-200092-5). Folktale, E-M.

Story Review Chart

Setting	Plot/Events	Characters	Theme
•	•	•	•

Cultural Paradigm Reference Classification Chart

Geographic Location	Economic System	Social System	Political System
•	•	•	•

The Loyal Cat is the story of how a temple in northern Japan got its name Hukuzo-ji, or the Cat Temple. A poor priest named Tetsuzan tends and lives in this secluded mountain temple. Priests at other temples in the area dress and behave impressively and sound very important when they recite their prayers. Consequently, many people visit their temples and bring valuable gifts. Although Tetsuzan knows many prayers, his gentle voice and unpretentious ways bring few gifts. Because Tetsuzan needs very little money, however, he is content with his humble life in the simple temple he cherishes.

One day, a band of playful monkeys carry a kitten up into a tree and torment it. When Tetsuzan chases the monkeys off, the kitten, named Huku, thanks the old priest for his kindness. Huku from then on lives in the temple and becomes Tetsuzan's loyal companion. When Huku grows up, he discovers that he can magically suspend objects in the air for as long as he wants. As the years go by, fewer and fewer visitors bring gifts to the temple, and Tetsuzan becomes so poor that he can no longer repair the temple. He also has to beg for food to feed Huku when all the mice leave for want of something to eat themselves.

One day, a young girl tells Tetsuzan that the lord of the nearby castle has died and that many priests have been asked by the lord's son to pray at the funeral. Huku thinks to himself that if Tetsuzan were to pray at the funeral, then people would see his goodness and honor him with many gifts. Tetsuzan then would have fine silk robes to wear, and Huku would again have plenty to eat. Huku then devises a plan to use his magical powers to help Tetsuzan.

Huku's first trick is to raise the dead lord's coffin and suspend it in the air. Despite the strenuous effort of the young lord's strongest men, the coffin cannot be to pulled back to Earth. Believing that a magic spell is behind the floating coffin, all the famous and powerful priests attending the funeral recite impressive prayers to break the spell. When none of them succeed, the young lord asks Tetsuzan to offer his prayer. As Tetsuzan softly prays in front of the funeral procession, only then does Huku allow the coffin to descend to the ground. When the young lord offers to give Tetsuzan as much gold as he wants, Tetsuzan modestly asks for only three pieces. Although this meager reward was enough to repair the temple and buy food, Huku really wanted Tetsuzan to ask for much more gold so that the temple would become rich and famous. Huku later realizes that Tetsuzan truly prefers a simple, quiet life, rather than one of wealth and fame.

Beautifully crafted color illustrations are lined in black and effectively convey the priest's ascetic way of life. They also show the manner of dress, conduct, and custom typical of the Japanese centuries ago.

Classroom Applications

What if another animal instead of the cat had come to the temple? Students can write their own versions of what would have happened in this story and what they would have renamed the temple. Tetsuzan preferred a humble way of life; students can list the advantages and disadvantages of living a simple, quiet life. The power of levitation would be an amazing and useful ability; students can write about, discuss, or draw what they would do if they could make an object or themselves float in midair.

 Uchida, Yoshiko, retold by. *The Magic Purse*. illustrated by Keiko Narahashi. Margaret K. McElderry Books, 1993. 32 pp. (ISBN 0-689-50559-0). Fairy Tale, E-M.

Story Review Chart

Setting	Plot/Events	Characters	Theme
•	•	•	•

Cultural Paradigm Reference Classification Chart

Geographic Location	Economic System	Social System	Political System
•	•	•	

A poor young farmer living in a small mountain village in Japan tries to save some money so that he can accompany his friends on a trip to a shrine. After working hard for several months, he still does not have enough money but decides to go anyway when he sees his friends depart. Trying to catch up with them, he takes what he believes is a shortcut.

As he walks down the path, the surroundings become increasingly unfamiliar. He soon realizes that he is in the dreaded Black Swamp, and before he can retrace his steps, a beautiful young girl comes to him from out of the swamp. She pleads with him to take a letter to her parents who live in the Red Swamp. At first afraid, the young man agrees to help when she explains that she is a prisoner of the ruler of the Black Swamp. She gives him an envelope and a small magic purse of gold coins. She tells the young man to spend as many coins from the purse as he wants but always to leave one so that the purse will become full again. Disappearing into the swamp, the girl calls out, "Don't forget me."

When the young man asks people how to get to the Red Swamp, they warn him that only death awaits those who go there. Urged on by his memory of the enchanting girl, he continues on until he reaches the Red Swamp. There an old man approaches in a small boat and asks for the letter from his daughter. After being handed the letter, the old man invites the younger man to go with him through the swamp to his home and meet his wife. Overjoyed to hear from their daughter, the couple repay the young man's kind deed with a sumptuous feast and gold coins.

After leaving the Red Swamp, the man continues his pilgrimage to the shrine, where he thanks the gods for his good fortune. When he finally returns home, he tells the people of his village about his strange and wonderful adventures. They then praise him for his compassion and courage. Remembering the girl who gave him the magic purse, the young man decides to share his gifts with the people of his village.

Evocative watercolors depict key events in the story and create a serene and bittersweet mood.

The young farmer's character, actions, and good fortune manifest the notion that those who are kind, good, honorable, and brave are rewarded and socially respected.

Classroom Applications

If you had a purse or bag that never ran out of money, what would you do? Offer the preceding question as a topic for small-group discussion. Have students list what good deeds they would do if they had a virtually unlimited supply of money. Another activity is for students to answer the following questions: What is a swamp? What plants and animals live in a swamp? and Do swamps differ in various geographic regions around the world?

 Esterl, Arnica. *Okino and the Whales*. illustrated by Mark Zawadzki. Harcourt Brace, 1995. 32 pp. (ISBN 0-15-20377-0). Contemporary Fiction, E-L.

Story Review Chart

Setting	Plot/Events	Characters	Theme
•	•	•	

Cultural Paradigm Reference Classification Chart

Geographic Location	Economic System	Social System	Political System
•		•	

While watching whales swim and breach in a bay near their home, Okino tells her son Takumi a story about his great-grandmother who became lost while playing on the beach as a young girl. In this story, the young girl's mother searches frantically in vain for her daughter. A seagull flying overhead tells the mother that her daughter is at the bottom of the sea with a large whale and that she can go to her if she brings a lamp to light the way. Knowing now where to look for her daughter, the mother bravely walks into the waves with the lit lamp.

After walking under the sea for some distance, the mother reaches the whale's palace. There she sees her daughter and other children hold hands and dance happily together. At that moment, a huge whale named Iwa, the Great Mother of the Ocean, asks her how she got into the palace and what she wants. Holding up her lamp, the mother says she only wants her daughter back. Impressed with the mother's courage and determination, Iwa gives her a task to complete before she will be allowed to take her daughter home. The task is to weave a coat made from the mother's lovely black hair that is large enough for Iwa to wear to keep warm.

The mother agrees to do the task. First, she cuts off all her hair and then starts weaving the coat. To make her hair grow back quickly, Iwa gives the mother special cream made of oil and ambergris. The mother works tirelessly for many years weaving the coat. By the time she finally finishes the coat, her daughter is a young woman. Pleased with the coat, Iwa orders two dolphins to take both mother and daughter back to shore.

The book's incredible illustrations vividly communicate the other-worldliness of the deep ocean and its denizens, particularly the majestic whale Iwa. The blues and greens blend to create an aura of serenity, beauty, and timelessness.

As an island nation, Japan is intimately tied to the ocean and all that lives there. *Okino and the Whales* highlights this geographic link between land and sea in a poetic way.

Classroom Applications

A study of ocean life—in particular, whales—is a logical follow-up activity. Students can begin by collecting information about different kinds of marine organisms. Then, they can draw a large profile of the ocean from shore to the deepest trenches. Finally, they can find small photographs (or make cutouts) of specific ocean creatures and paste them on the ocean profile where the organisms would normally live. The symbolism in this fantasy of growing up lends itself to classroom discussion.

 Paterson, Katherine. *The Tale of the Mandarin Ducks*. illustrated by Leo and Diane Dillon. Lodestar Books, 1990. 32 pp. (ISBN 0-525-67283-4). Folktale, E-M.

Story Review Chart

Setting	Plot/Events	Characters	Theme
•	•	•	•

Cultural Paradigm Reference Classification Chart

Geographic Location	Economic System	Social System	Political System
•		•	•

The Tale of the Mandarin Ducks is about how compassion and love triumphed over cruelty and evil in Japan long ago. The story begins when a callous, selfish lord orders his servant to trap a wild mandarin drake swimming in a pond on his property. The lord's chief steward, Shozo, fearing that captivity will kill the drake, urges his master to set it free. Shozo's master, however, wants the beautifully plumed duck to adorn his house so that he can impress his wealthy neighbors and guests.

Separated from his mate, who tends her nest full of eggs, the drake's colorful feathers fade, as does his health. Not wanting to see the drab, dying drake anymore, the lord has it taken to the kitchen. Yasuko, a kitchen maid, feels so sorry for the dying bird that she releases it into the forest. When the lord later discovers that his drake is missing, he blames Shozo and orders him to work in the kitchen as punishment. There he meets Yasuko, who wants to tell their cruel lord that she freed the drake. Appreciative of her offer, Shozo convinces her not to confess.

Soon, Yasuko and Shozo fall in love. When their lord learns of this, he accuses them of plotting to steal his precious drake and condemns both to death. While Yasuko and Shozo walk to their execution, two imperial messengers tell the lord that the emperor has banned the death penalty in accordance with the wishes of the merciful Buddha. They also notify the lord that he must send to the imperial court anyone he has sentenced to death.

While being escorted to the imperial court, Yasuko and Shozo escape their guards one night but become lost in the forest. The two imperial messengers find the couple—cold, tired, and frightened—and guide them to a small hut where they are safe. The next morning, Yasuko and Shozo find the grateful mandarin drake and his mate waiting outside the hut. There, deep in the forest and far from their unjust lord, Yasuko and Shozo raise their own family and live a long and loving life together.

Wonderfully inspiring illustrations drawn in a style reminiscent of Japanese paintings depict landscapes, buildings, people, and clothing characteristic of feudal Japanese society. Colors are predominantly earth tones, which help create a serene, almost magical setting that heightens the poignancy of the story.

The social contract between lord and servant underlies this story. One's obligation to this contract has limits, however, as Yasuko and Shozo show. Taken back in time to Japan's feudal past, the reader learns the value of compassion for others, self-sacrifice, and love.

Classroom Applications

Students might find it interesting to compare tales from various countries about animals with the magical ability to change themselves into human form and then help people in trouble. Also, students could undertake a natural history study of the mandarin duck and learn about its habitat, diet, behavior, and other related information. Students can also try to explain why people should be concerned about the welfare of others and why some people risk their own well-being and even their lives to help others.

Korea

Korea is located on the coast of northeast Asia, bordering the Sea of Japan. North and South Korea are situated between China and Japan.

 Heo, Yumi, retold by. *The Green Frogs: A Korean Folktale*. Houghton Mifflin, 1996. 32 pp. (ISBN 0-395-68378-5). Folktale, P-M.

Story Review Chart

Setting	Plot/Events	Characters	Theme
	•	•	•

Cultural Paradigm Reference Classification Chart

Geographic Location	Economic System	Social System	Political System
•		•	

Two frog brothers always do the opposite of what their mother asks them to do. If their mother asks them to be neat, they are messy; if she asks them to be quiet, they are noisy. Life goes on this way for some time. Then one day, their mother grows old and is dying. Knowing that her sons always do the opposite of what she asks, she asks them to bury her next to the stream in the shade. What she actually wants is to be buried on the hill in the sun. When their mother dies, the two frogs regret how they acted toward her in the past. As a parting gesture, then, they decide to follow her wishes and bury her by the stream. That night, it rains and the frogs are afraid that their mother's grave will wash away. They beg the stream to not wash away their mother's grave. This incident explains why frogs still croak today when it rains. This

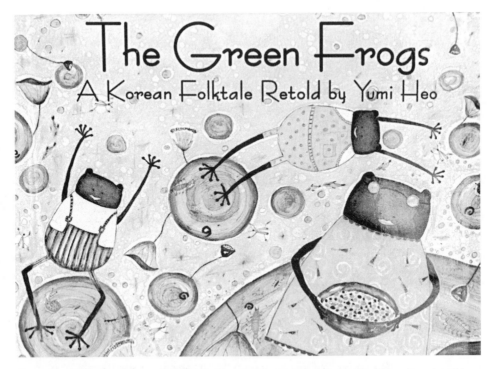

Cover illustration from THE GREEN FROGS. Copyright © 1996 by Yumi Heo. Reprinted by permission of Houghton Mifflin Company. All rights reserved.

imaginative pourqoi tale reminds us of two forms of social behavior that occur in many different cultures: The first is the propensity of young children often to do the opposite of what they are asked to do by others, especially adults. The second is regretting having mistreated others and then atoning for such behavior.

Fanciful illustrations in oil and pencil leap out at the reader and offer an unusual view of frogs. These humorous, flat-faced creatures with webless feet, surrounded by insects and lily pads, entreat the reader to have a closer look.

Classroom Applications

Using this story as a source of ideas, students can write or dictate their own pourqoi stories about how and why something came to be. For example, students may want to think up their own imaginative explanations for why flies fly, why frogs eat flies, or why frogs have webbed feet and hop. Older readers might be interested in studying frog biology (anatomy, behavior, habitat) or compiling a list of frog species from around the world, illustrated with photographs and labeled drawings. This information could be made into a poster presentation for their peers.

Kwon, Holly H., retold by. *The Moles and the Mireuk: A Korean Folktale*. illustrated by Woodleigh Hubbard. Houghton Mifflin, 1993. 32 pp. (ISBN 0-395-64347-3). Folktale, P-M.

Story Review Chart

Setting	Plot/Events	Characters	Theme
•	•	•	•

Cultural Paradigm Reference Classification Chart

Geographic Location	Economic System	Social System	Political System
•		•	

In this Korean folktale, a family of moles lives near a huge statue known as Mireuk. Mama and Papa mole believe that their daughter is the most nearly perfect mole in the "universe." Consequently, they want the best husband for her and devote considerable thought and effort to picking one.

First, Mama and Papa mole think that the King of the Moles would be the best husband, but then they realize that the Sky would be a better choice because he looks down on everything. When Papa visits the Sky, it tells him that the Sun is even more powerful because he hovers above him. So, off to the Sun Papa goes. But the Sun tells Papa that the Clouds often hide him from view. When Papa speaks to the Clouds, they tell him that the Wind is more powerful than they because it moves the Clouds around in the sky. The Wind, in turn, explains to Papa that, although it has great power, it is unable to blow over the huge statue of Mireuk. When Papa finally speaks to Mireuk, he learns that the statue fears only one thing—the mole who can dig away the earth beneath his feet and topple him over. So, Papa mole discovers in the end that the best husband for his daughter was close to home all the time—a fine young mole who lives nearby.

Illustrations throughout this story are highly stylized, brightly colored, and amusing.

Stories with morals typically delve into the social aspects of a culture. *The Moles and the Mireuk* reminds the reader that what people seek and desire most is often within easy reach and familiar. A second moral of this story is that greatness and power are often a matter of perspective.

Classroom Applications

This playful tale calls out to be acted out. It is replete with simple, readable dialogue and has a cast of characters befitting the acting talents of students. Costumes and props quickly made from paper cutouts and cardboard will add to the enjoyment and excitement of the performance.

 Han, Suzanne Crowder, retold by. *The Rabbit's Judgement*. illustrated by Yumi Heo. Henry Holt, 1994. 32 pp. (ISBN 0-8050-2674-6). Folktale, P-M.

Story Review Chart

Setting	Plot/Events	Characters	Theme
•	•	•	•

Cultural Paradigm Reference Classification Chart

Geographic Location	Economic System	Social System	Political System
		•	

This story, printed in both English and Korean, tells how a rabbit, in trickster tradition, saves a kind man from a hungry tiger. One day, a man discovers a very tired and hungry tiger in a deep pit. Unable to get out, the tiger pleads with the man to save him. Although the man feels sorry for the tiger, he is reluctant to help because, once free, the tiger might eat him. The tiger promises not to devour the man if he helps him. Reassured by the promise, the man lowers a log into the pit, and the tiger climbs out.

Once the tiger has been freed, hunger makes him forget his promise. Realizing the life-and-death predicament he is now in, the man tries to convince the tiger not to eat him but instead to be grateful for what he did. The tiger agrees, but only if they can find someone who agrees with the man. First, they ask a pine tree, but it asserts that people know nothing of gratitude because they cut down trees for their own benefit. Next, they ask an ox for its opinion. It, too, says that people know nothing of gratitude because they make oxen toil hard and eat them. Just when the tiger has heard enough and is about to pounce on the man and eat him, a rabbit hops by. The man begs for one last chance to prove that he should not be eaten. So, they explain the situation to the rabbit. To make a wise judgment, the rabbit asks the man and the tiger to return to exactly where they were before their problem first arose. The man goes to the edge of the pit, and the tiger jumps down into the pit. The rabbit reasons that their problem resulted when the man showed kindness and helped the tiger get out of the pit. Thus, he wisely concludes that their problem is solved if the tiger remains in the hole and the man continues his journey.

Highly stylized and imaginative illustrations playfully complement the story line. The main characters of the story are drawn in large, solid form and colored in muted earth tones. Myriad smaller creatures (worms, insects, birds) occupy the background of each engaging scene.

This story comments on the social contract through the cleverness of a trickster who teaches the value of kindness, gratitude, keeping one's word, and judging someone on the basis of what that individual does, rather than on a stereotype.

Classroom Applications

Divide the class into several groups. Have each group debate what the man's fate should be from different points of view—that of the tiger, the man himself, the ox, the tree, and the rabbit. Encourage students to go beyond the arguments offered in the book; for example, the tiger is justified in eating the man because it needs to regain its strength.

Nepal

Nepal is a landlocked country in the Himalayas between India and China.

 Margolies, Barbara A. *Kanu of Kathmandu: A Journey in Nepal.* Four Winds Press, 1992. 38 pp. (ISBN 02-762282-7). Informational, E-M.

Story Review Chart

Setting	Plot/Events	Characters	Theme
•	•	•	

Cultural Paradigm Reference Classification Chart

Geographic Location	Economic System	Social System	Political System
•	•	•	•

Eight-year-old Kanu takes his father's friends on a tour outside Kathmandu. Small farms and villages with bustling markets dot the countryside. Cities are alive with people working, children going to school, and everyone taking time in their busy schedule to relax. By visiting Nepal vicariously, readers learn about its religion, foods, clothing, and customs and about the imposing mountains that dominate this relatively small Asian country.

Photographs that vary in size and composition present a culturally aware portrait of a little-known country on the top of the world. The people and their country are realistically and respectfully portrayed. Words in Napali are scattered throughout the text and listed alphabetically on the final pages of the book. Maps of Nepal labeled in both English and Napali are inside the front and back covers.

The images of Nepal that most people have are largely based on its reputation as a mountain-climbing paradise and on the hardy Sherpas who help climbers scale the world's tallest peaks, such as Mt. Everest. This book provides a much broader and in-depth look at Nepal, its people, and their fascinating culture.

Classroom Applications

A classroom activity based on Kanu's role in this book involves children pretending to be tour guides. They could plan, for example, a trip for their parents or friends to take through their school. Another possibility is to construct Venn diagrams to compare rural and urban life in Nepal (or in any other country). This book can also serve as an impetus for a geography lesson that explores such questions as Where are the Himalayas? How were they formed? Where are the highest peaks? and What are their names (e.g., Mt. Everest)?

Thailand

Thailand is located in Southeast Asia. It is surrounded by Myanmar on the west and north, Laos on the north and east, and Cambodia and the Gulf of Thailand on the south.

Ho, Minfong. *Hush! A Thai Lullaby*. illustrated by Holly Meade. Orchard Books, 1996. 32 pp. (ISBN 0-531-09500-2). Poetry, P-E.

Story Review Chart

Setting	Plot/Events	Characters	Theme
•	•	•	•

Cultural Paradigm Reference Classification Chart

Geographic Location	Economic System	Social System	Political System
•		•	

Mother hushes all the animals so that Baby can sleep. A mosquito, lizard, cat, mouse, frog, pig, duck, monkey, water buffalo, and elephant all oblige and become quiet so that everyone can rest peacefully. But guess who isn't sleeping. Baby, of course! Throughout the story, Baby watches intently as Mother quiets down the animals and remains awake while all the animals and Mother are resting.

The lyrical rhythms of the text soothe the reader from one page to the next while the cut-paper and ink illustrations of varying perspectives, textures, and colors attract the reader's attention.

Classroom Applications

Using the word patterns modeled in this book, students can create their own lullabies. They can have fun dictating or writing one as a bedtime story for their parents, other family members, or themselves and read it when it's time for bed. Another classroom application is for students to listen to recorded lullabies from around the world and to put the lullabies they wrote to music.

 Oliviero, Jamie. *Som See and the Magic Elephant*. illustrated by Jo'Anne Kelly. Hyperion, 1995. 32 pp. (ISBN 0-7868-0025-9). Fiction, E-M.

Story Review Chart

Setting	Plot/Events	Characters	Theme
•	•	•	•

Cultural Paradigm Reference Classification Chart

Geographic Location	Economic System	Social System	Political System
•		•	

Today, Som See and her great-aunt Pa Nang are going to the Harvest Festival. On the way, Pa Nang shares a childhood story about Chang, the king's white elephant. Because the king had won so many battles riding on Chang's back, the elephant would bring good luck to those who touched his trunk. Pa Nang tells Som See that she once touched Chang's trunk.

The two return home from a wonderful day at the festival. Feeling tired, Pa Nang goes to her hammock to rest. But she becomes weaker and weaker. Anticipating her death, Pa Nang confides in Som See and tells her that she, Pa Nang, is about to go on a journey and not return. In a fading voice, she also tells Som See that her journey will be peaceful if she can touch Chang's trunk once again.

Hearing her great-aunt's wish, Som See decides to find Chang and bring him to Pa Nang. She follows monkeys deep into the rain forest and soon becomes lost. Not knowing in which direction to travel, Som See sits by a stream as her teardrops fall into the water. Then, magically, out of the water emerges Fon Pa, the Rain Fish, who says that what she seeks can be found in a palace. Following the fish's directions and walking until her legs ache, Som See comes upon the palace and climbs its crumbling stairs to the top of a tower. There she finds a brass bell and rings it.

Chang, the white elephant, arrives and takes Som See back to Pa Nang. Pa Nang awakens, touches Chang's trunk, and begins her journey. Chang returns to the forest, and Som See places the bell in the spirit house, a place of offerings. Although family and friends mourn Pa Nang's death, Som See knows that her journey will be peaceful.

Exquisite illustrations created by the colorful batik and direct dyeing techniques provide an uplifting backdrop to an otherwise somber story.

This sensitive intergenerational story delves into the respect and love a young child has for her great-aunt. Som See eloquently shows exemplary compassion and determination by fulfilling her dying great-aunt's final wish.

Classroom Applications

What is good luck? What symbols do people in the United States associate with good luck? What things are tokens of good luck in other countries? Students can discuss what people do around the world to bring themselves luck. Older students might want to offer their interpretations of what Pa Nang means when she says, "Luck doesn't last a lifetime." What experiences have influenced their views of good luck?

Tibet

Tibet is part of the People's Republic of China, bordering India, Nepal, and Bhutan on the south.

 Schroeder, Alan. *The Stone Lion.* illustrated by Todd L. W. Doney. Charles Schribner's Sons, 1994. 32 pp. (ISBN 0-684-19578-X). Fiction, E-L.

Story Review Chart

Setting	Plot/Events	Characters	Theme
•	•	•	•

Cultural Paradigm Reference Classification Chart

Geographic Location	Economic System	Social System	Political System
•	•	•	

When Drashi is 10 years old, his mother urges him to work as an apprentice for his older brother, Jarlo, who is a merchant. While working for his brother, Drashi always tries to treat customers honestly and fairly, but doing so sometimes leads to less profit. Such honesty so angers Jarlo that he orders Drashi and his mother to leave the village.

After a long trek into the foothills of the Himalayas, Drashi and his mother fortunately come across an abandoned hut, which becomes their new home. To warm the hut and cook food, Drashi has to scour the nearby mountain slopes for firewood. While searching one day for wood, he comes across a fierce-looking lion carved from stone. Drashi thinks it is the guardian of the mountain that his mother had told him about. As he prepares to pray to the lion, it asks him who he is and why he is there. Timidly at first, Drashi explains that he is just collecting firewood.

The lion orders Drashi to leave and to gather wood lower on the mountainside. Drashi respectfully replies that his mother told him not to cut down any living trees because doing so would eventually harm the mountain. Pleased by his response, the lion tells Drashi to hold a bucket under his stony chin and stroke his hard curly mane until the bucket is full. He admonishes Drashi not to trick him, otherwise he will be punished for his greed. Obeying the lion, Drashi's bucket soon catches a stream of gold and silver coins flowing from the lion's mouth. When the bucket is full, the boy immediately stops rubbing the lion's mane, and the lion tells Drashi to leave and not return.

When Drashi reaches home, he shows his mother the bucketful of coins. Overjoyed by their good fortune, the mother offers thankfulness to Vaishrevana, the god of wealth. News of their sudden prosperity quickly spreads. When Jarlo hears the news, he is perplexed by how his inept brother and old mother could have become so wealthy so quickly. Determined to find out, he and his wife visit them. Unable to lie about where their money came from, Drashi tells his brother about the stone lion.

The next day, Jarlo and his wife climb the mountain, and after many hours they find the stone lion. Jarlo rouses the lion and explains why he is there. Sensing Jarlo's insincerity, the lion tells Jarlo where to hold his bucket but warns him against any trickery. When the bucket is nearly full, Jarlo shakes it to make room for more coins, but a few spill out onto the rocky ground. Immediately, the coins stop flowing, and Jarlo asks why. The lion says that a large coin has become stuck in his throat. Jarlo greedily reaches into the lion's throat to get more coins. Suddenly, the lion's stony jaws clamp down tightly on Jarlo's arm, and all the coins in his bucket turn to ashes. For several days, Jarlo's arm remains trapped in the lion's mouth. Only after he finally admits his regret for being greedy and dishonest does the lion release him. Jarlo and his wife run headlong down the mountain to his brother's home. There, he apologizes to his brother. Drashi not only forgives his brother but also gives him the last of the coins from the stone lion.

Illustrations in this book vividly show the magnificent Himalayas.

Classroom Applications

Students can discuss how they or others they know feel about siblings and what they would do in the United States if they suddenly acquired wealth (e.g., won a lottery). Additionally, would they share their last few coins with siblings who treated them poorly? Students can also study what life would be like in the different mountains around the world. How do mountains differ? In what ways are they alike? How do mountains affect the ways people live? Students can locate Tibet in relation to the Himalayas and compare this story with other stories (e.g., *Kanu of Kathmandu*) that use the Himalayas as a geographic backdrop.

Vietnam

Vietnam is located in Southeast Asia and borders the South China Sea on the east, Laos and Cambodia on the west, and the People's Republic of China on the north.

 Lum, Darrell, retold by. *The Golden Slipper: A Vietnamese Legend*. illustrated by Makiko Nagano. Troll, 1994. 32 pp. (ISBN 0-8167-3406-2). Fairytale, P–M.

Story Review Chart

Setting	Plot/Events	Characters	Theme
•	•	•	•

Cultural Paradigm Reference Classification Chart

Geographic Location	Economic System	Social System	Political System
	•	•	•

In *The Golden Slipper*, Tam's stepmother demands that she toil tirelessly on her father's rice farm. This unbearable workload is further increased when her half-sister, Cam, is born. Tam's father, unable to prevent these cruelties to Tam, dies. After her father dies, Tam's stepmother becomes even harsher than before. To cope, Tam dreams of marrying a prince but knows this is unrealistic because only her half-sister, Cam, has a small dowry to offer a future husband.

One day, Cam goes with Tam to catch some prawns. While Tam works hard, Cam, as usual, plays. Completely exasperated, Tam weeps as she tries to remember her parents. When her tears fall, a lovely woman suddenly appears. She comforts Tam by saying that princesses don't cry. Tam replies that she hardly looks like a princess in her tattered clothes. The woman, however, reminds Tam of her kind and gentle heart and tells her to listen to the animals around her. Tam returns home with a deepened empathy for the animals living with her on the farm. She even shares her food with them.

At last, the Harvest Festival arrives. By giving Cam new clothes, her mother hopes the prince will notice Cam when he chooses his bride. Poor Tam, however, has been ordered by her stepmother to husk a cartload of rice before she can go to the festival. Knowing that this task will take more than a day to do, Tam becomes very disheartened. But after her stepmother and stepsister leave for the festival, the beautiful woman reappears. This time, she has brought birds with her to shake the rice free from their husks.

Then, suddenly and magically, Tam becomes clothed in royal garments with golden slippers on her feet. The old horse is transformed into a regal steed, and off they go to the festival. When they arrive, one slipper falls off her foot, but she cannot stop her horse to pick it up. The prince picks up the slipper and is so impressed by its beauty that he wants to meet the owner. All the women at the festival try on the slipper, but it fits none of them. Tam eventually comes forward, and the prince tries to put the slipper on her foot. It fits easily, they fall in love, and soon marry.

Regal golden orange and yellow in the illustrations foreshadow Tam's royal marriage. These colors appear in her dreams, in her animal friends, and in the clothing worn by the mysterious woman and later by herself and by the prince when they first meet.

This tale closely parallels the story of Cinderella. It communicates a universal theme about dreams coming true for those who are deserving.

Classroom Applications

Comparing various Cinderella stories (e.g., *The Korean Cinderella, Yen Shen: A Cinderella From China*) from around the world can be a fascinating and enlightening exercise. By doing so, students will begin to realize that different cultures have much in common. Ask groups of students to create contemporary Cinderella stories that take place in the country of their choice. What would Cinderella's shoes look like? How would Cinderella meet the prince? After the stories are finished, groups can compare their own stories. In what ways are their stories similar? How similar are the groups' stories to the traditional Cinderella stories?

 Keller, Holly. *Grandfather's Dream*. Greenwillow Books, 1994. 32 pp. (ISBN 0-688-112339-2). Contemporary Fiction, E-M.

Story Review Chart

Setting	Plot/Events	Characters	Theme
•	•	•	•

Cultural Paradigm Reference Classification Chart

Geographic Location	Economic System	Social System	Political System
•	•	•	•

This touching story tells of the people living in Tam Nong, a small village on the Mekong River of Vietnam. As the land along the river recovers from the long Vietnam

War, the people have to make a difficult choice between their traditions and progress. Grandfather tells young Nam about how large, beautiful, wild cranes returned each year in flocks so large they once filled the sky. But when the war came, the wetlands were drained so that soldiers would stay away. Most wild animals, including the cranes, also left to live in quieter, safer places. Grandfather explains to Nam that Vietnam is the true home of these magnificent birds, which bring good luck. He also speaks of his fervent dream that the cranes will return to their ancestral home soon; otherwise, they may never come back again.

Newly rebuilt dikes near Tam Nong are allowing the land to flood once again during the rainy season. However, farmers of the village want to use the wetland for growing rice, rather than as a home for the cranes. Thus, the village is split between those who want to grow more food and those who see the wetland as a way to bring the cranes back for good.

After the monsoon rains flood the land and the dry season is well under way, the cranes are seen flying in a large flock one morning toward the village. The sight of them in the sky makes Nam, Grandfather, and most other people in the village very happy. Grandfather then tells Nam that it is up to him now to make sure the cranes will return year after year.

The book's subtly colored illustrations of village life in the delta of the Mekong River of Vietnam express a sense of rejuvenation and hope.

Grandfather's Dream focuses on geography (river and wildlife), social customs, and people's attitudes. The values of traditions and living in harmony with the land are particularly apparent.

Classroom Applications

As a classroom activity, students can study about migratory birds by drawing maps and plotting their flyways over the United States. They can also invite individuals from a local wildlife conservation group or agency to come to their class and provide additional information about birds and what should be done to protect their habitats. Do the students have dreams about how to make the world a better place? What are they? In a poster session format, students can share their dreams and highlight what they need to do to actualize their dreams.

SUMMARY

This chapter examines recently published children's literature associated with nine Asian countries. Altogether, 35 books are reviewed, and they fall into nine literary genre, with folktales (15) predominating. The remaining books are distributed among eight other genre as follows: informational (5), contemporary fiction (3), poetry (3), fiction (3), fairytales (2), alphabet (2), historical nonfiction (1), and historical fiction (1). This variety of genres is nearly twice that of Africa. Also, children's literature about Asia tends to follow a strong folklore tradition, whereas that of Africa includes a significant body of contemporary fiction in addition to folktales.

The story review charts indicate that story characters are featured in nearly every book. Further analysis shows that these characters typically include one or more of the following: animals with humanlike or magical attributes, children (boys and girls), adolescents, adults/parents, the elderly, and spirits or godlike entities. The setting, plot/event, and theme are crucial in about 75% to 80% of the books reviewed. The setting is either the countryside, a small village, or a home. Plots and events typically encompass a hero/quest, learning a lesson, good overcoming evil, solving problems, and personal sacrifice leading to reward. Themes in these books include moral instruction, personal growth, trickery, intergenerational relationships, societal models of admirable character and behavior, and travel.

Characterizing the 35 books according to the transcultural paradigm also reveals a distinctive pattern. The social element is strongly developed in all 35 books reviewed. Moreover, relationships among the characters and the underlying themes in these books convey obvious social messages. The geographic component is apparent in most of the books reviewed (29), the economic component is found in just over half of the books (18), and the political component occurs even less frequently (14). The emphasis on social issues reflects the importance that Asian cultures have traditionally placed on personal conduct, the family, and interpersonal relationships. The relatively strong showing of the economic and political components stems from recent economic and political developments in the People's Republic of China and other Asian countries.

Although half a world away, Asia is where most people live. A judicious selection of children's books about Asia can help build a bridge for students to cross as they begin to explore and learn about the many peoples and cultures of Asia.

Suggested References

Agarwal, D. (1994). India, a visual journey. *Bookbird*, 32(4), 12-17. (India)

Agarwal, D. (1996). Contemporary Indian fiction in English: A colonial legacy. *Bookbird*, 34(4), 32-34. (India)

Broderick, K. (1995). Korea. *Book Links*, 4(3), 29-32. (Korea)

Cheevakumjorn, B. (1995). The rivalry of values in Thai children's books. *Bookbird*, 33(2), 11-17. (Thailand)

Chi, M. M-Y. (1993). Asserting Asian American children's self- and cultural identity through Asian American children's literature. *Social Studies Review*, 32(2), 50-55. (General)

Dickman, F. C. (1997). Reading the world: India. *Book Links*, 6(6), 36-39. (India)

Dowd, F. S. (1992). Evaluating children's books portraying Native American and Asian cultures. *Childhood Education*, 68(4), 219-224. (General)

Hsieh, D. (1995). Poems of the Shen Tong: Precocious children's verse in ancient China. *Bookbird*, 33(1), 26-29. (China)

Jafa, M. (1996). From goddess to prime minister: Changing images of women in Indian children's literature. *Bookbird*, 34(1), 6-12. (India)

Jin, J. (1996). Women in Chinese children's literature. *Bookbird*, 34(1), 17-21. (China)

Khorana, M. G. (1993). Break your silence: A call to Asian Indian children's writers. *Library Trends*, 41(3), 393-413. (General)

Kindersley, A. (1995). Looking for real children. *Bookbird*, 33(2). (Southeast Asia)

Lewis, J. Y. (1992). Reading the world: Japan. *Book Links*, 1(4), 24-26. (Japan)

Liaw, M. L. (1995). Looking into the mirror: Chinese children's responses to Chinese children's books. *Reading Horizons*, 35(3), 185-197. (China)

Lickteig, M. J. (1996). Books of Japanese Americans, books of Japan. *Multicultural Review*, 5(3), 26-33. (Japan)

Lo, S., & Lee, G. (1993). Asian images in children's books: What stories do we tell our children? *Emergency Librarian*, 20(5), 14-18. (General)

Louie, Y-Y. B. (1996). Children's literature in the People's Republic of China. *Reading Teacher*, 49(6), 494-496. (China)

Louie, Y-Y. B., & Louie, D. H. (1995). Chinese comics in transition. *Bookbird*, 33(3/4), 31-34. (China)

Marchetti, B. (1993). Japan's landscape in literature. *Journal of Geography*, 92(4), 194-200. (Japan)

Matsui, T. (1995). On the threshold of a new era in Vietnam. *Bookbird*, 33(2), 6-10. (Vietnam)

Pike, K. (1991). A fantastic flying journey—through literature. *Language Arts*, 68, 568-576. (General)

Richard, O., & MacCann, D. (1990, October). The Japanese sensibility in picture books for children. *Wilson Library Bulletin*, pp. 23-27. (Japan)

Salwi, D. M. (1997). A stranger in a strange world: Experience of an Indian science fiction writer. *Bookbird*, 35(4), 37-38. (India)

Shen, W., & Emrick, S. (1994). Teaching about China using language arts and social studies. *Southern Social Studies Journal*, 19(2), 55-65. (China)

Singkamanan, S. (1995-96). Other voices: Manga in Thailand. *Bookbird*, 33(3/4), 46-47. (Thailand)

Tajima, S. (1995). Hope in numbers: Cooperative book development in Asia. *Bookbird*, 33(2), 28-33. (General)

Takenaka, Y. (1995). Japan (I). *Bookbird*, 33(1), 52-57. (Japan)

Takenaka, Y. (1995). Japan (II). *Bookbird*, 33(2), 45-51. (Japan)

Tao, L., & Zuo, L. (1997). Oral reading practice in China's elementary schools: A brief discussion of its unique roots in language, culture, and society. *Reading Teacher*, 50(8), 654-665. (China)

Yoshida, J. (1997). Mother-daughter stories in Japan. *Bookbird*, 35(2), 6-11. (Japan)

CHILDREN'S BOOKS CITED
▼▼

Barry, D. (1994). *The rajah's rice: A mathematical folktale from India*. New York: Scientific American Books for Young Readers. (India)

Biddle, S., & Biddle, M. (1994). *The crane's gift*. Boston: Barefoot Books. (Japan)

Bond, R. (1991). *The cherry tree*. Honesdale, PA: Boyds Mills Press. (India)

Chang, C. (1994). *The seventh sister: A Chinese legend*. New York: Troll. (China)

Das, P. (1997). *I is for India*. Parsippany, NJ: Silver Press. (India)

Demi. (1990). *The empty pot*. New York: Henry Holt. (China)

Demi. (1992). *In the eyes of the cat: Japanese poetry for all seasons*. New York: Henry Holt. (Japan)

Demi. (1997). *One grain of rice: A mathematical folktale*. New York: Scholastic. (India)

Esterl, A. (1995). *Okino and the whales*. San Diego: Harcourt Brace. (Japan)

Goldstein, P. (1991). *Lóng is a dragon: Chinese writing for children*. San Francisco: China Books and Periodicals. (China)

Han, S. C. (1994). *The rabbit's judgement*. New York: Henry Holt. (Korea)

Heo, Y. (1996). *The green frogs: A Korean folktale*. Boston: Houghton Mifflin. (Korea)

Hillman, E. (1992). *Min-Yo and the moon dragon*. San Diego: Harcourt Brace. (China)

Ho, M. (1996). *Hush! A Thai lullaby*. New York: Orchard Books. (Thailand)

Hong, L. T. (1991). *How the ox star fell from heaven*. Morton Grove, IL: Albert Whitman. (China)

Hong, L. T. (1995). *The empress and the silkworm*. Morton Grove, IL: Albert Whitman. (China)

Keller, H. (1994). *Grandfather's dream.* New York: Greenwillow Books. (Vietnam)

Kwon, H. H. (1993). *The moles and the Mireuk: A Korean folktale.* Boston: Houghton Mifflin. (Korea)

Lee, J. (1990). *Legend of the Milky Way.* New York: Farrar, Straus & Giroux. (China)

Lum, D. (1994). *The golden slipper: A Vietnamese legend.* New York: Troll. (Vietnam)

Margolies, B. (1992). *Kanu of Kathmandu: A journey in Nepal.* New York: Four Winds Press. (Nepal)

Namioka, L. (1995). *The loyal cat.* San Diego: Harcourt Brace. (Japan)

Oliviero, J. (1995). *Som See and the magic elephant.* New York: Hyperion. (Thailand)

Paterson, K. (1990). *The tale of the mandarin ducks.* New York: Lodestar Books. (Japan)

San Souci, R. D. (1990). *The enchanted tapestry.* New York: Dial Books for Young Readers. (China)

Schmidt, J. (1994). *In the village of the elephants.* New York: Walker. (India)

Schroeder, A. (1994). *The stone lion.* New York: Charles Scribner's Sons. (Tibet)

Spagnoli, C. (1991). *Judge Rabbit and the tree spirit: A folktale from Cambodia.* San Francisco: Children's Book Press. (Cambodia)

Steele, P. (1991). *Journey through China.* New York: Troll. (China)

Tagore, R. (1992). *Paper boats.* Honesdale, PA: Caroline House. (India)

Teague, K. (1994). *Growing up in ancient China.* New York: Troll. (China)

Uchida, Y. (1993). *The magic purse.* New York: Margaret K. McElderry Books. (Japan)

Wells, R. (1992). *A to Zen: A book of Japanese culture.* New York: Simon & Schuster Books for Young Readers. (Japan)

Williams, L. (1995). *The long silk strand: A grandmother's legacy to her granddaughter.* Honesdale, PA: Boyds Mills Press. (Japan)

Yep, L. (1994). *The junior thunder lord.* Mahwah, NJ: BridgeWater Books. (China)

Zhensun, Z., & Low, A. (1991). *Young painter: The life and paintings of Wang Yani—China's extraordinary young artist.* New York: Scholastic. (China)

SUGGESTED CHILDREN'S BOOKS

▼▼▼

Breckler, R. (1996). *Sweet dried apples: A Vietnamese wartime childhood.* Boston: Houghton Mifflin. (Vietnam)

Brown, T. (1997). *Chinese New Year.* New York: Henry Holt. (China)

Climo, S. (1993). *The Korean Cinderella.* New York: HarperCollins. (Korea)

Davol, M. W. (1997). *The paper dragon.* New York: Atheneum. (China)

Day, N. Y. (1996). *Kanci and the crocodile.* New York: Simon & Schuster Books for Young Readers. (General)

Gajadin, C., & Tagore, R. (1992). *Amal and the letter from the king: Adapted from a play by Rabindranath Tagore.* Honesdale, PA: Boyds Mills Press. (India)

Galouchko, A. G. (1995). *Sho and the demons of the deep.* Toronto: Annick Press. (Japan)

Garland, S. (1993). *The lotus seed.* San Diego: Harcourt Brace. (Vietnam)

Garland, S. (1993). *Why ducks sleep on one leg.* New York: Scholastic. (Vietnam)

Ho, M. (1996). *Maples in the mist: Children's poems from the Tang Dynasty.* New York: Lothrop, Lee & Shepard Books. (China)

Hodges, M. (1992). *The golden deer.* New York: Charles Scribner's Sons. (India)

Hodges, M. (1994). *Hidden in sand.* New York: Charles Scribner's Sons. (India)

Ikeda, D. (1990). *The snow country.* New York: Knopf. (Japan)

Johnson, R. (1992). *Kenji and the magic geese.* New York: Simon & Schuster Books for Young Readers. (Japan)

Johston, T. (1990). *The badger and the magic fan: A Japanese folktale.* New York: G. P. Putman's Sons. (Japan)

Kodama, T. (1995). *Shin's tricycle.* New York: Walker. (Japan)

Kudler, D. (1997). *The seven gods of luck.* Boston: Houghton Mifflin. (Japan)

Lang, J. F. (1996). *The bee and the dream*: A Japanese tale. New York: Dutton Children's Books. (Japan)

Lattimore, D. N. (1997). *The fool and the Phoenix*: A tale of ancient Japan. New York: HarperCollins. (Japan)

Lawson, J. (1997). *Too many suns*. New York: Stoddart. (China)

Lawson, J. (1993). *The dragon's pearl*. Boston: Clarion Books. (China)

Lee, J. (1991). *Silent lotus*. New York: Farrar, Straus & Giroux. (Cambodia)

Louie, A. (1990). *Yeh Shen: A Cinderella story from China*. New York: Putnam. (China)

MacMillan, D. M. (1997). *Diwali: Hindu festival of lights*. Springfield, NJ: Enslow. (India)

Mado, M. (1992). *The animals*. New York: Margaret K. McElderry Books. (Japan)

McKibbon, K. (1996). *The token gift*. Toronto: Annick Press. (India)

Melmed, L. K. (1993). *The first song ever sung*. New York: Lothrop, Lee & Shepard Books. (Japan)

Melmed, L. K. (1997). *Little Oh*. New York: Lothrop, Lee & Shepard Books. (General)

Morimoto, J. (1992). *My Hiroshima*. New York: Puffin Books. (Japan)

Morris, W. (1992). *Future of Yen-Tzu*. New York: Macmillan. (China)

Reasoner, C. (1994). *A magic amber*. New York: Troll. (Korea)

Rhee, N. (1993). *Magic spring*. New York: Whitebird Books. (Korea)

San Souci, R. D. (1992). *Samuri's daughter*. New York: Dial Books for Young Readers. (Japan)

San Souci, R. D. (1993). *Snow wife*. New York: Dial Books for Young Readers. (Japan)

Say, A. (1991). *Tree of cranes*. Boston: Houghton Mifflin. (Japan)

Schroeder, A. (1994). Lily and the wooden bowl. Garden City, NY: Doubleday. (Japan)

Shepard, A., & Rosenberry, V. (1992). *Savitri: A tale of ancient India*. Morton Grove, IL: Albert Whitman. (India)

Tejima, K. (1990). *Ho-Limlim: A rabbit tale from Japan*. New York: Philomel. (Japan)

Yep, L. (1993). *The man who tricked a ghost*. Mahwah, NJ: BridgeWater Books. (China)

Yep, L. (1994). *Boy who swallowed snakes*. New York: Scholastic. (China)

Yep, L. (1996). *Tiger woman*. Mahwah, NJ: BridgeWater Books. (China)

Yep, L. (1997). *The dragon prince: A Chinese beauty and the beast tale*. New York: HarperCollins. (China)

Yolen, J. (1992). *Emperor and the kite*. New York: Putnam. (China)

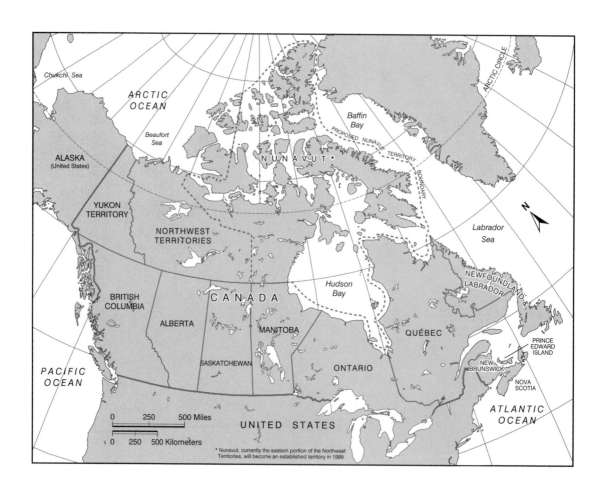

Chukchi Sea

ARCTIC
OCEAN

Baffin
Bay

Beaufort
Sea

PROPOSED NUNAVUT TERRITORY

ARCTIC CIRCLE

ALASKA
(United States)

N U N A V U T *

YUKON
TERRITORY

NORTHWEST
TERRITORIES

Labrador
Sea

BOUNDARY

BRITISH
COLUMBIA

C A N A D A

Hudson
Bay

NEWFOUNDLAND
LABRADOR

ALBERTA

MANITOBA

QUÉBEC

PRINCE
EDWARD
ISLAND

SASKATCHEWAN

PACIFIC
OCEAN

ONTARIO

NEW
BRUNSWICK

NOVA
SCOTIA

ATLANTIC
OCEAN

N

| 0 | 250 | 500 Miles |

| 0 | 250 | 500 Kilometers |

UNITED STATES

* Nunavut, currently the eastern portion of the Northwest
Territories, will become an established territory in 1999

4

Children's Books About Canada

CANADA

Canada is located north of the United States and extends above the Arctic Circle to the north, where it is bordered by the Beaufort Sea, the Arctic Ocean, and Baffin Bay. The country is bounded by the Labrador Sea and North Atlantic Ocean on the east and the Pacific Ocean and Alaska on the west.

Provinces and Territories

Alberta, British Columbia Inuit Nunavut Territory, (1999), Manitoba, New Brunswick, Newfoundland & Labrador, Northwest Territories, Nova Scotia & Prince Edward Island, Ontario, Quebec, Saskatchewan, Yukon Territory

EXAMINING THE CULTURAL REGION OF CANADA AND THE PATTERNS OF CHILDREN'S BOOKS

Like many English-speaking countries of the world, Canada has had a large increase in the number of children's books published within the past 10 years. Jobe (1989), in fact, claims that Canadian children have more books available for them than children in any other English-speaking country, receiving them from the United States, Great Britain, Australia, New Zealand, and Canada itself. Many of these Canadian books are now available in the United States as well. In addition, well-known Canadian authors and artists publish books in the United States. Are you surprised to learn that the popular writer Robert Munsch is Canadian?

American authors such as Marie Killilea, too, publish books geared to Canadian audiences. Publication information in the front of these books will mention "published simultaneously in Canada."

Canada is a huge, far-flung country stretching from the Atlantic to the Pacific, the second-largest country in the world. Its children's books reflect its diversity of locations, as well as its diversity of people. English, French, native peoples, and immigrants from the British Commonwealth make up most of the population.

Being farther north than the United States, its climate is colder, which is also reflected in its children's books. Both climate and geography influence the natural environment, dictating what animals and vegetation are present in nature and in children's stories. The Canadian picture books reviewed in this chapter have been selected to reflect these differences, giving American readers an opportunity to experience vicariously our fascinating neighbor to the north.

CHILDREN'S BOOKS REVIEWED

▼ Kusugak, Michael Arvaarluk. *Baseball Bats for Christmas*. illustrated by Vladyana Krykorka. Annick Press, 1990. 24 pp. (ISBN 1-55037-144-4). Contemporary Fiction, E-L[1]

Story Review Chart			
Setting	Plot/Events	Characters	Theme
•	•		

Cultural Paradigm Reference Classification Chart			
Geographic Location	Economic System	Social System	Political System
•		•	

[1]A = all ages, P = preschool, E = early elementary, M = middle elementary, L = late elementary

Arvaarluk, a 7-year-old Inuit boy, lives in an igloo in Repulse Bay on the Arctic Circle, where everything is ice and snow and no "standing-ups," as Arvaarluk's friends call trees, live. But one Christmas, Rocky Parsons, who flies in supplies in his trusty Norse-man plane, brings in six of them—Christmas trees. The boys have no idea what they are for, but when the manager of the Hudson's Bay store gives Arvaarluk a blue and red rubber ball for Christmas, his friend Yvo looks at the spindly trees and says, "I know what those things are for: baseball bats." So the boys cut off all the branches, fashion the trunks into bats, and play baseball for Christmas!

The author, an Inuit writer and children's storyteller, spent his first 11 years at Repulse Bay, and many of his books reflect this life among the children of the North. The artist, who emigrated to Canada from Czechoslovakia, stayed with the Kusugak family while painting the people of the North. She catches the flavor of life in this seemingly barren land, showing the fun of children's homemade games and the tradition of gift-giving your most favorite thing in the world to your very best friend, against a background of blue-shadowed snow and colorful northern lights.

Classroom Applications

What would your students give as gifts if they lived at Repulse Bay? Can they make up their own stories about it? How else could they use a Christmas tree? Divide the class into small groups and have them pretend to be Inuits who have received an evergreen tree for Christmas. What would each group decide to do with it?

 Carrier, Roch. *The Boxing Champion*. illustrated by Sheldon Cohen, and translated from French by Sheila Fischman. Tundra Books, 1991. 24 pp. (ISBN 0-88776-257-3). Contemporary Fiction, M-L.

Story Review Chart

Setting	Plot/Events	Characters	Theme
•	•	•	

Cultural Paradigm Reference Classification Chart

Geographic Location	Economic System	Social System	Political System
•		•	

Roch hates spring. In April, the hockey rink in his Quebec village of Sainte-Justine turns into a cow pasture again. The boys put their skates away, and the girls look for wildflow-ers in the grass. The Cotes children move into their summer kitchen and draw a big square on the floor for the boxing ring. Ten-year-old Roch hates boxing as much as he loves hockey, but he knows he will have to go up against the tough Cotes boys once again. This time he will be prepared, however, for with his mother's help he has ordered the Miracle Muscle Exerciser and Miracle Muscle Barbells, along with the Miracle Muscle Guide, which has been teaching him all winter long how to become a boxing champion.

When the nail-and-bottle bell rings for the first round that spring, Roch steps into the ring, ready to attack the youngest Cote boy. But when he opens his eyes again, he finds himself stretched out flat on the floor with a bleeding nose. Then a girl smiles down at him and tosses him some wildflowers. She is the prettiest girl in his class, and he has never dared talk to her. What a wonderful spring it's going to be after all, Roch decides.

Humorous cartoon-like drawings give readers a look at the inside and outside of Roch's house, room, school, and boxing ring from above, as well as straight on, as they enter the world of "the next French-Canadian boxing champion." Here is another amusing look at how children entertain themselves during the long, cold winters and springs of the Canadian north.

Classroom Applications

What winter games do your students know about? Can they invent one? Talk about how spring changes the land when the snow melts. Then have students look closely at the illustrations. What French words can they find within the pictures? Bring in a French dictionary and look up their meanings together.

 MacDonald, Hugh. *Chung Lee Loves Lobsters*. illustrated by Johnny Wales. Annick Press, 1992. 24 pp. (ISBN 1-55037-214-9). Contemporary Fiction, E-L.

Story Review Chart

Setting	Plot/Events	Characters	Theme
	•	•	•

Cultural Paradigm Reference Classification Chart

Geographic Location	Economic System	Social System	Political System
	•	•	

Five-year-old Bizzer and his 10-year-old brother, Wally, love to look at the live lobsters in their mother's restaurant in the fishing town on Prince Edward Island where they live. Once a month, old Mr. Chung Lee, the retired cook, comes in to buy a lobster for his dinner—a good healthy female. Their mother tries to sell him a cooked lobster, but he always takes a live one. She tells the boys afterward what a good cook Mr. Lee was when he worked there for 35 years.

The boys decide to follow Mr. Lee secretly to watch him cook and eat his lobster. He goes down to the shore, takes out chopsticks and a bowl, and begins scooping rice into his mouth. Then he takes the lobster from his cooler, but instead of cooking it, he walks out into the water about a meter, puts the lobster in the water, and lets it go. Bizzer is so upset that Mr. Lee has lost his monthly lobster that he runs down to the water's edge, crying.

A surprised Mr. Lee then tells the boys the story of how he came from China to Canada and worked in the restaurant cooking lobsters, putting them into boiling water, which gave them pain. Now he wants to restore some of the good he had taken away by releasing the one lobster he could afford every month to please the spirits of its ancestors he had hurt. Bizzer is puzzled because he thought Mr. Lee loved lobsters. The cook says, "I do, little boy." When Bizzer's mother finds out that the boys were watching Mr. Lee eat his dinner, she asks whether he enjoyed his lobster. Both boys answer together, "Yes, Mr. Chung Lee loves lobsters."

Watercolor illustrations on every other page bring to life the streets, restaurant, and shore of this Canadian fishing town. But it is the lesson Chung Lee teaches about living things that should touch the heart of the reader.

Classroom Applications

This is a story about appreciating the living creatures that give us food and about appreciating people who are different. Did your students understand it? Can they think of ways to appreciate the food they consume (e.g., learn about where a certain food comes from and how it is prepared; eat it all and not waste it)? What do they know about rice, for instance? Where did Mr. Lee get the rice he was eating? Bring in a hot plate and have the students help prepare a rice dish for eating.

 Sackett, Elisabeth. *Danger on the Arctic Ice*. illustrated by Martin Camm. Little, Brown, 1991. 28 pp. (ISBN 0-316-76598-8). Contemporary Fiction, E-L.

Story Review Chart

Setting	Plot/Events	Characters	Theme
•	•	•	

Cultural Paradigm Reference Classification Chart

Geographic Location	Economic System	Social System	Political System
•	•		

Although this story of the dangers a harp seal pup must face every spring when the sea ice breaks up is based on fact, today most seal pups are safe from human violence because of a treaty preventing their killing signed by Canada, the United States, and the European nations. Exquisite illustrations on every other page by nature artist Martin Camm portray the animals of this frozen world as the seal pup encounters an Arctic fox and a polar bear. Most dangerous, however, is the fur hunters in their boat, from whom the pup escapes just in time with the help of mother seal.

Classroom Applications

Suggest that the students create a diorama of the icy sea with icebergs and ice floes made from plaster of paris, Styrofoam, or cardboard sprayed with Christmas tree "snow." They can fashion Arctic animals from play dough, clay, or cardboard. Suggest that they make up stories about the Arctic animals they have created for another class to enjoy.

Harrison, Troon. *Don't Dig So Deep, Nicholas!* illustrated by Gary Clement. Owl Books, 1997. 32 pp. (ISBN 1-895688-60-4). Contemporary Fiction, P-E.

Story Review Chart

Setting	Plot/Events	Characters	Theme
	•	•	

Cultural Paradigm Reference Classification Chart

Geographic Location	Economic System	Social System	Political System
•			

Nicholas takes his blue shovel to the beach and begins digging a hole. A man in a deck chair looks over the top of his newspaper and tells Nicholas if he keeps digging like that he'll go through to Australia. Nicholas keeps on digging. Suddenly, out of the hole leaps a huge red kangaroo and then four more kangaroos with joeys in their pouches. Nicholas keeps on digging. A cinnamon-colored dingo runs out with four more dingoes following. They have a tug-of-war with a lady's hat. Next, a rude camel lumbers out with four more camels following. A flock of laughing kookaburras flies out followed by a flock of chattering cockatoos. Next come five furry koalas and four wooly wombats who help Nicholas dig. Finally, a procession of duck-billed platypuses emerges followed by six silent wallabies.

The beach is in an uproar, with animals everywhere howling, belching, laughing, and playing with beach toys, towels, wallets, and umbrellas. Then the sun goes down, and as it touches the horizon, the animals disappear back down the hole one by one. Nicholas fills it up and stamps it down. Nothing is left of the animals but their footprints and a white cockatoo feather. The man in the deck chair says to Nicholas, "See, I told you about digging through to Australia."

Humorous illustrations of animals leap, lumber, and bounce all over the pages, but no one on the beach seems to bat an eye. Finally, Nicholas walks down the beach in the footprints of wallabies and dingoes, whistling to himself.

Classroom Applications

Have your students pretend to dig through their own backyards and then dictate the story of what kinds of creatures might emerge. Can they illustrate their stories with drawings of the creatures? What if they lived in Australia? What Canadian animals might pop out of a hole they dug on an Australian beach? Give each student the challenge of finding out about a picture of her or his animal and being ready to pop it out of an imaginary hole on cue and tell about itself.

 Oliviero, James. *The Fish Skin.* illustrated by Brent Morrisseau. Hyperion, 1993. 40 pp. (ISBN 1-56282-401-5). Folktale, M-L.

Story Review Chart

Setting	Plot/Events	Characters	Theme
•	•	•	

Cultural Paradigm Reference Classification Chart

Geographic Location	Economic System	Social System	Political System
•	•		

In this retelling of a Cree Indian legend, Grandfather Sun moves in splendor across the sky but is distracted from his course when he sees his reflection in a large, clear lake. The longer he pauses to look at himself, the hotter it becomes for the Indian people camped by the lake. The land becomes parched, wolves are unable to howl, the turtle's shell cracks, and a young boy's grandmother becomes steadily weaker. The boy determines to find the Great Spirit who lives in a deep forest on the other side of the lake and to ask for help.

Morrisseau's haunting illustrations fill two-page spreads with the red and orange or purple and blue faces of Cree people, animals, and the Great Spirit. The Great Spirit reads the courageous boy's thoughts in his dreams and leaves him a magic fish skin. The boy slips into it, becoming a gigantic fish that dives into the lake, swallowing enough water to spit out at a cloud, which then rains on his people, restoring them all except the too slow turtle, whose shell remains cracked to this day.

Classroom Applications

Explanatory tales like this one, telling how animals came to look as they do, are common among native peoples. Can your children make up their own imaginary tales telling how animals they know came to look a certain way? Some children may want to dramatize this book tale, making masks for themselves to portray their roles as Grandfather Sun, the young boy, the grandmother, the gigantic fish, the wolves, the turtle, and the Indian people.

 Greve, Andreas. *The Good Night Story.* illustrated by Kitty Macaulay. Annick Press, 1993. 24 pp. (ISBN 1-55037-319-6). Contemporary Fiction, P-E.

Story Review Chart

Setting	Plot/Events	Characters	Theme
	•	•	

Cultural Paradigm Reference Classification Chart

Geographic Location	Economic System	Social System	Political System
	•	•	

Grandpa is such a good teller of good-night stories that he often puts himself to sleep. The boy who narrates this tale asks him to tell a quiet story with animals in it. "Go on," urges the boy at every pause. "Oh, all right," replies Grandpa, a phrase he repeats throughout the story. He starts by having a hunter stalking in the woods, but as soon as he mentions the word *deer*, a knock is heard at the door and a deer enters the bedroom. Next, Grandpa mentions a stag in the clearing, and of course a stag bangs on the door for admission. Then comes a rabbit, a wild boar, and finally a squirrel before Grandpa falls asleep.

But the animals are hungry, so the boy takes them all outside to stalk the hunter. The boar soon has him treed, and they all help themselves to the snacks in the backpack he has dropped. Then the boy starts to retell the same good-night story, and soon everyone is asleep, even the hunter in the tree. Humorous art in pen and ink and colored pencil decorates every page.

Classroom Applications

If students enjoyed acting out the previous tale, then here is another one made for the kind of dramatization called "story reenactment," in which everyone can participate while you read the tale. Have each student choose to be a deer, a stag, a rabbit, a wild boar, a squirrel, the hunter, the boy, or Grandpa. Everyone can make a simple mask or a headdress for a prop and take turns playing her or his role every time you repeat the story. As you read the story, let the different "animals" knock on the door and come in when they hear their name mentioned—or fall asleep when the boy tells the story.

 Keens-Douglas, Richardo. *Grandpa's Visit.* illustrated by Frances Clancy. Annick Press, 1996. 24 pp. (ISBN 1-55037-488-5). Contemporary Fiction, E-L.

Story Review Chart

Setting	Plot/Events	Characters	Theme
	•	•	•

Cultural Paradigm Reference Classification Chart

Geographic Location	Economic System	Social System	Political System
		•	

Jeremy is 7 years old when Grandpa comes unexpectedly to visit family in Canada from his Caribbean island. Although Grandpa is 84, he looks 74 and moves like 64. He brings presents for everyone, but when Jeremy sees that his is "just a ball" and not a secret ball radio or some other mechanical marvel, he goes to his room to play with his video games and computer and other electronic toys. As the days pass, Grandpa discovers that when Mom is in Dad is out, and when Dad is in Mom is out, and when Jeremy is in he runs straight to his room to play with his electronic gadgets.

Then one night, Grandpa investigates Jeremy's room and pushes the wrong buttons, causing everything in the house to "crash," including the computer, VCR, clock, and even the dishwasher. "Maybe a little fuse dat blow," says Grandpa. So the family is forced to light a few candles and make up their own entertainment. Grandpa picks up Jeremy's forgotten ball and tosses it to him and then to Mom and Dad. Then he teaches them how to play Donkey if they miss the ball. Soon, everyone is playing and laughing and talking together with the best time they have enjoyed since Jeremy was little. It is time for a change in their lifestyles, they realize, and Jeremy can't wait until they can all visit Grandpa on his island.

Classroom Applications

Encourage your students to talk about how they and their family members entertain themselves. Does anyone play games that involve talking with one another or having fun together? Teach them a circle game they can enjoy at home. Bring in a ball and have them play Donkey.

 Yolen, Jane. *Honkers*. illustrated by Leslie Baker. Little, Brown, 1993. 32 pp. (ISBN 0-316-96893-5). Fiction, P-E.

Story Review Chart

Setting	Plot/Events	Characters	Theme
	•	•	

Cultural Paradigm Reference Classification Chart

Geographic Location	Economic System	Social System	Political System
		•	

In this touching turn-of-the-last-century story, Betsy is 5 years old when her mother is having such a hard time waiting for the birth of a new baby that she and Daddy pack Betsy off on the train to Nana and Grandy's farm in the north. Before Betsy can show even a sign of homesickness, her grandparents tell her about a surprise in the barn: "Honkers," says Grandy. They are three Canada goose eggs found abandoned down by the river. Nana marks a "B" on the egg Betsy chooses for her own and teaches her to turn it twice a day.

When the geese finally hatch, they quickly imprint on Betsy and follow her everywhere, crying when she goes inside to eat. Baker's watercolor illustrations capture the feel of the era in browns and tans, contrasted here and there with Grandy's red checkerboard or Nana's red umbrella that Betsy uses to keep the nearly grown geese out of Nana's garden. Then it is fall and time for the birds to migrate south. Betsy's bird wants her to come too, but she can only watch as it runs a step and then is gone, flapping upward toward the sound of honkers overhead. The next day, Betsy, too, returns south on the train, following "the compass of her heart home."

Classroom Applications

A story like this can lead your students into an egg incubating activity. Fertile chicken eggs can usually be obtained from farms or the Cooperative Extension, but sometimes goose eggs are available. Hatched birds need to be returned to a farm, rather than kept by the children.

 Bouchard, David. *If You're Not From the Prairie . . .* illustrated by Henry Ripplinger. Atheneum, 1995. 32 pp. (ISBN 0-689-80103-3). Poetry, E-L.

Story Review Chart

Setting	Plot/Events	Characters	Theme
•	•		

Cultural Paradigm Reference Classification Chart

Geographic Location	Economic System	Social System	Political System
•	•		

"If you're not from the prairie, you don't know the sun," begins this hymn to the rolling prairie land of Canada by a boy in a red baseball cap. Sometimes harsh but always with a beauty of its own, the prairie comes to life in strikingly realistic landscape and figure paintings by one of Saskatchewan's foremost artists. The text, a book-length poem running opposite each page of painting, evokes memories of sun, wind, sky, flat land, grass, snow, trees, and cold. "If you're not from the prairie, you just can't know me," the boy tells the reader midway through the book and then goes on to describe himself.

Classroom Applications

Can your students relate to this boy? Have they experienced anything similar? Invite them to help you make a list of important environmental elements that surround their own lives, elements an outsider would need to experience in order to connect with. They can illustrate these elements by taking photographs of their environment or by drawing pictures of it to be placed in a scrapbook, along with their commentary for each illustration. If the class is studying natural environments like the prairie, suggest that students paint a large wall mural on newsprint showing seasons on the prairie as this book does.

 Manchur, Carolyn Marie, with Zola, Meguido. *In the Garden.* illustrated by Anne Hanley. Pemmican, 1993. 52 pp. (ISBN 0-921827-31-8). Contemporary Fiction, M-L.

Story Review Chart

Setting	Plot/Events	Characters	Theme
	•	•	

Cultural Paradigm Reference Classification Chart

Geographic Location	Economic System	Social System	Political System
	•	•	

Ten-year-old Joyce, a Metis Indian living with her family in the city with a backyard full of junk cars and couch grass, inherits from her grandmother, who has just died, a white handkerchief with blue forget-me-nots around the border. She misses Grandma a lot, but she cannot understand why Grandma gave her brother a coin collection, her older sister all her scarves, her second cousin a horsehair rug, and herself only a hand-kerchief. Then Joyce discovers a knot inside the handkerchief that turns out to be full of seeds, making Joyce determine then and there to grow a garden just like Grandma's.

Joyce's struggle to rip out the couch grass, chop down the carrigana hedge, and sieve the soil just-so is finally rewarded by a garden full of carrots, tomatoes, parsnips, beets, and a border of forget-me-nots. Then her father loses his job because of a strike, meaning the family will have to move. But they manage to stay a month—time enough to harvest and can the vegetables and make a potful of soup to be distributed to the tired, hungry strikers just before the strike ends. Joyce's father tells everyone proudly how his daughter grew the vegetables in her garden all by herself. The men clap; and Joyce claps too.

The art covering every page of the book is as striking and arresting as the story itself. Close-ups of Indian faces expressing sorrow, regret, surprise, joy, and determination draw the reader into the uncertain lives of these migratory workers living on the edge of the city, with glimpses of Grandma's garden and dreams of "the way it used to be."

Classroom Applications

Can your students tell stories of "the way it used to be" in the lives of their parents or grandparents? You can also use the book as a stepping-stone into a wonderful garden-ing activity for your students either inside or out. What would they like to grow?

 Eyvindson, Peter. *Jen and the Great One*. illustrated by Rhian Brynjolson. Pemmican, 1990. 48 pp. (ISBN 0-921927-0901). Contemporary Fiction, P-M.

Story Review Chart

Setting	Plot/Events	Characters	Theme
•	•	•	•

Cultural Paradigm Reference Classification Chart

Geographic Location	Economic System	Social System	Political System
•	•		

Jen, a Canadian Indian, loves the one remaining old-growth tree outside the city and often comes out to put her arms around it because it smells like Christmas. She calls it the Great One. Sometimes when she is very quiet, she can hear the Great One speak and tell about life before Big Businessman and Road Builder came to the valley and cut down all the Great Ones but this.

When Jen hears about the pollution that is poisoning everything, she brings back her friends to help. They pick up the pine cones, take out the seeds, and determine to grow and replant the seedlings. The Great One acknowledges their help by telling them that the children of the world give him hope. Realistic drawings cover every page, showing the beauty of the land before it was destroyed by "progress" and the return of natural beauty after the children restore the trees.

Classroom Applications

As a lead-in to environmental activities, this book can prompt your students to clean up their own environment and to plant trees. Take them on a walking trip to the largest tree around and have them take photographs, make bark rubbings, and collect leaves and seeds.

 Allen, Jonathan. *Mucky Moose*. Alladin Paperbacks, 1996. 32 pp. (ISBN 0-689-80651-5). Contemporary Fiction, P-M.

Story Review Chart

Setting	Plot/Events	Characters	Theme
•	•	•	

Cultural Paradigm Reference Classification Chart

Geographic Location	Economic System	Social System	Political System
		•	

This humorous animal story shows messy Mucky Moose in two-page cartoon-like drawings with gook hanging from his antlers and an odor that attracts flies, frogs, and skunks but wards off wolves that want to eat him. Every time the biggest wolf tries to attack, Mucky's terrible odor knocks the wolf flat on his back. Even a clothespin on his nose and a gas mask fail to help.

Classroom Applications

This is a fine story for dramatization, with students taking the parts of Mucky, the wolf, frogs, skunks, and birds. Have each student learn as much as possible about the animal she or he represents.

Kusugak, Michael Arvaarluk. *My Arctic, 1, 2, 3*. illustrated by Vladyanna Krykorka. Annick Press, 1996. 24 pp. (ISBN 1-55037-504-0). Counting Book, P-E.

Story Review Chart

Setting	Plot/Events	Characters	Theme
•		•	

Cultural Paradigm Reference Classification Chart

Geographic Location	Economic System	Social System	Political System
•			

Numbers from 1 to 10 and then 20, 100, and 1,000,000 are described by this acclaimed Inuit storyteller in terms of Arctic animals. One polar bear, two ringed seals, three killer whales, four bowhead whales, five Arctic foxes, and so on spring to life in the realistic illustrations on every page. Five pages at the end describe in more detail "The Arctic World of Michael Arvaarluk and His Family."

Classroom Applications

Have a follow-the-leader activity in which your students pretend to be each of these animals as you lead them across the tundra, ice, or river of your classroom floor. Be sure to describe aloud what the terrain is like you are all moving across so that students will know what motions to make. Then have your own counting-book activity, with groups of students role-playing the same animal moving across the room while the audience counts how many are in each group.

 Loewen, Iris. *My Kokum Called Today.* illustrated by Gloria Miller. Pemmican, 1993. 44 pp. (ISBN 0-921827-36-9). Contemporary Fiction, E-L.

Story Review Chart

Setting	Plot/Events	Characters	Theme
•	•	•	

Cultural Paradigm Reference Classification Chart

Geographic Location	Economic System	Social System	Political System
	•	•	

This first-person story told by an 11-year-old Cree Indian girl who lives in the city with her mother expresses her excitement to hear from her grandmother, her Kokum, that there's a Round Dance on the Reserve and she wants them to come. As the girl packs to go, she recalls the kindness of her Kokum, her wisdom and generosity with sick people, and how she takes the girl with her in the bush to gather plants for making medicine. Together, they make "bannock" bread and then dance the Round Dance all night long until the tired girl falls asleep in her Kokum's lap.

Classroom Applications

Bring in an Indian dance tape, have your students make drums, and do a Round Dance to the music. Realistic illustrations on every other page show how. This story can also lead into a cooking experience of making bannock bread.

 McLellan, Joe. *Nanabosho: How the Turtle Got Its Shell.* illustrated by Rhian Brynjolson. Pemmican, 1994. 48 pp. (ISBN 0-921827-40-7). Folktale, A.

Story Review Chart			
Setting	Plot/Events	Characters	Theme
	•	•	

Cultural Paradigm Reference Classification Chart			
Geographic Location	Economic System	Social System	Political System
	•		

Nanabosho, an Ojibway Indian trickster hero, goes fishing in this, one of a series of Nanabosho tales, but he doesn't have any luck until Turtle comes along. Turtle is a little green creature that has to hide from everyone because he has no shell. He tells Nanabosho where he can catch plenty of fish, and after Nanabosho has his fill, he rewards Turtle by painting a round rock and placing it on his back for a shell.

Classroom Applications

This story can lead to an art project of painting rocks like turtle shells. It should not, however, lead to a science project of bringing in a live turtle, if your students have carefully followed the introduction to the story about the Indian children who go with their grandparents to the city and see turtles for sale in a store. As the grandfather reminds the children before he recites the Nanabosho story: "Kitchie Manitou did not create turtles to be owned." Large, realistic drawings and a simple text in large type make this a story your older students can easily read independently.

 Killilea, Marie. *Newf.* illustrated by Ian Schoenherr. Philomel, 1992. 32 pp. (ISBN 0-399-21875-0). Contemporary Fiction, M-L.

Story Review Chart			
Setting	Plot/Events	Characters	Theme
•	•	•	

Cultural Paradigm Reference Classification Chart

Geographic Location	Economic System	Social System	Political System
•		•	

This beautifully written and illustrated story for older children is based on a legend about the Newfoundland dogs of the Gaspe Peninsula. On this wild and windswept coast, a huge black dog swims ashore and heads for a deserted fisherman's cottage for shelter. There, it finds a trembling white kitten, and the two become friends. The dog goes for a swim every day and brings back a fish for the two to eat. Twice, the dog has to rescue the kitten when it is swept out to sea by waves and later when it is buried under the snow in a blizzard. Two-page illustrations reveal the starkness of the landscape in every season and the loving friendship between dog and cat.

Classroom Applications

Ask your students for stories about their own animal pets or tales they have heard about animals befriending one another. Allow them to dictate stories for your transcription or to write and illustrate their own stories. Some students may want to talk into a tape recorder and later play back their stories for others. Other students may want to make up new stories about Newf's adventures.

 Larry, Charles. *Peboan and Seegwun.* Farrar, Straus & Giroux, 1993. 32 pp. (ISBN 0-374-45750-6). Folktale, M-L.

Story Review Chart

Setting	Plot/Events	Characters	Theme
•		•	

Cultural Paradigm Reference Classification Chart

Geographic Location	Economic System	Social System	Political System
•			

This Ojibway tribal legend tells the story of an old man sitting alone in his lodge, with the wind howling and the snow whipping around outside, when a young man stops to visit him. After smoking a pipe together, they each speak. The old man tells that his breath causes water to become hard as quartz. The young man tells that his breath makes flowers spring up everywhere. As they each describe the almost magical effects their actions create, it becomes evident that the young man is the spirit of spring and that the old man represents winter. Detailed full-page illustrations show Indians building canoes in spring, harvesting rice and berries in fall, and the icy face of Old Man Winter melting away as spring comes.

Classroom Applications

Your students may want to make cardboard carton dioramas of the seasons as shown in the illustrations and to tell stories about them.

 Dabcovich, Lydia. *The Polar Bear Son*. Clarion Books, 1997. 32 pp. (ISBN 0-395-72766-0). Folktale, M-L.

Story Review Chart

Setting	Plot/Events	Characters	Theme
•	•	•	

Cultural Paradigm Reference Classification Chart

Geographic Location	Economic System	Social System	Political System
	•	•	

An old Inuit woman lives by herself at the edge of the village but has no strong sons to provide for her. She tries to fend for herself but often has to depend on her neighbors for food. One day, she finds a little orphan polar bear out on the ice. She shares her food with him and names him Kunikdjuaq, her son. Children of the village love to play with him, tumbling in the snow.

When spring comes, he is big enough to go hunting and fishing for the old woman, returning with more fish than the Inuit hunters have caught. Even though she shares her bounty with the village, the hunters are angry because Kunikdjuaq is a better hunter than they are. In their jealousy, they decide to kill the bear.

The children warn the woman, and tearfully she sends her bear son away. Once more, she is alone, but this time when she is very lonely and hungry she goes far out on the ice early in the morning and calls for him. He comes to her, bringing salmon and seal, which they eat together. This goes on for many years. This story is still told by the Inuit about the old woman and the devoted bear who never forgot her.

Long horizontal sweeps of a brush paint gray, blue, and pink tints across white Arctic ice and snow in the two-page illustrations.

Classroom Applications

What other stories about polar bears can your students find? Challenge them to search the illustrations of this story carefully for other Arctic animals. Suggest that they put their finds together in the form of an illustrated mural of Arctic life.

 Zagwyn, Deborah Turney. *The Pumpkin Blanket*. Fitzhenry & Whiteside, 1995. 32 pp. (ISBN 0-88902-7412). Contemporary Fiction, P-M.

Story Review Chart

Setting	Plot/Events	Characters	Theme
•	•	•	

Cultural Paradigm Reference Classification Chart

Geographic Location	Economic System	Social System	Political System
	•	•	

No one knows where Clee's pumpkin blanket has come from. They hadn't noticed the northern lights shaking their folds above her bed when she was born, or the wind tossing a blanket inside the open door. They only know that she looks a lot like a pumpkin when she is bundled up inside it. When Clee is 3 years old, she wraps the blanket around her when she hears the coyotes yipping and yowling out back. She knows that her treasured blanket is coyote-proof. When she is 4, she makes a tent out of it to hide under when she is sent upstairs for bringing a baby worm to the dinner table. When she is 5, she dances with it outside like the fluttering autumn leaves as her French Canadian father harvests the vegetables.

Her father worries about her attachment to the blanket because he knows that Clee will go to kindergarten after Christmas and that she cannot take the blanket with her. He tells her there are 12 squares in her blanket, just as there are 12 pumpkins in the garden. Clee wants to make jack-o'-lanterns out of them for Halloween. Her father says that she can if they don't freeze before the end of October.

That night, the first freeze comes and kills the vines sheltering one of the pumpkins. Clee's father asks whether she will share her blanket with the exposed pumpkin, and she does. Her father carefully cuts the square from the blanket, and Clee covers the pumpkin. Next morning, another pumpkin is exposed, so Clee donates another square. Night after night, Clee gives square after square to save the pumpkins. Finally, only one square and one pumpkin are left. It is difficult for her to part with her beloved blanket, but she does.

When at last Clee and her father go out to harvest the pumpkins, the wind flips the blanket squares off every one and blows them up into the sky to be sewn together by the stars and draped over the moon. Lovely watercolor illustrations fill every page with the warm and colorful life of these French Canadians of the north.

Classroom Applications

Your students can create their own pumpkin blankets from squares of wallpaper to make a storytelling wall hanging. Have each student who contributes a square tell a tale about it. This story can also be dramatized with students pretending to be the 12 pumpkins.

 Mills, Judith Christine. *The Stonehook Schooner.* Key Porter Books, 1995. 32 pp. (ISBN 1-55013-719-0). Historical Fiction, M-L.

Story Review Chart

Setting	Plot/Events	Characters	Theme
•	•	•	

Cultural Paradigm Reference Classification Chart

Geographic Location	Economic System	Social System	Political System
•	•		

During the 1800s, schooners sailed from Canadian ports in Lake Ontario to rake stones from the bottom of the lake and transport them to cities such as Toronto, Oswego, and Rochester to be used for paving streets and building houses. It was dangerous, back-breaking work, but the stonehookers were proud of their skill and daring. In this story, young Matthew goes with his father for the first time, and they get caught in a fierce Great Lakes storm. Matthew lashes himself to the bowsprit and points the way for his father to steer safely back to shore.

The fury of the storm and the emotions of these French Canadian boatmen are captured in Mills's dramatic two-page illustrations.

Classroom Applications

Challenge your students to make up other adventure stories about Matthew and his father's schooner, the *Hannah May.* Suggest that they make a map of southern Canada, Lake Ontario, and northern United States, showing Canadian towns and the American lake ports, and draw lines showing where the stonehook schooners must travel.

 Sanderson, Esther. *Two Pairs of Shoes.* illustrated by David Beyer. Pemmican, 1990. 24 pp. (ISBN 0-921827-15-6). Contemporary Fiction, M-L.

Story Review Chart

Setting	Plot/Events	Characters	Theme
	•	•	•

Cultural Paradigm Reference Classification Chart

Geographic Location	Economic System	Social System	Political System
		•	

Maggie is a Cree Indian living with her mother on a reservation. For her eighth birthday, her mother gives her a pair of black patent leather shoes, just what she wanted. When she runs down the street to her Kokum's (grandma's) house to show her the shoes, her grandmother has to feel them all over because she is blind. Then she tells Maggie where to find the present she has for her—a pair of beautifully beaded moccasins. Tears come to Maggie's eyes as she remembers that her Kokum cannot see. How was she able to make such beautiful moccasins? The grandmother holds Maggie on her lap and tells her that from now on she must remember when and how to wear each pair.

Exceptional art graces every page of this story, with large close-ups of Indian faces against a shiny white background.

Classroom Applications

Bring in shoes of all sorts, including moccasins, for your students to pretend with. Can they demonstrate how they would walk differently in each type of shoe? Have a beading activity for those who are interested. Can anyone bead with their eyes closed?

 Munsch, Robert. *Where Is Gah-Ning?* illustrated by Helene Desputeaux. Annick Press, 1994. 32 pp. (ISBN 1-55037-982-8). Contemporary Fiction, P-E.

Story Review Chart

Setting	Plot/Events	Characters	Theme
	•	•	

Cultural Paradigm Reference Classification Chart

Geographic Location	Economic System	Social System	Political System
		•	

In this wild and wonderful Robert Munsch story, the little Chinese girl Gah-Ning pits her wits against her father's as she insists on going on a trip to Kapuskasing and he says no-way. So, she gets her bicycle and starts peddling down the road to Kapuskasing as a moose peers out of the pine trees smiling at her. When her father finds out, he jumps into his car and drives halfway to Kapuskasing before he catches her and brings her home.

Next, she gets her roller blades and starts out again. The brief text repeats the same dialogue every time her father asks, "Where is Gah-Ning?" This time, he jumps into his car and drives 50 km out of town before he catches her and brings her home. He tells her not to go on her bicycle, on a bus, on a skateboard, or in a helicopter. So, she goes downtown to the library where a clown is giving out balloons to the kids. Most kids take 1 or 2. Gah-Ning takes 300 balloons and floats out the door to Kapuskasing. When her father finds out, he jumps into his car and drives to a shopping mall in Kapuskasing just in time to catch Gah-Ning as she floats to Earth. "Daddy, you came shopping," she exclaims, "How nice!"

Desputeaux's brilliantly costumed cartoon-style characters match Munsch's words. Gah-Ning's red and pink sweatsuit with orange and yellow dots and matching headband set the tone. Tiny beads, pine needles, buttons, pieces of rice, pens, and pebbles trail behind as Gah-Ning dashes her way through life.

Classroom Applications

Here is a rollicking romp your students will want to imitate. They can do it on the playground in a reenactment Where Is Gah-Ning? game you can play with them. What other ways can they think of to travel? What are the safety problems involved? Some students may want to make a collage about this story by using beads, pine needs, buttons, and pieces of rice, pens, and pebbles, just as the illustrator did.

 Godkin, Celia. *Wolf Island.* Fitzhenry & Whiteside, 1993. 40 pp. (ISBN 1-55041-095-4). Factual Animal Story, M-L.

Story Review Chart

Setting	Plot/Events	Characters	Theme
•	•	•	

Cultural Paradigm Reference Classification Chart

Geographic Location	Economic System	Social System	Political System
•	•		

Wolf Island tells the true story of what happens on a small island in northern Ontario when a family of wolves that live there accidentally drift off the island in a raft they are investigating. Because they are the highest link in the food chain, every other living thing on the island is affected by their departure. The deer whose numbers are not kept in check by the wolves overpopulate and eat so much vegetation that the rabbits do not have enough. With fewer rabbits, there are fewer foxes. Then the deer start killing trees by eating tree bark in winter. Finally, the water between the mainland and the island freezes over, and the wolves are able to return and set the balance of nature straight again.

Colorful crayoned illustrations cover the pages, with brief paragraphs of text tucked in here and there.

Classroom Applications

Your students can make an illustrated food chain of animals and plants from their own area and tell what happens when one of the links is broken.

 Eyvindson, Peter. *The Yesterday Stone.* illustrated by Rhian Brynjolson. Pemmican, 1992. 44 pp. (ISBN 0-921827-24-5). Contemporary Fiction, M-L.

Story Review Chart

Setting	Plot/Events	Characters	Theme
	•	•	

Cultural Paradigm Reference Classification Chart

Geographic Location	Economic System	Social System	Political System
		•	

Her schoolmates laugh at the Indian girl Anna when she tells them to smile at the dandelions and watch them smile back. But her Caucasian friend Molly does not. Molly believes. Molly spends the afternoon smiling at every dandelion and says it is true. Anna still doesn't know whether she can trust telling Molly about her yesterday stone. This is the special stone her grandmother helps her find with a magnet—a magical stone that contains a world of stories, some imaginary and some real—about things that have happened. Her grandmother warns her that some people will not believe in a yesterday stone. Would Molly believe? At the end of the story, Anna takes the stone from her pocket and says to Molly, "I have something to show you."

Watercolor illustrations cover the pages, the most outstanding being the faces of the girls and the grandmother.

Classroom Applications

Do your students have any stones that are special to them? Take them on a stone hike where they can find yesterday stones of their own. What stories will the stones tell them? Students can write or dictate their stories and then illustrate them.

SUMMARY

Are you surprised about the wide variety of topics and characters, as well as the uniqueness of the stories? Americans often assume that Canadian children's books will be similar to those in the United States, just as they assume that Canada is like the United States, only colder. The truth is quite different. Canada is a unique country containing several strong cultural groups, including English, French, Asians, Inuits of the Arctic, and other indigenous people of the north and northwest coast.

A strong concern for the environment emerges from many stories, such as *Chung Lee Loves Lobsters*. Aren't you more surprised by the fact that Chinese live in Canada than by the ending? Or that Black Canadian city dwellers have relatives in the Caribbean islands? Or that when Canadian children dig a deep hole through Earth they don't come out in China but in Australia? Even Canadian Indians seem somehow different, with their contemporary lives in the city but strong ties to the reservation.

Sixteen of the 25 books reviewed about Canada are contemporary fiction, and 4 are folktales. The remaining five genres—historical fiction, fiction, poetry, informational, and counting book—are each represented by just 1 book.

The story review charts show that the principal story elements are plot/events (23) and characters (23). Setting was featured in 15 books, but discernible themes surfaced in only 4.

The cultural paradigm focus was evenly distributed, with geographic location being featured in 12 books, economic system in 13, and social system in 15. References to a political system were not evident in any of the books; could this be an indication that authors and publishers of Canadian children's books do not perceive them to be a forum for airing political issues?

Which story did you and your students find most unusual—the French Canadian boatmen who took rocks to Rochester, or the Inuit boys of Repulse Bay who made baseball bats out of Christmas trees? Whatever books about Canada your students read, both you and they will be rewarded with Canada's rich contribution to transcultural children's literature.

REFERENCES CITED

Jobe, R. A. (1989). Children's literature and teacher education in Canada. *Early Child Development and Care, 48,* 59-66.

SUGGESTED REFERENCES

Dawson, J. (1996). Telling it like it was in western Canada: Postcolonial historical fiction for children. *Bookbird, 34*(4), 24-28.

Ellis, S. (1984). News from the north. *Horn Book Magazine, 60*(3), 375-379.

Ellis, S. (1986). News from the north. *Horn Book Magazine, 62*(5), 626-628.

Jobe, R. A., & Sutton, W. K. (1992). Beyond Munsch: Canadian literature for children and young people. *Reading Teacher, 45*(8), 634-641.

Lewis, S. (1993). Best Canadiana. *Emergency Librarian, 20*(4), 12-14.

Lewis, S. (1994). Best Canadiana. *Emergency Librarian, 22*(4), 16-18.

Nist, J. S. (1989). Sharing and comparing award-winning picture books of English-language nations. *Early Child Development and Care, 48,* 49-57.

O'Connor, S. (1997). Two perspectives on Canadian science fiction: Science fiction in English-speaking Canada. *Bookbird, 35*(4), 12-17.

Wason-Ellam, L. (1988). Making literary connections. *Canadian Journal of English Language Arts, 11*(1), 47-54.

CHILDREN'S BOOKS CITED

Allen, J. (1996). *Mucky moose.* New York: Alladin.

Bouchard, D. (1995). *If you're not from the prairie . . .* New York: Atheneum.

Carrier, R. (1991). *The boxing champion.* Plattsburg, NY: Tundra Books.

Dabcovich, L. (1997). *The polar bear son.* New York: Clarion Books.

Eyvindson, P. (1990). *Jen and the Great One.* Winnipeg: Pemmican.

Eyvindson, P. (1992). *The yesterday stone.* Winnipeg: Pemmican.

Godkin, C. (1993). *Wolf island.* Markham, Ontario: Fitzhenry & Whiteside.

Greve, A. (1993). *The good night story.* Toronto: Annick Press.

Harrison, T. (1997). *Don't dig so deep, Nicholas!* Toronto: Owl Books.

Keens-Douglas, R. (1996). *Grandpa's visit.* Toronto: Annick Press.

Killilea, M. (1992). *Newf.* New York: Philomel.

Kusugak, M. (1990). *Baseball bats for Christmas.* Toronto: Annick Press.

Kusugak, M. (1996). *My arctic, 1, 2, 3.* Toronto: Annick Press.

Larry, C. (1993). *Peboan and Seegwun.* New York: Farrar, Straus & Giroux.

Loewen, I. (1993). *My Kokum called today.* Winnipeg: Pemmican.

MacDonald, H. (1992). *Chung Lee loves lobsters.* Toronto: Annick Press.

Manchur, C. M., & Zola, M. (1993). *In the garden.* Winnipeg: Pemmican.

McLellan, J. (1994). *Nanabosho: How the turtle got its shell.* Winnipeg: Pemmican.

Mills, J. C. (1995). *The stonehook schooner.* Toronto: Key Porter Books.

Munsch, R. (1994). *Where is Gah-Ning?* Toronto: Annick Press.

Oliviero, J. (1993). *The fish skin.* New York: Hyperion.

Sackett, E. (1991). *Danger on the arctic ice.* Boston: Little, Brown.

Sanderson, E. (1990). *Two pairs of shoes.* Winnipeg: Pemmican.

Yolen, J. (1993). *Honkers.* Boston: Little, Brown.

Zagwyn, D. T. (1995). *The pumpkin blanket.* Markham, Ontario: Fitzhenry & Whiteside.

SUGGESTED CHILDREN'S BOOKS
▼▼▼

Bouchard, D. (1994). *The meaning of respect.* Winnipeg: Pemmican.

Bourgeois, P. (1990). *Too many chickens.* Toronto: Kids Can.

Bourgeois, P. (1991). *Franklin fibs.* Toronto: Kids Can.

Carrier, R. (1991). *A happy New Year's Day.* Montreal: Tundra Books.

Cumming, P. (1993). *Out on the ice in the middle of the bay.* Toronto: Annick Press.

Daigneault, S. (1994). *Bruno in the snow.* New York: HarperCollins.

Gilman, P. (1990). *Grandma and the pirates.* Richmond Hill, Ontario: North Winds.

Gilmore, P. (1994). *Lights for Gita.* Toronto: Second Story Feminist Press.

Hundal, N. (1993). *November boots.* New York: HarperCollins.

Joose, B. M. (1991). *Mama, do you love me?* San Francisco: Chronicle Books.

Kovalski, M. (1990). *Pizza for breakfast.* New York: Morrow.

Kusugak, M. (1992). *Hide and snake.* Toronto: Annick Press.

Kusagak, M. (1993). *Northern lights, the soccer trails.* Toronto: Annick Press.

London, J. (1995). *The sugaring-off party.* New York: Dutton Children's Books.

McGugan, K. (1994). *Josepha.* Vancouver: Raincoast.

Morgan, A. (1991). *The magic hockey skates.* Don Mills, Ontario: Oxford University Press.

Munsch, R. (1991). *Show and tell.* Toronto: Annick Press.

Norman, H. (1997). *The girl who dreamed only geese.* San Diego: Harcourt Brace.

Sage, J. (1993). *Where the great bear watches.* New York: Viking.

Simmonds, P. (1995). *Freezing A B C.* New York: Knopf.

Stinson, K. (1991). *Who is sleeping in Aunty's bed?* Don Mills, Ontario: Oxford University Press.

Wallace, I. (1991). *Mr. Kneebone's new digs.* Toronto: Groundwood Books.

Yerxa, L. (1994). *Last leaf first snowflake to fall.* Vancouver: Douglas & McIntyre.

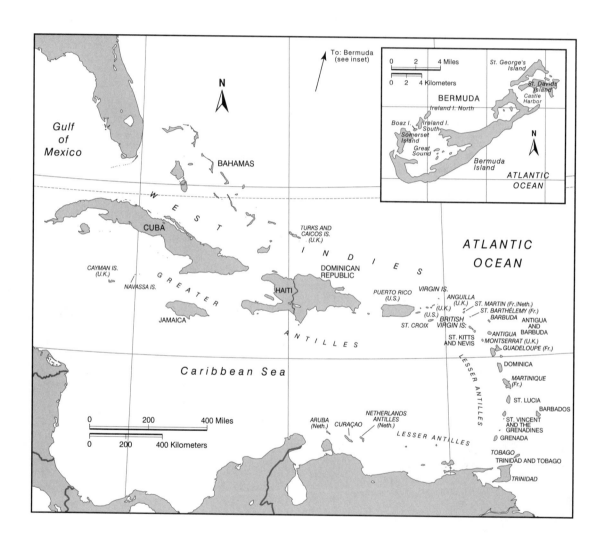

Gulf
of
Mexico

BAHAMAS

To: Bermuda
(see inset)

N

BERMUDA

0   2   4 Miles

0   2   4 Kilometers

*St. George's
Island*

*St. Davids
Island*

*Castle
Harbor*

Ireland I. North

Boaz I. *Ireland I.
South*

*Somerset
Island*

*Great
Sound*

*Bermuda
Island*

**ATLANTIC
OCEAN**

N

W

E

S

T

I

N

D

I

E

S

CUBA

TURKS AND
CAICOS IS.
(U.K.)

*ATLANTIC
OCEAN*

CAYMAN IS.
(U.K.)

NAVASSA IS.

G

R

E

A

T

E

R

DOMINICAN
REPUBLIC

HAITI

PUERTO RICO
(U.S.)

VIRGIN IS.

ANGUILLA
(U.K.)

ST. MARTIN (Fr./Neth.)

ST. BARTHÉLEMY (Fr.)

BARBUDA

ANTIGUA
AND
BARBUDA

JAMAICA

*BRITISH
VIRGIN IS.*

ST. CROIX
(U.S.)

ANTIGUA

MONTSERRAT (U.K.)

GUADELOUPE (Fr.)

ST. KITTS
AND NEVIS

A *N* *T* *I* *L* *L* *E* *S*

DOMINICA

MARTINIQUE
(Fr.)

Caribbean Sea

ST. LUCIA

BARBADOS

ST. VINCENT
AND THE
GRENADINES

L
E
S
S
E
R

A
N
T
I
L
L
E
S

GRENADA

ARUBA
(Neth.)

CURAÇAO

NETHERLANDS
ANTILLES
(Neth.)

LESSER ANTILLES

TOBAGO

TRINIDAD AND TOBAGO

TRINIDAD

0   200   400 Miles

0   200   400 Kilometers

5

Children's Books About the Caribbean

THE CARIBBEAN

The Caribbean is an archipelago of variously sized islands between the southeastern United States and northern South America. It is surrounded by the Gulf of Mexico to the west, the Atlantic Ocean to the north and east, and the Caribbean Sea to the south.

Countries

Anguilla, Antigua & Barbuda, Aruba, Bahamas, Barbados, Bermuda, British Virgin Islands, Cayman Islands, Cuba, Curaçao, Dominica, Dominican Republic, Grenada, Guadeloupe, Haiti, Jamaica, Martinique, Montserrat, Navassa Island, Netherlands Antilles, Puerto Rico, St. Kitts & Nevis, St. Lucia, St. Vincent & the Grenadines, Trinidad & Tobago, Turks & Caicos Islands, Virgin Islands

EXAMINING THE CULTURAL REGION OF THE CARIBBEAN AND THE PATTERNS OF CHILDREN'S BOOKS

When we think or hear about the Caribbean region, a collage of images comes to mind: idyllic islands, warm seas, balmy climate, beautiful sunsets, pristine beaches, lush vegetation, and congenial people. When examining a map, we see that the Caribbean consists of a few large islands (the Greater Antilles) and many smaller islands (the Lesser Antilles). Independent nations exist on all the larger islands (Cuba, Jamaica, Haiti, Dominican Republic, and Trinidad & Tobago), except for Puerto Rico, and about half of the smaller islands. The remaining small islands are territories of the United States, the United Kingdom, France, or the Netherlands.

Most current inhabitants of the Caribbean region can trace their ancestry to western Africa, western Europe, North America, India, Pakistan, or the indigenous peoples (Caribs) of the Caribbean region. The unique mix of cultures on these islands, together with the nature of island geography, has produced a varied collection of traditions, ideas, and attitudes.

Given our observations, the number of children's books available in the United States about a specific Caribbean nation or territory seems to be related to several factors. One factor is associated with the relative size of the U.S. co-culture. For example, the American Puerto Rican co-culture is one of the largest of Caribbean heritage. The largest number of transcultural Caribbean children's books available in the United States appears to be about Puerto Rico. Other associated factors are the amount of U.S. mass media attention a Caribbean nation receives, the current number of immigrants coming to the United States from a specific Caribbean nation, and the number of people who have lived in or visited a particular Caribbean nation and are writing children's books in the United States about that given Caribbean nation. For example, the stream of news reports during the last few years about Haiti and the influx of Haitian immigrants to the United States appears to have generated a greater than normal number of children's books about Haiti. Regardless of reasons why a general increase in the number of transcultural Caribbean children's books has occurred, it is important that this number continue to increase. Children who are exposed to these children's books will learn more about some of the closest neighbors of the United States.

COUNTRIES AND CHILDREN'S BOOKS REVIEWED

Antilles (Lesser)

The Lesser Antilles is a group of relatively small islands forming an arc from Puerto Rico in the north to the north coast of Venezuela in the south.

 Gershator, Phillis, retold by. *Tukama Tootles the Flute: A Tale From the Antilles.* illustrated by Synthia Saint James. Orchard Books, 1994. 32 pp. (ISBN 0-531-06811-0). Folktale, P-M.[1]

---

[1]A = all ages, P = preschool, E = early elementary, M = middle elementary, L = late elementary

Story Review Chart

Setting	Plot/Events	Characters	Theme
•	•	•	

Cultural Paradigm Reference Classification Chart

Geographic Location	Economic System	Social System	Political System
•		•	

Tukama, who lives with his grandmother, is something of a free spirit. Rather than obeying and helping his grandmother, he does what he wants. He leaves home early, plays at the beach and along a dangerous craggy shore all day, eats island fruit, plays his flute, and returns home late at night. Worrying incessantly about Tukama's welfare, his grandmother repeatedly gives him advice, which he arrogantly ignores.

One day when Tukama again returns late from his day of play, his grandmother warns him about a two-headed giant that comes at night to eat unruly boys. The next day, Tukama ventures off once again and, failing to heed his grandmother's warning, encounters a two-headed giant soon after the sun sets. Blocking Tukama from escaping, the giant compels the captive boy to play his flute. After each tune is played, the giant claims that he cannot hear the music. So, he beckons Tukama to come closer. Beginning at the giant's big toe, Tukama moves up to his huge knee, then to his massive chest, and finally to one of his immense noses. Now able to catch Tukama's scent, the giant grabs him and stuffs him into a bag. The giant then takes the bag home so that his wife can fatten up Tukama on johnnycakes.

Before going fishing the next day, the giant tells his wife to feed Tukama an extra helping of johnnycake so that he will be plump enough to eat for supper. After the giant leaves, Tukama plays his flute. This time, however, he turns the giant's little-by-little stratagem to his advantage by convincing the giant's wife he needs more room in the bag to play another tune. Once the bag becomes loose enough, Tukama escapes, rushes out of the giant's house to his home. Having learned his lesson, Tukama plays his flute for his grandmother, but only after he does his daily chores.

This delightful story highlights some social values that are held firmly by many Caribbean people. The message that children need to listen to their caregivers and to help them with their work comes across loud and clear. Another aspect of life in the Caribbean that receives attention is food. The story mentions several Caribbean staples, such as fish, johnnycake, and local fruits (tamarind, prickly pears, sea grapes, mangoes, and papaya). Also, a bit of island dialect occurs throughout the story, adding to its authenticity and charm.

The illustrator's bright, bold paintings effectively support the text. The broad brush strokes of faceless figures compel the reader to imagine the details of each character. Repeated use of various combinations of reds, browns, blues, greens, purple, yellow, black, and white helps link the individual scenes and events into a coherent story.

Classroom Applications

Students can do several classroom activities based on this book. For example, they can compare stories about giants, beginning with the familiar *Jack and the Beanstalk* tale.

They can also write about what lessons they have learned the hard way and then compare these lessons with Tukama's. Another activity is to have students sample several foods mentioned in the story as part of a Caribbean meal. Students can also study Caribbean music; by playing music recorded on CDs or cassettes, the class can compare the instruments, styles, rhythms, and lyrics of music in the United States with the different types of music heard in the Caribbean.

Bahamas

The Bahamas is located off the eastern and southern coasts of Florida.

 Yolen, Jane. *Encounter.* illustrated by David Shannon. Harcourt Brace, 1992. 32 pp. (ISBN 0-15-225962-7). Historical Fiction, E-M.

Story Review Chart

Setting	Plot/Events	Characters	Theme
•	•	•	•

Cultural Paradigm Reference Classification Chart

Geographic Location	Economic System	Social System	Political System
•	•	•	•

A Taino boy lives with his people on the island of San Salvador in the Bahamas. One night, he dreams of fearsome birds that symbolize three ships arriving the next day. The boy goes to the chief and begs him not to welcome the strangers from these ships, but the chief does not listen to him.

When the strangers come ashore, the boy sees that their appearances are unearthly. Again, he warns his people, but once again, they do not listen. Soon everyone, including the boy, becomes infatuated with the many trinkets the strangers give them. But the boy notices that the strangers are staring enviously at the Tainos' gold jewelry. They touch the gold jewelry, but the strangers avoid touching the Tainos' skin. When the boy accidentally cuts his hand on one of the strangers' metal swords, he looks around, but no one sees the impending danger.

The next day, the strangers take the boy and some other Tainos to their ships and set sail. The boy manages to slip unseen off the ship and into the ocean. He swims to a nearby island, where he tries to warn other people about the strangers. But no one listens. The boy eventually becomes a man, without land and his people. He continues to tell his story. But does anyone listen?

This fictional account of Columbus's 1492 landing on the island of San Salvador in the Bahamas offers an alternative perspective of the Taino/Columbus encounter—a view that hints at the disastrous consequences of the Europeans' arrival in the New World.

Beautifully rendered illustrations authentically represent the Taino people, former inhabitants of San Salvador. For example, the hair, facial features, and even the stools on which the chief and Columbus sit are depicted accurately. Painted in acrylic, the illustrations are also quite effective in conveying the historical significance of Columbus's arrival in the New World.

Classroom Applications

If someone took some of your family or friends away, took your home and your land, and gave you some trinkets in exchange, how would you feel? What would you do? Students can write their responses to these questions and share them in discussion groups. How do their own responses compare with the Taino boy's? Students can also compare what happened to the Tainos or Arawaks in the Bahamas with what happened to the Native Americans in the United States. What other indigenous people had lived or still live in the Caribbean? As students read books about other Caribbean nations, they can systematically study the indigenous people, compile their results into book form, and formally present copies of their class book to the other classrooms in the school.

Dominican Republic

The Dominican Republic occupies roughly the eastern two thirds of the large island of Hispaniola (Haiti is the other third), which lies between Cuba and Puerto Rico.

 Gordon, Ginger. *My Two Worlds.* photographs by Martha Cooper. Clarion Books, 1993. 32 pp. (ISBN 0-395-58704-2). Biography, E-M.

Story Review Chart			
Setting	Plot/Events	Characters	Theme
•	•	•	•

Cultural Paradigm Reference Classification Chart			
Geographic Location	Economic System	Social System	Political System
•	•	•	

A warm Spanish hello welcomes the reader to come along on a trip with 7-year-old Krisy Rodriguez and her sister Wendy. They are leaving New York City to visit relatives in the Dominican Republic for the Christmas holidays. Before departing, Krisy introduces the reader to her family members who are originally from the Dominican Republic. Unfortunately, only Krisy and Wendy can go on the trip this holiday.

The airplane ride to Puerto Plata, the city in the Dominican Republic where Krisy and Wendy will be staying, takes 4 hours. During the flight, Krisy looks out the window and watches the terrain slowly change beneath her. After the plane finally lands, Krisy and Wendy step into the Dominican Republic's bright sunlight and feel the warm embraces of their relatives. Once at their relatives' home, Krisy changes into her summer clothes and introduces her grandparents to the reader. While in the Dominican

Republic, Krisy speaks to everyone in Spanish. She also notes that people travel in different ways around the island and what animals are indigenous to Hispaniola.

When December 25 finally arrives, Krisy experiences a real island Christmas—lots of food to eat, games to play, and fun for everyone. The day after Christmas, Krisy continues enjoying herself by going to the beach, where she befriends tourists from Italy. A few days later, it is Krisy's birthday, which means even more celebrating. A tasty cake, exciting games, and many other birthday delights combine to make Krisy's birthday a happy one. Finally, Krisy and Wendy have to say good-bye and return to New York. After they arrive in snow-covered New York, Krisy and Wendy's family welcome them home. The story ends with Krisy saying how fortunate she is that she can live in two worlds.

This book tells of the special benefits of living in two worlds. Krisy quite matter-of-factly negotiates the transition from one culture to another and from one distinct geographic region to another. The reader learns through Krisy's words and experiences that although her two worlds differ in some ways, they are both important to her.

Photographs effectively complement Krisy's narration of her holiday trip and authenticate her two worlds. The colors, smiles, fun, emotions, and family togetherness clearly show Krisy's contentment with her life.

Classroom Applications

To extend this book into the classroom, each student can construct an individual photo essay ("A Day/Week in My Two Worlds") that tells about two special places (e.g., local mall and school, at home and at a grandparent's) or about two cities, states, or even countries. These essays can be used as a basis for planning imaginary or real trips for which students can identify things they want to see and do. Students can also discuss what they would pack, with whom they would travel, and how they would travel to and from their destinations. Another possibility is to have students interview (perhaps even videotape) classmates or other children in their school who have actually lived in two or more different places. Using the Internet to journey electronically to places where they would like to visit or live offers other interesting possibilities, such as communicating (via e-mail) directly with school-age children in other countries.

Haiti

Haiti occupies roughly the western third of the island of Hispaniola (the Dominican Republic is the other two thirds), which lies between Cuba and Puerto Rico.

 Lauture, Denize. *Running the Road to ABC.* illustrated by Reynold Ruffins. Simon & Schuster Books for Young Readers, 1996. 32 pp. (ISBN 0-689-80507-1). Contemporary Fiction, P-E.

Story Review Chart			
Setting	Plot/Events	Characters	Theme
•	•	•	•

Cultural Paradigm Reference Classification Chart

Geographic Location	Economic System	Social System	Political System
•	•	•	

In this story, six energetic children take the reader on a journey through their school. Early each morning, Dyesel, Milsen, Preneyis, Loud, Kousou, and Toutoun awake and get ready for school. After breakfast, with book bags and lunches in hand, the children race barefoot to school. On the way, they see people walking, hear animals making their morning noises, and survey the slopes of well-tended fields of coffee plants, corn, millet, and sugar cane. They trudge up hills and scamper down rocky ledges. Then they pass through a town bustling with early morning activity. The children quickly pass donkeys with loads; merchants with all sorts of goods; venders with hot, tasty breads; and people driving Jeeps and trucks. Once out of town, they walk on grass-covered roads that become bare dirt, then muddy, and eventually rocky. Do they slow down? No. The children continue their race to school. Hurt feet and twisted ankles can all be healed with nature's remedies. On and on they run, zipping by birds and butterflies. When all the children finally reach their school, they begin yet another journey—a journey to learn to read.

The story's lilting verses urge the reader from page to page and remind us of the love and eagerness children naturally have for learning.

Attractive illustrations done in gouache provide a portrait of the children's unbridled joy and anticipation as they go to school.

Classroom Applications

Ask the class, What do you see and do on your way to school? What do you like about learning at school? Students can create a wall map of the area where they live and trace their daily treks to school. They can also surround their mural with their writings on what they see on their daily journeys and what they like about learning in school.

 Williams, Karen Lynn. *Tap-Tap*. illustrated by Catherine Stock. Clarion Books, 1994. 34 pp. (ISBN 0-395-65617-6). Contemporary Fiction, E-M.

Story Review Chart

Setting	Plot/Events	Characters	Theme
•	•	•	

Cultural Paradigm Reference Classification Chart

Geographic Location	Economic System	Social System	Political System
•	•	•	

Sasifi gets up bright and early to go with her mother to market. But today is different because Sasifi is going to help her mother carry oranges to sell at the market. Soon after beginning their long walk, Sasifi asks her mother whether they can ride the *tap-tap*, or bus. Her mother says they will do what they always do and walk. This is the first time Sasifi carries a heavy basket on her head, and soon its weight lessens the previously imagined appeal of doing what mothers do on market day. Sasifi notices how others travel to market: Some walk, others go by donkey or horse, but many ride a tap-tap. Bolstered by her observation, she informs her mother that taking a tap-tap would be the best way to go to the market. Her mother responds by doubting whether Sasifi is really grown-up enough to help her. Sasifi assures her that she is indeed old enough.

After they finally reach the market, Sasifi learns from her mother how to pick a good place to sell their oranges, how to arrange the oranges to catch the customer's eye, how to convince customers to buy the oranges, and how to make change. After spending the morning learning the business of selling oranges, Sasifi takes over for the afternoon so that her mother can buy things they need at home. When mother returns, she is pleased to find that Sasifi has sold every orange and unexpectedly gives Sasifi a new hat and a few coins. Sasifi then surprises her mother by offering to pay for a trip home on the tap-tap.

Once they find a bus, Sasifi learns that a tap-tap leaves when it is full and not when a rider wants to leave. She also discovers that a tap-tap carries just about every-thing—people, animals, furniture—and stops when someone taps twice on the side of the bus. Sasifi has to stop the bus all by herself when a gust of wind blows her new hat off her head. Sasifi yells to the bus driver to stop, but the rushing wind and people talking drown out her voice. Then she firmly taps on the side of the bus twice, and the driver stops. Sasifi now can get her hat. Having learned about carrying a basket on her head, selling oranges in the market, and riding on the tap-tap, Sasifi ends her satisfy-ing day with a statement that she is not tired because she rode the bus.

Tap-Tap presents a child's view of a day of new experiences that teach much about life and growing up. Sasifi, like so many other children around the world, earnestly wants to partake in what she perceives to be adult activities and responsibil-ities. The book also provides insights into what motivates children to act as they do. Sasifi asks, for example, to ride the tap-tap because many others do—even though she knows her mother will say no. Very importantly, this book provides a window for viewing common cultural themes, including language (some French words appear in the text), market experiences typical of many countries in the Caribbean and else-where, shared routines of everyday life, passage from childhood to adulthood, and the informal process of socialization.

Soft pastel watercolor illustrations respectfully depict the people and places of Haiti. Rather than being highly realistic, the portraits of Sasifi and her mother tend to be impressionistic. In contrast, the landscapes are reminiscent of folk art. Overall, the illustrations communicate a sense of community and a studied understanding of the subtleties of island life in the Caribbean.

Classroom Applications

Several themes of this book can be explored profitably in the classroom. Because many children ride buses to school, they can compare their bus rides with Sasifi's. Studying transportation in general or buses in particular might lead to some interesting discoveries. Similarly, students can compare shopping in a mall with shopping in an open-air market. Another fruitful activity is to have a market day in school. Students can buy and sell things they have made and use "money" they have designed and printed as the instrument of economic exchange. Through a market simulation, students can learn firsthand about advertising, profit and loss, competition, and other basic business practices and economic principles common around the world.

Jamaica

Jamaica is located south of Cuba in the northwestern part of the Caribbean Sea.

 Hanson, Regina. *The Face in the Window.* illustrated by Linda Saport. Clarion Books, 1997. 32 pp. (ISBN 0-395-78625-8). Contemporary Fiction, E-M.

Story Review Chart			
Setting	Plot/Events	Characters	Theme
	•	•	•

Cultural Paradigm Reference Classification Chart			
Geographic Location	Economic System	Social System	Political System
		•	

On her way to school, Dora and her two friends, Lureen and Trevor, stop to pick mangoes in Miss Nella's yard. There they see Miss Nella chase something that does not appear to be there at all and then go into her house. Because the coast seems clear, Lureen and Trevor throw stones at the mangoes to knock them down. Dora hesitates to throw stones and questions whether she should do so. After her friends accuse her of being afraid and threaten to walk to school without her, Dora also tosses a stone at the tree. She hits Miss Nella's door instead. Miss Nella immediately looks out her window and sees Dora. Dora's friends then ask her whether she looked into Miss Nella's eyes, and she says, "Yes." "Oh, no!" her friends reply. They then tell her that her seeing Miss Nella's eyes can only bring bad luck.

At school, Dora continues to think about her pending bad luck, and her friends continue to taunt her. Consequently, Dora goes home from school alone. After she gets home, the rain comes down heavily, and Dora begins to believe that her bad luck brought the bad weather. As day turns into evening and evening into morning, the rain intensifies. Dora is now certain that she has caused this deluge. She tells her parents that the rain will never end and that she is responsible. Her parents patiently explain to her that Miss Nella is ill in her mind and ask Dora to think what she should do about hitting Miss Nella's door. Dora thinks she should apologize, providing her parents accompany her to Miss Nella's. So they all go to Miss Nella's and Dora gives her something sweet to eat. After Dora returns home, she makes more tasty treats to give to Miss Nella. Later, Dora goes by herself to Miss Nella's to deliver her gift of food.

This compassionate story communicates the message that people should try to understand their fears and to offer kindness to those in need. It also realistically portrays the genuine sensitivity and compassion that island people typically have for another, the parents' concern that their children learn to do what is right, and the importance of children respecting their elders. Additionally, this story shows how peer pressure can lead children to misbehave.

Pastel illustrations effectively depict the familiar dilemma children face when trying to decide what to do—listen to their peers and fit in or listen to their parents and do what is right.

Classroom Applications

Encourage students to talk about and compare experiences they have had similar to Dora's—doing what their peers expect and want and doing what their parents and their conscience tell them. Students can also discuss those times when they were afraid of something and what they did to overcome their fear, how they have extended kindness to someone in need, and how they have apologized to others.

 Gunning, Monica. *Not a Copper Penny in Me House.* illustrated by Frane Lessac. Boyds Mills Press, 1993. 32 pp. (ISBN 1-56397-050-3). Poetry, P-E.

Story Review Chart

Setting	Plot/Events	Characters	Theme
•		•	•

Cultural Paradigm Reference Classification Chart

Geographic Location	Economic System	Social System	Political System
•	•	•	

This anthology of poems tells of daily life in a traditional Jamaican village. From the easy-to-read poem "Country Christmas," the reader learns that preparing meals, attending the John Canoe Festival, and sprucing up homes are all part of the Christmas holiday in Jamaica. Also, not having "a copper penny in me house" is not an impediment in a community where trust sometimes substitutes for money. Other poems in this book are similarly straightforward yet convey many fascinating insights about varied facets of rural life in Jamaica. For example, the reader discovers what grandparents do on Sundays, how the sun bleaches clothes, how to make soap from plants, what it is like to have school outside under a tree, and what to expect on Christmas Eve at the market. Although the poems are specific to Jamaica, the general concepts presented, such as the vitality and importance of the extended family, the exuberance of Christmas celebrations, and the enjoyment of communal activities, are shared by many Caribbean nations.

Illustrations, done in gouache, use a folk art style common to the Caribbean. Additionally, the bold and brilliant color combinations highlight the distinctive vegetation, styles of housing, and community activities of Caribbean life.

Classroom Applications

This book suggests numerous ideas for related classroom activities. Students can enumerate and discuss similarities and differences of how certain holidays are celebrated in various Caribbean nations, as well as in the United States. Another possible activity centers on the special preparation of holiday meals, which students will readily recognize as a nearly universal tradition.

 Hanson, Regina. *The Tangerine Tree*. illustrated by Harvey Stevenson. Clarion Books, 1995. 32 pp. (ISBN 0-395-68963-5). Contemporary Fiction, E-M.

Story Review Chart

Setting	Plot/Events	Characters	Theme
•		•	•

Cultural Paradigm Reference Classification Chart

Geographic Location	Economic System	Social System	Political System
•	•	•	

This story opens with Ida asking her father why he is packing his suitcase. She learns that he is going to New York to work. She asks whether she can go too, but her parents tell her she cannot. When Ida sees her father pack his guitar, she is afraid he will never return home. To allay her fears, Ida's parents explain that her father has to go because they need money to pay rent, buy school uniforms, and provide a better life for her than what they had as children. They also tell Ida that her father is taking his guitar to play Jamaican music when he gets lonely. Their reassurance still does not lessen Ida's worries about the impending breakup of the family.

To avoid the anguish of saying good-bye to her father, Ida runs to her tangerine tree and cries. Her two older brothers, Delroy and Basil, offer to take care of her and even to make her a kite. Even their concern for her does not help. Finally, her father walks out to the tree where Ida is and gives her a present. Ida opens it and finds the book *Stories of Ancient Greeks*, which belonged to her brothers when they were younger. He tells her that when she can read the book all by herself, he will return home. Ida thinks that the wait will be forever because she cannot read. But he reminds her that she already knows a few letters and that learning the rest won't take too long. He also tells Ida that while he is away, Delroy will care for the bananas, Basil will tend the yams, and she will take care of the tangerine tree. He also asks Ida to pick the tasty fruit and to help her mother sell it at the market.

While her father finishes packing, Ida squeezes some tangerine juice into a bottle. When it is time for her father to leave, the entire family walks to the bus stop, where they exchange heartfelt good-byes, and Ida gives her father the sweet juice. After everyone returns home, Ida sees her mother standing alone with her head slumped down. Ida gently leads her mother to the tangerine tree and asks her to read aloud the book her father just gave her. Ida proclaims that she will learn to read her book as soon as possible so that she can write her father to tell him it is time to come home.

The Tangerine Tree poignantly describes the strength of a family forced to separate by dire economic conditions and how each member of the family must cope with the separation. It also informs the reader that many immigrants coming to America to work for a better life have to leave behind families. Another aspect of family separation beautifully portrayed in this book is Ida's view of place and time. At first, she doesn't know where New York is, nor can she comprehend how long her father will be gone. Only when she sees him pack his guitar, which she knows is very important to him, does she realize it will be a long time before he will be back, if at all. When Ida's father gives each of the children a responsibility to assume, they realize that they need to be strong and do what they can to keep the family together. These efforts to sustain the family tell of the trials and tribulations of separation experienced by many families around the world.

Acrylic illustrations sensitively convey the agony a family feels in coming to terms with a necessary but distressfully long separation. Helping soothe these sad moments somewhat is the beauty of the verdant landscape of Jamaica. Sunlight filtering into the home, colorful flowers, lush forests, and orange-colored tangerines create a serene backdrop during a time of anguish mixed with hope and love.

Classroom Applications

Students can discuss their experiences with writing to, or receiving letters from, family or friends. The history of the immigrant experience in the United States also offers a wealth of opportunities for further inquiry. Ellis Island National Park, for example, maintains an Internet Web site for visitors to peruse and learn about how and why millions of people came to the United States as immigrants. Also, students can study the implications of other historic places, such as Goree Island off the coast of Senegal in Africa. They can compare the differences between coming to the United States as immigrants versus coming to the United States as slaves.

Martinique

Martinique is located in the Lesser Antilles between the islands of Dominica and St. Lucia at the eastern end of the Caribbean Sea.

 San Souci, Robert D. *The Faithful Friend.* illustrated by Brian Pinkey. Simon & Schuster Books for Young Readers, 1995. 40 pp. (ISBN 0-02-786131-7). Folktale, E-L.

Story Review Chart			
Setting	Plot/Events	Characters	Theme
	•	•	•

Cultural Paradigm Reference Classification Chart

Geographic Location	Economic System	Social System	Political System
		•	

This story of loyalty and magic takes place in the late 19th century on the small island of Martinique. When Monsieur Duforce's wife dies at childbirth and he faces raising his newborn son, Clement, being wealthy allows Monsieur Duforce to hire a French widow to care for his son. The widow also has a newborn son, named Hippolyte. Clement and Hippolyte become close as children and grow up like brothers. When a young man, Clement falls in love with a portrait of a woman named Pauline. He asks Hippolyte to help him find her so that he can propose marriage. Hippolyte cautions Clement that beauty can be deceiving and that Pauline's uncle, Monsieur Zabocat, is rumored to be a wizard. Clement ignores these warnings, and the two begin their journey to find Pauline. They come across the deceased body of a beggar. Hippolyte thinks they should bury him properly, and Clement agrees. Eventually, they arrive at Monsieur Zabocat's home in Macouba. After dinner, Clement proposes marriage to Pauline and she accepts. Monsieur Zabocat, however, strenuously objects because he intended to take his niece to France to marry a man of his choice. Boldly, Pauline tells her uncle that she is old enough to marry any man she chooses and that she chooses Clement. Monsieur Zabocat angrily orders Clement, Hippolyte, and Pauline to leave his home at once and vows revenge upon them.

The three depart for Clement's home. Clement reassures Pauline that his father will warmly welcome her as a future daughter-in-law. Tired by the long journey, all three decide to rest. While Clement and Pauline nap, Hippolyte hears sounds of distant drums and follows their foreboding beat to a band of zombies. He overhears their sinister plot to kill Clement and Pauline. He also hears their curse: Whosoever tells of their plans will turn to stone. After Hippolyte manages to thwart the zombies, he uncovers their new plan, which involves poisoned mangoes. But once again, the loyal Hippolyte foils their evil intentions. Still undaunted, the zombies concoct a third stratagem; this time, they send a serpent to kill the couple on the evening of their wedding day. Hippolyte discovers this diabolical scheme too.

Soon after reaching home, Clement marries Pauline. Monsieur Zabocat attends their wedding, pretending to have forgiven the bride and groom. Hippolyte, wary of the zombies' latest intrigue, goes to the honeymoon chamber with a cutlass and kills the serpent coiled on their bed. The serpent magically disappears. Clement then enters the room to find Hippolyte with a cutlass in his hand. He rashly assumes that Hippolyte was going to kill him out of envy. At first, Hippolyte does not defend himself because of the zombies' curse. But when he feels Clement's contempt for him, he recounts the zombies' murderous intentions. As their curse comes true, Clement's anger subsides, but it is too late, for his dear friend has turned completely to stone. Clement frantically cries out that he is willing to do anything to bring Hippolyte back to life. Just then, a stranger claims that he can restore Hippolyte to life, but only if Clement accepts the curse on himself. Knowing that Hippolyte has saved his life more than once, Clement agrees. The stranger starts to direct the curse to Clement but, at the last moment, touches Monsieur Zabocat, who instantly turns to stone. The stranger then identifies himself as the beggar they had buried and explains that he has come back to life to repay their kindness. The story ends with Clement, Hippolyte, and their wives living happily together and their children sustaining their fathers' friendship.

The underlying massage of this story is how love and loyalty overcome barriers imposed by economic status and racial heritage and allow two men to sustain a friendship throughout their lives and, thereafter, through their children.

Oil paintings and scratchboard illustrations wonderfully meld the story together. The choice of colors in the paintings helps create the nurturing atmosphere of a lush, tropical island. The scratchboard style, in contrast, helps impart the emotions and moods of the story. For example, Clement's and Hippolyte's facial expressions and postures convey a sense of melancholy when they bury the beggar, whereas Zabocat's face shows vengeful anger at Clement's marriage proposal.

Classroom Applications

As an in-class activity, students can reflect on what friendship means. They can discuss what they each look for in a friend, what they believe their friends think about them, and what they believe are universal qualities of friendship. The Internet and its e-mail capability can provide a way for students to initiate and nurture friendships with "Net pals" who live in various countries around the world.

Puerto Rico

Puerto Rico is located east of the Dominican Republic.

 Nodar, Carmen Santiago. *Abuelita's Paradise.* illustrated by Diane Paterson. Albert Whitman, 1992. 32 pp. (ISBN 0-8075-0129-8). Contemporary Fiction, E–M.

Story Review Chart

Setting	Plot/Events	Characters	Theme
•	•	•	•

Cultural Paradigm Reference Classification Chart

Geographic Location	Economic System	Social System	Political System
•	•	•	

In the rocking chair her grandmother Abuelita left her, Marita rocks and recalls the many stories her grandmother shared with her. The stories were about when her grandmother was a young girl and lived in Puerto Rico. In one such story, Abuelita goes with her father to the fields. There she gaily dances among the ever-so-tall stalks of sugar cane. Then she hears her father cutting them down and begins to cry. Her father tells her that the sugar cane is like her hair and will grow back. After her father finishes working in the fields, the two head home chewing on the sweet pieces of sugar cane. After they arrive home, father takes a siesta and Abuelita lures a honey creeper bird to come close by putting sugar on the kitchen table. Abuelita also tells other stories, like plucking chicken feathers, making feather pillows, identifying island plants, and telling about the history of pirates and forts. Embraced by her mother's arms, Marita tells her mother stories about what she will do when she visits her grandmother's beloved Puerto Rico.

This captivating intergenerational book engagingly tells a story through the eyes of a child who reminisces about her grandmother's own storytelling. These fond memories raise many questions in Marita's mind: Will Marita's mother tell her stories? Will she one day tell Marita's future children stories? Will Marita one day go to Puerto Rico? Will Marita tell her future children and grandchildren stories? The reader is left thinking that, like life, the stories will continue.

Watercolor illustrations gently shift the reader's attention from one setting to the next and from one period of time to another. They also aptly portray the characters' ranges of emotions expressed or implied in the story.

Classroom Applications

Ask the class, Has someone ever told you stories about things that happened long ago? Where did these stories take place? Were these stories told in a special place? Interviewing older relatives or friends about their childhoods can help build and strengthen transgenerational relationships. Suggest that students write narrative accounts of stories they have heard from parents, grandparents, and other older relatives and put them in a class book. Older students can also study such topics as sugar cane, rain forests, and pirates.

 Jaffe, Nina. *The Golden Flower: A Taino Myth From Puerto Rico.* illustrated by Enrique O. Sánchez. Simon & Schuster Books for Young Children, 1996. 32 pp. (ISBN 0-689-80469-5). Folklore, E-M.

Story Review Chart

Setting	Plot/Events	Characters	Theme
•	•	•	•

Cultural Paradigm Reference Classification Chart

Geographic Location	Economic System	Social System	Political System
•		•	

With people seated all around him, a Taino chief opens this story with a tale about how the island of Puerto Rico, or Boriquen, as it once was called, came to be. According to legend, a Taino boy is walking one day on the desert plain below the mountain on which he lives. Everything from the top of the mountain to the plains below is barren of trees, flowers, and water. But this day is special. Floating in the winds is a seed. The boy swoops it into his hand and puts it into his pouch.

For many days, the boy puts many seeds into his pouch, until one day he decides to plant them. Those he plants on top of his mountain become lush trees and flowers, including a unique golden flower. The golden blossom of this special flower eventually grows into a large sphere. Not knowing what it is, the boy and others stay away from it. But one day, two men by chance find the object, which is really a pumpkin. Because they believe that it might have special powers, they race each other to get it first. The two men fight over the pumpkin and tug on it until the vine snaps. The pumpkin then rolls down the mountain and bursts open. Out of it gushes the sea and all its denizens. The level of the ocean rapidly rises until only the top of the densely vegetated mountain is visible. Now, the Taino have plants to cultivate, water for their crops, fish to catch, and all sorts of wonderful things resulting from the birth of the island of Puerto Rico.

This creation myth's lead character is a child. It is intriguing that a child, rather than an omnipotent god, initiates the chain of events leading to the birth of the island. Also fascinating is how the content of the story emphasizes island geography, whereas the act of storytelling reflects the social importance of this creation myth.

Illustrations done in acrylic and gouache are cast in earth tones that, in combination with an inventive style, imbue the entire book with an intense, naturalistic sense.

Classroom Applications

What better way to follow up this story than to have students tell their own fanciful versions of how something with which they are familiar might have been created. Students can also write stories on the creative uses of pumpkins; planting pumpkin seeds and tending the seedlings can provide students with a follow-up to compare fact and fantasy.

Most cultures around the world have creation myths. By comparing these myths, students can gain insight into why human cultures create myths and how myths transcend time and place.

 Ichikawa, Satomi. *Isabela's Ribbons*. Philomel, 1995. 32 pp. (ISBN 0-399-22772-5). Contemporary Fiction, E–M.

Story Review Chart			
Setting	Plot/Events	Characters	Theme
	•	•	

Cultural Paradigm Reference Classification Chart			
Geographic Location	Economic System	Social System	Political System
		•	

In this story, Isabela combines her love for hair ribbons and her fondness for playing hide-and-seek. Her many-colored ribbons blend with the richly hued tropical environment, making it difficult for her two adult and animal playmates to find her. Her dog

Samantha, adult neighbor Patria, and Grandma look for her among the hibiscus flowers, banana trees, and limbs of the flamboyant tree.

One day, when Isabela has no one to play with, she takes a basket of ribbons and climbs a mango tree. Seated among the boughs, she realizes that she is not having any fun by herself. A parrot perches in the tree but soon flies away. Then a wondrous thing happens: The top of the tree magically becomes the bottom of the sea. Isabela and her ribbons all become fish. They see sunlight and swim toward it. To their surprise, they see children playing beneath the mango tree. Isabela decides to share her fish with them, and so she throws her streaming ribbons out of the tree. The children grasp and grapple for the ribbons and then find their newfound friend, Isabela. Isabela and her friends end the story by wearing all the ribbons and playing together.

Colorful pictures vividly illustrate the delightfulness of this story. From the plants in which Isabela hides to the bright colors of her ribbons, the watercolor paintings effectively intertwine plot and setting.

Classroom Applications

What games do you like to play? How do you make friends? How do you keep friends? These are natural questions for students to think about. Each student can contribute a dictated or written response regarding these and other similar questions to a class book on friendship. Students can also find out what games are played in different countries and how to play them by e-mailing inquiries to students in schools around the world.

 Dorros, Arthur. *Isla*. illustrated by Elisa Kleven. Dutton Children's Books, 1995. 32 pp. (ISBN 0-525-45149-8). Contemporary Fiction, P-M.

Story Review Chart

Setting	Plot/Events	Characters	Theme
•	•	•	•

Cultural Paradigm Reference Classification Chart

Geographic Location	Economic System	Social System	Political System
•		•	

Rosalba goes on an imaginary trip with her grandmother Abuela to the island nation where she was born. Like two birds, they fly over an island that looks emerald green and is warm year round. They eventually end up at the home of Rosalba's uncle Fernando, aunt Isabela, and cousin Elena. After warm welcomes, Abuela shows Rosalba the house and tells her many family stories recounting her life on the island long ago.

Then the two fly to the rain forest, where they see an abundant and gorgeous array of flora and fauna. They compare this serene site to a bustling old city. Like two acrobatic birds, they do loops and rolls in the air as bedazzled people on the ground look on with amazement. Venturing on, they soar over the harbor; below, they see cruise ships and an old historic building. From there, they fly over the city. Abuela informs Rosalba about the many changes that have occurred in the city since she was young. She suggests that they change their course and visit an open-air market. After watching the people sell and buy all kinds of goods, it's off to the beach to swim and be with their relatives. Rosalba and Abuela go into the water and find many different kinds of fish. Now it is time to be fish. They jump up and about and say they are flying fish. After their exciting adventures, they return to have dinner with Fernando, Isabela, and Elena. The time has come for Rosalba and Abuela to fly back to New York. With the stars guiding them, they are soon back home in bed. Abuela tells Rosalba that they can visit their island anytime, and Rosalba says she cannot wait to return.

This imaginative intergenerational story portrays the warm attachment between a grandmother and her granddaughter. Abuela shares an important part of her life with Rosalba, who in turn makes Abuela's fondly remembered experiences part of her own memories. The text also intersperses Spanish words throughout the story. They are clearly defined in context and also appear in a glossary.

Classroom Applications

Students can write, draw, or dictate where they would fly with Abuela if she offered to take them anywhere in the Caribbean. Would it be to Puerto Rico, the Bahamas, Haiti, or somewhere else? What would they do? After finishing these stories, students can share them with their peers in a storytelling circle or on a poster display.

 Picó, Fernando. *The Red Comb*. illustrated by Maria Antonia Ordóñez. BridgeWater Press, 1991. 48 pp. (ISBN 0-8167-3539-5). Folklore, E-M.

Story Review Chart

Setting	Plot/Events	Characters	Theme
•	•	•	•

Cultural Paradigm Reference Classification Chart

Geographic Location	Economic System	Social System	Political System
•	•	•	

Vitita lives in Rio Piedras, where she listens quietly to all the conversation going on in the village. The person she most likes to listen to is her neighbor, Siña Rosa Bultron. One day while doing her chores, Vitita discovers a runaway slave woman hiding under the steps of her porch. The woman's hair is uncombed, and her clothes are tattered and worn. When Vitita asks her who she is and what she is doing, the woman runs away. Vitita tells Siña Rosa about the woman. Siña Rosa instructs her not to tell her father, but to leave food for the woman each night in the fork of the mango tree. Vitita returns home and follows Siña Rosa's instructions. After the third night, the woman finally eats the food left for her. Night after night, Vitita and the woman follow the same routine. One evening, Vitita decides to leave something special for the woman. It is a red comb that Vitita's godmother had given her.

Later, Vitita overhears another conversation. This time, it is about the runaway slave woman. Padro Calderon, a slave hunter, tells Vitita's father about the woman's escape and asks whether he can spend the night in the mango tree to try to recapture her. Vitita goes to Siña Rosa for advice. Siña Rosa takes charge and outwits the slave hunter. The next evening, Calderon attempts another scheme, but once again Siña Rosa thwarts his plan. Vitita's father finally asks Calderon to take his slave hunting elsewhere.

A few weeks later, Siña Rosa announces to the village that her niece will come to live with her. A lovely woman wearing a red comb in her hair comes to the village and eventually becomes happily married to a man living there. The story ends with Vitita telling her grandchildren their favorite Siña Rosa story, the one about the red comb.

Loosely based on historical facts, this embellished story is about an event that happened in Puerto Rico years ago. The story provides insights into the island's culture, including enduring friendships among the people, willingness to help those in need, children's respect for elders, and acting justly. Expressive illustrations highlight the beauty found in small island villages. Mango trees, banana trees, and a starlit evening sky all contribute to a serene island setting.

Classroom Applications

Helping others is important to any social system around the world. Students can list in what ways they may have helped others and how others may have helped them. Older students can research the history of slavery in the United States and, in particular, how slaves helped one another escape to freedom.

 Delacre, Lulu. *Vejigante Masquerader.* Scholastic, 1993. 40 pp. (ISBN 0-590-45776-4). Contemporary Fiction, E-L.

Story Review Chart			
Setting	Plot/Events	Characters	Theme
	•	•	•

Cultural Paradigm Reference Classification Chart			
Geographic Location	Economic System	Social System	Political System
•	•	•	

Ramón wants to be a masquerader during the February carnival celebration, but he does not have a costume, which is required. Costumes enable festival goers to play pranks without being recognized and thereby escape retribution!

Getting a costume, however, is a major problem for Ramón. His mother has neither the time to make him one nor the money to buy him one. So Ramón secretly makes his own. He learns to sew from a seamstress and earns money to buy a mask by doing her errands. All goes well until he goes to pick up his mask and finds that he does not have quite enough money. The mask maker, Don Migue, tells Ramón to take the mask but to return next week to work off what he owes. Happily, Ramón returns home and eagerly awaits the big day.

The carnival soon arrives, and Ramón gets to be a *vejigante*. He passes among the crowd, and not even his family recognizes him. Then he sees and follows the daring El Gallo's group. He shadows them and works up the courage to challenge a mean goat—one that even the bravest of El Gallo's group would not confront. Although the goat's horns shred Ramón's costume, El Gallo's group praise his bravery. They invite him to be a member of their *vejigante* group, but Ramón still has a problem: How can he parade with them the next day with his costume ruined? Ramón sadly returns home and tells his mother everything. She consoles him with a reminder that "persistence is the key," and together they repair the costume so that he can fulfill his dream.

Vejigante Masquerader offers a simple reminder that if one continues to work hard, then dreams can become reality. Also, this book is a frolicking introduction to the carnival, which most Caribbean cultures celebrate at some time and in some form.

Classroom Applications

Mixed watercolor, colored pencil, and pastel illustrations radiate the festive feelings associated with a Caribbean carnival. Students can create their own classroom carnival by following the instructions at the end of the book and make their own *vejigante* masks. Ask the class, Do we wear masks during anytime of the year in the United States? Halloween and Mardi Gras can be discussed as examples.

St. Lucia

St. Lucia is located in the Lesser Antilles, between Martinique to the north and St. Vincent and the Grenadines to the south.

 Orr, Katherine. *My Grandpa and the Sea*. Carolrhoda Books, 1990. 32 pp. (ISBN 0-87614-409-1). Contemporary Fiction, E-M.

Story Review Chart			
Setting	Plot/Events	Characters	Theme
•	•	•	•

Cultural Paradigm Reference Classification Chart			
Geographic Location	Economic System	Social System	Political System
•	•	•	

A young girl tells about her grandfather, who had been making his living from the sea until new big fishing boats drive him out of business. A nephew offers him a partnership on one of the new fishing boats, but he refuses. Grandfather says that people should not take more than they need from the sea. He tries driving a taxi for a while and helping his wife with her new bakery, but neither proves successful. Feeling that his place is the sea, Grandfather tries to figure out what he can do. While sipping his seamoss drink, he suddenly realizes that the answer is right in front of him; he can start a seamoss farm. Soon, Grandfather's seamoss farm is set up near shore and the crop is growing well. He harvests the crop, dries and packages it, and sells it for a tidy profit. Grandfather does quite well with his business and shares his wisdom with his granddaughter by telling her that the head should always serve the heart.

This inspiring story of a grandfather and his perseverance to earn a living and not compromise his principles is a lesson to all. Faced with limited options, he uses his ingenuity to follow his heart, a lesson he passes on to his granddaughter and to all those who read this story. Illustrations complement the story and highlight the natural beauty of the island and the surrounding ocean.

Classroom Applications

Students can study the fascinating field of aquaculture by constructing a Venn diagram to compare the similarities and differences of aquaculture and agriculture. They can share their results with their peers. Older students might research the problem of overfishing of the oceans. Students can also discuss what they would do if they were in a situation where they must either make money but compromise their principles or be unemployed but remain true to their ideals.

Trinidad and Tobago

Trinidad and Tobago are two islands (Trinidad is larger) located close to each other south of the Lesser Antilles and just off the northern coast of Venezuela.

 Joseph, Lynn. *Coconut Kind of Day: Island Poems.* illustrated by Sandra Speidel. Puffin Books, 1992. 30 pp. (ISBN 0-14-054527-1). Poetry, E-M.

Story Review Chart

Setting	Plot/Events	Characters	Theme
•	•	•	

Cultural Paradigm Reference Classification Chart

Geographic Location	Economic System	Social System	Political System
•			

The poems in this book recount everyday events in the life of a young girl in Trinidad. She begins with her walk to school and on the way says hello to the man selling fruit. Then she tells about her brother, who swims in Mayaro Bay, and her mother, who has gone off to market to sell figs. At school, the young girl and her best friend Jasmine race snails, but their teacher rebukes them for racing snails in her class. On the way home, she and her friends get tropical fruit ice cream in Popsicle form. Then it's off to ask their male peers whether they can play cricket. Told that it is a male sport, the girls decide that they will have a team for both boys and girls when they get older. Farther on the way home, she meets her father and eats coconut jelly beneath the coconut trees. Then she and Jasmine see the fishermen pulling their nets to land. They try their hand at hauling a net to shore, only to be defeated by a large wave. As the sun begins to set, the ibis fly by. Later in the evening, steel drums are heard, and the *jumbi*, or bogeyman, comes out. Finally, the sleepy schoolgirl says good night to all the sounds of the evening.

The lyrical words catch the timeless wonder of an eventful day in the island life of a young schoolgirl. The illustrations, likewise, reflect the essence of the characters and the idyllic landscape of a Caribbean island.

Classroom Applications

Students can write poems about one of their school days. Afterward, they can see in what ways their days are similar to those of the poem's lead character. The class can additionally read their poems while accompanied by Caribbean music.

 Binch, Caroline. *Gregory Cool*. Dial Books for Young Readers, 1994. 32 pp. (ISBN 0-8037-1577-3). Contemporary Fiction, E–M.

Story Review Chart

Setting	Plot/Events	Characters	Theme
•	•	•	•

Cultural Paradigm Reference Classification Chart

Geographic Location	Economic System	Social System	Political System
•		•	

Gregory travels all the way from the United States to visit his grandparents on the island of Tobago. They meet him at the airport, and his grandmother is delighted that she finally gets to kiss and embrace her grandson. On the way to his grandparents' home, Gregory feels the sultry air of the tropics and inhales the island aromas, neither of which he finds pleasant. He wishes he were back home with his parents and friends and wonders whether he can endure a whole month in Tobago.

His grandparents' home is a small house, and his room has a curtain behind which he can hang his clothes. He goes to sleep and in the morning meets his cousin

Cover illustration from GREGORY COOL by Caroline Binch. Copyright © 1994 by Caroline Binch. Used by permission of Dial Books for Young Readers, a division of Penguin Books USA Inc.

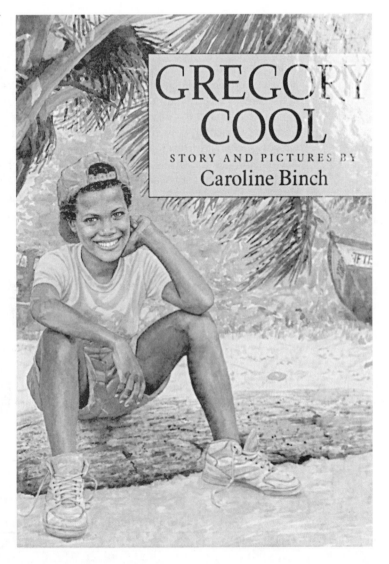

Lennox at breakfast. Gregory doesn't like the food, but he does drink juice. After breakfast, Lennox takes Gregory outside to show his cousin around and offers to take him swimming. Gregory declines and stays by himself in the yard. With no television or bicycle, Gregory decides to spend the next day again in the yard. Later that day, Grandmother comes outside and tells Gregory and Lennox that they are all going to the beach. After a ride on a bus, they arrive at a gorgeous beach. Gregory goes into the water but frantically swims to shore when he mistakes dolphins for sharks. Lennox now has the upper hand and tells Gregory that he is not cool. Gregory goes off and gets a drink of coconut water from a fisherman. Later, when he asks for more coconut water, Lennox points at the coconuts atop a nearby tree and quickly scampers up the trunk. Gregory tries to follow but is unable to match his cousin's climbing skill. The two boys then go for a swim and pretend to be sharks and stingrays. On returning home, they decide to walk up a hill and watch the moon rise. Gregory takes off his sneakers and goes barefoot like his cousin. On their way back to the house for dinner, Lennox tells Gregory that now he is cool.

Getting used to any new environment takes time, patience, and support. This period of transition can become even more difficult in a different country. Although Gregory feels out of place early on, he gradually feels more at home as he explores his new environment with his cousin. *Gregory Cool* accurately portrays everyday life in a rural island community. The grandparents are shown to be patient, kind, and wise; the land and sea prove to be effective medicines for homesickness.

Watercolor and pencil illustrations reflect the closeness of the people and the beauty of the island of Tobago.

Classroom Applications

Ask the class, If you didn't have a television to watch or your friends to play with, what would you enjoy doing on an island such as Tobago? Have the students look carefully at the pictures and write or draw what they would like to do if they could stay with Gregory's grandparents for a week. Comparing sharks and dolphins or preparing and tasting coconut water are other activities in which the students can engage.

 Joseph, Lynn. *An Island Christmas.* illustrated by Catherine Stock. Clarion Books, 1992. 32 pp. (ISBN 0-395-58761–1). Contemporary Fiction, E-M.

Story Review Chart

Setting	Plot/Events	Characters	Theme
•		•	•

Cultural Paradigm Reference Classification Chart

Geographic Location	Economic System	Social System	Political System
•		•	

The excitement of an island Christmas is something to see and experience. Rosie's mother reminds her of the many preparations that need to be made. Instead of going to the beach, Rosie picks sorrel fruit, from which her mother will make a tasty Christmas drink. While picking fruit, she meets the sugar cane man selling his canes for 10 cents each. He stops what he is doing and helps Rosie pick the best fruit. They then go to Rosie's house, and before the sugar cane man leaves, he gives Mama the largest cane he has.

The next day, Tantie comes over to fix black currant cake, and Rosie's brother joins them. By evening, all the delectable cakes have been baked, and the sound of a band can be heard. The *parang* band, with its rhythmic sounds, plays Christmas music at each house. People dance and sing and then offer the musicians food. When the band finishes, it moves on to the next house. As the rush and excitement of Christmas Eve build, Rosie's mother does the last-minute cooking, and Daddy does the last-minute shopping. Then Rosie and her brother repaint their Christmas tree white and decorate it. Next, they go up into their tree house to make some Christmas presents.

With everything finally ready for Christmas Eve and Christmas Day, the whole family sings their favorite Christmas songs before they go to sleep. The next morning, they wake up early, run downstairs, and open their gifts. There they find a toy drum, a truck, and other gifts. After the family is dressed, relatives arrive. Soon it's off to church. Family, food, and fun are what a real island Christmas is all about.

An Island Christmas nicely captures the anticipation and flavor of an island Christmas. From the particular emphasis on food preparation to going to church with relatives, this story conveys the strong family togetherness that typifies an island holiday celebration. Expressive watercolor illustrations are appealing invitations to spend Christmas with Rosie and her family.

Classroom Applications

Ask the class, Can you think of foods that are associated with certain holidays, celebrations, or special times? What about Thanksgiving, a birthday, or Hanukkah? Have students write about the foods they associate with a special day of celebration and about the other preparations necessary to make that day complete and enjoyable.

 Joseph, Lynn. *Jasmine's Parlour Day.* illustrated by Ann Grifalconi. Lothrop, Lee & Shepard Books, 1994. 32 pp. (ISBN 0-688-11487-3). Contemporary Fiction, E-M.

Story Review Chart

Setting	Plot/Events	Characters	Theme
•	•	•	

Cultural Paradigm Reference Classification Chart

Geographic Location	Economic System	Social System	Political System
•	•	•	

When Jasmine wakes up, her mama reminds her that it is Parlour Day, the day she goes to the beach to help sell food at their *parlour*, or concession stand. Filled with excitement, Jasmine hurriedly dresses and offers to carry the sugar cakes her mama made to sell. Jasmine cannot balance the basket on her head the way her mama does, so she steadies it with her hands. Along the way, they pass coconut trees, breadfruit trees, and two iguanas.

When they arrive at Maracus Bay, Jasmine and her mama set up their parlour. Jasmine lines up the fish on beds of ice while mama readies the scale for weighing food.

Then Jasmine takes some sugar cakes over to the parlour of her best friend's mother. There she and her best friend Michelle share some sweets and venture off to see who else has arrived. They listen to the sounds in conch shells, see unpleasant Miz Barrows, and stop at Derek's parlour. Because Derek must stay with his mother's parlour, the two girls give him a large piece of sugar cake. Then off Jasmine and Michelle go to see Carlos, and what a sight to see. He is juggling fruit! They give him some sugar cake and leave. The sun is rising, the temperature is climbing, and the cars are arriving with people ready to go to the beach. It is now time for Jasmine and Michelle to return to their parlours to work. On their way, Jasmine unthinkingly gives a sugar cake to Miz Barrows, who responds with a nicer than usual grunt. Jasmine rejoins her mama, surrounded by the bright sounds of people selling and buying sugar cakes and fish.

Jasmine typifies many children living in the Caribbean. Her enthusiasm for a daily event, her willingness to help with adult work, and her kindness toward others are but a few of the social graces valued by Caribbean cultures. The book's scenes in and around parlours are quite realistic and inviting. The extensive preparation and range of goods to sell and the cooperative spirit of parlour vendors are just a few everyday characteristics of Caribbean markets.

Vibrant illustrations express much of the thrill and enjoyment that Jasmine and other story characters attach to Parlour Day. They also meld the surrounding land and seascapes into a peaceful setting.

Classroom Applications

Have students find out what kinds of goods are sold around the world at parlours, outdoor markets, and concession stands. If they could design and run their own stands, what would they sell? How would they display and sell their goods? Students can set up their own stands and "sell" their actual or pretend goods in the classroom.

U.S. Virgin Islands

The U.S. Virgin Islands are located east of Puerto Rico.

 Gershator, Phillis. *Rata, Pata, Scata, Fata: A Caribbean Story.* illustrated by Holly Meade. Little, Brown, 1994. 32 pp. (ISBN 0-316-30470-0). Contemporary Fiction, P-E.

Story Review Chart

Setting	Plot/Events	Characters	Theme
•	•	•	

Cultural Paradigm Reference Classification Chart

Geographic Location	Economic System	Social System	Political System
•		•	

Junjun, a young boy, much prefers dreaming to working. When his mother asks him to get some fish, he wishes they would come to him. He tries repeating his magic words "rata-pata-scata-fata" a few times, and soon a fisherman drops a fish near him. He takes it to his mother, who is pleased with the fish. She then sends him to fetch their goat. Junjun looks high and low for the goat but to no avail. He then says his magic words again, sits down, and the goat soon comes to him and nibbles on his straw hat. With the goat beside him, Junjun heads home for lunch. In the afternoon, Mother asks Junjun to pick some tamarinds. Junjun thinks about how high he would have to climb in the tree to pick them, so once more he utters his magic words. Almost immediately, a gust of wind blows some tamarinds off the tree and into Junjun's pail.

Each time Junjun brings things to his mother, he tells her what has happened. She pays faint tribute to Junjun's magic words and continues with her many chores. With the day nearly over, Mother tells Junjun to do one more chore. She explains that because there has been little rain for several days, he must fetch water from the well. Complaining that he is too tired, he instead asks his mother to say his magic words. She does, and the rain makes the sound of "rata-pata-scata-fata" as it falls all around them.

Collages of torn, softly colored paper add a whimsical touch to the playful magic in this charming story.

Classroom Applications

Rhyming magic words, playful action and dialogue, and a lighthearted story line make this is an ideal book for children to dramatize using simple props. Students can also talk about their wishes and the magic words they might use to make their wishes come true.

Caribbean: General

Mitchell, Rita Phillips. Hue Boy. *illustrated by Caroline Binch. Dial Books for Young Readers, 1993. 26 pp.* (ISBN 0-8037-1448-3). *Contemporary Fiction, E-M.*

Story Review Chart

Setting	Plot/Events	Characters	Theme
•	•	•	•

Cultural Paradigm Reference Classification Chart

Geographic Location	Economic System	Social System	Political System
		•	

Hue Boy is shorter than his friends. Keeping a watchful eye on his height, Hue Boy's mama measures him each day, but he does not seem to grow any taller. She wishes Hue Boy's dad were home; he certainly would know what to do. Unfortunately, Hue Boy's dad works off the island and so cannot be there to help his son.

Mama gives Hue Boy plenty of fruits and vegetables to eat. Also, his grandmother makes him some new clothes and tells him he will grow into them. Hue Boy's neighbor Carlos also has a suggestion: He tells Hue Boy that he can become taller by doing stretching exercises. So Hue Boy does the suggested exercises, but he still does not grow any taller. One day at school, the other children taunt Hue Boy about his height. His teacher tells him to ignore them and not to worry. Concerned about how other children are treating him, Hue Boy's mother takes him to see a wise man, a doctor, and a healer. They each give their opinions on what to do. Hue Boy tries to follow everyone's advice, but to no avail. One day, Hue Boy goes to the harbor and sees an incredibly large ship. Then he sees a tall man walking toward him. The man turns out to be his father, who has come home at last. Together, they walk through the village and Hue Boy finally feels tall.

Many children can relate to this story. Feelings of inadequacy about one's appearance and uncertainty about being accepted by peers are emotions experienced by most children. The book also tells how people living in an island village willingly cooperate to help solve each other's problems. Although the advice does not always work, one senses that the people truly care enough to take the time to show their concern for one another.

Illustrations in *Hue Boy* reflect the genuine affection that island people characteristically have for children. Most noticeable is the strong commitment to the extended family in which many close relatives actively nurture children. Thus, we see a mother's worried look, a grandmother's proud face, and a father's loving smile.

Classroom Applications

Everyone has personal problems. Students can write about problems that they have had or that someone they know has had and suggest possible solutions. Ask the class, Are all problems perceived in the same way? Can a problem have more than one solution? Do people in other countries view problems and find solutions to them in the same way as you do? Students can share their answers to these questions in discussion groups.

 Stow, Jenny. *The House That Jack Built*. Dial Books for Young Readers, 1992. 32 pp. (ISBN 0-8037-1090-9). Poetry, P–E.

Story Review Chart

Setting	Plot/Events	Characters	Theme
•		•	

Cultural Paradigm Reference Classification Chart

Geographic Location	Economic System	Social System	Political System
•		•	

This version of the well-known story "The House That Jack Built" takes place on a Caribbean island. Although the basic story line is familiar, the characters, setting, and innumerable details have a distinct Caribbean flavor, which is reinforced by numerous collages done in paint, ink, and crayon. Jack's Caribbean-style house nestled amid hibiscus and palm trees creates an inviting and tranquil scene.

Classroom Applications

Students can compare several versions of the story "The House That Jack Built," focusing primarily on the setting. Ask the class, Are the houses built of the same materials and in the same way? How do Jack's finished houses differ from one location to another? What kinds of plants, if any, surround the houses? Answers to these and other questions can be shared in group discussions. A follow-up activity is for students actually to construct from cardboard boxes their own "house that Jack built." They can decide on which changes they would have to make to their house if they moved it to different climates around the world.

 Linden, Ann Marie. *One Smiling Grandma*. illustrated by Lynne Russell. Dial Books for Young Readers, 1992. 26 pp. (ISBN 0-14-055341-X). Counting Book, P-E.

Story Review Chart

Setting	Plot/Events	Characters	Theme
•	•	•	•

Cultural Paradigm Reference Classification Chart

Geographic Location	Economic System	Social System	Political System
•		•	

This delightful counting book presents vignettes about a young girl and her grandmother living in a Caribbean community. The story opens with the grandmother rocking on the porch. This is followed by the young granddaughter with hair ribbons counting humming birds, steel drums, flying fish, market ladies, conch shells, sugar apples, coconuts, and mongooses. The story ends with the granddaughter napping on her grandmother's lap.

Classroom Applications

One Smiling Grandma contains eye-filling two-page spreads that take the reader on a visually stimulating Caribbean excursion. Young students will enjoy counting along with the story, reading and developing their own Caribbean counting book. For example, teachers can bring in one conch shell, two Caribbean postcards, three travel books on the Caribbean, and four real mangoes for the students to taste. Once students complete their Caribbean counting book, they can develop a U.S. counting book.

SUMMARY

Of the 24 books reviewed for this chapter, 21 are associated with 10 countries and 3 with the Caribbean region generally. Contemporary fiction is the predominant genre (15), whereas only 4 books belong to the folktale genre. Relatively few books fall into each of the other three genres found: poetry (3), historical fiction (1), and counting book (1).

In all 24 books reviewed, the authors tend to emphasize the characters; in 20 books, the settings and plot/events are featured. Themes are evident in 16 books. The theme that emerges most frequently stresses the importance and resiliency of the extended family and the common practice of helping those in need through sharing and offering personal support. Overall, most books about the Caribbean clearly contain at least three of the four major story elements. Consequently, children reading these books will find engaging, multifaceted books that vividly portray the richness of many Caribbean cultures.

Applying the transcultural paradigm to the books about the Caribbean reveals that references to a social system are obvious in all 24 books reviewed. As one might expect for a region identified with subtropical islands, geographic location plays an important role in 20 books. The economic system is featured in 11 books, and the political system in just 1 book.

SUGGESTED REFERENCES
▼▼

Ballenger, C. (1996). Learning the ABC's in a Haitian preschool: A teacher's story. *Language Arts,* 73(5), 317-323. (Haiti)

Bello, Y. (1993). Caribbean American children's literature. In V. J. Harris (Ed.), *Teaching multicultural literature in grades K-8* (pp. 245-265). Norwood, MA: Christopher Gordon. (General)

Caines, H., McDonald, C., & Miller-Lachmann, L. (1995). Understanding Haiti. *Multicultural Review,* 4(1), 25-27, 58-63. (Haiti)

Canadian International Development Agency. (1992). *Children's literature: Toward understanding the Caribbean. A curriculum guide for grades K-8.* Toronto: UNICET Canada. (General)

Day, F. A. (1997). *Latina and Latino voices in literature for children and teenagers.* Portsmouth, NH: Heinemann. (General)

Gutierrez, M. (1992). Ideology in literature: Images of social relationships within Puerto Rico's historical context in "Isolda's Mirror," a short story by Rosario Ferre. *Social Studies,* 83(1), 12-16. (Puerto Rico)

Headlam, A. L. (1990). *Examining cultural relevancy in the "Doctor Bird Readers": Text analysis from the perspective of Jamaican children.* Paper presented at the annual meeting of the International Reading Association. (Jamaica)

Mestre, L. S., & Nieto, S. (1996). Puerto Rican children's literature and culture in the public library. *Multicultural Review,* 5(2), 26-38. (Puerto Rico)

Rosell, J. F. (1996). Cuba. *Bookbird,* 33(3/4), 58-63. (Cuba)

Wald, K., & Bacon, B. (1981). New literacy for new people: Children and books in Cuba. *Journal of Reading,* 25(3), 251-260. (Cuba)

CHILDREN'S BOOKS CITED
▼▼

Binch, C. (1994). *Gregory cool.* New York: Dial Books for Young Readers. (Tobago)

Delacre, L. (1993). *Vejigante masquerader.* New York: Scholastic. (Puerto Rico)

Dorros, A. (1995). *Isla.* New York: Dutton Children's Books. (Puerto Rico)

Gershator, P. (1994). *Rata, pata, scata, fata: A Caribbean story.* Boston: Little, Brown. (U.S. Virgin Islands)

Gershator, P. (1994). *Tukama tootles the flute: A tale from the Antilles.* New York: Orchard Books. (Antilles)

Gordon, G. (1993). *My two worlds.* New York: Clarion Books. (Dominican Republic)

Gunning, M. (1993). *Not a copper penny in me house.* Honesdale, PA: Boyds Mills Press. (Jamaica)

Hanson, R. (1995). *The tangerine tree.* New York: Clarion Books. (Jamaica)

Hanson, R. (1997). *The face in the window.* New York: Clarion Books. (Jamaica)

Ichikawa, S. (1995). *Isabela's ribbons.* New York: Philomel. (Puerto Rico)

Jaffe, N. (1996). *The golden flower: A Taino myth from Puerto Rico.* New York: Simon & Schuster Books for Young Children. (Puerto Rico)

Joseph, L. (1992). *Coconut kind of day: Island poems.* New York: Puffin Books. (Trinidad & Tobago)

Joseph, L. (1992). *An island Christmas.* New York: Clarion Books. (Trinidad & Tobago)

Joseph, L. (1994). *Jasmine's parlour day.* New York: Lothrop, Lee & Shepard Books. (Trinidad & Tobago)

Lauture, D. (1996). *Running the road to ABC.* New York: Simon & Schuster Books for Young Children. (Haiti)

Linden, A. M. (1992). *One smiling grandma.* New York: Dial Books for Young Readers. (General)

Mitchell, R. (1993). *Hue boy.* New York: Dial Books for Young Readers. (General)

Nodar, C. S. (1992). *Abuelita's paradise.* Morton Grove, IL: Albert Whitman. (Puerto Rico)

Orr, K. (1990). *My grandpa and the sea.* Minneapolis, MN: Carolrhoda Books. (St. Lucia)

Picó, F. (1991). *The red comb.* New York: BridgeWater Press. (Puerto Rico)

San Souci, R. D. (1995). *The faithful friend.* New York: Simon & Schuster Books for Young Children. (Martinique)

Stow, J. (1992). *The house that Jack built.* New York: Dial Books for Young Readers. (General)

Williams, K. (1994). *Tap-tap.* New York: Clarion Books. (Haiti)

Yolen, J. (1992). *Encounter.* San Diego: Harcourt Brace. (Bahamas)

SUGGESTED CHILDREN'S BOOKS

▼▼

Agard, J., & Nichols, G. (1994). *Caribbean dozen: A collection of poems.* London: Candlewick Press. (General)

Burden-Atmon, D., & Jones, K. (1993). *Carnival.* New York: Simon & Schuster. (General)

Burgie, I. (1992). *Caribbean carnival: Songs of the West Indies.* New York: Morrow. (West Indies)

Crespo, G. (1993). *How the sea began: A Taino myth.* New York: Clarion Books. (Puerto Rico)

Gonzalez, L. (1994). *Bossy Gallito: A traditional Cuban folk tale.* New York: Scholastic. (Cuba)

Hallworth, G. (1996). *Down by the river: Afro-Caribbean rhymes, games, and songs for children.* New York: Scholastic. (General)

Lessac, F. (1994). *Caribbean alphabet: An island ABC.* New York: Morrow. (General)

McKinley, Y. (1995). *Taste of the Caribbean.* New York: Thomson Learning. (General)

Mohr, N. (1996). *Old Letivia and the mountain of sorrows.* New York: Viking. (Puerto Rico)

Pitre, F. (1993). *Juan Bobo and the pig: A Puerto Rican folktale.* New York: Dutton Children's Books. (Puerto Rico)

San Souci, R. D. (1992). *Sukey and the mermaid.* New York: Macmillan. (General)

Wolkstein, D. (1997). *Bouki dances the Kokioko: A tale from Haiti.* San Diego: Gulliver Books. (Haiti)

6

Children's Books About Central America, Mexico, and South America

CENTRAL AMERICA

Central America is a group of small countries located between Mexico on the north and Colombia, South America, on the south. It is bordered on the east by the Caribbean Sea and on the west by the Pacific Ocean.

Countries

Belize, Costa Rica, El Salvador, Guatemala, Honduras, Nicaragua, Panama

MEXICO

Mexico is a large North American country bordered on the north by the United States and on the south by Guatemala and Belize. On the east it is bordered by the Gulf of Mexico and the Bay of Campeche and on the west by the Pacific Ocean.

SOUTH AMERICA

South America is a continent located south of the Caribbean Sea and Panama and north of the Drake Passage and Antarctica. It is bordered on the east by the Atlantic Ocean and on the west by the Pacific Ocean.

Countries

Argentina, Bolivia, Brazil, Chile, Colombia, Ecuador, French Guiana, Guyana, Paraguay, Peru, Suriname, Uruguay, Venezuela

EXAMINING THE CULTURAL REGION OF CENTRAL AMERICA, MEXICO, AND SOUTH AMERICA AND THE PATTERNS OF CHILDREN'S BOOKS

As we examine children's picture books about the cultural region of Central America, Mexico, and South America, we realize that we are dealing with a vast area of different countries. The common thread that pervades the literature of many of these countries is their Hispanic background. Spanish explorers and conquistadors brought the Spanish language and culture to most of these countries, with the exception of Belize and Guyana, once British colonies; Suriname, once a Dutch colony; French Guiana, still a French colony; and the large country of Brazil, once a Portuguese colony.

Many of these colonizers intermarried with the indigenous peoples, creating over the years a new people and culture altogether. Other indigenous people either retreated to areas in the mountains difficult to reach or were never encountered in the first place, such as those in the Amazon jungle. Several countries on the east coast of Central and South America, including Brazil, experienced an influx of Africans brought originally as slaves by the colonizers. In addition, Europeans from several countries emigrated to South America, especially after World War II.

We hope, as we examine children's books about the area, to see evidence of this rich mix of people. It is our special hope that these books present the peoples and cultures as they truly are, and not in the stereotypical manner frequently encountered in the past. We remember only too well when Mexicans were portrayed as peons in serapes and sombreros, when few books featured modern urban stories, and when countries other than Mexico were depicted mainly through their folktales. As Ramsey (1987) notes:

> It is not easy to represent the complexities of various cultures, common human issues, and appealing characters in a fifteen-to-twenty page children's book. Many authors who have tried to portray a broad range of human experiences have been criticized for presenting stereotypical or unrealistic portraits. Some authors work so hard to present a political or social statement that the stories sound dogmatic and lose their appeal to young children. No one book is ideal, and, in fact, no single author has managed to address all the issues satisfactorily. Teachers will need to select books that together present a comprehensive perspective of the country and the world. (p. 70)

Chapter 1 discusses these issues at some length, offering Figure 1.7, "Guidelines for Identifying, Evaluating, and Selecting Transcultural Children's Literature" to assist the reader in selecting the best books available. Especially important is the author's perspective. Is the author a member of a society or cultural region written about in the book? Although such authors may possess biases of their own, they are usually more knowledgeable about their own people and cultures than outsiders.

As you consider the books reviewed in this chapter, keep these points in mind. The books you finally choose for your own bookcase should present a comprehensive perspective of each culture, as noted by Ramsey (1987). Also needed is a balance of types, such as folktales, contemporary fiction, and historical fiction, and of topics that interest children, such as stories about families, animals, music, and especially characters and situations with which they can identify.

COUNTRIES AND CHILDREN'S BOOKS REVIEWED

Central America: El Salvador

El Salvador is located on the curved western edge of Central America, bordered by the Pacific Ocean. It is bordered on the north by Guatemala, on the north and east by Honduras, and on the southeast by the Gulf of Fonseca, across which lie Honduras and Nicaragua.

 Argueta, Manlio. *Magic Dogs of the Volcanoes.* illustrated by Elly Simmons. Children's Book Press, 1990. 32 pp. (ISBN 0-89239-129-4). Fiction Based on Folklore, E-M.[1]

Story Review Chart			
Setting	Plot/Events	Characters	Theme
•	•	•	•

Cultural Paradigm Reference Classification Chart			
Geographic Location	Economic System	Social System	Political System
•	•		

On the slopes of El Salvador's volcanoes live the *cadejos*, the magic dogs that look like wolves but are not and that can make themselves invisible. The people who live on the slopes of the volcanoes love these magic dogs because they have always protected the people from danger and misfortune.

But Don Tonio and his 13 brothers do not like the magic dogs because they believe that the dogs have enchanted the people so that they will not work hard for the brothers anymore. They decide to send an army of lead soldiers up the slopes to hunt the dogs. Although the soldiers search all night, they find nothing because the dogs have made themselves invisible. But when the soldiers begin to trample the morning glories on which the dogs live, the dogs take action.

The dogs enlist the help of their great-great-grandparents, the volcanoes Tecapa, with his steaming hat, and Chaparrastique, with her dress made of water. The volcanoes agree to help, and soon Tecapa fans himself with his hat until the ground gets so hot that the soldiers' feet begin to melt. Chaparrastique shakes her dress, and drops of water turn to steam on the lead soldiers, who quickly retreat down the mountains.

---

[1]A = all ages, P = preschool, E = early elementary, M = middle elementary, L = late elementary

Don Tonio and his brothers run away, and the *cadejos* and people of the villages put on a huge fiesta that is later remembered as a national holiday. From that day on, there is peace on the volcanoes of El Salvador.

Colorful folk art in bright yellow, red, blue, and green watercolors, gouache, pastels, and colored pencil grace every other page of the tale. Its theme of antiviolence and caring for natural life in the shadow of huge volcanoes makes this a fine teaching tale for the children of El Salvador because it appears in Spanish on the lower half of each page, and for your students as well.

Classroom Applications

A project on Central America can include a diorama in a cardboard box illustrating this story. Make the volcanoes from plaster or papier-mâché, and bring in toy soldiers or make cutouts of people and the magic dogs. Suggest that your students learn what other countries in the world have volcanoes that people live near, such as Italy and Japan. How do these people deal with the danger from eruptions?

Central America: Guatemala

Guatemala is located south of Mexico, bordered on the west and north by Mexico; on the east by the Caribbean Sea, Belize, and Honduras; and on the southeast by El Salvador. The Pacific Ocean borders Guatemala on the southwest from Mexico to El Salvador.

Castaneda, Omar S. *Abuela's Weave*. illustrated by Enrique O. Sanchez. Lee & Low Books, 1993. 32 pp. (ISBN 1-880000-00-8). Contemporary Fiction, E-M.

Story Review Chart			
Setting	Plot/Events	Characters	Theme
•	•	•	•

Cultural Paradigm Reference Classification Chart			
Geographic Location	Economic System	Social System	Political System
	•	•	

In the mountainous highlands of Guatemala, Mayan villages dot the landscape. Scenes of life in a farming village shown in blues and greens contrast with the bright, multicolored cloth woven on traditional backstrap looms by the girl Esperanza and Abuela, her grandmother. They are making *huipil* blouses and tapestries to be sold in the city market on Fiesta de Pueblos. But Esperanza is worried that their hand-loomed weavings cannot compete with machine-woven goods. She is even more worried that no one will buy from her grandmother because of a birthmark on her face that has helped circulate the rumor that she is a witch.

When the great day comes, Esperanza carries a large basketful of woven goods on her head to the bus stop while her grandmother walks behind, completely encased in a long black robe. Although the market stalls are filled when Esperanza arrives, she finds a niche between two stalls and hangs her goods from their board slats. But where is Abuela? And who will notice their old-fashioned hand weaving when the other stalls are filled with lovely machine-woven Guatemalan designs?

But people do notice: both tourists and Guatemalans. They look with wonder at the beautiful tapestries and blouses. Even Abuela appears and removes her covering when she sees people smiling and buying everything she and her granddaughter have to offer. On the bus ride back home, Abuela sits with Esperanza and does not even try to cover her face.

Classroom Applications

Standing up for the things one believes in is the theme of this sensitive story. What things would your students stand up for in their lives even if people might laugh at them? How would they deal with rumors like the one directed against Abuela? Bring in small looms and let the students try their hand at weaving as well.

 Grifalconi, Ann. *The Bravest Flute*. Little, Brown, 1994. 32 pp. (ISBN 0-316-32878-2). Contemporary Fiction, E-M.

Story Review Chart

Setting	Plot/Events	Characters	Theme
•	•	•	•

Cultural Paradigm Reference Classification Chart

Geographic Location	Economic System	Social System	Political System
	•	•	

A boy from a Mayan village in the mountains of Guatemala must lead the parade to town on New Year's Day, playing his bamboo flute all the way. Can he do it? It will be his first task of service to the community and bring honor on him and his family. But he is hungry and exhausted from working the rocky soil and having so little to eat. Even the seed corn is gone. It will take all the strength he can muster to lead the parade with a bass drum strapped on his back while he plays his flute all the way to the steps of the cathedral where the elders will be seated. Can he make it?

In purples and pinks and blues, this stirring story takes the reader from the boy's mountain village over the winding footpath through the hills as gaily-dressed people stream from their lonely mountain homes to fall in behind them. To keep the drum held high, the boy bends over as he moves forward, almost staggering but never missing a step. Can he make it? Now he is walking on soft leaves laid out on the city streets and being pelted with flowers and paper streamers as people cheer. Now he passes the stern faces of the elders in black and red robes. But his breath begins to fail.

Suddenly, a new flute is thrust into his hands: a master flute all black and silver. The widow of the old master flutist has given him her husband's flute! The sweetest music he has ever heard comes out of it. He is swept forward by his own playing. Now he is kneeling with the elders on the top step of the cathedral, the brave new flute in one hand and a bag of coins awarded by the elders in the other. Now he can buy food for his family and seed corn for the year to come.

Classroom Applications

Indian flute music from the western United States, Mexico, and the Andes is available on tapes and CDs. Use this music as a background as you and the class read *The Bravest Flute* together. The story can be dramatized by students falling in line one behind another as they march around the room. Suggest that different students alternate in the boy's role, playing a tonette flute.

 Smith-Ayala, Emilie. *Clouds on the Mountain*. illustrated by Alice Priestley. Annick Press, 1996. 32 pp. (ISBN 1-55037-472-9). Contemporary Fiction, M-L.

Story Review Chart

Setting	Plot/Events	Characters	Theme
•	•	•	

Cultural Paradigm Reference Classification Chart

Geographic Location	Economic System	Social System	Political System
•		•	

Here is Guatemala from a different perspective—that of a Canadian family who spend their winters in a town close to the mountains. The three boys can hardly wait for the big day when school is out and they can take their annual hike up the mountain to the waterfall. Abel fills the water bottles in preparation. Axelito washes mangoes and grapes. Mama makes tuna and avocado sandwiches. But Bram has his arm in a cast from his fall off the monkey bars at school, and all he can do is watch.

Then they start off across the soccer field, around a farmer's cornfield, and up the path to the mountain where they begin their climb. Freddie, the new little black puppy, nestles down in Abel's pack and falls asleep. Just as they hear the sound of falling water in the distance, three black clouds roll over the mountain. Mama wants to go back, but the boys persuade her to push on.

Just as they are eating lunch at the waterfall, a gigantic purple cloud with flashes of fire comes boiling over the mountain and releases its fury on them. Rain pours down, lightning splits the sky, and instantly they are soaked to the skin. Mama scoops up Axelito, Abel grabs Bram by his good arm, and they stumble their way down. Abel has to stop to find Freddie, who has scrambled out of his pack. Finally, they take refuge in a rock overhang to catch their breath. But icy torrents of rain soon push them on.

At the foot of the mountain, they must cross a river, now roiling with water, but Mama holds them high as they cross two by two. At last, they are safe and warm in their home, wondering whether Chac, the Mayan rain god, saw them on the mountain and was sorry.

Classroom Applications

Although mountain climbing may not be an appropriate activity, you and your students can still experience a hike through the mountains of Guatemala as a "follow-the-leader" trip around the playground or the school building. You be the leader and call out the movements everyone behind you must make as you demonstrate them: "Take giant steps around the cornfield," "now swim the river," "climb up over rocks," "time to sit down for lunch," "now everybody up and hurry back down the mountain," as you repeat the whole sequence. Invite your students to learn more about the Maya of Guatemala and their beliefs; then they can make up their own stories about a pretend visit to Abel, Axelito, and Bram.

 Volkmer, Jane Anne. *Song of the Chirimia: A Guatemalan Folktale.* translated by Lori Ann Schatschneider. Carolrhoda Books, 1990. 40 pp. (ISBN 0-87614-592-6). Folktale, M-L.

Story Review Chart

Setting	Plot/Events	Characters	Theme
	•	•	

Cultural Paradigm Reference Classification Chart

Geographic Location	Economic System	Social System	Political System
		•	•

The Mayan king Clear Sky would do anything for his beloved daughter Moonlight. When she falls into a state of depression and he learns that she needs to marry before her sorrow will leave, he invites all the young bachelors to the central plaza so that his daughter can choose a husband. Some bring gifts of jade, some of gold or pottery or birds. Each one parades before Moonlight, but she does not smile.

After everyone has left, a poor young man walks into the plaza. He brings no gifts, but he is singing a joyful song. Moonlight lifts her head and smiles. The king calls the young man, known as Black Feather, over to his daughter. She tells him she will marry him if he can make his song become as one with the birds. He promises her that he will learn to sing like the birds but that it will take time—three full moons.

Black Feather begins his quest deep in the woods where the birds never stop singing. But no matter how hard he tries, he just cannot learn to sing as they do. The Great Spirit of the Woods takes pity on him and tells him to cut off a tree branch and give it to him. The Spirit sets the branch ablaze, fashioning it into a long hollow pipe with holes in one side. He calls it a *chirimia* and tells Black Feather to learn to play it well. This he does, producing sounds so melodious that even the birds stop singing to listen. When he returns to the palace, Moonlight is enchanted by the beautiful melody, and soon they are married. Even today, the song of the chirimia can be heard by travelers who visit Guatemala.

Stylized illustrations of Mayan people in profile like those carved on Mayan temples stand out against a white background, along with Mayan glyphs and symbols—all in full color. Appearing next to each English paragraph is a Spanish translation of the story.

Classroom Applications

Can your students pick out the Spanish words that say the same thing as English words? Clear Sky is *Cielo Claro*, and Moonlight is *Luz de Luna*. Night is *noche*, silent is *silencio*, and song is *melodia*. What other words can they decipher? Bring in a Spanish language tape and a flute music tape to make their word quest more enjoyable.

Central America: Nicaragua

Nicaragua is located in Central America south of Honduras, bordered on the north by Honduras, on the east by the Caribbean Sea, on the south by Costa Rica, and on the west by the Pacific Ocean.

 Garay, Luis. *Pedrito's Day*. Orchard Books, 1997. 32 pp. (ISBN 0-531-09522-3). Contemporary Fiction, P-M.

Story Review Chart			
Setting	Plot/Events	Characters	Theme
•	•	•	•

Cultural Paradigm Reference Classification Chart			
Geographic Location	Economic System	Social System	Political System
	•	•	

Pedrito's father, Pedro, has gone north to work, and now only Pedrito, little Pedro, is at home with his mama and his *abuela*, grandmother. He helps by shining shoes in the market while his mother sells Abuela's tortillas and tamales. But if he only had a bicycle, he could help so much better! He keeps some of the coins he earns stashed in his shoe-shine box for the bicycle, and he knows that his father will also contribute money when he is big enough to own a bicycle.

Just as he is about to get a shoe-shine customer, Tia Paula asks Pedrito to run an errand for her. She gives him a bill and asks him to get change from Tia Blanca. On the way, some older boys ask Pedrito to join them in a game of soccer in the street. He is thrilled to be asked and quickly joins them. When he returns to his shoe-shine box, he

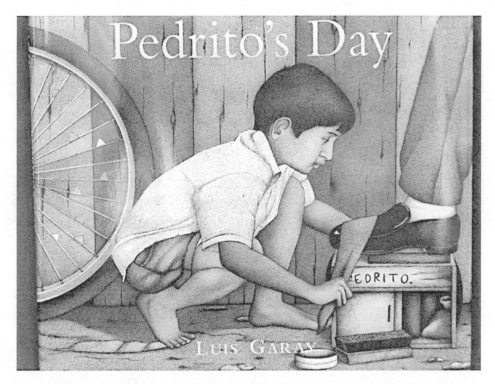

Cover of PEDRITO'S DAY by Luis Garay. Jacket illustration copyright © 1997 by Louis Garay. Reprinted by permission of Orchard Books, New York.

remembers the errand and reaches into his pocket but the money is gone. He searches the street where they played, without finding it.

The miserable boy tries to think of a way to explain the loss to Tia Paula. Perhaps he could say a robber took the money or a bird flew away with it. Or perhaps he should just run away. Finally, he knows what he must do: He tells her he lost the money. But before she can get angry, he says he will replace it with his bicycle money, and he counts out the coins into her hand. Now, half of his hard-earned money is gone, and so are the shoe-shine customers.

Pedrito and Mama talk about the lost money on the way home and how he was a baby to lose it but brave to admit it and replace it. A letter awaits them from Pedro with money for the rent and—surprise—some to put aside for Pedrito's bicycle. He is big enough now.

Nicaraguan artist Garay's carefully crafted illustrations against a textured background on every other page make the marketplace so real that the reader can almost smell the flowers, fruits, and corn husk tamales. But especially revealing are Pedrito's facial expressions as he faces his loss and struggles with his moral dilemma to account for it.

Classroom Applications

What would your students have done had they lost money that had been entrusted to them? The theme of this story is an important discussion topic. Have them consider Pedrito's initial excuses. Why do they think he chose not to use them? What would have happened had he told one of these lies to Tia Paula? Have the students ever experienced anything similar?

Central America: Panama

Panama is located at the southern end of Central America, between Costa Rica and Colombia. To the north is the Caribbean Sea, and to the south the Pacific Ocean, with the Panama Canal cutting the narrow country in two as it connects these two bodies of water.

 Palacios, Argentina. A *Christmas Surprise for Chabelita*. illustrated by Lori Lohstoeter. Troll, 1993. 32 pp. (ISBN 0-8167-3132-2). Contemporary Fiction, P-M.

Story Review Chart

Setting	Plot/Events	Characters	Theme
	•	•	

Cultural Paradigm Reference Classification Chart

Geographic Location	Economic System	Social System	Political System
	•	•	

When Chabelita is a little girl, her mother leaves her with her grandparents because she must go away to teach. Chabelita is sad but enjoys accompanying her grandfather to the market every day, where he goes to chat with his friends. Sometimes they go to the riverbank to buy oranges from the *campesinos*, the people from the country who bring their fruits and vegetables on boats, or to the post office for mail. Chabelita is most excited when a package arrives for her from her mother: a beautiful red dress and shiny black shoes to wear for a special occasion.

That occasion comes quickly: Chabelita's first day at school. Then, when her mother comes home for a weekend, she reads the little girl her own favorite poem: *Caperucita Roja*—Little Red Riding Hood in Spanish. Chabelita loves it so much that she memorizes it and recites it in school. Her teacher asks her to recite it at the Christmas pageant as the youngest child in the program. If only her mother could be there.

On the night of her performance, Chabelita does not forget a single line. Then a lady with a big bouquet of red carnations comes forward—her mother with "Red carnations for my Little Red Riding Hood"—a Christmas surprise she will never forget.

Lohstoeter's realistic oil paintings of the people of Panama on the streets, in the market, and in the school audience help North American readers identify closely with people from another culture who nevertheless display the same values, needs, sorrows, and joys they do.

Classroom Applications

Can your students imagine what will happen next with Chabelita and her mother during this Christmas holiday? Have them dictate to you another story about Chabelita's experiences. As a tie-in, suggest that they learn how other Central and South American countries celebrate Christmas.

 Markun, Patricia Maloney. *The Little Painter of Sabana Grande*. illustrated by Robert Casilla. Bradbury Press, 1993. 32 pp. (ISBN 0-02-762205-3). Contemporary Fiction, E-M.

Story Review Chart

Setting	Plot/Events	Characters	Theme
	•	•	

Cultural Paradigm Reference Classification Chart

Geographic Location	Economic System	Social System	Political System
•		•	

Sabana Grande, a small village in the mountains of Panama, is so small that only seven whitewashed adobe houses stand there alongside a stream. Now that school is out, Fernando, who lives in the middle house, is going to do something important for the first time: He is going to paint pictures from the paints his teacher has taught him to make from the natural ingredients around him—black from charcoal, blue from berries, yellow from dried grasses, and red from clay. His pictures will be like the ones he learned to make in school with crayons.

There sits the paint, stirred and waiting in four bowls. There lie his paintbrushes in three sizes. But what is he going to paint on? There is no paper in his house, nor in any of his neighbors' houses. He looks longingly at the white outside walls of his house, but Papa says no and Mama agrees. Finally, his father cannot stand to see his son so miserable, so he gives in and allows Fernando to paint on the white walls of their house.

Fernando's first picture is of a gorgeous red-flowering poinciana tree just beginning to bloom on the mountainside. One by one, his neighbors come out to see what he is doing. On one branch of the tree, he paints a black toucan with a large yellow bill. On another, he paints a brown sloth hanging upside-down by its toes. The neighbors bring out chairs and drink coffee as they watch Fernando's scene unfold. Soon word spreads to Santa Marta on the other side of the mountain, and some of its people hike over to watch as a painted vine with huge purple flowers begins creeping up the wall on the other side of the door.

Next Fernando paints a white-faced monkey and a red and yellow rooster so lifelike that it looks about to crow. Señora Alfaro wants Fernando to paint her house.

Señor Remon too. Fernando just nods. He knows there are six more houses to paint before the school vacation is finished.

Realistic illustrations reveal the beauty of the setting as Fernando's creativity captures its beauty on the walls of the simple thatched houses.

Classroom Applications

This story, based on a true happening, can inspire your students to become involved in painting—not on classroom walls, but on easels or sheets of paper with paints they, too, have prepared from natural materials. If they want to paint on outside walls, provide wide brushes and buckets of water.

Mexico

Mexico is located south of the United States and north of the Central American countries of Guatemala and Belize. It is bounded on the east by the Gulf of Mexico and the Caribbean Sea and on the west by the Gulf of California and the Pacific Ocean.

 Aardema, Verna. *Borreguita and the Coyote*. illustrated by Petra Mathers. Knopf, 1991. 32 pp. (ISBN 0-679-80921-X). Folktale, E–M.

Story Review Chart

Setting	Plot/Events	Characters	Theme
	•	•	•

Cultural Paradigm Reference Classification Chart

Geographic Location	Economic System	Social System	Political System
		•	

This tale from the city of Ayutla, in western Mexico, tells a trickster story about a little ewe lamb and the coyote that attempts to eat her. Usually, the coyote is the trickster in folktales, but in this case the tables are turned. The first time Coyote tries to eat Borreguita, she persuades him to come back when she has finished eating the clover in the field, for she is thin as a bean pod now. He agrees, saying, "*Esta bien.*" That is good.

Next time, Borreguita persuades him that cheese tastes better than lamb and that she will show him how to get some down by the pond at night when the moon is high. That night, Coyote jumps into the pond and paddles out to the bright round "cheese" glowing in the middle of the pond. It is the reflection of the moon, and all he gets is a mouthful of water.

Next day, Coyote catches Borreguita up in the cliffs and scrambles up to eat her. But before he gets there, she lies down on a ledge on her back with her legs straight up, braced against a rocky overhang above her. She tells Coyote that she is holding up the mountain and that if she lets go, it will come tumbling down. She persuades Coyote to hold it up for her while she goes for help. Of course, she never returns.

Her final trick comes when Coyote at last has her cornered in the pasture. She agrees to let him eat her if he will swallow her whole. When Coyote opens his mouth wide, the lamb runs forward and butts the inside of his mouth so hard that it sends him rolling backward with one big toothache. From that day on, Coyote never bothers Borreguita again.

Classroom Applications

Folktales like this lend themselves well to oral storytelling, and especially to dramatic reenactments. Your students may want to share this humorous tale with others by putting on a simple puppet show with lamb and coyote hand puppets made from mittens, from paper bags with ears attached and faces painted on, or by using stuffed animals. Or, they may want to be the actual coyote and lamb with brown- and white-eared headbands.

Read the story aloud several times for the class to become familiar with the plot incidents. Make your voice sound low and gruff for Coyote and high and sweet for Borreguita. Give everyone who wants to play one of the roles a chance. Tape-record the drama for the actors to listen to how they sound; they may want to repeat their performances to make their voices sound even more interesting. Some students may want to look for other coyote or wolf folktales from other cultures.

 Kroll, Virginia. *Butterfly Boy.* illustrated by Gerardo Suzán. Boyds Mills Press, 1997. 32 pp. (ISBN 1-56397-371-5). Contemporary Fiction, E-L.

Story Review Chart

Setting	Plot/Events	Characters	Theme
	•	•	

Cultural Paradigm Reference Classification Chart

Geographic Location	Economic System	Social System	Political System
		•	

Every afternoon, Emilio wheels his grandfather Abuelo outside into the sunshine and reads to him. Abuelo cannot walk or talk because he has had a stroke, but Emilio can tell by the gleam in Abuelo's eyes that he understands words. Then one day, Abuelo points with his good hand. Five crimson, brown, and white butterflies are fluttering around the side of the garage, landing, flitting up, and landing again. Emilio can tell that his grandfather is smiling inside even though his mouth can no longer show it.

After that, the two of them watch the butterflies together every afternoon. Emilio gets within inches of them, and they do not fly away. Mrs. Salazar, the next-door neighbor, calls him "Butterfly Boy." But when autumn comes, the butterflies dis-

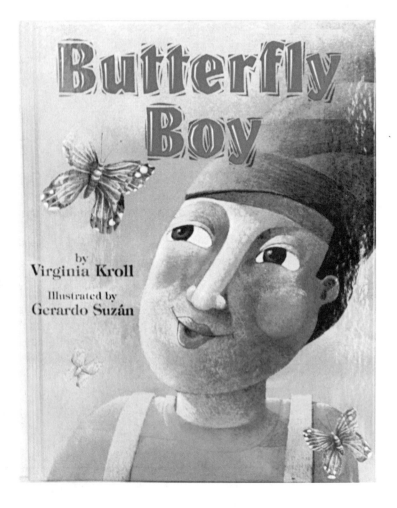

appear, not to return again until the following spring. Emilio brings home a library book about butterflies and shows his grandfather a picture of their butterflies—red admirals. They like to sun themselves on bright white surfaces, he reads. Then one afternoon, the butterflies return. Emilio sees two of them on the school playground and races home to tell his grandfather. Once outside, Abuelo points at the garage with his good hand. Emilio gasps to see that it is blue! His father has painted it blue to match their house. "You can't!" cries Emilio to his father. But it is already done.

Now, five red admirals are flitting about, turning circles in the air. Emilio looks around wildly, sees the laundry hanging from the clothesline, grabs a white shirt, and puts it on. Then he stands as stiff as a statue with his arms outstretched. The butterflies fly closer and closer. One finally lands on Emilio's shoulder. Then another one lands on his other shoulder, and one on his chest. Mrs. Salazar looks over her fence and says, "Incredible, Butterfly Boy."

Emilio's father finally gets the point and says that he is going back to the hardware store to buy white paint. Mrs. Salazar asks him to save some for her fence. The corners of Abuelo's mouth turn up, and his eyes dance and twinkle "like twilight stars."

Unusual, surrealistic illustrations in blue overtones fill two-page spreads, giving the story an almost mystical touch. Have your students comment on the pictures. What do they think about the large hats worn by Abuelo and Emilio, with birds, stars, flowers, and clouds in the different ones? What about the picture of Abuelo floating through the air with butterfly wings on his back?

Emilio's attention to his physically impaired grandfather, even though his parents believe that Abuelo does not understand words anymore, is a true transcultural phenomenon. Grandchildren the world over have a special affection for their grandparents, frequently reflected in children's literature. The young and the old of every culture have special bonds.

Classroom Applications

You may want to visit a nursing home with your students to talk with the residents or to dramatize one of the students' favorite stories. Not only do these residents have a need to associate with children, but the youngsters themselves have a reciprocal need to be with older adults. The story can also be a lead-in to a butterfly project, such as raising a butterfly from a caterpillar and then letting it go.

 Winter, Jonah. *Diego*. illustrated by Jeanette Winter, and translated by Amy Prince. Knopf, 1991. 40 pp. (ISBN 0-679-81987-8). Biography, E-L.

Story Review Chart

Setting	Plot/Events	Characters	Theme
•	•	•	•

Cultural Paradigm Reference Classification Chart

Geographic Location	Economic System	Social System	Political System
		•	•

The life of the famous Mexican muralist Diego Rivera takes on legendary proportions in this simple tale in English and Spanish as illustrated by Winter's framed miniature paintings at the top of every page. In his early childhood, Diego falls seriously ill and is nursed back to health by an Indian healer, Antonia, in her hut in the mountains. The jungle animals become his friends. A wild parrot becomes his pet.

When he returns home, his parents give him a box of colored chalk for a homecoming gift. Immediately, Diego begins drawing with the chalk—everywhere, even on the walls. So his father makes him a studio with blackboards covering every wall. Soon they too are filled with his drawings. But at school, he has a difficult time concentrating on his lessons, with his mind back in the jungle among his animal friends.

At home, Diego plays with toy soldiers he himself has created: 5,000 of them! But his special love is for colorful things like the paintings on the walls of the church. His parents have the good sense to send him to art school even though he is several years younger than the other students. Yet he finds it boring to draw from models. He prefers to paint from the rich life of the common people around him: people at cemeteries on the Day of the Dead; people dressed in fiesta costumes. When he witnesses soldiers shooting down striking workers, he paints that too. He is determined to help the poor people of his country who are struggling for equality.

His years abroad in Paris make him homesick for Mexico. But his travels to Italy open his eyes to the wonderful murals by the masters that he sees in cathedrals. When he returns to Mexico, he begins painting huge murals on the walls and ceilings of government buildings, schools, hospitals, everywhere, depicting the story of the Mexican people. He paints day and night, even falling asleep on his scaffold. Into his murals goes everything he has ever seen: Antonia's hut, the jungle, fiestas, the Day of the Dead, soldiers in the street. He becomes world famous, his art making his people proud to be Mexicans even today.

Classroom Applications

As noted in the cultural paradigm chart, this story has political overtones as Rivera uses his art for political statements against the tyranny he sees around him. Your students can create their own mural across a wall from paints or wet chalk on a long roll of wrapping paper. Have them choose a theme of importance in their lives, discuss how they can illustrate the theme, and then use space on the paper for each student to develop her or his idea. Themes like preserving the environment by planting trees, or cleaning up a park, or building a new playground together, or celebrating an important milestone in the community can be illustrated in this way. Be sure to accept whatever the students produce, even scribbles. Bring to class art books showing some of Rivera's murals to give the students inspiration.

 Ada, Alma Flor. *Gathering the Sun: An Alphabet in Spanish and English*. illustrated by Simón Silva, and translated by Rosa Zubizarreta. Lothrop, Lee & Shepard Books, 1997. 40 pp. (ISBN 0-688-13903-5). Poetry, E-L.

Story Review Chart

Setting	Plot/Events	Characters	Theme
•		•	•

Cultural Paradigm Reference Classification Chart

Geographic Location	Economic System	Social System	Political System
	•		•

Cover from Gathering the Sun:
An Alphabet in Spanish and Eng-
lish *by Alma Flor Ada, illustrated
by Simón Silva, 1997. New York:
Lothrop, Lee & Shepard Books, a
division of William Morrow & Co.,
Inc. Printed with permission from
William Morrow & Co., Inc.*

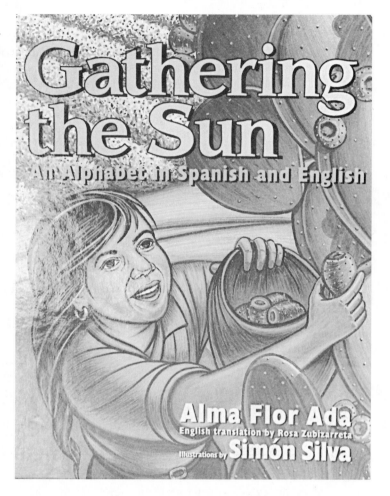

This gorgeously illustrated book of poems for every letter of the Spanish alphabet is a celebration in color and verse of Mexican farmworkers and the fruits and vegetables they harvest both in Mexico and across the border in the southwestern United States. Brush strokes of orange and red sweep across two-page spreads honoring the farmworkers' hero Cesar Chavez and the great Mexican Pyramid of the Sun and the Calendar Stone. Brief poems from A, *Arboles* ("Trees") to Z, *Zanahoria* ("Carrot") are rhymed in Spanish and translated into English.

A poem to a carrot, you may wonder? But as the stalwart worker walks off the last two-page spread of carrots clear to the horizon, with a sleeping toddler in one arm and a basket of carrots in the other, he, along with the carrot, is the embodiment of the book's theme: gathering the sun. "The carrot hides/ beneath the earth./ After all, she knows/ the sun's fiery color/ by heart."

Beets, peaches, cherries, lettuce, prickly pears, and tomatoes are also dignified and glorified by words and breathtaking colors sweeping from field to horizon, always with families together sharing labor and love. Fathers pick peaches, harvest asparagus, and read with their children. Mothers grow carnations, roll biscuit dough, and wrap enchiladas with children helping. The poem "Honor" says it all: "Honor is the work/ we do in the fields./ Honor is a family/ who loves and cares for one another/ . . . "

Classroom Applications

Do your students know the joy of working together with their hands in the earth? Help them start a garden in the classroom. Beans grow the quickest, but any vegetable seeds will do. Be sure to grow them in a common garden or large container so that several children can work together. If a field trip to a commercial vegetable grower is feasible, be sure to visit beforehand and then take your students. Help them discover that vegetables and fruits come from the earth and that they are harvested by people who work in the fields, an honorable occupation.

 Ober, Hal. *How Music Came to the World.* illustrated by Carol Ober. Houghton Mifflin, 1994. 32 pp. (ISBN 0-395-67523-5). Folktale, E-L.

Story Review Chart

Setting	Plot/Events	Characters	Theme
	•	•	

Cultural Paradigm Reference Classification Chart

Geographic Location	Economic System	Social System	Political System
•		•	

This Aztec explanatory myth, based on a poem from a 16th-century Nahua manuscript, brings together two great Aztec gods: Tezcatlipoca, the sky god; and Quetzalcoatl, the wind god. Ober's brilliant oil pastels fill every page with Aztec-style depictions of the action, accompanied by a brief text at the bottom. The wind god is cajoled into going to the House of the Sun to bring back singers and musicians to wake up the silent Earth.

Climbing a twisted rope bridge to the House of the Sun, the wind god must find his way through a maze of streets to the great courtyard, where he locates flute players in gold, minstrels in blue, lullaby singers in white, and love song singers in red. The sun tries to prevent them from leaving, but the wind god blows up such a storm that the musicians must run to his lap for protection. Then he carries them back to Earth and releases them. Earth has been filled with music ever since.

Classroom Applications

Explanatory myths have been told by every culture. Storytellers have repeated them, and scholars have collected and translated them. Now they are finding their way into more and more children's picture books. What myths can your students discover about other cultures? How do they compare with this one? Your students may wish to collect a scrapbook of creation myths about how things on Earth came to be. Some may want to invent myths of their own about the creation of things in their own environment.

 Czernecki, Stefan, and Rhodes, Timothy. *The Hummingbirds' Gift*. illustrated by Stefan Czernecki, and straw weavings by Reyes de Silva and Juan Hilario Silva. Hyperion, 1994. 32 pp. (ISBN 1-56282-604-2). Folktale, E-L.

Story Review Chart

Setting	Plot/Events	Characters	Theme
•	•	•	•

Cultural Paradigm Reference Classification Chart

Geographic Location	Economic System	Social System	Political System
	•	•	

This unusual tale comes from the Tarascan Indians of central Mexico living in the lyrically named village of Tzintzuntzan, Place of the Hummingbirds. Their village is famous for its flowers and for the hundreds of hummingbirds attracted to the blooms. In fact, each page of the story is bordered by a frame of stylized flowers.

One year, the rain fails and the flowers wither. The farmer Isidro is worried because his crop of wheat is shriveling into yellow straw. His wife, Consuelo, concerned because the hummingbirds are dying from lack of flower nectar, wants to find a way to help them. Together they come up with a plan.

Isidro takes his burro and two large clay pots along the dry riverbed all the way to the lake, which still holds some water. He fills the pots and returns home. There Consuelo mixes the water with clay, molds the clay into tiny pots in the shapes of flowers, and bakes them in the sun. Then she and her children paint the pots all the colors of the flowers once in her garden. They fill them with sugar water and place them in the branches of the bushes. Soon hummingbirds are buzzing around the pots, drinking their fill. Isidro fetches water ever day, and the children keep the little pots filled. The hummingbirds are saved, but what about the farmer's own children? The cupboard is almost bare.

When the hummingbirds sense Consuelo's anxiety, they fly off to the dried up wheat field and bring back small bits of straw. When a small pile has been gathered, the birds settle at Consuelo's feet and begin to weave the straw into beautiful little figures. She can sell the figures at the Day of the Dead, Consuelo realizes, and quickly enlists her family to make more. They create tiny dancers, musicians, skeletons, and birds. Gifts like this will be bought by the villagers to give to their children to honor the dead.

Half of every page is now devoted to photographs of the real woven figures mentioned in the text. The opposite pages contain colorful folk art-like paintings showing Day of the Dead events. Everyone admires the little straw figures, and Consuelo is able to earn enough money to last all year. Even after the rain returns, Isidro,

Consuela, and their family continue to weave the tiny figures as a reminder to their children and their children's children of the hummingbirds' gift.

Classroom Applications

Just as the children of Mexico help their families by accomplishing such real tasks in times of need, so your students can find ways to help people through their own arts and crafts. The craft products they make from play dough or clay or the easel paintings or collages they create can decorate the walls of children's wards in hospitals and residents' rooms in nursing homes or be part of a craft show the school puts on to raise money for trees to plant around the school or for new library books.

Tarascan families still make their little straw figures and still tell this tale of how they came to be. Your students may want to create their own stories afterward about how they, too, came to help people by bringing the beauty of arts and crafts into people's lives.

 Presilla, Maricel E., and Soto, Gloria. *Life Around the Lake.* illustrated by embroideries of the women of Lake Patzcuaro. Henry Holt, 1996. 32 pp. (ISBN 0-8050-3800-0). Nonfiction, M-L.

Story Review Chart

Setting	Plot/Events	Characters	Theme
•			

Cultural Paradigm Reference Classification Chart

Geographic Location	Economic System	Social System	Political System
•	•		

This unique picture book depicts the life of the Tarascan people, who live along the shores of Lake Patzcuaro in central Mexico, through their illustrated embroideries. Every other page describes an aspect of their life, followed by a lovely full-page embroidery photograph of the scene: fishermen in boats using butterfly nets; José Guadalupe weaving a new net; potters making ceramics, women weaving rebozos and ponchos, and men making palm fiber hats; the Santa Cruz Ranch; women making fresh corn tortillas to be sold door to door; a marriage ceremony; the Dance of the Old Men in their white-face masks; the fiesta of Corpus Christi; the Day of the Dead celebration; the women embroiderers of Tzintzuntzan.

Not only are the people making a living selling these wonderful embroideries, but they are also making a statement about their environment: that its beauty and usefulness need to be preserved. The lake is being polluted with agricultural runoff, introduced fish are killing off native species, and dredging is killing important plants.

Classroom Applications

That the beauty of craft products can preserve the beauty in nature may be a new concept for your students. Can they apply it to their own environment with arts and crafts projects as they did after reading *The Hummingbirds' Gift*? Because the same Mexican people are involved, these two books can be used together to complete a picture of life in rural Tarascan villages.

 Parkison, Jami. *Pequeña the Burro.* illustrated by Itoko Maeno. MarshMedia, 1994. 32 pp. (ISBN 1-55942-055-3). Contemporary Fiction, E–M.

Story Review Chart

Setting	Plot/Events	Characters	Theme
	•	•	

Cultural Paradigm Reference Classification Chart

Geographic Location	Economic System	Social System	Political System
		•	

Pequeña lives in Chapultepec Park, the great park in Mexico City where people flock for picnics; to visit the zoo, the theater, the bullring, and the castle; to listen to mariachi bands; and for their children to ride the burros. Although Pequeña is the littlest burro, Maria Alverez chooses her for her birthday party early Sunday morning in the park.

At first, Pequeña is excited to be chosen, but then Bonito, the gloomiest burro in the corral, tells her that Maria is the daughter of Captain Alverez, the great *charro* rider, and that he will be watching Pequeña like a hawk in case she should be frightened by a bursting balloon and drop one of the children or get tired in the hot sun and faint.

That seed of doubt begins to make Pequeña very nervous. When she sees her reflection in a window, she suddenly realizes that she is *only* a burro, as common "as a washrag," as useless "as a broken toy." That is, until Sabio, the oldest burro, begins reciting a litany of accomplishments that burros can be proud of: They have helped build Mexico; transported settlers; hauled bricks; pulled plows; hauled gold and silver down mountain trails . . .

On Sunday morning, Pequeña's owner dresses her for the party with red satin bows in her mane and a yellow cart hooked to her shoulder harness. A mariachi band plays, a feast fills one table, and children flock around Pequeña for a ride in her cart or on her back. After lunch, everyone gathers around a large concrete picnic table with a piñata dangling above it. While children on the table jump up and down with excitement, a blindfolded Maria breaks open the piñata with a sturdy pole.

Just as the candy spills out, another loud crack sounds, and the table breaks in two, with Maria caught under one of the concrete slabs. The piece is too heavy to move by hand, but then Captain Alverez spies Pequeña, who has carried a rope over to the table. He hitches the burro to the concrete slab, and with great effort she manages to pull it off the little girl. In grateful thanks, Pequeña is allowed to march in Mexico's Independence Day parade, leading the column of charro riders to the shouts of people who recognize her as the burro that saved the little girl.

Classroom Applications

Talk with your students about important roles they have had to play. Were they nervous or afraid? What did they do to relieve their feelings? Do animals have such feelings? How can one tell? A party with a piñata is certainly an exciting affair for children everywhere. If you plan one for your students, be sure to include other Mexican activities throughout the year so that piñatas do not become stereotypical of everything Mexican.

South America: Argentina

Argentina is located in the southern half of South America, stretching from Bolivia and Paraguay in the north to Cape Horn, the tip of South America, in the south. It is bordered on its entire western length by Chile, and on the east by Brazil and Uruguay and the Atlantic Ocean all the way south to Cape Horn.

 Brusca, Maria Cristina. *My Mama's Little Ranch on the Pampas*. Henry Holt, 1994. 32 pp. (ISBN 0-8050-2782-3). Nonfiction, E-L.

Story Review Chart

Setting	Plot/Events	Characters	Theme
•	•	•	

Cultural Paradigm Reference Classification Chart

Geographic Location	Economic System	Social System	Political System
	•	•	

Maria Cristina Brusca's first year as a child on her mother's ranch on the pampas outside Buenos Aires comes alive in this first-person narration with watercolor illustrations. Maria's father works in the city, but she, her mother, and her brother Guillermo stay on the ranch all summer. They handle such chores as opening the windmill, feeding the pigs, and helping mend the fences so that her mother can buy cows. Maria's horse helps push the cattle into a chute for branding as Maria heats the branding iron, but the *gauchos* ("cowboys") do the rest.

In May, Maria is allowed to drive her mother's sulky into town with her brother. After shopping, they visit the general store, The Stab, and dance the *malambo* to old Victrola music while the gauchos laugh. Many adventures ensue, including being "bombed" by seagulls when she and her brother try to make a bird egg collection; seeing the frightening *la luz mala* when they are out hunting for armadillos; and helping the vet deliver a calf by caesarean. All Maria needs to do is rattle the feed bucket, and her horse, Pampero, comes galloping up to her as she contemplates the wonderful and scary year she has just experienced.

Classroom Applications

Spanish words and phrases are explained on the end pages in illustrations and brief paragraphs. Have your students compare Argentine cattle ranching with U.S. cattle ranching. Can the class also make up a story about a year on such a ranch?

South America: Bolivia

Bolivia is a landlocked country located in central South America. It is bordered on the north and east by Brazil, on the south by Paraguay and Argentina, and on the west by Peru and Chile.

 Topooco, Eusebio. *Waira's First Journey.* Lothrop, Lee & Shepard Books, 1993. 40 pp. (ISBN 0–688–12054–7). Historical Fiction, M-L.

Story Review Chart

Setting	Plot/Events	Characters	Theme
•	•	•	

Cultural Paradigm Reference Classification Chart

Geographic Location	Economic System	Social System	Political System
	•	•	•

The author's story about his own people, the Aymara Indians, takes place long ago, before the Spanish conquered Bolivia. Every year, they travel to the market in Topojo to barter for items they cannot grow at home. This is Waira's first long trip. They travel with their llama pack animals and camp along the way. One stop they make is to the stone ruins of Tiwanaku for Waira to see the city their ancestors built long ago. She looks closely at the Sun Gate, with its carvings of suns and condors, and the Moon Gate, made from a single gigantic piece of stone. The city was destroyed by the eruption of a distant volcano and the waters of Lake Titicaca that covered the city for hundreds of years.

They stop at a house along Lake Titicaca to barter their wool, dried potatoes, and llama meat for dried fish, maize, and vegetables. Waira strikes up an acquaintance with Sushi, a boy her age, and eventually gives him a llama to ride to visit her.

Finally, they arrive at Topojo, where Aymaras come in from all directions in llama caravans. Waira's family plans to barter for fruit, pottery, and tools. First, Waira watches the condor dances and receives a condor feather from one of the dancers. The impressive two-page scene of the market on the high plains is filled with hundreds of people and their produce. But finally, Waira's family finishes their transactions and heads homeward again.

Classroom Applications

What more can your students learn about the llama and its value to the people of the Andes? If a zoo is nearby, plan a field trip to see a llama. Because they are such good pack animals, llamas are also making an appearance as trail animals in the western United States. What can your students learn about the condor? In the United States, it is nearly extinct, except for newly released birds in the Grand Canyon area.

South America: Brazil

Brazil is a large country located in the center of South America, bordered on the north by Venezuela and Colombia; on the west by Peru, Bolivia, Paraguay, and Argentina; on the south by Uruguay; and on the east by the Atlantic Ocean.

 Jordan, Martin, and Jordan, Tanis. *Amazon Alphabet*. Kingfisher, 1996. 40 pp. (ISBN 1-85697-666-1). Alphabet Book, P-E.

Story Review Chart			
Setting	Plot/Events	Characters	Theme
•			•

Cultural Paradigm Reference Classification Chart			
Geographic Location	Economic System	Social System	Political System
•			

This striking alphabet book with a two-page spread for each letter shows large, exquisite pictures of Amazon animals. The *Aa agouti* is "eating Brazil nuts." The *Cc caiman* drowses in the sun with two butterflies from the preceding page resting on its snout. Can your students recognize that the eagle and the frog shown are completely different species from those in North America? Animals such as the kinkajou, red ouakari, yapok, and black Zorro make this book an excellent science reference for new animals as well. Notes at the end give more information about each animal.

Classroom Applications

Making their own alphabet scrapbooks is a fascinating and challenging project for students. Perhaps they would like to assemble one on each new culture they learn about. They can use tracing paper to trace over the outlines of these animals, coloring them in and cutting them out for their own books. Or they may want to assemble a science scrapbook of similar species of animals, such as caimans, alligators, and crocodiles.

 Lewin, Ted. *Amazon Boy*. Macmillan, 1993. 32 pp. (ISBN 0-02-757383-4). Contemporary Fiction, E-M.

Story Review Chart

Setting	Plot/Events	Characters	Theme
•	•	•	•

Cultural Paradigm Reference Classification Chart

Geographic Location	Economic System	Social System	Political System
•	•		

Green, jungly watercolor art covers every inch of the two-page scenes as Paulo, who lives in a thatched house on stilts on the banks of the Amazon River, gets to go downstream with his father to the great city of Belem near the mouth of the river. It is the first time he has ever gone downriver, and his excitement rises as he hears the old river steamer blow its whistle.

When Paulo awakens the next morning, they are entering the harbor, with its old stone fort and throng of fishing boats jam-packed along the pier. Every kind of fish imaginable is coming off the boats, balanced in wooden boxes atop the heads of the fishermen. One man carries only one huge fish—a *filhote*, Paulo's father tells him. They used to be twice that size, but all the big ones have been caught, and soon they will all be gone, he notes.

Paulo and his father wander through stalls of dried snake tails and porpoise jaws, folk cures for aches and fevers. People sell blue crabs, jungle fruits, and bottles of yellow *tucupi*.

When Paulo returns home and goes fishing in his own canoe, he finds that he has hooked something really big. As he pulls it in hand over hand, he realizes that he has hooked a *filhote* bigger than his canoe. It will make them rich when they take it to Belem! It will take three men to carry it on their heads! Then he remembers his father's words. He looks down at the great whiskered face, gently removes the hook, and watches as the fish slides silently back into the dark water.

Classroom Applications

What would your students have done? Do any of them go fishing? Do they let their catches go free? Why is this important these days? Have them find out what other fish and other animals are endangered and make posters about them.

 Papi, Liza. *Carnavalia! African-Brazilian Folklore and Crafts.* Rizzoli, 1994. 48 pp. (ISBN 0-8478-1779-2). Fiction, Folklore, and Crafts, M–L.

Story Review Chart

Setting	Plot/Events	Characters	Theme
•	•		

Cultural Paradigm Reference Classification Chart

Geographic Location	Economic System	Social System	Political System
		•	•

For the first 29 pages of this fascinating book, 7-year-old Mourrice and his nanny join in with carnival revelers on the streets of their northeastern Brazilian village. The boy learns the meaning of the first celebration *Reisado* as the Three Kings and their retinue dance many traditional dances for him.

Nanny takes him to a performance of the play *Jump My Cow*, with its Christmas-story origins and its African-Brazilian double meanings. It is about who has power in Brazilian society and who doesn't, done in cow, bull, horse, and dog costumes. When the big carnival occurs for 4 days in February, Nanny helps Mourrice make a different costume for each day.

As they watch the parade on the first day, suddenly *Frevo* dancers appear and go wild with their gyrations. On the second day, a king, queen, princesses, and one prince dance the *Congo*. On the third day, the *Mocambique* is danced over crossed sticks representing swords and with costumed men representing battling Portuguese and Africans. Finally, on the fourth day, the *Maracatu* is performed crowning the men who had once been kings in Africa.

Papi, a Brazilian artist, brings these dances to life with her vibrant, hand-colored woodcut prints. Black, brown, and white men and women in carnival costumes whirl across pages as streamers and confetti rain down.

Classroom Applications

Pages 30 to 48 give directions for making carnival crafts such as *Reisado* and *Cangaceiro* hats, the *Jump My Cow* cow mask and "winding sheet" to cover its body, flags, a *Frevo* umbrella, and *Congo* snakes. Your students may want to make these carnival crafts.

The story is a study of the history of Brazil as well, with slaves from Africa brought by the Portuguese settlers finally gaining their freedom in 1888, and the blending of these races through intermarriage with one another and the native Brazilians. As a class, discuss slavery and where it has occurred around the world. Then have students contrast this story with our own history.

 Cherry, Lynn. *The Great Kapok Tree: A Tale of the Amazon Rain Forest*. Harcourt Brace, 1990. 32 pp. (ISBN 0-15-200520-X). Contemporary Fiction, P-M.

Story Review Chart

Setting	Plot/Events	Characters	Theme
•		•	•

Cultural Paradigm Reference Classification Chart

Geographic Location	Economic System	Social System	Political System
•	•		

A man with an ax over his shoulder walks into the middle of an Amazon rain forest. He stops at the base of a huge kapok tree and begins to chop the trunk. The wood is very hard, and soon the man grows tired. When he sits down to rest against its large but-tress roots, the hum of the forest lulls him to sleep.

As he sleeps, denizens of the tree and forest come out one by one and whisper in his ear. The boa constrictor tells him the tree is a tree of miracles where generations of its ancestors have lived and not to chop it down. Bees buzz in the man's ear about the flowers that live in the tree and need their pollination. A troop of monkeys tells him that when the roots of trees die, the rains wash the soil away and a desert results. A toucan, a macaw, and a cock-of-the-walk fly down to tell him what happens once people start to chop down trees in a rain forest: Only ruins remain. A jaguar asks him not to cut down the tree, or else where can he find his dinner? Tree porcupines tell him how trees produce oxygen and that he will be destroying that which gives them all life. Anteaters remind him that what happens tomorrow depends on what he does today. A sleepy sloth asks him how much beauty is worth. Finally, a child from the Yanomamo tribe asks him to look at all of them with different eyes when he wakes up.

The man awakens with a start to find all the creatures of the forest staring at him. He is surrounded by strange and beautiful plants hanging from the tree like jewels. He stands up, picks up his ax, and is about to swing it once again when he turns back and stares at the child and the animals. Then he drops the ax and walks out of the forest.

Classroom Applications

This stirring story calls out to be dramatized. Your students can take the parts of each rain forest creature who whispers in the man's ear and pleads for the great kapok tree to be spared. They can wear animal masks, talk through paper bag puppets they have made, or hold up animal figures that state their case. To bring the moral of this story closer to home, change its location to a nearby woods and have the animals be famil-iar woodland animals. How can the death of a large woodland tree affect each animal the students represent?

South America: Colombia

Colombia is located in the northwestern corner of South America. It is bordered on the north by Panama and the Caribbean Sea, on the east by Venezuela and Brazil, on the south by Peru and Ecuador, and on the west by the Pacific Ocean.

 Torres, Leyla. *Saturday Sancocho.* Farrar, Straus & Giroux, 1995. 32 pp. (ISBN 0-374-36418-4). Contemporary Fiction, P–M.

Story Review Chart			
Setting	Plot/Events	Characters	Theme
	•	•	

Cultural Paradigm Reference Classification Chart

Geographic Location	Economic System	Social System	Political System
	•	•	

Every Saturday, Maria Lili can't wait to make her favorite chicken *sancocho* ("stew") with her grandparents. But one Saturday, they discover that there is no food in the house but a dozen eggs: no vegetables, no chicken, and no money to buy any. This does not deter Mama Ana, her grandmother, who puts the eggs in a basket and goes to market with Maria Lili for a lesson in bartering.

First, they persuade Don Eugenio to give them a bunch of green plantains for six eggs. Then, Doña Carmen at the next stand gives them 4 pounds of thick cassava for six plantains. Don Mateo reluctantly takes 2 pounds of cassava for six ears of corn, but Mama Ana gives him a couple of eggs to make him feel better. Doña Dolores wants all the corn for eight carrots, but Mama Ana persuades her to take just three ears.

They trade their remaining eggs for onions, tomatoes, garlic, and cumin, but still they lack one important ingredient: a chicken.

Her clever grandma has Maria Lili help divide up everything equally between two baskets. Then, she offers one to Doña Petrona for a chicken and finally gets her to agree. Don Fernando sees Maria Lili carrying one of Mama Ana's hand-knit bags over her shoulder and suggests that she trade it for one of his wooden ladles and a colorful spinning top. Not long after they arrive home, the water is boiling and the ingredients are added for a delicious *sancocho*.

Classroom Applications

Your students, too, can make this stew by following the recipe at the end of the story. They may want to compare Maria Lili's market experience with others they have encountered vicariously through books set in Africa and other countries. What about shopping for fresh vegetables in the United States? If a farmers' market is available, plan a field trip there to purchase the ingredients for a cooking experience back in the classroom.

South America: Peru

Peru is centrally located on the Pacific coast of South America, bordered on the north by Ecuador and Colombia, on the east by Brazil and Bolivia, on the south by Chile, and on the west by the Pacific Ocean.

 Ehlert, Lois. *Moon Rope.* Harcourt Brace, 1992. 36 pp. (ISBN 0-15-255343-6). Folklore, P-E.

Story Review Chart

Setting	Plot/Events	Characters	Theme
•	•	•	

Cultural Paradigm Reference Classification Chart

Geographic Location	Economic System	Social System	Political System
	•	•	

Few folktales can compete in beauty with Ehlert's *Moon Rope*, with its large two-page spreads of stylized collage animals in silver, gold, or turquoise against glossy backgrounds in green, blue, magenta, black, coral, or plum. The simple text appears in large white typeface in English and in a silver typeface in Spanish against the colored background. The stylized animals and flowers were inspired by ancient Peruvian textiles, jewelry, and ceramic vessels. They tell a clever explanatory tale about a fox who wants to go to the moon and a mole who reluctantly accompanies him.

Often folktales are too long and complicated for youngest students. Not this one. Its simple words get straight to the point, and even the youngest listeners enjoy the stylized designs of the animals. Fox wants to go to the moon, but he does not want to go alone, so he persuades Mole to come along. Mole does not really want to go, but his stomach likes the idea of the huge worms Fox tells him are up there. Fox decides to climb up a grass rope he has made to lasso the moon.

Fox's first attempt is a failure as the rope falls back and hits him on the nose. Finally, he gets some birds to carry the rope up and hitch it onto the crescent moon. Up climb Fox and Mole, "paw over paw and claw over claw." Fox keeps his eyes on the moon and finally arrives at his destination. But Mole keeps looking back to Earth until he suddenly loses his grip and falls on a bird who has been following them. The bird carries him back to Earth, where all the creatures laugh and tease him so much that he digs a deep tunnel to hide in.

These days, Mole comes out only after dark and has nothing to do with foxes. And Fox? The animals say that, on a clear night, they can see Fox's face in the full moon looking down on Earth. Can you? His eyes, ears, and nose are faintly visible within Ehlert's large silver moon on the last page.

Classroom Applications

It is important to read stories like this in both languages for students to gain the full, almost magical effect of this folktale. Also, be sure to read the story as many times as the students want it repeated. "Repetition is a necessary part of young children's learning. . . . Have them sit close and try to identify the animals as they appear in the story" (Beaty, 1997, p. 177).

Afterward they can create their own animal collages if you have ready a tableful of colored metallic paper cut into geometric shapes, along with glue and colored construction paper for backing. Some students may want to tell you their own Fox and Mole stories after they complete their collages.

South America: Venezuela

Venezuela is located on the northern coast of South America, bordered on the north by the Caribbean Sea, on the east by Guyana and Brazil, on the south by Brazil, and on the west by Colombia.

Kurusa. *The Streets Are Free*. illustrated by Monika Doppert. Annick Press, 1995. 48 pp. (ISBN 1-55037-370-6). Contemporary Fiction, M-L.

Story Review Chart

Setting	Plot/Events	Characters	Theme
•	•	•	•

Cultural Paradigm Reference Classification Chart

Geographic Location	Economic System	Social System	Political System
		•	•

The large, modern city of Caracas, like many other cities in South America, has no more room for the hundreds of people who flock there every year for work and a better life. So the people move up onto the hillsides, building shacks of tin and wooden planks, hoping eventually to improve their lives enough to move down into the city. These shanty towns are called *barrios*, and this story is based on a true happening in the barrio of San Jose de la Urbina.

Cheo, Carlitos, Camila, and the other children in the barrio have no place to play. Hopscotch, soccer, baseball, and tag are games they seldom enjoy. When they play ball in the street, the ball gets lost in people's laundry or trapped on their roofs. Kites are soon tangled in hydroelectric wires. Truck drivers yell at them in the narrow barrio streets, and women with brooms chase them away.

A house that has been converted to a library is their only refuge. There, they decide to go down to city hall and ask to see the mayor about their playground. They make a banner that says WE HAVE NOWHERE TO PLAY. WE NEED A PLAYGROUND. But at city hall, the children nearly cause a riot when a guard calls the police because they won't leave, and their mothers hurry to defend them. The mayor finally appears, and the children ask him to come look at the lot they want for their playground. He says he is too busy at that moment, but a woman reporter comes with the children, afterward publishing an article about the children who "take on city hall."

This article actually brings the mayor out to cut a ribbon at the entrance to the vacant lot reserved for THE CHILDREN'S PARK OF SAN JOSE. When Camila realizes the mayor is here only because of the upcoming election, she knows nothing more is going to happen.

But the children refuse to give up. Why can't the people of San Jose build it themselves, they want to know? They talk with older brothers, who talk with uncles and fathers, and finally the men of San Jose bring cement, bricks, buckets, old tires, sheets of aluminum, and wooden boards. The women contribute food and support, and soon the playground is a reality. On the fence, the children put up their own sign: SAN JOSE PLAYGROUND. EVERYBODY COME AND PLAY.

Classroom Applications

Such a story calls for an ongoing discussion about the power of people to affect elected officials, as well as what children can do to bring about needed change in their community. Your older students may want to try their own hand at writing a newspaper article for a class newspaper or making banners and signs.

SUMMARY

The large number of current children's books about Central America, Mexico, and South America is often surprising to teachers who are accustomed to the limited number available only a few years ago. This chapter presents an overview of 25 books about 11 countries and belonging primarily to either contemporary fiction (12) or folktales (6). One to three books fall into each of the following other genres: nonfiction, historical fiction, poetry, biography, and alphabet book.

Characters and plot/events are the story elements stressed in nearly every reviewed book, whereas setting is conspicuous in 17 of the books and theme in 12.

When considering the cultural paradigm, the social component is clearly discernible in 19 books and economic issues surface in 14, whereas geography and political themes are apparent in about a third of the books reviewed.

Your students should have no trouble identifying with Esperanza from Guatemala who helps her ostracized grandmother sell her weaving; Pedrito the shoe-shine boy from Nicaragua who replaces the money he loses from his own bicycle savings; Fernando from Panama who paints trees and flowers on the outside walls of his house; Emilio from Mexico, the "butterfly boy" who helps his impaired grandfather enjoy life again; Maria from Argentina who herds cattle on her mother's ranch; Waira the Bolivian Indian girl who gives her llama to a new friend; Paulo the Amazon boy who lets the large but endangered river fish he catches go free; and Cheo, Carlitos, and Camila, the Venezuelan barrio children who defy city hall to finally get their own playground.

Who could forget them? When students learn about other cultures from the experiences of children like themselves, they never forget them. For, as also noted by Ramsey (1987):

> Stories introduce children to unfamiliar people in a personalized and appealing fashion. By involving the children with characters and situations that they can identify with, books increase children's appreciation of other ways of life and help them see unfamiliar people as individuals. (p. 69)

REFERENCES CITED
▼▼

Beaty, J. B. (1997). *Building bridges with multicultural picture books*. Upper Saddle River, NJ: Merrill/Prentice Hall.

Ramsey, P. G. (1987). *Teaching and learning in a diverse world: Multicultural education for young children*. New York: Teachers College Press.

Suggested References

Agosto, C. (1997, May). Reading the world: Brazil. *Book Links*, 13-15. (Brazil)

Barrera, R. B., & de Cortes, O. G. (1997). Mexican American children's literature in the 1990s: Toward authenticity. In V. J. Harris *Using multiethnic literature in the K-8 classroom* (pp. 129-153). Norwood, MA: Christopher-Gordon. (Mexico)

Brandao, A. L. (1997). Walking in a new way: Brazilian children's and young adult science fiction. *Bookbird*, 35(4), 26-30. (Brazil)

Day, F. A. (1997). *Latina and Latino voices in literature for children and teenagers*. Portsmouth, NH: Heinemann. (General)

Freeman, Y. S. (1998). Providing quality children's literature in Spanish. *New Advocate*, 11(1), 23-38. (General)

Ramero, P. A., & Zancanella, D. (1990). Expanding the circle: Hispanic voices in American literature. *English Journal*, 79(1), 24-25. (General)

Rodriguez, A. O. (1995). Voices of children's poetry in Latin America. *Bookbird*, 33(1), 1-16. (General)

Saccardi, M. (1997). The art of Mexico. *Book Links*, 6(6), 49-55. (Mexico)

Silva-Diaz, M. C. (1995-96). Cidlil: The Venezuelan documentation center for children's literature. *Bookbird*, 33(3-4), 102-103. (Venezuela)

Silva-Diaz, M. C. (1997). Rites of initiation in recent Latin American narratives. *Bookbird*, 35(2), 21-26. (General)

Thierry, M. P. (1996). What is wrong with Chile school children's understanding of written texts? *Journal of Adolescent and Adult Literacy*, 40(1), 14-21. (Chile)

World Reference Atlas. (1996). New York: Dorling Kindersley.

Children's Books Cited

Aardema, V. (1991). *Borreguita and the coyote*. New York: Knopf. (Mexico)

Ada, A. F. (1997). *Gathering the sun: An alphabet in Spanish and English*. New York: Lothrop, Lee & Shepard Books. (Mexico)

Argueta, M. (1990). *Magic dogs of the volcanoes*. San Francisco: Children's Book Press. (El Salvador)

Brusca, M. C. (1994). *My mama's little ranch on the pampas*. New York: Henry Holt. (Argentina)

Castaneda, O. S. (1993). *Abuela's weave*. New York: Lee & Low Books. (Guatemala)

Cherry, L. (1990). *The great kapok tree: A tale of the Amazon rain forest*. San Diego: Harcourt Brace.

Czernecki, S., & Rhodes, T. (1994). *The hummingbirds' gift*. New York: Hyperion. (Mexico)

Ehlert, L. (1992). *Moon rope*. San Diego: Harcourt Brace. (Peru)

Garay, L. (1997). *Pedrito's day*. New York: Orchard Books. (Nicaragua)

Grifalconi, A. (1994). *The bravest flute*. Boston: Little, Brown. (Guatemala)

Jordan, M., & Jordan, T. (1996). *Amazon alphabet*. New York: Kingfisher. (Brazil)

Kroll, V. (1997). *Butterfly boy*. Honesdale, PA: Boyds Mills Press. (Mexico)

Kurusa. (1995). *The streets are free*. Toronto: Annick Press. (Venezuela)

Lewin, T. (1993). *Amazon boy*. New York: Macmillan. (Brazil)

Markun, P. M. (1993). *The little painter of Sabana Grande*. New York: Bradbury Press. (Panama)

Ober, H. (1994). *How music came to the world*. Boston: Houghton Mifflin. (Mexico)

Palacios, A. (1993). *A Christmas surprise for Chabelita*. New York: Troll. (Panama)

Papi, L. (1994). *Carnavalia! African-Brazilian folklore and crafts*. New York: Rizzoli. (Brazil)

Parkison, J. (1994). *Pequeña the burro*. Kansas City, MO: MarshMedia. (Mexico)

Presilla, M. E., & Soto, G. (1996). *Life around the lake*. New York: Henry Holt. (Mexico)

Smith-Ayala, E. (1996). *Clouds on the mountain.* Toronto: Annick Press. (Guatemala)

Topooco, E. (1993). *Waira's first journey.* New York: Lothrop, Lee & Shepard Books. (Bolivia)

Torres, L. (1995). *Saturday sancocho.* New York: Farrar, Straus & Giroux. (Colombia)

Volkmer, J. A. (1990). *Song of the chirimia: A Guatemalan folktale.* Minneapolis, MN: Carolrhoda Books. (Guatemala)

Winter, J. (1991). *Diego.* New York: Knopf. (Mexico)

SUGGESTED CHILDREN'S BOOKS

▼▼

Aardema, V. (1991). *Pedro and the padre.* New York: Dial Books for Young Readers. (Mexico)

Ada, A. F. (1991). *The gold coin.* New York: Macmillan. (Central America)

Ada, A. F. (1997). *The lizard and the sun: An old Mexican folktale.* New York: Bantum. (Mexico)

Ancona, G. (1994). *The piñata maker; El pinatero.* San Diego: Harcourt Brace. (Mexico)

Barbot, D. (1991). *A bicycle for Rosaura.* Brooklyn, NY: Kane-Miller. (Venezuela)

Brusca, M. C. (1991). *On the pampas.* New York: Henry Holt. (Argentina)

Charles, D. (1992). *Chancy and the secret of fire.* New York: Putnam. (Peru)

Bunting, E. (1996). *Going home.* New York: Harper-Collins. (General)

Burton, A. (1996). *Journey of the nightly jaguar.* New York: Simon & Schuster Books for Young Readers. (Mexico)

Czernecki, S., & Rhodes, T. (1992). *The sleeping bread.* New York: Hyperion. (Guatemala)

Darling, K. (1996). *Amazon ABC.* New York: Lothrop, Lee & Shepard Books. (Brazil)

Dawson, Z. (1996). *Postcards from Brazil.* Chatham, NJ: Raintree Steck Vaughn. (Brazil)

Gerson, M.-J. (1994). *How night came from the sea.* Boston: Little, Brown. (Brazil)

Gerson, M.-J. (1995). *People of the corn.* Boston: Little, Brown. (Mexico)

Gollub, M. (1994). *The moon was at a fiesta.* New York: Tambourine Books. (Mexico)

Grossman, P. (1994). *Saturday market.* New York: Lothrop, Lee & Shepard Books. (Mexico)

Guy, G. F. (1996). *Fiesta!* New York: Greenwillow Books. (Mexico)

Haskins, J., & Benson, K. (1996). *Count your way through Brazil.* Minneapolis, MN: Carolrhoda Books. (Brazil)

Hewitt, S. (1996). *The Aztecs.* San Francisco: Children's Book Press. (Mexico)

Hurwitz, J. (1993). *New shoes for Silvia.* New York: Morrow. (Central America)

Johnston, T. (1994). *The tale of Rabbit and Coyote.* New York: Putnam. (Mexico)

Krupp, R. R. (1996). *Let's go traveling in Mexico.* New York: Morrow. (Mexico)

Lecher, D. (1992). *Angelina's magic yarn.* New York: Farrar, Straus & Giroux. (South America)

Maitland, K. (1994). *Ashes for gold.* Greenvale, NY: Mondo. (Mexico)

Martinez, A. C. (1991). *The woman who outshone the sun.* San Francisco: Children's Book Press. (Mexico)

McCunney, M. (1997). *Mario's Mayan journey.* Greenvale, NY: Mondo. (General)

McDermott, G. (1997). *Musicians of the sun.* New York: Simon & Schuster Books for Young Readers. (Mexico)

Mora, P. (1997). *Tomas and the library lady.* New York: Random House. (General)

Patent, D. H. (1996). *Children save the rain forest.* New York: Dutton Children's Books. (Costa Rica)

Patent, D. H. (1996). *The Quetzal: Sacred bird of the forest.* New York: Morrow. (Mexico)

Steele, P. (1997). *Aztec news.* Cambridge, MA: Candlewick Press. (Mexico)

Vidal, B. (1991). *The legend of El Dorado.* New York: Knopf. (Colombia)

Winter, J. (1996). *Josefina.* New York: Harcourt Brace Juvenile Books. (Mexico)

Wisniewski, D. (1991). *Rain player.* New York: Clarion Books. (Mexico)

Wood, M. (1994). *Growing up in Aztec times.* New York: Troll. (Mexico)

CHAPTER

7

Children's Books About Eastern Europe

EASTERN EUROPE

Eastern Europe occupies the eastern half of continental Europe between Germany, Austria, and Italy on the west and the Ural Mountains in Russia to the east. To the south lie Greece and Turkey; to the north, the Baltic Sea and Scandinavia.

Countries

Albania, Belarus, Bosnia & Herzegovina, Bulgaria, Croatia, Czech Republic, Estonia, Georgia, Hungary, Latvia, Lithuania, Macedonia, Moldova, Poland, Romania, Russian Federation, Slovakia, Slovenia, Ukraine, Yugoslavia

EXAMINING THE CULTURAL REGION OF EASTERN EUROPE AND THE PATTERNS OF CHILDREN'S BOOKS

The designation of Eastern Europe is a political artifact resulting from World War II and the Cold War. After nearly 50 years behind the Iron Curtain, Eastern Europe today is emerging as a diverse group of independent countries that are undergoing fundamental political and economic reform. Unfortunately, this upheaval has been accompanied in some countries by bloody civil wars based on long-standing ethnic hatreds that had been largely held in check by the totalitarian governments of Eastern European countries and ultimately by the former Soviet Union.

Except for the Russian Federation (Russia), most countries belonging to Eastern Europe are small to medium in size. The people are primarily Slavic historically, linguistically, and culturally (people of Western Europe, in contrast, can trace their roots back to the Roman Empire). Eastern European cultures, customs, and attitudes have much in common with their western neighbors. Consequently, the children's literature of Eastern Europe and Western Europe share many of the same plots, themes, character types, and styles of illustration. Long-standing Slavic cultures and relatively recent major historic events (e.g., World War II, the Holocaust, the Cold War), however, have produced a distinct body of children's literature about the eastern half of Europe. The bulk of English-language children's books set in Eastern Europe focus on Russia. A relatively modest number of books have stories about the Czech Republic, Poland, Romania, and Ukraine; fewer still, about other Eastern European countries. This pattern can be attributed largely to an interplay of several factors: (a) the degree of media attention a country receives in the United States, (b) the extent of immigration from a particular country to the United States, and (c) the level of political and economic stability within a country. As the modern world becomes more integrated, it becomes increasingly important that our bookshelves hold children's books reflecting the various cultures, attitudes, traditions, and values of a major region in Europe that managed to endure and remain hopeful despite nearly a century of great turmoil, oppression, and suffering.

COUNTRIES AND CHILDREN'S BOOKS REVIEWED

Czech Republic

The Czech Republic is a landlocked country bordered by Germany on the west and north, Poland on the northeast, Slovakia on the southeast, and Austria on the south.

 Wisniewski, David. *Golem*. Clarion Books, 1996. 32 pp. (ISBN 0-395-72618-2). Legend, M-L.[1]

---

[1]A = all ages, P = preschool, E = early elementary, M = middle elementary, L = late elementary

Story Review Chart

Setting	Plot/Events	Characters	Theme
•	•	•	•

Cultural Paradigm Reference Classification Chart

Geographic Location	Economic System	Social System	Political System
•		•	•

This story unfolds in the Jewish ghetto of Prague in the 1500s. The chief rabbi, Judah Loew ben Bezalel, searches for a way to rid his people living in the Jewish ghetto of persecution. While asleep, the written word *golem* is revealed to him. Realizing he now has a way to help his people, the rabbi plans to create a golem, or protector, out of clay. Late one evening, he takes his son-in-law and a student scholar outside the ghetto's gates to the clay banks of the river Vltava. There the three men pile up a

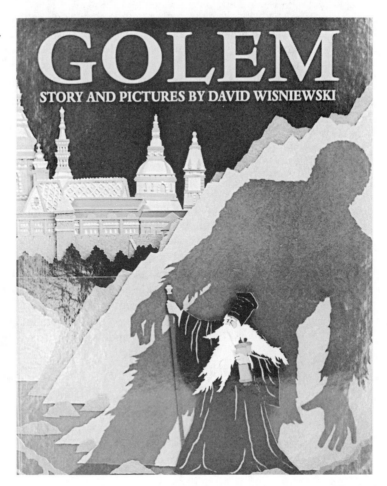

Cover, from GOLEM by David Wisniewski. Copyright © 1996 by David Wisniewski. Reprinted by permission of Clarion Books/Houghton Mifflin Company. All rights reserved.

mound of clay. With only his hands as tools, the rabbi sculpts the clay into a massive human figure. He then chants a spell and writes the word *emet* ("truth") on the golem's forehead. After transforming into a human-like being, the golem follows the rabbi back to the ghetto, where he is told that he was given life to protect the Jewish people and that, once his purpose is fulfilled, he will return to his earthen state.

When the rabbi shows the immense golem to his people, they initially are frightened. After he assures them that the golem is meant to protect them and renames it Joseph, the people's fears diminish. The golem capably serves as protector by aggressively fending off perpetrators of violence who enter the ghetto at night. In contrast with his combative nocturnal nature, during the day the golem peacefully smells roses, watches sunrises, and delights in other wonders. But the more the golem protects the ghetto, the more fearful the people outside the ghetto become of the Jews living inside. The relatively few who terrorized the ghetto before the golem arrived have therefore grown into a huge mob bent on the ghetto's destruction.

As violence against Jews increases, so does the golem's size and power until it frightens everyone living outside the ghetto. The emperor summons the rabbi to his castle and asks him whether he and the golem plan to enslave the entire city. The rabbi replies emphatically no and says he would never inflict on anyone what has been wrongly done to him and his people. After the rabbi reveals the golem's true purpose, the emperor offers to guarantee the safety of all who live in the ghetto if the golem is destroyed. The rabbi agrees to the emperor's offer and returns to the ghetto to speak with the golem. Knowing what the rabbi will say, the golem pleads not to be turned back to clay. But the rabbi, bound by his agreement with the emperor, reaches out and erases the *e* from the word *emet* on the golem's forehead. Only the word *met* remains, and it means death. Because life has become so precious to him, the golem again begs to be allowed to live. His pleas are to no avail, however, and he crumbles into a mound of clay, which the rabbi, his son-in-law, and a student carry to the attic. They then respectfully cover the clay with worn prayer books and lock the door as they leave. But behind the locked door remains the golem, who will arise again if ever needed.

This powerful legend tells of an artificial being that, having saved a mistreated people, is denied life and its enjoyment. *Golem*, then, is a story about self-sacrifice for the greater good of a people and its culture.

Illustrations made of cut paper colored in earth tones dramatically convey the plight of an oppressed people and the love, wisdom, and faith that free them. Imaginative use of geometric shapes overlain or surrounded by jagged cuts of paper enhances the fearfulness of the golem's supernatural transformation from clay into a three-dimensional superhuman and then back to clay.

Classroom Applications

Students can discuss their experiences of making a sacrifice for someone else. How did they feel about the situation? Creating cut-paper illustrations that depict these situations and fashioning superheroes from clay can provide students with an opportunity to act out those situations. Older students can study the founding of the modern state of Israel as a safe and secure homeland for Jews who survived the horrors of the Holocaust in Europe.

Sis, Peter. *The Three Golden Keys*. Doubleday Books for Young Readers, 1994. 32 pp. (ISBN 0-385-47292-7). Contemporary Fiction, E-M.

Story Review Chart

Setting	Plot/Events	Characters	Theme
•	•	•	•

Cultural Paradigm Reference Classification Chart

Geographic Location	Economic System	Social System	Political System
•		•	

Swept off course during a hot-air balloon ride, the author describes descending into a vaguely familiar but deserted city. He soon recognizes the city as Prague, where he grew up as a boy. Although he manages to find his family's house, which is full of old but fond memories, he cannot open the door because of the three padlocks on it. He feels compelled to find the three keys, but no one is around to help him except for the black cat he remembers having as a pet when he was young.

The cat beckons him to follow. While walking down the streets that were his winter playground, he recalls his sister's birthday and Christmastime with his family. Eventually, he wanders toward the city's castle, but first he stops off at the library, a place he loved to visit as a child. He enters the deserted, silent building and sees the librarian and various characters mysteriously emerge from the bookcases. The librarian gives him a scroll, with a golden key attached, that tells of the legend of Prince Bruncvik's magical sword. Leaving the library, the author follows the cat down the streets in old Prague, which evoke thoughts of summer games, piano lessons, and freshly baked bread. The cat then escorts him into a garden, which magically transforms into a royal court where plants assume the shapes of the emperor and his entourage. The emperor opens another scroll containing a second gold key. This time, the scroll recounts the story of an artificial man, or golem, who defended the Jews of Prague. Next the cat directs the man through streets that remind him of autumn joys and scenes. They then enter a clock tower in the town square and climb up into a domed room where several mythical robots walk out of the woodwork. One of these robots holds the third and final scroll, which contains the last golden key. The scroll tells another story from the man's childhood—a story about a strange machine that hides in the clock tower. With the three golden keys now in his possession, the man follows his cat across a bridge that reminds him of springtime delights. Finally, he returns to his family's house, unlocks the door, and enters to hear his mother's voice, the sounds of the streets, and the life of a city he had left so long ago.

This book reaffirms the value of one's cultural and social roots, which begin growing in childhood and support and nourish throughout one's life. Events in the book seem to symbolize moving from childhood to adulthood in a process that transcends both time and place and that largely defines what it means to be human. Thus, books like *The Three Golden Keys* not only remind us how much we appreciate our own social and cultural background but also tell us that people elsewhere value theirs as well.

Illustrations in this book imaginatively take the reader on a journey back to childhood. Their muted colors create an atmosphere of mystery and solitude as the mind traces its memories to the past. Fanciful buildings, streets, bridges, and other urban structures reflect the perceptions, fascinations, and simple joys of childhood. Images hidden within and emerging from familiar objects symbolize how the physical world helps elicit fond recollections of a longed-for time and place.

Classroom Applications

Students can interview their caregivers or family friends about their own childhoods, which can be written down or tape-recorded (create a living history). Another activity involves writing stories on scrolls about places the students would like to remember when they become adults; they can base their stories on actual or fictionalized events that occurred in their favorite place(s). While writing these stories, students can listen to music written by composers from what was once Czechoslovakia (now Czech Republic and Slovakia); Dvorak's *Slavonic Dances* and Smetna's *Ma Vlast* are two possibilities. When finished, students can tell their stories to one another and visit Web sites about Prague and the Czech Republic.

Poland

Poland is bordered by Germany on the west, the Baltic Sea on the north, Lithuania, Belorussia, and Ukraine on the east, and Slovakia and the Czech Republic on the south.

 Nerlove, Miriam. *Flowers on the Wall.* Margaret K. McElderry Books, 1996. 32 pp. (ISBN 0-689-50614-7). Historical Fiction, E-M.

Story Review Chart

Setting	Plot/Events	Characters	Theme
•	•	•	•

Cultural Paradigm Reference Classification Chart

Geographic Location	Economic System	Social System	Political System
•	•	•	•

This story sadly tells of the life of a Jewish family living in Warsaw, Poland, as the Holocaust engulfs Europe. It is a story of love and hope that ultimately ends in tragedy. Rachel lives with her mama, papa, and older brother Nat in a cold, drab, one-room basement apartment. Rachel's father, Jacob, owns a dry goods store in Warsaw, but he has very few customers because Jewish-owned businesses are being boycotted. So, for another night, Rachel and her family go to bed hungry.

Eventually, Jacob has to close his shop, which his landlord then rents to a businessman who is not Jewish. To earn enough money to survive, Jacob and Nat get permits to work as *tragarz* ("porters"). Although horse-drawn wagons and carts usually are hired to haul heavy loads, it is less expensive to hire Jewish porters because they do not require the care that horses do. Having to work all day, Nat no longer can go to his *cheder* ("school"). Each morning, Rachel's mother goes to the employment office to find temporary jobs available for Jewish women. Having outgrown her shoes and with no money to buy new ones, Rachel cannot go outside. So she stays by herself inside the apartment.

To occupy the lonely time when her family has gone to work each day, Rachel cleans the apartment and looks at picture books on her parents' bookshelf. Then one evening, Jacob brings Rachel some paints and small brushes. When Rachel points out that they need paper to paint on, her father suggests that the walls need to be decorated. So together they begin painting flowers on the walls. Day after day, Rachel spends hours painting flowers of every color. Soon a veritable garden grows on the walls inside a once very dreary apartment. Unlike her painted flowers, however, Rachel and her family do not survive the Holocaust.

Muted watercolors cast the Warsaw ghetto in somber, foreboding tones. They convey an unsettling sense of the political, economic, and social injustices and cruelties inflicted on Jewish families struggling to preserve what they held dear and true. These illustrations are compelling reminders of the worst and best of humanity.

Classroom Applications

A host of classroom activities are appropriate as follow-up for *Flowers on the Wall*. Older students can draw or trace, color, and label maps of Europe to show the expansion, decline, and end of Axis domination in Europe from 1939 to 1945 and the locations of major concentration camps. They also can visit the U.S. Holocaust Memorial Museum in Washington, DC, over the Internet. A discussion of the causes, major events, and key participants of the civil rights movement in the United States can help students better appreciate and understand the struggle against injustice, prejudice, and hatred in a more familiar place and time. Finally, on a personal level, ask students to imagine what they individually might feel and do if other people or even their government mistreated them because of their race, religion, or ethnic background.

 Wild, Margaret. *Let the Celebrations Begin!* illustrated by Julie Vivas. Orchard Books, 1991. 32 pp. (ISBN 0-531-05937-5). Historical Fiction, E-M.

Story Review Chart

Setting	Plot/Events	Characters	Theme
•	•	•	•

Cultural Paradigm Reference Classification Chart

Geographic Location	Economic System	Social System	Political System
•	•	•	•

The story begins with Miriam and other women quietly planning a party for the children when the concentration camp they are in is liberated (presumably, in Poland). Her young, emaciated friends David and Sarah ask Miriam to tell them what it was like to live in a home of love and security—a home with plenty of food, toys, and a warm bedroom all to oneself. Miriam realizes that David and Sarah desperately want some toys of their own to play with. So she and the women in the camp secretly make stuffed animals and dolls at night out of anything they can find—bits of clothing, buttons, some thread, tufts of wool, discarded rags. Then one day, rumors of the war's end come true. Friendly soldiers liberate the camp, and Miriam and other survivors celebrate with a special party when the children get their toys.

Let the Celebrations Begin! tells about a horrific period of history when the social fabric in Europe and elsewhere was ripped apart and how a few, against all odds, began to stitch it back together with compassion and dignity. This story also shows the reader how the noble and resilient human spirit manages to survive and transcend abject misery, destructive hate, and incomprehensible inhumanity.

Illustrations starkly show shaved heads, emaciated bodies, gaunt faces, and threadbare clothing, all of which attest to the brutal existence those in concentration camps had to endure.

Classroom Applications

This emotional and inspiring book can serve to introduce younger students to the Holocaust. Follow-up study could address such questions as, What was the Holocaust, and why did it occur? What was the purpose of the concentration camps? and What consequences did the Holocaust have (e.g., the founding of the state of Israel). The U.S. Holocaust Memorial Museum is a superb source of background information for teachers and may be accessed on the Internet.

Romania

Romania is located in south central Europe, bordered by Hungary and Yugoslavia on the west, Ukraine on the north and east, the Black Sea also on the east, and Bulgaria on the south.

 Hooper, Maureen Brett. *The Christmas Drum.* illustrated by Diane Paterson. Boyds Mills Press, 1994. 32 pp. (ISBN 1-56397-105-4). Contemporary Fiction, E-M.

Story Review Chart			
Setting	Plot/Events	Characters	Theme
•	•	•	•

Cultural Paradigm Reference Classification Chart

Geographic Location	Economic System	Social System	Political System
•	•	•	

Peter awakes on Christmas Eve morning, realizing that tonight he has to lead the *colindat*, a group of musicians that parades through his village house to house, playing instruments and singing carols. His papa is working in a factory in the city and probably will not make it home in time to perform with the colindat. When Papa left to go to the city, he told Peter to take his place and to play his *duba* ("small drum").

Filled with self-doubt, Peter looks at the duba on his bed and worries about his ability to lead the colindat like his father. He then goes into the kitchen to ask his grandfather, mother, and sister Anna whether they believe he is good enough to lead the colindat. They assure him he is. Still unconvinced of his ability, he goes to the bus stop, hoping his papa is back, but he is not. While waiting at the bus stop, Peter thinks about his rehearsal sessions with the colindat. He remembers the band members questioning his abilities because he is too young and too small. Their skepticism only intensifies his own doubts about himself.

Evening arrives, and Peter goes to join the colindat. Once assembled, all await in silence for Peter to start the procession. Suddenly, he freezes and is convinced he cannot do it. Then his duba says he can and he does. Peter's drumming gets the colindat under way, and he confidently leads its playing. Praises abound; never before have the villagers heard a drummer such as Peter. At the end of the evening, the colindat arrives at Peter's house, where they play for his family. Peter sings a solo of his favorite Christmas carol, which deeply moves his family. Then Papa suddenly appears and whirls Peter around. He is so pleased with Peter's singing and playing and the praises from the villagers that he tells Peter the drum is now his. The story ends with Peter and his duba going to bed and whispering good night to one another.

This story of Christmas describes the customs of caroling, music making, and community celebration in Romania. It also paints a familiar and moving portrait of a boy overcoming self-doubt and growing up a little as a result. Finally, the loving and supportive family round out this story about the customs and social relationships of an Eastern European country we probably know too little about.

Watercolor illustrations present endearing images that trace the change in a child's outlook from self-doubt to one of confidence. The cozy scenes in Peter's home accentuate the social context that supports his growing up. Additionally, each page is bordered with Christmas holly, enhancing the festive mood of the story.

Classroom Applications

Ask the class, Have you ever doubted your ability to do something? Have students identify situations, places, and people that increase their self-doubts. Ask them to offer their classmates ideas on how to overcome self-doubt and increase self-confidence. Students might also act out scenarios in which they are unsure of themselves at first but then manage to replace self-doubt with confidence. Younger students might want to listen to Christmas carols (or other comparable ceremonial music) from around the world and perhaps play along with simple musical instruments. Family holiday traditions and important family-centered events can also be a lively source of experiences for students to discuss and share with one another. Students can take turns describing how their families or their friends' families celebrate special holidays or events.

 Matthews, Wendy. *The Gift of a Traveler.* illustrated by Robert Van Nutt. BridgeWater Press, 1995. 32 pp. (ISBN 0-8167-3656-1). Fiction, E-M.

Story Review Chart

Setting	Plot/Events	Characters	Theme
•	•	•	•

Cultural Paradigm Reference Classification Chart

Geographic Location	Economic System	Social System	Political System
•		•	

Christmas at the turn of the century in the mountains of Romania provides the backdrop for a story of family tradition and continuity. At her mother's insistence, Christine reluctantly visits her great-grandmother, Anica, to help decorate her tree on Christmas Eve. After hanging the last decoration, Great-Grandmother gives Christine a key to a drawer in her large cupboard. Inside the drawer is a most unusual ornament, one Great-Grandmother has kept since she was a young girl. She then tells Christine how she got the decoration and why she has kept it all these years.

One Christmas Eve long ago, Anica went with her father, brother, and two sisters into the forest to cut down a Christmas tree. On the way home, while searching for pine cones to make an ornament, she became separated from the others. She then encountered a wolf and a stranger, who helped her find her father. The stranger said that he was a traveler and that the wolf, Sasha, was his friend. After they all returned to Anica's home, she invited the traveler and Sasha to stay for Christmas dinner with her family. After her brother and sisters hung on the tree the decorations they each had made, Anica felt dejected because she hadn't anything to give the tree. Late into the night, the traveler told wonderful stories and played a musical instrument while everyone sang along. When it was time to go to bed, the traveler thanked Anica for her friendship and trust and then went out into the stable with Sasha to sleep. In the morning, Anica awoke to find a beautiful Christmas tree ornament in her room. Believing that the traveler had given it to her as a gift, she went to the stable to thank him, but both he and Sasha were gone and without leaving any footprints in the snow.

After telling this magical story, Great-Grandmother explains to Christine that she has kept the ornament with her always—during her childhood in the mountains, when she married and moved to Bucharest, and finally when she came to America. Now that she is 90 years old, she thinks it is time to give the ornament to Christine, who can keep and cherish it as she has.

Full-page paintings meld the past and present into a moving story of family traditions that span nearly a century and extend from Romania to America. Numerous images of Romanian hearth and home, clothing, and customs create an air of authentic celebration.

Central to this story is the importance of cultural legacy—the passing of family history and traditions from generation to generation and from place to place to establish cultural continuity and identity.

Classroom Applications

How are the same or comparable special occasions, such as Christmas, celebrated in different parts of the world? Students can explore this question by thinking about their own family celebrations and then researching how others in the world celebrate the same or similar occasions. If craft making is associated with such an event, students can make appropriate objects and show them to others.

 Silverman, Erica. *Gittel's Hands*. illustrated by Deborah Nourse Lattimore. BridgeWater Press, 1996. 32 pp. (ISBN 0-8167-3798-3). Fiction, E-M.

Story Review Chart

Setting	Plot/Events	Characters	Theme
•	•	•	•

Cultural Paradigm Reference Classification Chart

Geographic Location	Economic System	Social System	Political System
•	•	•	

A father-daughter relationship is the central theme of this story. Yakov lives with his only daughter, Gittel, in a modest house in a *shtetl* ("Jewish village") near the Carpathian Mountains of Romania. Gittel is an industrious and obedient daughter, and she always helps those in need. Yakov loves his daughter and proudly sings her praises to any and all. But Gittel is modest about her abilities and finds her father's boasting embarrassing and nearly impossible to live up to.

During one particularly long winter, Yakov runs out of hay to feed his horse, which he uses to deliver fresh water to his customers. Already in debt to Reb Raya, the hay merchant, and unable to pay for more hay, Yakov asks Reb Raya to hire his daughter as a seamstress in exchange for hay. Reb says he will only hire the best seamstress. In response, Yakov unthinkingly claims that Gittel can embroider a perfect matzo cover from only a rag and thread. Reb Raya agrees to hire Gittel if she makes a perfect matzo cover; but if she does not, he will take Yakov's water barrel in trade for some hay. Reb Raya gives Gittel a rag and some thread; but when she asks for a needle, he refuses because it was not part of the deal with her father.

Although Gittel is distressed about being unable to make a matzo cover, she is more concerned about a dove stuck in the chimney. She quickly frees the bird, cleans its sooty feathers, and lets it go. Reb Raya and Yakov return to find that Gittel has not made a matzo cover. When she tries to explain why, Yakov tells her to be silent. He then urges Reb Raya to hire his daughter as a cook and brags that she can prepare a holiday feast from only table scraps. Reb Raya accepts the offer, but if Gittel fails to cook a feast, he will take Yakov's wagon in exchange for hay. Reb Raya gives Gittel an egg, a piece of cheese, and some milk but refuses to provide firewood because that is not part of their arrangement. Although discouraged, Gittel's concern soon turns to an emaciated cat she finds. After she feeds the cat, Reb Raya and Yakov return and discover that she did not prepare a feast as promised. Yakov pleads for one more chance to convince Reb Raya to hire his daughter. This time, Yakov proclaims that she can make plates, candlesticks, and even a silver Elijah's cup. Reb Raya agrees but only if he gets Yakov's horse if she fails. Knowing she cannot possibly make the silver objects her father expects, Gittel worries about what will happen to him when he has to give his horse to Reb Raya. As she gazes forlornly out her window, she sees a beggar shivering in the cold. Concern for her father gives way temporarily to the more immediate needs of the beggar; she gives him her shawl and brings him into her house.

The beggar responds to her kindness by waving his hands in the air, and instantly metal-working tools and bars of silver materialize on the table. He then patiently teaches Gittel how to make candlesticks and plates and watches her fashion an exquisite Elijah's cup. Seeing sincere compassion in the beggar's eyes, Gittel realizes that he must be none other than the prophet Elijah. By the next morning, Gittel has made everything Yakov said she would. Reb Raya eagerly agrees to hire Gittel, but she finally speaks her mind and says she cannot work for a man who cheated her father. The assertive daughter and her amazed, proud father return home but not without the barrel, wagon, and horse that are rightfully theirs.

This story provides a glimpse into everyday life in a shtetl, a small Jewish community in Eastern Europe. Although the houses, clothing, and objects of daily life are drawn in a stylized manner, the simple yet loving character of shtetl life is evident. The relationship between a father and his daughter reveals many personal attributes valued in Jewish culture, including tradition, love, respect, kindness, and growth.

Suggestive of Marc Chagall's paintings, the illustrations are quite stylized and imaginative. Bold patterns and vivid colors create a whimsical setting in which the principal characters confront problems in life in a lighthearted way.

Classroom Applications

Gender roles are clearly drawn in this story. See whether students can identify and compare the ways Gittel (a young woman), Yakov (her father), and Reb Raya (a businessman) behave. Can they decide whose behavior changes the most and why? Ask students to talk about what they have done recently that surprised themselves, their families, or their friends and why. Students can tell about problems they have had that resulted from exaggerating the truth or making promises they could not keep. How could these problems have been avoided? Also, students can read about Jewish traditions or invite a rabbi to come to the class to explain Jewish traditions and define common Hebrew words.

Russian Federation (formerly part of the Soviet Union)

The Russian Federation is divided into two regions: European Russia and Asiatic Russia. European Russia extends from Finland, the Baltic states, Belarus, Ukraine, and the Black Sea in the east to the Ural Mountains in the west, with Georgia and Kazakhstan on the south. Asiatic Russia extends from the Ural Mountains on the east to the Pacific Ocean on the west, with the Arctic Ocean on the north and Kazakhstan, Mongolia, and China on the south.

 Trivas, Irene. *Annie . . . Anya: A Month in Moscow.* Orchard Books, 1992. 32 pp. (ISBN 0-531-05452-7). Contemporary Fiction, E-M.

Story Review Chart

Setting	Plot/Events	Characters	Theme
•	•	•	•

Cultural Paradigm Reference Classification Chart

Geographic Location	Economic System	Social System	Political System
•	•	•	

This is a story about 5-year-old Annie, who travels with her parents to Russia, where her mom and dad work in a hospital for a month. Although she really does not want to go, Annie does not want to stay home either. When the family arrives in Moscow, the wide city streets, huge hotel, strange Russian language, and restaurants without her favorite peanut butter and bananas conspire to make Annie feel very homesick. Her father tries to comfort Annie by singing her to sleep. The next day, Annie and her parents go sightseeing in Red Square and visit old churches. The unfamiliar sights and sounds of Moscow, however, do not make Annie feel any less grumpy. Her father says she has jet lag, but Annie isn't buying that. She really wants to go home. The next day, they go to the circus by subway. Annie loves going up and down the tall escalators in the subway stations. The fun and excitement she has at the circus help her forget momentarily what she doesn't like about being in Moscow. Then they go shopping, which is not much fun because the lines are long and there is not much to buy. Later, watching Russian television is also not enjoyable because the only words Annie knows are *da* for "yes" and *nyet* for "no." Will Annie ever enjoy Moscow?

The next day, when Annie's mom and dad go to work, they take her to a day care center. They leave her with Nadya, who cares for a group of children Annie's age. For the first few days, Annie stubbornly sits by herself and just watches the other children play.

Then one day, Nadya introduces Annie to her daughter Anya. The two girls play together and make up songs, and Anya teaches Annie many Russian words. The two become very good friends. From then on, Annie can't wait to return to day care, where she can play with the children and learn more Russian words. Then one evening, Nadya and Anya take Annie home with them, where she meets Anya's *babushka* ("grandmother") and papa.

Eventually, the day arrives when Annie and her parents have to leave Russia and return home. Nadya invites Annie and her mom and dad to a going-away party. Annie and her parents exchange gifts with Anya and her family. Then they enjoy a traditional Russian meal together. Annie and Anya finally hug and say *dosvidanye* to each other, which means "until we meet again."

The social component of the transcultural paradigm is clearly evident in this story that introduces the reader to the Russian culture, including language, family life, customs, and attitudes.

Wonderful watercolor illustrations effectively complement key events in the story. They also reveal the changes in a young girl as she becomes acquainted with and better appreciates another culture and its people.

Classroom Applications

Most children find visiting large cities to be appealing and memorable. Determine which two or three cities most students in the class have visited. Also find out which cities most would like to visit. Use Venn diagrams to compare Moscow, Russia, with a city in the United States that most have visited or at least know something about. Similarly, compare the two or three cities that most in the class want to visit. Students can also make passports and plan a trip to Moscow. They can study the places that Annie visited and map out a pretend itinerary for themselves. Building a dictionary of Russian words may prove interesting, and students can start by copying the Cyrillic alphabet from an unabridged English-language dictionary. They then can compare the Cyrillic and English alphabets in terms of letter-phoneme pairings (e.g., what Cyrillic letter sounds like *m*?).

 Mayer, Marianna, retold by. *Baba Yaga and Vasilisa the Brave*. illustrated by Kinuko Y. Craft. Morrow Junior Books, 1994. 40 pp. (ISBN 0-688-08500-8). Fairytale, P-L.

Story Review Chart			
Setting	Plot/Events	Characters	Theme
	•	•	•

Cultural Paradigm Reference Classification Chart			
Geographic Location	Economic System	Social System	Political System
	•	•	•

After her father's death, Vasilisa has to live with her stepmother and stepsisters. Although Vasilisa is supposed to inherit money from her father, the stepmother instead spends it on herself and her two daughters. Penniless, Vasilisa is forced to work day and night doing household chores and catering to the whims of her stepmother and stepsisters. Despite her hardships, she remains kind and caring, unlike her stepmother and stepsisters. To help her cope with her grim situation, Vasilisa seeks comfort from a doll that her mother made for her before she died. This simple, tiny doll magically comes to life and gives Vasilisa the love and companionship she needs.

One day, the stepmother realizes that her two daughters are ready to marry. But how can she marry them off with lovely Vasilisa around, making them appear even uglier than they really are? Using her witchcraft, the stepmother permanently extinguishes all the candles in the house and then sends Vasilisa to get a light from the notorious Baba Yaga, who lives deep in the forest. Frightened and feeling helpless, Vasilisa tells her doll that Baba Yaga will never let her return home. Nonetheless, the two journey to Baba Yaga's house in the forest.

When Vasilisa reaches the cottage, she finds it surrounded by the gruesome bones of Baba Yaga's previous victims. Baba Yaga invites the innocent Vasilisa into her home and tells the girl she must perform several tasks or otherwise end up as tomorrow's dinner. After Baba Yaga leaves early the next day, Vasilisa and the doll work together to complete the seemingly impossible tasks set before them. On her return, Baba Yaga is so impressed with what Vasilisa has accomplished that she gives her even more to do the next day. Once again, Vasilisa and her loyal doll team up to finish all their chores. More than pleased with what Vasilisa has done, Baba Yaga finally lets her return home and even gives her a glowing skull to light her way home and to give to her stepmother.

After arriving home, Vasilisa hands the light to her stepmother, who suddenly catches on fire and disappears, along with her two daughters. Frightened, Vasilisa runs out of the house and goes to a nearby village. There she meets and decides to live with a childless woman who treats her lovingly, as if she were her real daughter. A few years later, Vasilisa weaves some fabric for her adoptive mother to sell at the market. Overwhelmed by the fabric's wondrous beauty, the mother gives it instead to the czar as a gift. The fabric is then sent to some tailors, who are told to make a garment for the czar from it. The tailors, however, think that only the person who wove such gorgeous fabric is worthy of cutting it. When asked who wove the cloth, Vasilisa's adoptive mother says Vasilisa. On meeting each other, Vasilisa and the czar fall in love and become happily married. Despite all that Vasilisa has as the czar's wife, she still carries her doll with her and thinks about Baba Yaga every now and then.

Although details of each Cinderella tale vary (e.g., a doll and Baba Yaga, rather than a fairy godmother; a piece of fabric, rather than a glass slipper), the underlying message seems universally valid and understood: Happiness comes to those who are good and do good.

Craft's illustrations in oils, watercolors, and gouache are done in exquisite, eye-catching detail. They also exhibit elements of style, composition, and color reminiscent of Russian folk art.

Classroom Applications

Will the real Cinderella please stand up. Students can do a comparative study of different Cinderella stories (*The Golden Slipper* [Vietnam] and *Chinye: A West African Folk Tale*
[West Africa]). They can begin by listing the attributes of the main characters in each
story and then identify and compare key events and settings. Students can also combine elements from different Cinderella stories to create their own versions.

 Polacco, Patricia. *Babushka Baba Yaga*. Philomel, 1993. 32 pp. (ISBN 0-339-22531-5).
Fiction, E-M.

Story Review Chart

Setting	Plot/Events	Characters	Theme
•	•	•	•

Cultural Paradigm Reference Classification Chart

Geographic Location	Economic System	Social System	Political System
•	•	•	

A morose, lonely Baba Yaga longingly watches the people in the village from the edge
of her forest domain. Although embittered by the false and vindictive stories people
tell of her wickedness and cruelty, especially to children, Baba Yaga yearns for a child
whom she can hold, care for, and love. Unable to endure this need another day, Baba
Yaga disguises herself as a *babushka* ("Russian grandmother"). She then goes into the
village, where she befriends a young mother who has a son named Victor but no
babushka to care for him while she is away at work. Baba Yaga offers her services for a
place to stay and a little food. Victor's mother agrees to this arrangement.

Each morning after finishing her chores, Baba Yaga takes Victor to the edge of
her forest, where she tells him stories, sings songs, and just sits and daydreams with
him. As the love between Victor and Baba Yaga grows stronger each day, she becomes
increasingly content with her new life. Then one day, the other babushkas in the village
tell stories to their grandchildren. One tells the legend of the horrible, ugly, and wicked
Baba Yaga who comes at night to take naughty children away from home. That night,
Victor becomes so frightened by what he has heard that Baba Yaga decides to leave
before the boy finds out her real identity.

As the days pass, Victor returns to the edge of the forest to help him remember
his dear babushka. But one fateful day, he is surrounded by a pack of vicious wolves
that no one in the village can chase off. When Victor's mother frantically pleads for
someone to save her son, Baba Yaga emerges from the forest and quickly rescues the
crying boy. Victor immediately recognizes his babushka and hugs her. The people in
the village celebrate their good fortune and apologize to Baba Yaga for misjudging her.
They even welcome her to stay and live once again in the village.

In Russia, the socialization and well-being of children have traditionally relied on the resources of the extended family. In particular, the affection and care afforded to children through the mother-grandmother alliance plays an important role in raising children.

Colorful and imaginative illustrations show a gregarious people and their traditional clothing, homes, and customs. The result is an appealing vignette of past life in a small Russian village.

Classroom Applications

Because so many different Baba Yaga stories (e.g., *Baba Yaga and Vasilisa the Brave, Matreshka*) have been written, students may find it interesting to compare the various ways the Baba Yaga is portrayed. Is she an evil witch, a loving grandmother, or something else? Students can look specifically at the Baba Yaga in this story and recall experiences of how people are sometimes misjudged by what others say about them or how they look instead of what they actually do.

 Polacco, Patricia. *Babushka's Doll*. Simon & Schuster Books for Young Readers, 1990. 34 pp. (ISBN 0-671-68343-8). Fiction, P-M.

Story Review Chart

Setting	Plot/Events	Characters	Theme
	•	•	•

Cultural Paradigm Reference Classification Chart

Geographic Location	Economic System	Social System	Political System
		•	

A *babushka* ("Russian grandmother") cares for her granddaughter Natasha, who is very impatient with others when she wants something. Even though her babushka has many chores to do around the house, Natasha thinks that playing, being entertained, and being fed always come first. Rather than getting angry, the wise babushka teaches Natasha to act more kindly toward others and to imagine how others see her. To put her instruction to the test, Babushka entices Natasha to play with the doll she once played with as a young girl. The doll is enchanted, however, and comes to life. Eventually, the doll's mischief, temper tantrums, and endless demands to do this and that wear Natasha to a frazzle. When Babushka returns home, she finds Natasha crying and reassures her that she only had a bad dream. When told that she can play with the doll whenever she wishes, Natasha politely declines. Having served its purpose, the doll winks at Babushka as it is being put back on the shelf.

This story highlights the role that tradition and the extended family play in raising children in Russia, where socialization, self-discipline, and a realistic self-image are important to growing up.

Acrylic, colored marker, and pencil illustrations capture the close and nurturing relationship between Babushka and her granddaughter. Also depicted is the sometimes painful experiences a child has to endure when learning how to interact with others.

Classroom Applications

Many children have a favorite toy, such as a stuffed animal, doll, or action hero. What if that toy could come to life and teach children how to get along better with family members and friends. Ask students to imagine such toys and what lessons on good behavior they should teach. Younger students can draw their enchanted toys or make stick puppets of them and then write or dictate stories about what they learn from their toys. Similarly, students can share with each other what their grandparents have taught them. Are grandmothers generally alike the world over, and in what ways are they similar and different? To begin answering these questions, students can compare their own grandmothers or those of their friends to babushkas depicted in numerous Russian stories (e.g., *Russian Girl*, *Babushka Baba Yaga*, and *Annie . . . Anya: A Month in Moscow*).

 Kimmel, Eric A., adapted by. *Bearhead: A Russian Folktale.* illustrated by Charles Mikolaycak. Holiday House, 1991. 32 pp. (ISBN 0-8234-0902-3). Folktale, E-M.

Story Review Chart

Setting	Plot/Events	Characters	Theme
•	•	•	•

Cultural Paradigm Reference Classification Chart

Geographic Location	Economic System	Social System	Political System
•		•	

An old woman living in a Russian forest finds a creature with the head of a bear and the body of a human baby. She takes it home to show to her husband. He thinks they should return it to the forest, but the woman insists on keeping it. She names it Bearhead. The infant grows into a large, strong, loving, and obedient son. One day, Bearhead's father receives a letter from Madame Hexaba ordering him to become her servant. Because Bearhead fears that his father will never return home, he goes in his father's place. When Hexaba first meets Bearhead, she tests his ability to work for her. She tells him to clear the dinner table as quickly as possible. Taking her command quite literally, Bearhead simply tosses the table and everything on it out the window in the blink of an eye. Hexaba repeatedly gives Bearhead more tasks to do. Although he completes every task, he does them in ways Hexaba never intended.

At her wit's end, Hexaba finally tells Bearhead to collect a large debt from a goblin that lives in a lake. She expects that this fearsome goblin will rid her of troublesome Bearhead once and for all. On his way to the lake, Bearhead frees a small bird from a snare and puts it into his pocket. When he reaches the lake, the goblin challenges Bearhead to a stone-throwing contest. If Bearhead throws a stone farther, he can have anything he wants. If he looses, he must dwell at the bottom of the lake with the goblin. Secretly substituting the small bird in his pocket for a stone, Bearhead's throw far outdistances the goblin's. Bearhead claims his prize—a wagon filled with gold and the goblin's tall green hat—and returns to Hexaba's abode. Seeing the goblin's green hat bobbing in the window above the door, Hexaba becomes so frightened that she tells what she believes to be the goblin to take all the gold and never return. Of course, Bearhead once again faithfully obeys Hexaba's orders. He returns home and gives all the gold to his loving parents. Realizing that he wants to be with other bear-people, Bearhead leaves his parents to begin a new life.

This whimsical and imaginative folktale tells of the close relationship that develops between Bearhead and his proud adoptive parents. Humorous aspects of the story provide moments of comical relief. Also, a strong parental devotion runs throughout the story. No matter what, they cherish their unusual son, who relies on his naïveté and gentle nature to make the best of each situation.

Watercolor and colored pencil illustrations humorously show Bearhead overcoming one predicament after another with enthusiasm, childlike innocence, and some good luck.

Classroom Applications

Sometimes a person is feared, laughed at, or shunned because he or she appears strange or acts differently. The *Bearhead* story, however, reminds us not to judge others before we really know them. Ask students to recall instances when they may have misjudged or mistreated someone else. Can they suggest how to get to know someone else? Can students also recall when they themselves have been misjudged because others simply did not know them well enough? Students can discuss why people are different, why such differences are good, and why it is important to get to know someone rather than judge that person from first impressions and what others say.

 Isadora, Rachel, retold by. *Firebird*. Putnam, 1994. 32 pp. (ISBN 0-399-22510-2). Fairytale, E-M.

Story Review Chart

Setting	Plot/Events	Characters	Theme
•	•	•	•

Cultural Paradigm Reference Classification Chart

Geographic Location	Economic System	Social System	Political System
•		•	

Young Prince Ivan lives near a forest where an enchanted tree with magical fruit grows. Everyone avoids the forest because those who enter do not leave. When Ivan

Cover of Firebird *by Isadora, R. 1994. Used by permission of G. P. Putnam's Sons, New York, NY.*

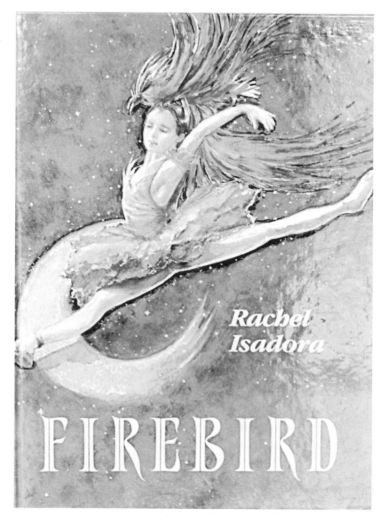

becomes a young man, he decides to go into the forest and find the enchanted tree. He wanders deeper and deeper into the forest and eventually is unable to go any farther. After night falls, he sees a light, which he approaches cautiously. At last, he sees the tree and next to it a beautiful creature, a firebird that is part woman and part bird. Starstruck, Ivan captures the firebird but then frees it after realizing how terribly frightened it is. Thankful for his compassion, she gives him one of her red tail feathers and tells him to wave it if he ever needs her help.

Ivan later encounters 10 princesses; the prettiest one tells him their sad story. All 10 princesses, the prince is told, sought the magic tree but were captured by Katschei, an evil sorcerer. Oblivious to their dangerous predicament, the princesses proceed to dance with Ivan. Suddenly, an enraged Katschei and his monsters appear.

But just as quickly, Ivan remembers the firebird and waves its red feather. The firebird appears and stuns Katschei and his monsters long enough for Ivan to destroy them all. The firebird then flies away. Ivan returns to his palace and marries the prettiest of the 10 princesses. The story ends with Ivan returning to the edge of the forest to recall longingly the firebird.

This story tells of an idealized, enchanted love—a love proved by freeing rather than possessing the other individual, a love requited in time of need, and a love imprinted permanently in one's memory. Such love, because of its selfless and chaste qualities, is admired and held up as an ideal.

Incredible illustrations evoke strong emotions. Whether depicting enchantment, beauty, joy, gratitude, or longing, the artistic combination of colors, style, and technique creates a romanticized world longed for but just out of reach.

Classroom Applications

Love is a complex and confusing emotion that everyone struggles to understand. Students can use the *Firebird* story as a source of questions about the nature of love. For example, why is Ivan captivated by the firebird, and why does he fall in love with her? Why does he capture the firebird and then free her? Why does the firebird give Ivan one of her feathers? Why does the firebird rescue Ivan but then fly away, never to see him again? and Why does Ivan visit the forest at the end of the story? Students can offer answers to these and other similar questions for class discussion. While reading the story, students can listen to *The Firebird Suite* by Igor Stravinsky. They can also pick parts based on the story and make up dance steps to the music. Watching *The Firebird Ballet* on videotape can lead into a general discussion of ballet.

 Chekhov, Anton. *Kashtanka*. adapted from a new translation by Ronald Meyer, and illustrated by Gennady Spirin. Gulliver Books, 1994. 30 pp. (ISBN 0-15-200539-0). Fiction, E-M.

Story Review Chart

Setting	Plot/Events	Characters	Theme
•	•	•	•

Cultural Paradigm Reference Classification Chart

Geographic Location	Economic System	Social System	Political System
•	•	•	

This story tells of a dog's loyalty for her master despite the allure of an exciting life in the circus. It begins one cold winter night when Kashtanka goes outside with her master, the cabinetmaker Luka Alexandrych. While they walk through the snow-covered streets, Kashtanka has a grand time barking at, chasing after, and howling at what she sees on the streets. In all the excitement, however, she becomes separated from her master and frantically runs up and down the street, looking for him.

Taking shelter in a doorway from the falling snow and cold, Kashtanka curls up and begins to whimper. The door opens behind her, and out walks a rotund little man who dusts the snow off her back and leads her inside. After the stranger has his dinner, he gives Kashtanka the leftovers, which she greatly appreciates because it is more than her previous master had ever given her. Despite the bountiful meal, she still fondly recalls the pungent aromas in the cabinetmaker's apartment. When her new master goes to bed, Kashtanka lies down, closes her eyes, and reminisces about the fun she had playing with the cabinetmaker's son, Fedyuska.

Early the next day, Kashtanka explores the apartment and finds a goose and a cat living there. A great commotion and noise fill the apartment until the man calls the goose and cat by their names and orders them back to their appointed places. He then tells Kashtanka that she must learn to live peaceably with her new roommates. He also decides to name her Auntie. Later, the stranger has the goose, the cat, and a sow perform amusing tricks involving a bell, a pistol, and a hoop. To end their performance, the goose sits on the sow's back and the cat stands on the goose's back to form a pyramid. Although these tricks are entertaining and she has plenty of good food, Kashtanka continues to be homesick.

Eventually, the stranger teaches Kashtanka tricks: walking on her hind legs, dancing, howling to music, ringing a bell, shooting the pistol, and even substituting for the goose in the pyramid trick. Then one evening, the stranger takes his animals and Kashtanka to a circus where they perform all their tricks. During Kashtanka's part of the performance, a child's voice in the audience calls out to her. Turning to face the familiar voice, Kashtanka catches sight of a boy and his father. She instantly recognizes them and dashes toward them. Reunited at last with Fedyuska and his father, Kashtanka follows them home as she recalls her recent experiences but dismisses them as a dream.

This story by Anton Chekhov explores the dilemma of deciding in which of two worlds, each with advantages and disadvantages, to live. In the end, loyalty and love win out over creature comforts and the glamour of the circus. Kashtanka's story also provides glimpses into urban life in Russia, presumably before the Russian Revolution.

Illustrations in this book are artistically superb. They sensitively portray a wide range of emotions felt by the various characters of the story. Meticulously painted scenes in the cabinetmaker's workshop, the stranger's apartment, and streets of a Russian city combine to hold the reader's attention and stir the imagination.

Classroom Applications

Dorothy chants repeatedly the heartfelt words "There's no place like home" in the classic story *The Wizard of Oz*. A similar longing underlies the touching story of Kashtanka the dog. Students can describe their own feelings about being away from their homes, families, and friends. What do they miss the most and the least? What do they do to get over feeling homesick? While away from home, what do they imagine their families and friends back home think about and do? What do they like the most about going away from home and later returning home?

We frequently think about our feelings toward our pets, but how do our pets feel about us, and what do they like and dislike about living with us? In a related activity, students can write about what they believe their pets (real or imagined) feel about them and about living with their families.

As another activity, students can learn more about the famous Russian Circus and perhaps even watch a video of one of its fabulous performances. Students then can ask and answer follow-up questions, such as, What kinds of animals perform in the Russian Circus? How do the clown acts differ from those seen at circuses touring the United States? and Do any children perform on the trapeze?

 Arnold, Katya, adapted by. *Knock, Knock, Terenok: A Traditional Russian Tale.* North-South Books, 1994. 28 pp. (ISBN 1-55858-329-7). Folktale (cumulative rhyme), P-E.

Story Review Chart

Setting	Plot/Events	Characters	Theme
•	•	•	•

Cultural Paradigm Reference Classification Chart

Geographic Location	Economic System	Social System	Political System
•		•	•

A fly finds a hut and makes it her home. Then a mouse comes along and moves in. A frog joins them and makes it a household of three. Then a duck arrives, followed by a rabbit. Soon a fox comes along, and then a pig. A wolf crowds into what little space remains. Then a bear tries to barge in, but there is no more room. The bear says he could live just fine on the roof. But the others are not so sure because of the bear's immense weight. Disregarding their concern, the bear plops down on the roof. And what do you think happens? Right, the hut collapses, but everyone gets out without a scratch.

Cumulative rhymes punctuate this comical tale with predictable sentence structure and story line. Watercolor illustrations reinforce the meaning of the text by showing that, as available space in the hut decreases, the size of each new occupant increases. Close scrutiny of the illustrations reveals that Lenin's portrait hangs in the house. When the house finally falls apart, Lenin's picture also breaks. This whimsical tale, therefore, could symbolically represent the fall of the former Soviet Union.

Classroom Applications

Students can try writing their own cumulative rhyming stories modeled after this one from Russia. They can also compare their cumulative rhymes to the Caribbean version of *The House That Jack Built* and to the familiar rhyme "I Know an Old Lady." Older students can discuss how this rhyme symbolizes in a lighthearted way what happened to Russia between its first and second revolutions (1918-1991).

Piumini, Roberto. *The Knot in the Tracks.* illustrated by Mikhail Fedorov, and translated from Italian by Olivia Holmes. Tambourine Books, 1994. 32 pp. (ISBN 0-688-11167-X). Fiction, E-M.

Story Review Chart

Setting	Plot/Events	Characters	Theme
•	•	•	•

Cultural Paradigm Reference Classification Chart

Geographic Location	Economic System	Social System	Political System
•		•	

Petrushka, a railroad worker, faithfully and carefully tends a desolate stretch of tracks of the Trans-Siberian Railroad. The only people he ever sees are passengers on the train that speeds by his hovel once every week. Besides being lonely, his job is made even more difficult by the harsh Siberian weather.

His job gets even harder when he checks the tracks one evening and finds them tied into a knot. Squatting beside the twisted track is a grotesque demon with huge hands and hairy ears. The demon calls himself Rashka, and he tells Petrushka that it was he who tied the rails into a knot. Petrushka pleads with the demon to untie the tracks so that the next train can pass by safely. Rashka agrees to do so only if Petrushka makes him some hot orange and mint tea. Having neither oranges nor mint, Petrushka has to walk for 3 days to a mountain valley where mint and oranges grow. He rushes back to the railroad track, brews the tea, and serves it to Rashka. Pleased with the tea, the demon unties the tracks with his magical powers. A few days later, Petrushka again finds the tracks knotted. This time, the demon demands 100 red stones as the price for untying the track. Petrushka has to journey for several days before finding the red stones. He races back just in time to give them to Rashka, who angrily finds that several are missing. Petrushka swears in the name of the saints that he brought back 100 stones. Fearful of what the saints might do to him, Rashka unties the tracks and searches for the missing stones himself. He finds them lying between the tracks, and just as he picks them up, the train runs him over. Needless to say, Petrushka is overjoyed with this fortunate turn of events; his problems are finally over.

This story tells of how trickery and supernatural powers are defeated by selfless, steadfast devotion to one's obligations and religious beliefs. The description of the Siberian wilderness provides a geographic context in which this story unfolds.

Stylistically rendered illustrations depict the desolate Siberian steppe and surrounding mountains. Also shown are Petrushka's simple clothing, his austere cottage, and a steam-powered train that has linked Siberia with European Russia for decades.

Classroom Application

The Circumbaikal Railway (formerly the Trans-Siberian Railroad) is known around the world. Drawing a map of Siberia and labeling the major cities along the railway and the distances between them will help students better appreciate the immensity of Russia, and Siberia in particular. Students can find out more about the Circumbaikal Railway on the Internet. They can also compare this railway with the one built in the United States in the late 1800s to connect cities on the east and west coasts and those in between.

 Ayres, Becky Hickox. *Matreshka*. illustrated by Alexi Natchev. Doubleday Books for Young Readers, 1992. 32 pp. (ISBN 0-385-30657-1). Fairytale, P-M.

Story Review Chart

Setting	Plot/Events	Characters	Theme
•	•	•	•

Cultural Paradigm Reference Classification Chart

Geographic Location	Economic System	Social System	Political System
•		•	

Kata lives with her grandfather in a Russian forest. On her way home from a village where she sells wooden bowels and spoons that her grandfather makes, Kata gives an elderly woman some of her food. To repay this kindness, the old woman gives Kata a wooden doll named Matreshka, which contains four other dolls, each nested inside the next larger one. Kata puts Matreshka into her apron pocket and continues home.

When a winter storm overtakes Kata, she heads toward a flickering light in the forest. There she sees a strange-looking house built on stilts shaped like chicken legs. Kata opens the wooden gate in the fence surrounding the house, walks up the stairs, and knocks on the door. Baba Yaga, an evil witch, invites Kata inside. She gives her some soup and locks her in a room. Baba Yaga then prepares the ingredients for a magic spell to turn Kata into a goose for dinner. Unable to escape from the locked room, Kata becomes frightened. The Matreshka doll calls out to Kata and offers to help her unlock the door. For each step of the escape from Baba Yaga's house, the next smaller doll helps Kata get past an obstacle. The last and smallest doll tricks Baba Yaga to say a magic spell that turns her into a harmless frog. Kata finally reaches home with her Matreshka doll, which she plays with and keeps in her pocket just in case.

Receiving particular attention in this story are social values: being kind to others, helping older family members with work, and good triumphing over evil. Also emerging from this story is the familiar message that good things sometimes come in small packages.

Brightly colored watercolor illustrations accentuate key events in the story through the marvelous facial expressions of the characters. Kata's cherub-like face and Baba Yaga's gnarled features vividly embody the images of good and evil.

Classroom Applications

Baba Yaga makes yet another appearance in this story. This time, however, she embodies evil and lacks redeeming qualities. Comparing the different ways Baba Yaga is portrayed in various Russian folktales (e.g., as a surrogate grandmother in *Babushka Baba*

Yaga, as a helpful witch in *Baba Yaga and Vasilisa the Brave*) may remind students that we should judge others on the basis of their individual characters and actions rather than on labels or names given to them. Can students recall other storybook characters that are good in some stories but just the opposite in others?

Nested dolls have long been associated with Russian folk art. Students can design on paper their own nested dolls and create stories to go along with them. Their stories can follow the Matreshka plot, in which overcoming each problem requires a smaller but no less determined doll.

 Gilchrist, Cherry, retold by. *Prince Ivan and the Firebird*. illustrated by Andrei Troshkov. Barefoot Books, 1994. 32 pp. (ISBN 1-56957-920-2). Fairytale, E-M.

Story Review Chart

Setting	Plot/Events	Characters	Theme
•	•	•	•

Cultural Paradigm Reference Classification Chart

Geographic Location	Economic System	Social System	Political System
•	•	•	

The story begins as King Vyslav discovers that someone has been stealing his prized golden apples. After all attempts to guard his apples prove ineffective, the king promises his kingdom to whichever of his sons can catch the thief. The oldest son, Prince Dmitri, is the first to try, but he falls asleep under the golden-apple tree. On awaking the next morning, he sees that more apples are missing. The king then bids his second oldest son, Prince Vassily, to stand guard by his precious tree. But he, too, falls asleep, and still more apples are missing.

With so few apples remaining, the king desperately summons his youngest son, Prince Ivan, and asks him to save what is left of his golden apples. Accepting the challenge, the young prince manages to remain awake to see a wondrous light emanating from the Firebird. He then sees the beautifully plumed bird pluck apples from the king's tree. Just as Ivan grasps the bird, it flies away, leaving him clutching a single tail feather. The next morning, Ivan tells his father that the Firebird has been stealing his apples and shows him the feather, which is so exquisite that the king wants the creature for himself. The two older princes, envious of Ivan's success, ride off in search of the Firebird. Ivan, wanting to prove his mettle, pleads with his father for permission to seek out the Firebird. Although fearful that harm may come to Ivan, the king reluctantly acquiesces to his youngest son's request.

Soon after beginning his quest, Ivan encounters a large gray wolf that agrees to take him to the walled palace of King Dolmat, who keeps the Firebird in a golden cage. The wolf warns Ivan to take only the bird and to leave the golden cage; otherwise, he will not return alive. Ivan disregards the wolf's warning and is captured. King Dolmat tells Ivan that, to avoid being executed, he must bring him the Horse With the Golden

Mane, for which he will give Ivan the Firebird. The wolf next takes the young prince to the kingdom of King Afron, the owner of the Horse With the Golden Mane. Once again, Ivan ignores the wolf's advice on how to steal the horse and is captured. King Afron offers Ivan his freedom and the horse if he brings him Princess Helen the Fair. This time, the wolf itself seizes the princess as she walks through a garden. On the trip back to King Afron's kingdom, Ivan and the princess fall in love. When Ivan laments that he cannot give up his new love, the wolf magically transforms himself into a likeness of the princess, whom Ivan then gives to King Afron and receives the horse and a pardon in return. After escaping from the king, the wolf rejoins Ivan and the princess. Now Ivan cannot part with the horse, and so the wolf changes into a likeness of the horse, which Ivan presents to the king in exchange for the Firebird and his life.

Ivan has nearly accomplished his quest and much more: He has not only the Firebird to give to his father but also the love of Princess Helen and the Horse With the Golden Mane. Having returned to where they first met in the forest, Ivan and the wolf say good-bye to each other. Ivan's two older brothers, returning home dejected and empty-handed, find their younger brother asleep in the forest. When they see that he has the Firebird, a lovely princess, and a magnificent horse, they brutally kill him out of resentment and jealousy. They then divide up the spoils of their treacherous deed and return home.

Days later, the wolf comes upon Ivan's corpse. To bring him back to life, the wolf forces a raven to bring him the waters of life and death. After sprinkling these magical waters over Ivan's remains, Ivan comes back to life. Quickly, he rushes home just in time to prevent his brother Prince Vassily from marrying Princess Helen. When King Vyslav learns from the princess what his two oldest sons did to Ivan, he has both of them condemned to a dungeon for the rest of their lives. Ivan marries his beloved Princess Helen and regains the Horse With the Golden Mane. The king, of course, at long last has his prize possession, the Firebird.

Father-son and sibling relationships, loyalty, personal growth through experience, and making hard choices imbue this story of the Firebird with strong social messages. Also present are economic themes: coveting valuable things and obtaining them by any means possible—barter, theft, and even murder.

Striking illustrations create exotic, romanticized settings in which color, composition, and style are preeminent. They not only enliven the printed words of the story but also stir the imagination of the reader.

Classroom Applications

There are numerous versions of the folktale about the firebird and Prince Ivan (e.g., *Firebird*, by R. Isadora; *Firebird: A Russian Folktale*, by Demi; *Prince Ivan and the Firebird*, by B. Lodge). After reading these folktales, students can compare them with respect to their overall plots, key events, character development, supporting characters, and underlying themes. The firebird and Prince Ivan stories can serve as a fitting entry into the realm of symbols and symbolism. First, use familiar symbols, such as the flag of the United States and logos on clothing, to introduce students to the concept of *symbolism*. Have students find other symbols and tell the class what they believe each symbol means or stands for. Next, students can think about what the firebird symbolically represents, as well as the quest that Ivan undertakes to find, capture, and save or free the firebird. Look for other books laden with symbolism for students to explore.

 Kendall, Russ. *Russian Girl: Life in an Old Russian Town.* Scholastic, 1994. 40 pp. (ISBN 0-590-45789-6). Photo Essay, E-M.

Story Review Chart

Setting	Plot/Events	Characters	Theme
•	•	•	

Cultural Paradigm Reference Classification Chart

Geographic Location	Economic System	Social System	Political System
•	•	•	

This book takes the reader on a journey with Olga Surikova, a 9-year-old girl who lives in an old Russian town called Suzdal. The itinerary begins by meeting Olga's immediate family: her mother, father, and older brother. The next stop is a history and geography lesson of Suzdal and central Russia. Olga then takes the reader to her school, where she studies Russian, English, mathematics, and other courses. After school, Olga and her brother Ivan visit their *babushka's* ("grandmother's") farm and help out with the chores. Additional stops include their father's woodshop and mother's nursing practice at home, a Russian Orthodox Church, a monastery, playing in the winter snow, and a birthday party at home. The book ends with recipes for two popular Russian dishes, an introduction to the Cyrillic alphabet and common Russian words, and a historical summary of Suzdal, Russia, and Russian culture and people.

This books weaves various geographic, social, and economic elements to tell about contemporary life in a small Russian city.

Photographs capture much of the essence of Russia, its people, and their culture. The scenes photographed typically show people, places, and events in realistic and informative settings.

Classroom Applications

Ask the class, How does Olga's life compare with yours? Students should find many similarities: She goes to school, has a family, and has a loose tooth. Students can describe what their day is like and compare it with Olga's. Using Venn diagrams, they can also note similarities, such as daily meals, as well as some subtle and not so subtle differences, such as favorite foods and language.

 Langton, Jane, retold by. *Salt: A Russian Folktale.* illustrated by Ilse Plume. Hyperion, 1992. 42 pages. (ISBN 1-56282-681-6). Folktale, E-M.

Story Review Chart

Setting	Plot/Events	Characters	Theme
•	•	•	•

Cultural Paradigm Reference Classification Chart

Geographic Location	Economic System	Social System	Political System
•	•	•	•

In this Russian folktale about a wealthy merchant and his three sons, Fyodor and Vasily, the two oldest sons, are clever, confident, and favored by their father. The youngest son is called Ivan the Fool because he continually asks silly questions.

Wishing to increase his wealth, the merchant loads two of his large, fast-sailing ships with valuable cargo. He then gives Fyodor and Vasily each one of these ships and tells them to sail to distant lands, sell the cargo, and bring back gold, silver, and jewels. Watching his older brothers depart motivates Ivan to want a chance to prove himself too. So he asks his father for a ship loaded with cargo to sell. At first, his father believes that Ivan is too foolish to be trusted with so much responsibility. But after pleading with his father, Ivan gets a small ship filled only with wooden spoons. Ivan proudly sails off to find customers for his modest cargo and answers to his "silly" questions.

Ivan encounters a severe storm but manages to sail his ship to the safety of an island. There he discovers salt and wisely replaces his cargo of spoons with it. He then sails on to the port ruled by a wealthy czar and falls in love with his daughter Marushka. She is very thin, weak, and sad because she finds the tasteless food prepared by the cooks inedible. Ivan, knowing that salt can make food taste better, shows the czar the flavor-enhancing crystals. The czar is not very interested, however, because the salt looks just like sand, which is everywhere in his kingdom. Consequently, the czar disparages Ivan's offer by saying, "Who would want to buy more?"

Fulfilling his obligations as host, the czar invites Ivan to dinner. This gives Ivan a chance to go to the kitchen and prove the value of salt by adding it to the soup. When Marushka sips her salted soup, she miraculously becomes well. Seeing his daughter's restored appetite, the czar offers Ivan gold, silver, and jewels for saving his daughter from starvation and for the salt. Ivan requests Marushka's hand in marriage, and she desires to marry him as well. The czar agrees to their marriage, and the couple set sail for Ivan's home.

During the long journey, Ivan and Marushka encounter his brothers, Fyodor and Vasily. They lost their cargo, and their ships are slowly sinking. Both brothers and their crews scramble aboard Ivan's ship. When they learn of Ivan's good fortune, they angrily throw Ivan overboard, lock Marushka in her cabin, and divide Ivan's hard-earned treasure between them. They get more than they bargained for, however, when Marushka's sadness over Ivan's apparent death produces a spate of tears that gradually fills the ship, threatening to sink it. While the two brothers fight over what to throw overboard to keep the ship afloat, the crew tosses all the treasure into the sea.

In the interim, Ivan manages to reach an island, where he finds a giant. Although greatly outsized, Ivan outwits the giant, who agrees to carry him home. When Ivan finally arrives home, he confronts his brothers and marries his beloved Marushka. Although Ivan has no treasure to prove his worthiness, he does know the whereabouts of an island of salt. Hearing this, Ivan's father now calls his youngest son Clever Ivan because salt is worth more than gold.

The recurring theme of sibling rivalry appears in this story from old Russia. In particular, the story examines how brothers should treat one another and what happens when those obligations are violated. The plot and character development also explore the notion of the unlikely hero whose mental strengths overcome risks and dangers to achieve deserved rewards.

Framed with a golden scrolled border, colored-pencil drawings resemble religious icons characteristic of the Russian Orthodox Church. The stylized rendering of decorative motifs, clothing, and architecture re-creates a time and place reminiscent of medieval Russia.

Classroom Applications

Sibling rivalry is a recurring theme in children's stories set in Russia (e.g., *Tsar Saltan, Baba Yaga and Vasilisa the Brave, Prince Ivan and the Firebird*). See whether students can explain, on the basis of these stories, why brothers or sisters compete against, fight with, and perhaps even hurt one another. Can students think of ways that siblings might settle disagreements more peacefully, avoid fighting, and help each other more?

Common table salt is one of those substances that humans everywhere and from prehistoric times to the present have come to depend on. Students can investigate what salt is, where it is found naturally, why human blood and the sea are salty, and how people around the world obtain and use salt. Problems associated with salt offer yet another set of questions for students to ponder. For example, What impact does too little or too much salt have on human health? How does salt impair the quality of soil and water? and Why does salt damage roads and cars?

 Pushkin, Alexander. *The Tale of Tsar Saltan.* illustrated by Gennady Spirin. Dial Books for Young Readers, 1996. 28 pp. (ISBN 0-8037-2001-7). Fairytale, E-M.

Story Review Chart			
Setting	Plot/Events	Characters	Theme
•	•	•	•

Cultural Paradigm Reference Classification Chart			
Geographic Location	Economic System	Social System	Political System
•	•	•	•

Tsar Saltan takes the hand of the youngest of three sisters in marriage. Although the two older sisters are invited to live with the couple, they are still terribly jealous of their sister, the new tsarina. Adding to their jealously is the couple's genuine happiness and news of their child-to-be.

The marriage takes a turn for the worst, however, when the tsar goes with his men to fight a war. The tsarina is left alone with her two older sisters. They become enraged when their younger sister has a son, who will one day be tsar. With the help of their cousin, the two conniving sisters plot to do away with the tsarina and the young prince. They begin by intercepting the tsar's and tsarina's communications. They then rewrite one of the tsar's messages into an order to his knights to kill his wife and child. The knights, weeping at the prospect of having to kill their beloved tsarina, nonetheless seal the tsarina and young prince in a barrel and cast them into the sea.

Instead of meeting a dismal fate at the bottom of the ocean, the tsarina and her son wash ashore on a deserted island. A magical swan rescues them and years later builds a beautiful new kingdom for the now grown-up prince, Sarevitch, to reign over. All is well until a ship is blown off course and lands on the shores of Sarevitch's kingdom. The prince, hearing about his father's kingdom from the shipwrecked crew, wants to return with them to see it. But to do so, the magical swan first turns the prince into an insect.

The prince, disguised as an insect, returns to his father's kingdom aboard a ship. The ship's crew tells the tsar and his court about the new kingdom. The tsar, still believing that his wife and child are dead, wishes to visit the new kingdom. The conniving sisters, however, dissuade him from going.

When the prince returns to his kingdom, he asks the swan to help him. The swan grants him three wishes, the third of which is for a beautiful princess who turns out to be the swan itself. Meanwhile, the king, after hearing more about the new kingdom, finally sails to the new kingdom. There he finds his beloved wife, long-lost son, and new daughter-in-law. The king remains in the new kingdom and lives happily with his family once again. Although his wife's two sisters are forgiven, their evil deeds are not forgotten, and so the two sisters are forbidden to enter the new kingdom.

This happy-ever-after story highlights the social component of the cultural paradigm. As in other similar tales from Russia and elsewhere, jealousy and greed motivate older siblings to conspire against and harm their younger perceived rival. In the end, however, good and justice prevail, with the youngest rewarded with love, status, and wealth.

Elegant watercolor illustrations help the reader connect with the characters in this story of sibling rivalry, treachery, love, and the triumph of good over evil.

Classroom Applications

Planning and creating imaginary "worlds" is a common childhood experience. Students can pretend they have discovered an uninhabited island where they can create an island nation. Divide the class into several small groups. After drawing a map of the island, each group can decide where to put physical structures, such as buildings, streets, airport, and harbor. Each group also can decide what to call their new nation, what kind of government to set up, how people on the island will make a living, and many other major and minor details. Each group can showcase its nation before students in other classes. Students can pick which island nation they would prefer to visit and on which island they would like to live.

Milhous, Katherine, and Dalgliesh, Alice, collected for Once Upon a Time (Charles Scribner's Sons, 1938). *The Turnip*. illustrated by Pierr Morgan. Paper Star, 1990. 32 pp. (ISBN 0-698-11426-4). Folktale, P-E.

Story Review Chart

Setting	Plot/Events	Characters	Theme
•	•	•	•

Cultural Paradigm Reference Classification Chart

Geographic Location	Economic System	Social System	Political System
•	•	•	

In the tradition of "Jack and the Bean Stalk," Dedoushka plants a turnip seed and waits for it to grow. The result is much more than he expects—so much more, in fact, that he is unable to pull the huge turnip from the ground despite all effort. He then asks his wife, Baboushka, for help. With all their strength, she pulls on him and he pulls on the stubborn turnip, but it won't budge. So they call their granddaughter Mashenka for more help. All three pull with all their strength but still cannot wrest the turnip from the ground. Next, they call on the dog Geouchka for an extra tug. Despite their strenuous struggle to uproot the giant turnip, it holds tenaciously to the earth. Becoming increasingly exasperated, they ask the cat Keska for its help, but to no avail. Finally, they enlist the help of a tiny field mouse. At last, all six working as one manage to extract the gigantic turnip from the soil, and so into a pot of boiling water it goes.

For most of its 1,000-year history, Russia has been a land of peasants who toil on countless small farms. This story paints their exhausting and hard life in a lighthearted manner. Implicit in the story, however, is the importance of teamwork and cooperation in which even the smallest contribution can make the difference between success and failure.

Colorful cartoon-like drawings highlight the engaging actions of the characters and show traditional clothing of the Russian peasants and evocative images of a former agrarian life.

Classroom Applications

Working with others to solve problems is a strategy that everyone needs to learn and strengthen. Use this story about a stubborn turnip to entice students to undertake a fun cooperative problem-solving activity. Divide the class into small groups. Give each group a turnip (or comparable object) that they must do something to by using only certain tools and materials (e.g., move a turnip from one box to another without touching it with their hands). In a similar activity, students can recall problems they and other members of their families or friends solved by working together. They then can go on to describe those problems, explain how they solved them, and tell why working together is a good way to solve problems.

This humorous turnip story can also lead to a study of gardening. If an agricultural cooperative extension office or garden club is nearby, ask a representative to come to class and talk about the basics of gardening (e.g., preparing the soil, planting seeds, controlling weeds and insect pests).

Ukraine

The Ukraine is located in southeastern Europe and is surrounded by Romania, Slovakia, and Poland on the west, Belorussia on the north, and the Russian Federation on the east.

 Czernecki, Stefan, and Rhodes, Timothy. *Nina's Treasures*. illustrated by Stefan Czernecki. Hyperion, 1990. 40 pp. (ISBN 1-56282-487-2). Fiction, E-M.

Story Review Chart

Setting	Plot/Events	Characters	Theme
•	•	•	•

Cultural Paradigm Reference Classification Chart

Geographic Location	Economic System	Social System	Political System
•	•	•	

In this Ukrainian folktale, a woman named Katerina lives with her chicken, Nina, in a cottage near the village of Zelena. Surrounding her modest home is a large garden where she grows vegetables and flowers of almost every kind. Her favorite flowers are poppies because she uses their black seeds to decorate the delicious breads and cakes she bakes for the spring festival. Every Saturday, Katerina goes to the village to trade her flowers and Nina's eggs for flour, sausages, cream, and honey and for cornmeal for Nina to eat during the long, cold winter.

When summer wanes and the chill of fall arrives, Katerina harvests the fruits, vegetables, and flower seeds in her garden. She puts the seeds in a safe place so that she will have them to plant next spring. Nina, unconcerned with having enough to last her until spring, eats all the seeds she can find in the garden. During the winter, Nina lays eggs and Katerina uses them in the breads, cakes, and cookies she bakes for the villagers. Eventually, the flour runs out, and Katerina has to use cornmeal for her baking. Because the winter is colder and longer than usual, the cornmeal also runs out. With nothing to eat, Nina becomes so thin that Katerina must give her for food the seeds set aside for spring planting.

When spring finally arrives, however, no seeds are left for planting a new garden and Katerina has no money for buying more food. Nina, regretting that she ate so much seed during the fall, tries to make amends. So one night Nina lays eggs that are painted with beautifully colored flowers. The next day, Katerina takes these eggs to the village and trades them for everything she and Nina need. Although neither Nina nor any other hen in the village would ever lay such gorgeous eggs again, the grandmothers of Zelena paint colorful flowers on eggs before the spring festival every year thereafter.

Brightly colored and stylized floral designs appear in every illustration and help create an imaginative and cheerful backdrop.

Classroom Applications

Ukrainian egg painting (*pysanky*) has long been admired by people from all over the world. Students can study Ukrainian folk art and then try their own egg paintings. The finished products can be made into mobiles for display in the classroom.

"I should have!" is a common refrain of self-criticism. Similarly, we tend to do what leads to quick and easy short-term gain, rather than what may seem harder but in the long term proves much more beneficial. Students can dictate or write about those situations when they failed to do something that, in hindsight, they should have. Can they also come up with some rules of thumb, on the basis of these experiences, for helping them decide more wisely what they should or should not do?

Yugoslavia (former)

The former Yugoslavia was located in south central Europe and bordered by the Adriatic Sea and Italy on the west, Austria and Hungary on the north, Romania and Bulgaria on the east, and Albania and Greece on the south.

 UNICEF. I *Dream of Peace: Images of War by Children of Former Yugoslavia.* HarperCollins, 1994. 80 pp. (ISBN 0-06-251128-9). Contemporary Children's Essays and Poems, M-L.

Story Review Chart			
Setting	Plot/Events	Characters	Theme
•	•	•	•

Cultural Paradigm Reference Classification Chart			
Geographic Location	Economic System	Social System	Political System
•	•	•	•

This book is a collection of writings and drawings by children who tell about their personal experiences with the brutality and devastation caused by the recent civil war in the former Yugoslavia. Their eloquent words and poignant drawings bear witness to their fears, lost innocence, and suffering. But their resiliency is also evident as they hope for a future free of war.

This book dramatically shows the tragic consequences of war as it tears asunder the social fabric of a society: Neighbors become enemies, families are torn apart by hatred and prejudice, and the most vulnerable become helpless victims.

Children's drawings and photographs provide powerful and memorable testimony of the horrendous agony and destruction wrought by war.

Classroom Applications

Students can discuss their views about civil strife and how they can help prevent children like themselves from becoming victims of war. One such strategy is to develop a class Web page that invites children from around the world to express their concerns and ideas.

SUMMARY

A review of the variety of children's books about countries of Eastern Europe reveals some key patterns. Most stories reviewed have well-defined plot/events and well-developed characters. Stories with a discernable theme are somewhat less common, as are stories in which the setting plays a key role. One common theme in these books centers on a hero of worthy moral character who goes on a quest and relies on bravery, initiative, intellect, and special help to overcome dangers or evil or both and is rewarded with status, wealth, enlightenment, and personal contentment. Admiration of the hero or heroine might be surprising, given 50 years of totalitarian rule in Eastern Europe, where individual greatness was frowned on if it did not directly and primarily benefit the well-being of the nation. Many of the hero/quest stories reviewed (particularly those set in Russia), however, are based on mythic heroes, indicating that the heroic ideal endured and continued to be valued for its own sake despite efforts by the state to promote the welfare of society at the expense of the aspirations and needs of the individual. A profound shift in focus from the collective to the individual, however, is well under way in many Eastern European countries. The educational system in the Russian Federation, for example, is undergoing a fundamental change in which an ideological, highly bureaucratic system is giving way to "an openly child-centered view of teaching and learning" (Pratt, 1996, p. 26).

In terms of the transcultural paradigm, the social component is the most prevalent and well developed aspect of books associated with Eastern Europe. Particularly evident are the relationships between children and other family members, including grandparents. Geographic location comes in a close second, with the events of a story often unfolding in a forest, rural village, or city. Economic issues generally play a minor role and are usually limited to the hardships of poverty and economic transactions involving simple barter. The notion of wealth, its benefits and acquisition, appears occasionally. Political themes likewise surface infrequently, but when they do, they usually involve benevolent rulers (kings, tsars, princes, princesses). Although too few books are available from which to form definitive conclusions, books with events set in the Czech Republic, Poland, or the former Yugoslavia seem to stress crucial political and moral issues that stem from relatively recent historic events (anti-Semitism, World War II, the Holocaust, and civil war stemming from ethnic hatred).

In addition to including a representative sample of children's books from the eastern regions of Europe, one would be wise to set aside plenty of space for books yet to be published that will go beyond the rich folktale tradition. Further developments in Russia, Poland, Hungary, the Czech Republic, and the rest of Eastern Europe are likely to lead to changes in the nature of children's literature associated with these countries. As has happened in the United States and elsewhere, more authors will write and publish more children's books about contemporary themes.

REFERENCES CITED
▼▼

Pratt, L. (1996). Dialogues about literacy education in Russia. *Language and Literacy Spectrum, 6,* 23-26.

SUGGESTED REFERENCES
▼▼

Baloghova, M. (1995). Milan Rufu's little prayers. *Bookbird, 33*(1), 37-38. (Slovenia)

Creuziger, C. (1996). *Childhood in Russia: Representation and reality.* Lanham, MD: University Press of America. (Russia)

DeCoker, G., et al. (1993). Teaching about the former Soviet Union: Activities and resources. *Social Studies and the Young Learner, 5*(4), 1-4. (Soviet Union)

Eklof, B. (1986). *Russian peasant schools officialdom, village culture, and popular pedagogy, 1861–1914.* Berkeley: University of California Press. (Russia)

Elkonin, D. E. (1988). *Further remarks on the psychology bases of the initial teaching of reading.* North-Holland: Elsevier Science. (General)

Hutarova, I. (1995-96). Suk's library of children's literature. *Bookbird, 33*(3-4), 97-98. (Czech Republic)

Immroth, B. (1990). A U.S.-U.S.S.R. colloquium on library service to children. *Journal of Youth Services in Libraries, 3*(3), 209-218. (General)

Jaquelska, J., & Niedziela, S. (1995-96). In Warsaw and in Auschwitz: Children's books helping to build the future. *Bookbird, 33*(3-4), 94-96. (Poland)

Komaromi, G., & Rigo, B. (1994). Hungary. *Bookbird, 32*(4), 51-54. (Hungary)

Long, R. (1984). Soviet children's books: Expanding children's views of the Soviet Union. *Journal of Reading. 27*(5), 418-422. (Russian Federation)

Mahony, A. (1997, May). 1997 Caldecott Medal winner: David Wisniewski. *Booklinks.* (Poland)

Mazi-Leskovar, D. (1997). Charlie needs a cloak: The viewer and the reader. *Bookbird, 35*(1), 34-36. (Slovakia)

McEneaney, J. E. (1997). Teaching them to read Russian: Four hundred years of the Russian *bukvar. Reading Teacher, 51*(3), 210-226. (Russia)

Opravilova, E. (1989). Books as educational media for small children in Czechoslovakia. *Early Child Development and Care, 48,* 67-73. (former Czechoslovakia)

Povsic, F. F. (1981). Non-Russian tales from the Soviet Union. *Reading Teacher, 35*(2), 196-202. (Soviet republics)

Povsic, F. F. (1981). Russian folk and animal tales. *Reading Teacher, 35*(3), 329-343. (Russia)

Povsic, F. F. (1982). Hungary: Children's fiction in English. *Reading Teacher, 35*(7), 820-828. (Hungary)

Povsic, F. F. (1982). Russia: Children's fiction in English for elementary school children. *Reading Teacher, 35*(4), 466-474. (Russia)

Prosalkova, J. (1997). Bits and pieces about 20th-century Russian science fiction. *Bookbird, 35*(4), 22-25. (Russia)

Rearick, W. D. (1982). How Bulgaria views and promotes children's literature. *Reading Teacher, 35*(5), 538-543. (Bulgaria)

Rutkiewicz, E. (1997). Decorative art for children: Polish school of illustrations. *Bookbird, 35*(1), 32-34. (Poland)

Stevkova, M. (1989). Co-publishing illustrated children's books in the socialist countries. *Early Child Development and Care, 48,* 75-77. (Soviet republics)

Swierczynska-Jelonek, D. (1995–96). Other voices: What Polish children actually read. *Bookbird, 33*(3/4), 45-46. (Poland)

Zilkova, M. (1995–96). In defense of "bad" books: A view from Slovakia. *Bookbird, 33*(3/4), 40-44. (Slovakia)

CHILDREN'S BOOKS CITED

▼▼

Arnold, K. (1994). *Knock, knock, terenok: A traditional Russian tale*. New York: North-South Books. (Russia)

Ayers, B. H. (1992). *Matreshka*. New York: Doubleday Books for Young Readers. (Russia)

Chekhov, A. (1994). *Kashtanka* (R. Meyer, Trans.). New York: Gulliver Books. (Russia)

Czernecki, S., & Rhodes, T. (1990). *Nina's treasures*. New York: Hyperion. (Ukraine)

Gilchrist, C. (1994). *Prince Ivan and the firebird*. Boston: Barefoot Books. (Russia)

Hooper, M. B. (1994). *The Christmas drum*. Honesdale, PA: Boyds Mills Press. (Romania)

Isadora, R. (1994). *Firebird*. New York: Putnam. (Russia)

Kendall, R. (1994). *Russian girl: Life in an old Russian town*. New York: Scholastic. (Russia)

Kimmel, E. A. (1991). *Bearhead: A Russian folktale*. New York: Holiday House. (Russia)

Langton, J. (1992). *Salt: A Russian folktale*. New York: Hyperion. (Russia)

Matthews, W. (1995). *The gift of a traveler*. New York: BridgeWater Press. (Romania)

Mayer, M. (1994). *Baba Yaga and Vasilisa the brave*. New York: Morrow Junior Books. (Russia)

Milhous, K., & Dalgliesh, A. (1990). *The turnip*. New York: Paper Star. (Russia)

Nerlove, M. (1996). *Flowers on the wall*. New York: Margaret K. McElderry Books. (Poland)

Piumini, R. (1994). *The knot in the tracks* (O. Holmes, Trans.). New York: Tambourine Books. (Russia)

Polacco, P. (1990). *Babushka's doll*. New York: Simon & Schuster Books for Young Readers. (Russia)

Polacco, P. (1993). *Babushka Baba Yaga*. New York: Philomel. (Russia)

Pushkin, A. (1996). *The tale of Tsar Saltan*. New York: Dial Books for Young Readers. (Russia)

Silverman, E. (1996). *Gittel's hands*. New York: BridgeWater Press. (Romania)

Sis, P. (1994). *The three golden keys*. New York: Doubleday Books for Young Readers. (Czech Republic)

Trivas, I. (1992). *Annie . . . Anya: A month in Moscow*. New York: Orchard Books. (Russia)

UNICEF. (1994). *I dream of peace: Images of war by children of former Yugoslavia*. New York: HarperCollins. (former Yugoslavia)

Wild, M. (1991). *Let the celebrations begin!* New York: Orchard Books. (Poland)

Wisniewski, D. (1996). *Golem*. New York: Clarion Books. (Czech Republic)

SUGGESTED CHILDREN'S BOOKS

▼▼

Arnold, K. (1994). *Baba Yaga and the little girl*. New York: North-South Books. (Russia)

Arnold, K. (1996). *Baba Yaga: A Russian folktale*. New York: North-South Books. (Russia)

Demi. (1994). *Firebird: A Russian folktale*. New York: Henry Holt. (Russia)

Falk, B. B. (1993). *Grusha*. New York: HarperCollins. (Russia)

Gabler, M. (1994). *Tall, Wide, and Sharp-Eye: A Czech folktale*. New York: Henry Holt. (Czech Republic)

Gliori, D. (1994). *Snow child*. New York: Scholastic. (Russia)

Jaffe, N. (1992). *In the month of Kislev: A story for Hanukkah*. New York: Viking Children's Books. (Poland)

Kimmel, E. A. (1993). *Baba Yaga: A Russian folktale*. New York: Holiday House. (Russia)

Kimmel, E. A. (1994). *I-know-not-what, I-know-not-where: A Russian tale*. New York: Holiday House. (Russia)

Lodge, B. (1993). *Prince Ivan and the firebird: A Russian folktale*. Dallas, TX: Whispering Coyote Press. (Russia)

Matas, C. (1993). *Daniel's story*. New York: Scholastic. (Russia)

Mochizuki, K. (1997). *Passage to freedom: The Sugihara story*. New York: Lee & Low Books. (Lithuania)

Moroney, L. (1990). *Elinda who danced in the sky: An Eastern European folktale from Estonia*. San Francisco: Children's Book Press. (Estonia)

Obermon, S. (1993). *The always prayer shawl*. Honesdale, PA: Boyds Mills Press. (Russia)

Philemon, S., & Vijtech, A. (1996). *Marushka and the Month brothers*. New York: North-South Books. (Russia)

Rael, E. O. (1993). *Marushka's egg*. New York: Macmillan Children's Books. (Russia)

Shepard, A. (1997). *The sea king's daughter: A Russian legend*. New York: Atheneum Books for Young Readers. (Russia)

Ushinsky, K. (1992). *How a shirt grew in the field*. New York: Clarion Books. (Russia)

Werner, V. (1992). *Petrouchka*. New York: Viking Children's Books. (Russia)

Winthrop, E. (1994). *Vaslissa the beautiful*. New York: HarperCollins. (Russia)

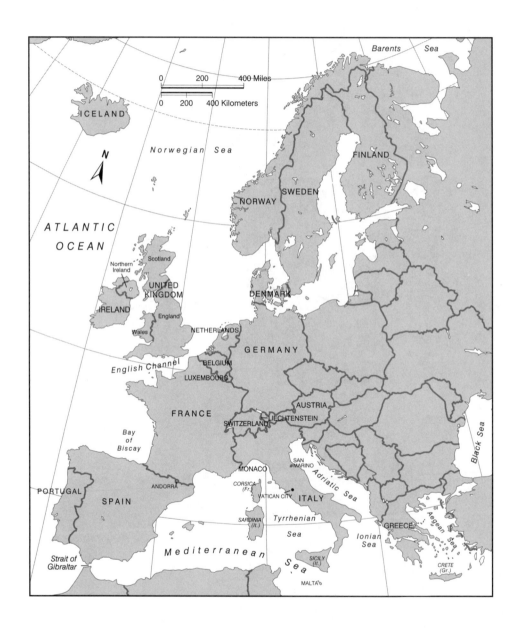

ICELAND

Barents Sea

Norwegian Sea

FINLAND

SWEDEN

NORWAY

ATLANTIC
OCEAN

Scotland

Northern
Ireland

UNITED
KINGDOM

IRELAND

England

Wales

DENMARK

NETHERLANDS

English Channel

GERMANY

BELGIUM

LUXEMBOURG

FRANCE

AUSTRIA

LIECHTENSTEIN

SWITZERLAND

Bay
of
Biscay

Black Sea

MONACO

SAN
MARINO

Adriatic Sea

PORTUGAL

SPAIN

ANDORRA

CORSICA
(Fr.)

VATICAN CITY

ITALY

Aegean Sea

GREECE

SARDINIA
(It.)

Tyrrhenian

Sea

Ionian
Sea

Mediterranean

Sea

SICILY
(It.)

CRETE
(Gr.)

Strait of
Gibraltar

MALTA

N

0   200   400 Miles

0   200   400 Kilometers

8

Children's Books About Western Europe

WESTERN EUROPE

Western Europe occupies the western half of continental Europe and the islands of the United Kingdom and Ireland. It is bordered on the east by Russia, Poland, Czech Republic, Slovakia, Hungary, Slovenia, Croatia, Bosnia, and Albania; on the west by the Norwegian Sea and Atlantic Ocean; on the north by the Arctic Ocean; and on the south by the Mediterranean Sea.

Countries

Austria, Belgium, Denmark, England, Finland, France, Germany, Greece, Iceland, Ireland, Italy, Liechtenstein, Luxembourg, Monaco, the Netherlands, Northern Ireland, Norway, Portugal, Scotland, Spain, Sweden, Switzerland, Wales

EXAMINING THE CULTURAL REGION OF WESTERN EUROPE AND THE PATTERNS OF CHILDREN'S BOOKS

The countries of Western Europe tend to be familiar to Americans. The ancestors of many Americans migrated from Western Europe; thus, Americans still have ties to the people there and may even exchange visits with them. English is spoken by many of the people; thus, one might expect to encounter numerous children's books written in English to be published in these countries. Child rearing in Western European cultures seems similar to our own; thus, one might also expect their children's literature to feature topics and subject treatment similar to those in our own books.

When we examine Western European children's literature, however, we are surprised to find that this is not necessarily the case. Child rearing, even in England, is different from that in the United States (as discussed in Avery's "Two Patterns of Childhood," 1984), producing youngsters with very different attitudes and behaviors, especially toward adults. The independence of American youngsters often contrasts with the obedience and respect of European children. Storybooks and picture books for children reflect this difference; few of them feature such topics as "self-concept" or "feelings" or "inner-city conflicts." Instead, with the exception of books from England published for the U.S. market, most children's books in Western Europe reflect each country's unique culture, folklore, and history.

Many European book illustrations, too, reflect a different purpose from those in American books—not so much for appealing to young children's sensibilities as to expressing artistically the illustrators' feeling for the subject. Whereas many American artists approach their book illustrations from a child's point of view, many European artists approach from their own perspective.

Some books reviewed in this chapter are clearly European in their composition and treatment of the subject. Others are more obviously American: set in European countries but by American authors and artists. Can you tell the difference? Let your students help you discover the differences and similarities in Western European books as they enjoy these exciting new additions to the world of children's literature.

COUNTRIES AND CHILDREN'S BOOKS REVIEWED

Austria

Austria is located in the eastern part of Western Europe, landlocked by Italy, Switzerland, Germany, the Czech Republic, Slovakia, and Hungary.

 Nichol, Barbara. *Beethoven Lives Upstairs.* illustrated by Scott Cameron. Orchard Books, 1993. 48 pp. (ISBN 0-531-06828-5). Historical Fiction, M-L.[1]

---

[1]A = all ages, P = preschool, E = early elementary, M = middle elementary, L = late elementary

Story Review Chart

Setting	Plot/Events	Characters	Theme
•		•	

Cultural Paradigm Reference Classification Chart

Geographic Location	Economic System	Social System	Political System
		•	•

Ten-year-old Christoph writes to his uncle from Vienna in 1822 that a madman has moved in upstairs. Thus begins a fascinating 3-year correspondence between Christoph and his uncle Karl about Ludwig van Beethoven, deaf musical genius but eccentric tenant. Christoph's father has recently died, and his mother has rented out

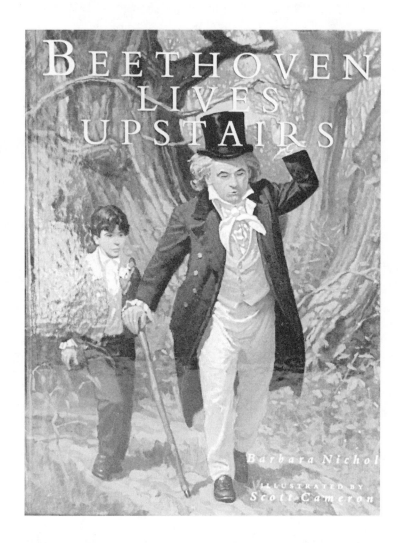

From BEETHOVEN LIVES UPSTAIRS by Barbara Nichol, illustrated by Scott Cameron. Jacket Illustration © 1993 by Scott Cameron. Reprinted by permission of Orchard Books, New York.

the upstairs flat to Beethoven. Christoph describes true incidents from Beethoven's life in this fictitious correspondence, telling how he takes off the legs of his piano and sits on the floor to play so that he can feel the music; or pours water on his head as he stamps his feet as if he were marching.

The uncle explains to the boy that Beethoven is working on a symphony and so hears music in his head all day long. Beethoven nicknames Christoph "The Gatekeeper" for his habit of sitting on the doorstep, and gives him two tickets for the performance of his new Ninth Symphony, "Ode to Joy." Christoph is surprised by the music and wonders how a man so troubled and tempestuous could have a heart so full of joy.

Nichol is also the author of the award-winning cassette/CD *Beethoven Lives Upstairs* (see Appendix B). Cameron's full-page oil paintings on every other page showing the boy and the master in 19th-century Vienna are reminiscent of N. C. Wyeth's, one of his favorite turn-of-the-century illustrators; they give the correspondence a wonderful 19th-century air full of the gloominess of candlelit rooms, as well as the brilliant pomp of Vienna street scenes.

Sensitive students may discover how much more formal are interpersonal relationships between mother and son, boy and uncle, boy and Beethoven, and how respect for a great artist crosses all social lines, even those of royalty.

Classroom Applications

Your students may want to choose cultural heroes of their own and write letters describing make-believe visits of the heroes to their own homes. They will surely want to hear a recording of Beethoven's Ninth Symphony that was written in Christoph's house.

 Varvasovszky, Lasio. *Henry in Shadowland*. translated by David R. Godine. David Godine, 1990. 16 pp. (ISBN 0-87923-785-6). Contemporary Fiction, E-M.

Story Review Chart

Setting	Plot/Events	Characters	Theme
•		•	

Cultural Paradigm Reference Classification Chart

Geographic Location	Economic System	Social System	Political System
		•	•

Black paper cutouts of a dragon and a princess lure Henry into a fanciful world of pretend: a child's shadow theater inside a shadowbox, a toy unfamiliar to most American children. Henry has been helping his mother's friend Paul cut out little figures from black paper and mount them on toothpick holders and then watching Paul strut their shadows across a back-lit sheet of white paper inside the shadowbox theater.

Suddenly, Henry finds himself stepping into the shadowbox and interacting with life-size shadow figures. Is it a dream? Henry gives Princess Gundi his sweater so that he can see her better but ends up painting Firetooth the Dragon every color in his paint box. Firetooth tells him the story of how everything in Shadowland came to be black when Mr. Light overslept and Mr. Shadow took over.

Henry persuades them all to join him in painting all of Shadowland, creating a riotous colorfest with blue trees, yellow swimming pool water, and a polka-dot person. But when Henry finally leaves his fantasy land, all its inhabitants come along.

One-dimensional illustrations of characters appear here and there within the text or in comic strip-like boxes against a white background on oversize pages—very different from most American book illustration (with the exception of Maurice Sendak's).

Henry's outfit of knee pants and long socks, along with a sweater vest, gives him a definite Austrian or German appearance. Although Henry's own world is contemporary, Shadowland figures drive old-fashioned cars and high-wheeled bicycles.

Classroom Applications

Issues such as single-parent families (Henry's), abduction of children (Princess Gundi), and her father the king's concern are topics for discussion. Here is also a chance for students to consider the contrasts between old and new, Austria and America, and what might happen if Mr. Light overslept in this world and Mr. Shadow took over. Students might create their own shadowboxes to find out.

Denmark

Denmark is located in the northern part of Western Europe, bordered by the North Sea, the Baltic Sea, and Germany.

 Anderson, Hans Christian. *The Snow Queen.* illustrated by Mary Engelbreit. Workman, 1993. 48 pp. (ISBN 1-56305-438-8). Folktale, E-L.

Story Review Chart			
Setting	Plot/Events	Characters	Theme
•	•	•	•

Cultural Paradigm Reference Classification Chart			
Geographic Location	Economic System	Social System	Political System
•	•	•	

Anderson's classic folktale *The Snow Queen* comes to life again in this lively new edition. The rather long tale of the little boy Kay, who is stolen away by the icy Snow Queen, and his dear friend Gerda, who searches until she finds him, takes the reader through several substories: "The Mirror and Its Fragments" that become lodged in Kay's eyes and heart so that his heart turns cold; "The Flower Garden of the Woman Who Could Conjure" where Gerda escapes the conjurer's trap when she remembers the power of roses; "The Prince and the Princess" who offer Gerda help after the talking crows bring her to them; "The Little Robber Girl" who lends Gerda a talking reindeer to carry her north; and "The Lapland Woman and the Finmark Woman" who understand Gerda's powers and show her the way to "The Snow Queen's Castle and What Happened There at Last."

Mary Engelbreit's full-page illustrations for each substory are rimmed with stylized borders like window frames around ornate scenes from long ago. From the warmth of cozy flower-decked rooms and tile-roofed house with a stork on the chimney to the icy beauty of the frozen northland, Engelbreit's scenes transport the reader into a fairytale world of goblins, witches, and animal helpers where good triumphs over evil.

Classroom Applications

Students are intrigued by the idea of a magic mirror dropping to Earth and shattering into "a hundred million million pieces" so small they can lodge in a person's eye or heart and cause good to shrink away and evil to become magnified until the power of love melts them away. Have the class make up their own tales with this motif. Values, ethics, and morals of the characters are a principal focus, but students can also extract information about the topography and climate of Denmark, Lapland, and Finland and the basic needs of people for special clothing and shelter in the frigid winter. Like *Hansel and Gretel*, it is a story that lends itself well to dramatization.

England

England is located in the most western part of Western Europe as an island surrounded by the North Sea, English Channel, Atlantic Ocean, Irish Sea, and Norwegian Sea. Known as the United Kingdom, it includes Scotland to the north, Wales to the west, and Northern Ireland across the Irish Sea north of Ireland.

 Lewis, Kim. *Floss*. Candlewick Press, 1992. 24 pp. (ISBN 1-56402-010-X). Contemporary Fiction, P-E.

Story Review Chart

Setting	Plot/Events	Characters	Theme
•		•	

Cultural Paradigm Reference Classification Chart

Geographic Location	Economic System	Social System	Political System
•	•		

Floss is a young border collie that must give up her carefree life in the city with children and balls in the park to learn the hard work of herding sheep on a farm far away.

Her owner, an old man, takes Floss by train out to the farm where his son raises sheep and needs a new young dog to replace Old Nell, who is too old to work. Floss learns how to run wide, lie down, walk behind, shed, and pen the sheep. But one day when the farmer's children are out playing soccer, she runs off to join them, showing off her nose kicks and best passes.

Realistic illustrations by the author on every page show the sheep grazing, being herded, and then escaping when Floss forgets her lessons. Half pages of simple text tell the story of how she finally learns to work so well that the farmer runs her in the dog trials at the fair. Only the children are disappointed that there is no time for Floss to play with them. When their father comes to realize that Floss also needs the children, he gives her a nod and lets her go for a bit, showing off her nose kicks and best passes.

This is a story of economics shown in the muted colors of the heather-covered hills of Northumberland, where nothing much grows except sheep and where the author lives on a sheep farm. Everyone must work hard, including animals. But then comes a time for play, and even animals may join in.

Classroom Applications

Have students tell stories about their own dog pets. Can they find out what dog skills are used by people in the United States (e.g., police dogs for drug-sniffing, guard dogs, search dogs, racing dogs).

 Munro, Roxie. *The Inside-Outside Book of London*. E. P. Dutton, 1996. 48 pp. (ISBN 0-14-055810-1). Travel, A.

Story Review Chart

Setting	Plot/Events	Characters	Theme
•			

Cultural Paradigm Reference Classification Chart

Geographic Location	Economic System	Social System	Political System
	•		•

This unique travel book presents 12 sites of contemporary London in large two-page illustrations. Wordless except for a label, the detailed pictures show both an outside and an inside view of the site from the perspective of a sightseer looking down, out, or even from center-stage. The reader, for example, views the British Museum from across the street and then a close-up of Egyptian mummies inside; Waterloo Station from above the tracks and then from inside a train compartment; a New Oxford Street umbrella shop from outside in the rain and then inside among baskets and racks of umbrellas.

The sightseer goes to Trafalgar Square via Regent Street by climbing the steps of a red double-deck bus and viewing the winding London streets from inside the bus. The Houses of Parliament seen from across the river open up to the House of Commons viewed from the gallery by flipping the page. Ask your students to view the outside of the dome of St. Paul's Cathedral and then the inside by turning the page. Can they guess what the boy and girl are doing on the bench at opposite sides of the dome? The last page describes each site in detail, calling this final one the "Whispering Gallery."

Classroom Applications

Children usually have more of an eye for detail than adults. See what unusual items your students can pick out from each of these wonderfully executed pictures. Can they then make up their own stories about sightseeing in London? Also have them discuss some differences in a monarchy like England's and a democracy like America's. What comparable sites might an English sightseer visit in Washington, DC?

 French, Vivian. *Lazy Jack*. illustrated by Russell Ayto. Candlewick Press, 1995. 32 pp. (ISBN 1-56402-130-0). Folktale, E-M.

Story Review Chart			
Setting	Plot/Events	Characters	Theme
	•	•	•

Cultural Paradigm Reference Classification Chart			
Geographic Location	Economic System	Social System	Political System
	•	•	

England is the home of "Jack tales," folktales with Everyman Jack as the principal character, and "Jack and the Beanstalk" is the best-known example. Jack is usually an innocent young man who bumbles through life in a series of incidents but always ends up with the prize. The comical Lazy Jack is a boy so sleepy that he goes through the entire story without opening his eyes. His mother routs him out of bed every morning to go to work, but every evening he loses his daily pay on the way home. So his mother carefully instructs him each night how to carry it home.

Still, Jack can't seem to get it right, losing the coin he earns from the builder off the end of his nose; pouring the jug of milk from the farmer into his pockets; carrying the wedge of cheese from the dairyman on his head, where it melts; wrapping the puppy from the baker in a wet cloth; tying the fish he earns from the fishmonger with a piece of string and dragging it home; and finally carrying the donkey from the grocer on his back, causing the merchants to roar with such laughter that they each decide to hire Jack for 1 day of the week, and this time he knows how to take home his pay.

Ayto's cartoon-like drawings of English village life in olden days carry the humor of the story right to the climax, where the mother repeats her tired refrain of "You are a *silly* boy," but the merchants shout "OH, NO HE'S NOT!" and hire him on the spot.

Folktales like this usually have a lesson to teach, and this time it is not about laziness. Do your students recognize how hard Jack works every day? The value of laughter is what this tale highlights. While illustrating labor and production of goods, as well as payment in kind, the tale demonstrates that abilities such as making people laugh are worthy attributes—a real transcultural lesson.

Classroom Applications

Because formula tales like this with their repetitive dialogue ("I know what to do. My mom told me.") are easy to remember, they lend themselves well to oral storytelling. Give your students a chance to learn this valuable skill. They may even want to make up their own stories, substituting contemporary jobs, payment in kind, and comical responses of their own Jacks.

 Pyle, Howard, and Borgenicht, David. *The Legend of King Arthur.* illustrated by Luigi Galante, Simone Boni, and Francesca D'Ottavi. Running Press, 1996. 56 pp. (ISBN 1–56138–503–4). Legend, M-L.

Story Review Chart

Setting	Plot/Events	Characters	Theme
	•	•	

Cultural Paradigm Reference Classification Chart

Geographic Location	Economic System	Social System	Political System
			•

One of the great legends of England, this version of the ancient Celtic tale of King Arthur is a shortened retelling of the children's classic by Howard Pyle. Divided into five brief parts, it describes (a) Merlin's vision of the death of Arthur's father while Arthur is still a baby; (b) the great tournament 18 years later, in which knights of the kingdom joust and the Archbishop of Canterbury puts them to the test of kingship; (c) the miracle of the sword that young Arthur, a squire, secretly pulls from the anvil and then he learns of his ancestry; (d) the contest itself, in which all the knights and nobles try to pull the sword from the anvil but only Arthur prevails; and (e) the crowning of Arthur in the cathedral.

Although this tale for older children is not the better known Knights of the Roundtable story, its pictures and words make it just as dramatic. Realistic illustrations spreading across oversize pages give characters a lifelike quality and emotional depth. From Merlin's incantation creating the shining sword-in-the-stone to the knights' jousting tournament, splendid scenes seem to splash across the pages, carrying the drama of the unknown boy, soon-to-be-king.

The political system of ancient England, where a king's crown depends on intrigue as much as royal blood and the succession to the throne can be a bloody battle, comes to life in this dramatic tale.

Classroom Applications

Can your students find any parallels in contemporary succession controversies? They may want to try their own hands at dramatizing the story; it lends itself well to play-acting. Or they may want to consider what makes this story a legend and to find out whether legends are true.

 Hollinshead, Marilyn. *The Nine Days Wonder.* illustrated by Pierr Morgan. Philomel, 1994. 32 pp. (ISBN 0-399-21967-6). Historical Fiction, E–L.

Story Review Chart

Setting	Plot/Events	Characters	Theme
•		•	

Cultural Paradigm Reference Classification Chart

Geographic Location	Economic System	Social System	Political System
		•	•

Will Kemp, the merriest dancer in old England, was a real actor and dancer in Shakespeare's plays during the reign of Queen Elizabeth I. In 1600, he boasted that he could dance all the way from London to Norwich, 117 miles away, in 10 days or less, sleeping only at night. No one believed him, and people placed their bets that he could not do it. This rollicking story, based on Will's actual diary, carries him tripping, twirling, and capering across the countryside with his friend Tom Slye playing pipe and drum and with George Sprat, the mile keeper, disparaging every step he takes.

But Will lets nothing stop him—not a bear-baiting contest, two fighting horses, a pain in his hip, a road full of muck, a sky full of snow, the streets full of people, or the gates of the city. He dances skimble-skamble, lippity-loppity, swig-a-swag, higgledy-piggledy, and jig-a-jog with bells on right up to the house of the Lord Mayor of Norwich. Then he sits down and writes a book about it.

Pierr Morgan, the illustrator, went to England to retrace the steps of Will Kemp, where she met a group of morris dancers who still carry on Will's tradition. Her gouache paintings catch not only the flavor of Elizabethan England with its half-timbered houses, thatch-roofed cottages, hedgerows, and hamlets but also the reactions of the people and animals Will meets.

The Nine Days Wonder is a swirling tour through old England, showing plump country lasses, fainthearted louts, and crowds so thick that the Lord Mayor of Norwich has to hire wifflers with sticks to keep them back. Historically accurate words and pictures help students identify social classes and role status. Mention of the Lord Mayor and Lord Chief Justice hint at a governing system under Queen Elizabeth. But recreation and a man's belief in himself seem to be the principal focuses of this story.

Classroom Applications

Bring in some ankle bells and morris dancing tapes and let your students test their own talents by dancing a country jig. Some children may want to play a toy flute and a drum or tambourine to keep time.

France

France is located in the western part of Western Europe, bordered on the west by the Atlantic Ocean, on the north by the English Channel, on the east by Germany, and on the south by Spain and the Mediterranean Sea.

Axworthy, Anni. *Anni's Diary of France*. Whispering Coyote Press, 1994. 32 pp. (ISBN 1-879085-58-5). Fictional Travel, M-L.

Story Review Chart

Setting	Plot/Events	Characters	Theme
•		•	

Cultural Paradigm Reference Classification Chart

Geographic Location	Economic System	Social System	Political System
•	•		

A fine introduction to France for older children, *Anni's Diary of France* records a trip to France taken by the girl Anni, along with her mother and father, as a diary illustrated with drawings and photographs bordering every page. This is definitely a child's-eye view of France, from the outdoor cafes of Paris, where Anni notes that even the dogs are well dressed, to the bell tower of Notre Dame Cathedral, where she sticks out her tongue like one of the gargoyles.

A street artist draws a caricature of Anni outside the Pompidou Center for Art and Culture while Anni makes a drawing of him: *tres bien* ("very good"). She learns the language as she goes along. In Normandy, she is charmed by the House of Broken Crockery. In Brittany, she gets covered with a "sea monster's" coating of green algae paste to be washed away by a warm seawater bath. In the Loire Valley, she sleeps in a four-poster bed in a castle inn, just like a princess. In Loches, the family stays with a French family and the daughter Angela takes Anni to school for a day.

By car, boat, bike, and on foot, the family visits medieval towns, fishing villages, and even the Futurescope theme park, but Anni's most memorable times are spent riding horseback in the marshy Camargue, eating and even helping prepare wonderful French food wherever they go, and participating fully in the life around her.

Anni's Diary of France is also a lighthearted look at France's economic system, showing housing from castles to cave dwellings; natural resources of soil, water, flora, and fauna; goats and cheese production and cowboys and bullfights. A glossary of French words is included on the end pages.

Classroom Applications

Take your students on their own tour, perhaps a field trip to a museum, park, or zoo, and have them record their adventures in illustrated diaries like Anni's.

 Le Tord, Bijou. *A Blue Butterfly: A Story About Claude Monet.* Doubleday, 1995. 32 pp. (ISBN 0-385-31102-8). Biography, E-L.

Story Review Chart

Setting	Plot/Events	Characters	Theme
•		•	

Cultural Paradigm Reference Classification Chart

Geographic Location	Economic System	Social System	Political System
•			

The author-artist journeys to France to visit Monet's garden in Giverny and then to Paris to view his paintings in preparation for this book. Then she herself uses the same eight colors as Monet used (silver white, cobalt violet light, emerald green, ultramarine extra-fine, vermilion, cadmium yellow light and dark, and lemon yellow) to paint the impressionistic watercolor illustrations in this book.

Each two-page spread shows a lovely scene of flowers "like tiny jewels or little stars leaping from the sky," or trees, or buildings, or the sea, with Monet standing to one side, brush in hand, painting the scene. One sentence of simple text describing how he painted is placed like a poem in the far left corner. The title comes from the last page, where Monet is dazzled by the light he holds on his brush "like a blue butterfly."

Classroom Applications

Challenge your students to use these same Monet colors on paintings of their own. Take them outside—perhaps to a park or garden—to paint grass, trees, flowers, and sky. If an art museum is nearby, take the class on a field trip there to view a real Monet painting. If not, bring in an art book from the library, showing Monet's paintings.

 Anholt, Laurence. *Camille and the Sunflowers: A Story About Vincent van Gogh.* Barron's, 1994. 28 pp. (ISBN 0-8120-6409-7). Historical Fiction, E-L.

Story Review Chart

Setting	Plot/Events	Characters	Theme
•		•	

Cultural Paradigm Reference Classification Chart

Geographic Location	Economic System	Social System	Political System
•		•	

"Where Camille lived, the sunflowers grew so high they looked like real suns" begins this delightful tale of a little boy's friendship with the painter Vincent Van Gogh, who visits his village one summer to paint. Camille's father, the village postmaster, helps the destitute painter by lending him pots and pans and furniture for his rented house. Camille brings him a huge bunch of sunflowers. Vincent, as the painter calls himself, rewards their friendship before the summer is out by painting pictures of the postmaster, Camille, and of course, the sunflowers. The village children laugh at Camille's picture, which he takes to school to show them, and later tease Vincent and throw stones at him because he "plays with paints all day" instead of working.

Cover of Camille and the Sunflowers: A Story About Vincent van Gogh *by Laurence Anholt, illustrated by Laurence Anholt, 1994, Hauppauge, NY: Barron's. Reprinted with permission of Barron's Educational Series, Inc.*

Based on true accounts of Van Gogh's life and his paintings, this story brings out the fears that people often express when someone is different from themselves. Illustrations in pen and ink and watercolors have a definite European flavor, with barefoot Camille in his blue cap and jacket running through a field of gigantic sunflowers, or Camille's glorious dream scene of the Sunflower Man at night with candles stuck on his hat, painting the stars. Small reproductions of Van Gogh's works appear as he shows them to Camille, so even though Camille's bunch of sunflowers eventually wilts, there they are again in a glorious painting!

Classroom Applications

Bring in postcards or print reproductions of Van Gogh's works for your students to comment on. Would they like to try their own hands at painting flowers in a vase? Bring in some sunflowers (artificial flowers will do if sunflowers are out of season) as props.

 Zolotow, Charlotte. *The Moon Was the Best*. illustrated by Tana Hoban. Greenwillow Books, 1993. 32 pp. (ISBN 0-688-09940-8). Travel, P-M.

Story Review Chart

Setting	Plot/Events	Characters	Theme
•			

Cultural Paradigm Reference Classification Chart

Geographic Location	Economic System	Social System	Political System
•		•	

This is a simple story of the special things a mother remembers about her visit to Paris so that she can tell her little girl when she returns: "the things I'd like if I were there." Renowned photographer Tana Hoban captures a girl's-eye view of Paris on every other page, and the author writes the mother's remembrances in single sentences of large type on the opposite pages.

Child readers will relate to the girl rolling a hoop under the flowering chestnut trees; the man feeding pigeons who cluster at his feet, on his lap, and even on his shoulder; the lady carrying long loaves of bread under her arm like sticks; and the carousel with white animals waiting for the music to begin. They will especially respond to the mother's reply when her daughter asks what was the best: "The moon was the best," as the title states, because it was the same moon shining on her little girl, and she knew they weren't so far apart after all. A list of photograph locations in Paris is included.

Classroom Applications

How is Paris different from London? How are photographs different from paintings? What makes a great city great? All of these questions can be explored if your students show interest. The class may also want to discuss or illustrate locations in their own city, town, or rural area that would be attractive to a visitor.

 Dunrea, Olivier. *The Tale of Hilda Louise.* Farrar, Straus & Giroux, 1996. 32 pp. (ISBN 0-374-37380-9). Fiction, M-L.

Story Review Chart

Setting	Plot/Events	Characters	Theme
	•	•	

Cultural Paradigm Reference Classification Chart

Geographic Location	Economic System	Social System	Political System
		•	

Hilda Louise is a little French girl who lives in an orphanage in Paris in the early 1900s because she has lost her parents, and her only other relative, an uncle, cannot be found. As much as she loves the other 109 orphans and Madame Zanzibar, the director, she longs for a family of her own. Then one day while in the garden, Hilda Louise suddenly floats into the air. Soon she is turning somersaults in the air and doing death spirals.

But one day, a strong gust of wind blows her up and over the walls of the orphanage, out over the city, past the Eiffel Tower, and down through an open garret window, where she lands in the arms of a red-haired artist painting at an easel. It is her uncle. From then on, she lives happily in her uncle's studio and never floats again. But when she returns to the orphanage for a visit, Madame Zanzibar mentions that Marian Lee has begun to float—and there she is up near the ceiling polishing the brass chandelier.

This whimsical story comes to life in the simple but effective full-page oil paintings by the author, showing Hilda Louise using her newfound talent to help others and finally to help herself. Scenes from Paris of the 1900s, with its chimney-potted rooftops and pinafore-clad little girls, give the tale a definite French flavor. The acceptance by the people of Hilda Louise's eccentric behavior is very French as well. Ask your students what Americans might have done if this had happened in New York City.

France's social system is definitely reflected in the story, showing a concern for children and the family.

Classroom Applications

Would any of your students like to fly? Talk about how people fly today with hang gliders, parasailing, and ultralights. Bring in a video of these types of craft and have children make up their own stories of flying. Discuss the concept of an *orphanage* with your students. Was the one in the story a good one? How can they tell?

 De Maupassant, Guy, and Halperin, Wendy Anderson. *When Chickens Grow Teeth.* Orchard Books, 1996. 32 pages. (ISBN 0-531-09526-6). Fiction, M-L.

Story Review Chart

Setting	Plot/Events	Characters	Theme
	•	•	

Cultural Paradigm Reference Classification Chart

Geographic Location	Economic System	Social System	Political System
	•	•	

This farcical Guy de Maupassant tale retold by Wendy Halperin owes as much to its wonderfully realistic watercolors as it does to the words. Repeated pictures of the characters as in a comic strip border the two-page spreads, bringing an entire French village to life. A window of text is tucked between the top and bottom rows. This is the story of Toine, a fat, jolly cafe keeper who eats as much as he sells, and his scrawny, complaining wife, Colette, who raises chickens behind the cafe and raises her voice whenever she sees her husband loafing with his friends.

One day, Toine falls off a ladder, injures his back, and becomes bedridden for a spell. His friends gather around with fruit from the forest, a game of chess, and gossip. Not Madame Colette. She decides that she needs help hatching her eggs and puts Toine to work. "I'll hatch eggs when chickens grow teeth," declares Toine, but soon he has five eggs on pillows under each of his enormous arms. Tiny pictures show each separate egg and each separate friend tiptoeing around so as not to disturb the eggs.

What a day when the eggs hatch and most of the village turns out to see! Toine is a "father" now and tends his flock as proudly as any parent. And Madame Colette? Even she has to smile.

Your students can learn as much about French village life from the pictures as they can from the story. The social system is the focus here, looking at interpersonal relations, the friendship and caring of a close-knit community, and the miracle of birth and parenthood—even of chickens.

Classroom Applications

Would your students enjoy hatching eggs in an incubator as a project?

Germany

Germany is located in the central part of Western Europe. It is bordered on the north by the North Sea, Denmark, and the Baltic Sea and lies west of Poland, the Czech Republic, and Austria, north of Switzerland, and east of France, Luxembourg, Belgium, and the Netherlands.

 Heuck, Sigrid. *A Ghost in the Castle.* illustrated by Bernard Oberdieck. Annick Press, 1994. 28 pp. (ISBN 1-55037-331-5). Fiction, M-L.

Story Review Chart

Setting	Plot/Events	Characters	Theme
	•	•	

Cultural Paradigm Reference Classification Chart

Geographic Location	Economic System	Social System	Political System
		•	

"Once upon a time . . . " begins this story, to the delight of listeners who expect a fairy story to commence. But this is a fictional tale of a white owl belonging to a small traveling circus in medieval Germany. The circus has acrobats and clowns, an elephant, and a camel, but the children in the towns the circus visits are especially fascinated by the big white owl who sits so motionless in her little cage that they cannot tell whether she is alive or not until she blinks.

One day, the gardener of a nearby castle approaches the owner of the circus and proposes to purchase the rare owl. His master is disturbed at night by a noisy ghost in the castle and has offered a reward to anyone who can rid the castle of the ghost. The gardener knows that the ghost is, in fact, a horde of rustling mice who come out of the walls at night to scamper around the halls. So the owl is purchased and set free in the castle attic to do her work. She has never caught a mouse in her life, but just the sight of the spooky white bird frightens the mice back into their holes.

The master gives the gardener his reward, but then the owl begins hooting at night, making such a frightening sound that the master has to pay the gardener again to rid the castle of this more monstrous ghost. That night, the gardener opens the attic window and the great white bird finally flies off to its freedom.

Detailed drawings of children and animals, circus wagons, and castle rooms against a filmy textured background evoke a bygone era. The focus here is the social system, with values, ethics, and morals the emphasis.

Classroom Applications

What people will do for money and their cruel treatment of animals are subjects your students can discuss. Has anyone visited a modern circus or zoo? Students may be able to discuss whether animals should be caged. And what can they find out about white owls?

 Fisher, Leonard Everett. *Gutenberg*. Macmillan, 1993. 16 pp. (ISBN 0-02-735238-2). Biography, M-L.

Story Review Chart

Setting	Plot/Events	Characters	Theme
	•	•	

Cultural Paradigm Reference Classification Chart

Geographic Location	Economic System	Social System	Political System
	•		•

Born in Mainz, Germany, between 1394 and 1399, Johann Gutenberg is known today as the inventor of the modern printing press with moveable type. As the large black-and-white paintings of this brief book show, Gutenberg, a successful goldsmith and gemstone cutter, becomes obsessed with the idea of printing words mechanically and making many copies of them. As an expert at making metal punches to create intricate jewelry designs, he puts this skill to work secretly making individual letters of lead and casting them into metal strips of the same size and thickness. The printing press itself he models after wine presses. In his day of hand-lettered books laboriously scratched out by monks and scribes, Gutenberg wants to become the only master printer of Europe.

Word of his experiment leaks out to the partners who have invested in his business. Eventually, he is forced to borrow more money from Johann Fust, a Mainz lawyer who sees great business possibilities in Gutenberg's press. In 1454, Gutenberg begins printing his famous Bible, a page of which appears as this book's frontispiece. At this moment, Fust steps in and demands repayment of his loan, taking Gutenberg to court over it. Because the printer has no money, Fust takes over Gutenberg's shop and finishes printing and selling the Bible himself for a handsome profit.

The book's large, dark illustrations with close-ups of medieval men from the waist up show Gutenberg and his helpers next hammering together a new shop with new presses for a new edition of the Bible that would come out 3 years later. He continues printing and training young men to become apprentices until the end of his life in 1468. But his invention allows millions of people to be reached by the same printed words at the same time, thus putting an end to the Middle Ages and shaping the modern age.

Classroom Applications

Featuring an economic system wholly different from ours, this book takes the reader back in time to the birth of modern technology. Have your students make the journey with you through books, CD-ROMs, and videotapes to determine what life was like and how goods were manufactured in those far-off days (see Appendix B). Then take a field trip to a print shop or newspaper pressroom to see how modern printing is done. The class may want to set up a desktop shop in the classroom and print their own books or newspapers.

 Berenzy, Alix. *Rapunzel*. Henry Holt, 1995. 32 pp. (ISBN 0-8050-1283-4). Folktale, M-L.

Story Review Chart

Setting	Plot/Events	Characters	Theme
	•	•	•

Cultural Paradigm Reference Classification Chart

Geographic Location	Economic System	Social System	Political System
		•	

Folktales have many variants, and this familiar tale is based on the original German story that predates the tale told by the Brothers Grimm. In this account, the girl Rapunzel is named for a blue flowering plant that is eaten as salad greens by her mother before she is born. But the greens have been stolen from the garden of an ancient fairy, Mother Gothel, who then claims the baby as her own and locks her in a tall stone tower. As Rapunzel grows into maidenhood, her long, golden braids are the only means for entering her room at the top. Mother Gothel comes during the day, but the king's son, who has discovered her secret, comes every night to visit her, calling the familiar refrain: "Rapunzel, Rapunzel, let down your hair for me."

Large, dramatic colored-pencil and paint illustrations on black paper make use of light and shadow to create the dark mood and atmosphere of this tale as the old fairy discovers the prince and drags Rapunzel far away to a barren desert where she is left to fend for herself. The prince is blinded when he leaps from the tower and lands in a thorn bush. But both of these lovers keep the faith and are eventually reunited in the desert, now blooming with rapunzel flowers and with the twin children Rapunzel has borne. Her tears of joy fall on the prince's eyes, restoring his sight, and of course, they live happily ever after.

Classroom Applications

Fairytales like this, with their stereotyped characters, have much to teach contemporary children. Ask your students what moral this tale has to teach; you may be surprised to hear they recognize that the stealing at the outset created the problem and understand that someone must pay the consequences or that good triumphs over evil if one never loses faith. As an easily remembered tale with strong characters and dialogue, *Rapunzel* is a favorite for dramatization by children, as well as for oral storytelling by them.

 Carle, Eric. *Walter the Baker.* Simon & Schuster, 1995. 32 pp. (ISBN 0-689-80078-9). Fiction, P-E.

Story Review Chart

Setting	Plot/Events	Characters	Theme
	•	•	

Cultural Paradigm Reference Classification Chart

Geographic Location	Economic System	Social System	Political System
	•		•

Walter is the best baker in the whole duchy in this simple story for younger children. Carle's colorful collage cutouts of medieval people, houses, and the castle of the duke and duchess practically burst from the stark white pages of the tale—a Carle trademark. Everyone loves Walter's sweet rolls, especially the duke and duchess, until the day the cat spills the milk and Walter makes his dough with water. The duke is so upset over the taste of the rolls that he wants to banish Walter forever, but he gives Walter one more chance—if he can make a roll through which the rising sun can shine three times. What a struggle Walter has pulling, pounding, and twisting the dough. Finally, he flings it against the ceiling in a fit of anger. But the contrary dough plops down with its own twist into just what the Duke ordered: Walter has invented the pretzel!

Classroom Applications

Let your students enjoy the story, and then challenge them with questions about what they do when they are frustrated because something does not turn out as they wanted it to. What do they think about a ruler who would "banish" someone because his rolls do not taste good? A new vocabulary word and concept for most youngsters. Best of all, this story can lead to a wonderful cooking adventure for your students as they take on the role of Walter the baker.

Greece

Greece is located in the eastern Mediterranean between the Aegean Sea and the Ionian Sea, south of Albania, Macedonia, and Bulgaria.

 Marshall, Laura. *The Girl Who Changed Her Fate.* Atheneum, 1992. 32 pp. (ISBN 0-689-31742-5). Folktale, M-L.

Story Review Chart

Setting	Plot/Events	Characters	Theme
	•	•	

Cultural Paradigm Reference Classification Chart

Geographic Location	Economic System	Social System	Political System
		•	

Eleni, the heroine of this strange folktale, seems to be plagued with bad luck; everywhere she goes, destructive things happen to her and those around her. She discovers instead that she is ill-fated and must change her fate by going to the mountaintop where the fates live, finding her own fate, offering the fate a gift, and asking the fate to change her fate. This difficult task is wonderfully illustrated with strongly textured oil paintings of

Greeks in peasant costumes, white-walled villages, and the colorful Greek landscape divided into interesting vertical pictures with text embedded within the scenery.

After many hardships, Eleni finally finds her fate, a spectacular demon-like being who rejects Eleni's gift of bread with such rage that it finally exhausts her, and in that moment, she sees Eleni's innocence. Giving Eleni a ball of silk thread, the fate instructs her to keep it until someone comes seeking it and then to demand its weight in gold. When a young man asks for the thread for his sister's wedding dress, no amount of gold tips the balance scale until he steps on the scale himself. Eleni accepts his gold and himself as her own bridegroom and lives happily ever after.

This story features the social system, with its values, ethics, and family structure. It also seems to speak to the question of why bad things happen to good people.

Classroom Applications

Can your students apply the teaching of this tale to their own lives? Do they know of someone who seems to have "bad luck," or is it "bad fate"? How was Eleni finally able to change her fate? "Hands" and "giving" play important roles here. Can your students use their hands symbolically, just as Eleni's sisters did?

 Aliki. *The Gods and Goddesses of Olympus.* HarperCollins, 1994. 48 pp. (ISBN 0-06-023531-4). Legend, M-L.

Story Review Chart

Setting	Plot/Events	Characters	Theme
		•	

Cultural Paradigm Reference Classification Chart

Geographic Location	Economic System	Social System	Political System
		•	

The most impressive feature of this book is Aliki's gouache paintings of the gods and goddesses of Mount Olympus adapted from Greek vase paintings and sculptures and filling every page with their fantastic histories and accomplishments. Minimal text describes the tumultuous lineage and lives of Zeus, Hera, Hephaestus, Aphrodite, Ares, Poseidon, Athena, Hermes, Artemis, Apollo, Hades, Demeter and Persephone, Dionysus, and Hestia.

The social system, with its norms and roles and family relationships, is featured here.

Classroom Applications

Discuss with your students how these immortals affected the lives of the mortals in ancient Greek mythology and how they are remembered today. Suggest that each student choose one of the gods or goddesses and make up a story about the character.

Chelepi, Chris. *Growing Up in Ancient Greece.* illustrated by Chris Molan. Troll, 1994. 32 pp. (ISBN 0-8167-2720-1). Historical Nonfiction, M–L.

Story Review Chart

Setting	Plot/Events	Characters	Theme
•			

Cultural Paradigm Reference Classification Chart

Geographic Location	Economic System	Social System	Political System
	•	•	

This well-illustrated, easily understood book about ancient Greece makes a fine companion volume to *The Gods and Goddesses of Olympus*. Simple paragraphs on Athens, life in the country, learning at home, going to school, ceremonies and festivals, clothing, inside a house, shopping, food, warriors, growing up in Sparta, and getting married give students enough pertinent information for them to reconstruct a house or put on a play about life in Athens. Illustrations showing both boys and girls taking part in the life around them help modern children identify with ancient Greeks. It focuses on the social and economic systems.

Classroom Applications

Have small groups of students construct their own homes inside cardboard boxes and then tell stories about their lives there.

 Pastuchiv, Olga. *Minas and the Fish.* Houghton Mifflin, 1997. 32 pp. (ISBN 0-395-79756-X). Fiction, P–E.

Story Review Chart

Setting	Plot/Events	Characters	Theme
•	•	•	•

Cultural Paradigm Reference Classification Chart

Geographic Location	Economic System	Social System	Political System
	•	•	

Little Minas lives with his father and brothers by the sea. The thing he wants most of all is to be big like them and to go out on their boat fishing with them. But they always tell him he's too little and must wait until he gets bigger and learns to swim.

Then one day, the brothers Antonis and Giorgos catch in their nets a very strange fish with huge teeth and eyes that change colors. They tie it to their mast while they haul in their nets. When they get home and show Minas their strange catch, he stares at it over the boat rail while the brothers go ashore to drink their morning coffee. Suddenly, the fish speaks to Minas, saying that if he lets it go free, it will give Minas a wish. The startled boy finally agrees, saying that he wants to be big like his brothers and to know how to swim. The fish agrees, and Minas unties it.

Suddenly, Minas is as big as his brothers. The fish tells him to jump in and proceeds to teach him how to swim. This accomplished, it is about to swim home when Minas wants to swim there, too, so the big fish takes him on its back and swims into the depths. At this point, illustrations are two-page spreads of gloriously colorful undersea creatures: striped and spotted fish, shrimps, crabs, and jellyfish; a giant eel and an octopus; and the scary fish of the abysmal depths.

When the fish finally takes Minas home again, his brothers do not recognize him and accuse him of being the one who stole their fish. He jumps into the water to escape and calls to the fish to make him little again. When he emerges, Minas is back to his own size, but he can still swim! The brothers are amazed and invite him to go on the boat with them and help with the nets. Minas is finally happy.

Classroom Applications

If your students are as fond of fish as Minas, this is the time to set up an aquarium in the classroom. Take a field trip to an aquarium store and have students help choose the fish and learn to take care of them. Do they understand the lesson that Minas learned through his encounter with the fish and his brothers: that drastic changes can cause more trouble than little changes?

 Yolen, Jane. *Wings*. illustrated by Dennis Nolan. Harcourt Brace, 1991. 32 pp. (ISBN 0-15-297850-X). Legend, M-L.

Story Review Chart

Setting	Plot/Events	Characters	Theme
	•	•	

Cultural Paradigm Reference Classification Chart

Geographic Location	Economic System	Social System	Political System
		•	•

The Greek legend of Daedelus and Icarus comes to life in this retelling through Yolen's storytelling skills and Nolan's dramatic full-page watercolor paintings. Daedelus, the great artist and prince of Athens who invents the ax, bevel, and awl and whose statues are so lifelike they almost move, is so full of pride that he angers the gods. Or as Yolen puts it: "A man who hears only praise becomes deaf." When his carelessness causes the death of a young prince, Daedelus is banished from Athens forever.

Eventually, Daedelus sails to the island of Crete, where King Minos employs him to build a labyrinth to hide the terrible Minotaur, a monster with a bull's head and man's body and who eats human flesh. Meanwhile, Daedelus marries a Crete woman and fathers a son, Icarus. When Theseus, another prince of Athens, comes to Crete to slay the Minotaur, Daedelus tells him how he can penetrate the labyrinth. King Minos finds out, and once again Daedelus is banished: This time, he is locked up in a high prison tower at the edge of the sea with his son.

Ever the idea master, Daedelus coaxes the birds he sees to come to his window, where he plucks some of their feathers and eventually constructs pairs of wings for himself and his son. When it is time for their escape, he warns his son not to fly too low or the water will soak the feathers, nor too high or the sun will melt the wax holding the feathers together. But his son, glorying in his freedom, flies higher than the birds and higher than the clouds until the sun melts the wax and Icarus plunges into the sea.

Nolan shows the gods who monitor human behavior as shadowy heads and hands in the clouds in every illustration.

Classroom Applications

As your students follow the gods' feelings as the story unfolds, can they predict what may happen next? They may also want to invent and fly their own paper airplane wings. Can they compare the political system's monarchy showing a king's total control over his subjects with the social system's morality as enforced by the gods of ancient Greece? Pride is Daedelus's downfall, but what about Icarus?

Iceland

Iceland is an island nation situated in the North Atlantic Ocean, southeast of Greenland and northwest of Scotland.

 McMillan, Bruce. *Nights of the Pufflings.* Houghton Mifflin, 1995. 32 pp. (ISBN 0-395-70810-9). Informational, E–M.

Story Review Chart			
Setting	Plot/Events	Characters	Theme
•	•	•	

Cultural Paradigm Reference Classification Chart			
Geographic Location	Economic System	Social System	Political System
•			

Every August on Heimaey Island off the coast of Iceland, a strange real-life drama takes place. Hundreds of young puffin birds known as pufflings emerge from underground burrows to take their first flight to the ocean, where they will spend the winter—at sea. For 2 weeks in August, the young birds venture forth every night on their maiden flights. But often the lights of the island village confuse them, and they crash-land on a village street instead of splash-landing in the ocean. Because they cannot take off from flat ground, they run around trying to hide from destruction by cats, dogs, and cars.

This is the photographic story of Halla, her friend Arnar Ingi, and the other village children who sleep late during the day in order to stay up all night rescuing the pufflings. Armed with flashlights and cardboard cartons, they scurry around the streets of the village, gathering up the stranded pufflings. The next day, they hike down to the beach with their boxes of birds and release them one by one, holding them up so that they get used to flapping their wings, and then, *einn-tveir-prir* ("one-two-three"), swinging each one between their legs and launching it high into the air on the last swing. Every night for 2 weeks, Halla and her friends perform this exciting life-saving task, captured in outstanding color photographs by McMillan. The importance of geographic location is dramatically portrayed in this unique photo story.

Classroom Applications

Do any of your students have an anecdote to tell about staying up all night to see or help a wild creature? Have students find out more about puffins and other seabirds of the north. Suggest that they draw pictures of the birds and tell about them.

Ireland

Ireland is an island bordered by the Atlantic Ocean on the east, Northern Ireland on the north, the Irish Sea on the west, and located just west of the island of Great Britain.

 Akerman, Karen. *The Banshee.* illustrated by David Ray. Philomel, 1990. 32 pp. (ISBN 0-399-21924-2). Folktale, E-M.

Story Review Chart			
Setting	Plot/Events	Characters	Theme
•			

Cultural Paradigm Reference Classification Chart			
Geographic Location	Economic System	Social System	Political System
		•	

Here is a night song in prose about a little Irish village tucking itself in for the night, and the spirit-like Banshee that drifts on the wind from house to house, looking for a lonely soul to keep her company. Who will it be? Not the young mother and her baby, the blacksmith and his cat, the farmer and his mare, the innkeeper and his wife, the woodland owl and the grandmother, the father and his sleeping daughter, or the farmer and his cows. So the Banshee turns away and disappears with the fading night.

Told with large type in a sentence or two beneath Ray's soft acrylic paintings, *The Banshee* portrays a quiet, peaceful time when candles lit homes and gas lamps illuminated dark streets.

Classroom Applications

Ask your students to tell what the Banshee might see in contemporary homes if she looked in their windows on a moonlit night. Can they see what makes this Irish night so peaceful, rather than scary? Are any of them afraid of the dark? What makes it scary?

 Hodges, Margaret. *Saint Patrick and the Peddler.* illustrated by Paul Brett Johnson. Orchard Books, 1997. 40 pp. (ISBN 0-531-07089-1). Folktale, E–M.

Story Review Chart

Setting	Plot/Events	Characters	Theme
•	•	•	

Cultural Paradigm Reference Classification Chart

Geographic Location	Economic System	Social System	Political System
	•	•	

No review of Irish stories can be complete without a tale about Saint Patrick. This particular folktale is a variant of the old English "Pedlar of Swaffam," which itself is a variant of a tale told in ancient Persia. When the author first heard the Irish version told here and learned that Saint Patrick had actually worked 6 years on a farm near Ballymena, where her grandfather had also had a farm, she placed the peddler in Ballymena.

This poor peddler who walks the roads of Ireland selling his wares from door to door has no wife, no horse, no dog to keep him company. He sleeps by himself in a wee house on a farm near Ballymena. But he welcomes anyone who stops by his door, and he tells each visitor stories of Saint Patrick working in the field nearby, who could even have lived in a house like his. One visitor is a boy, Danny, who notices words inscribed on the peddler's iron cooking pot. But the peddler cannot read even his own language, and these words are in Latin. The boy determines to learn the meaning of the words.

Meanwhile, the potato crop fails, and hard times come to everyone. No one has money to buy the peddler's wares. Then one night, the peddler has a dream of Saint Patrick telling him to go to the city of Dublin and to stand on the bridge over the River Liffey. There he will hear what he is meant to hear. Three times, the peddler has the same dream, and at last he goes to Dublin and stands on the bridge.

A fat butcher stands at the entrance to his shop, watching the peddler. Finally, the butcher walks over and asks the peddler why he is standing there. The peddler tells him his dream, at which the butcher laughs uproariously. Then he responds that he, too, has had a dream three nights in a row in which Saint Patrick tells him to go to Ballymena and dig under an iron pot in a poor cabin on a farm near there. But he would never believe such nonsense.

The peddler hurries back to Ballymena, digs under his pot, and finds another pot full of gold. At that moment, the boy Danny appears and translates the words on the pot that say: "Here I stand, old and good, with something better under me."

So the peddler becomes a rich man with a wife, a dog, and a horse. But he still opens his house to visitors and tells them tales about Saint Patrick, who could have lived in a house like his.

Classroom Applications

Searching for buried treasure has always intrigued humankind. Your students can make up their own tales of buried treasure if they like this one. Or they might hide a "treasure" somewhere in the classroom and write notes with clues for their classmates to find it. Books are treasures for everyone to enjoy. You yourself might "bury" a new book and post clues around the room for the students to discover where you have hidden the next book you plan to read to them.

 McDermott, Gerald. *Tim O'Toole and the Wee Folk.* Puffin Books, 1990. 32 pp. (ISBN 0-14-050675-6). Folktale, P-E.

Story Review Chart

Setting	Plot/Events	Characters	Theme
	•	•	

Cultural Paradigm Reference Classification Chart

Geographic Location	Economic System	Social System	Political System
		•	

Told in typical folktale fashion with a truly Irish lilt, this tale about Tim O'Toole and his wife, Kathleen, who are so poor that they have not a penny or a potato between them, takes Tim up and down the country, searching for work but finding none. So he stretches out to rest in the clover by the side of the road and there discovers a troop of wee folk all dressed in green, laughing, piping, and dancing. As any good Irishman would, Tim demands their treasure, and they give him a little gray goose that lays golden eggs. Unfortunately for Tim, he stops to rest on the way home at the McGoons' home, boasting of his good fortune, and the McGoons switch geese on him when he is asleep.

When he returns to scold the little men for tricking him, they give him a tablecloth that produces an unending supply of food and drink. But he stops once more at the McGoons' home, and the McGoons make the same switch while he is sleeping. On his third visit to the wee folk, they discover what has happened and tell Tim to wear a strange green hat and to boast to the McGoons that it is magic. The trick works, for when the McGoons pick up the hat, the wee folk pour forth and beat the McGoons about the shins and ankles with little blackthorn clubs until they return Tim's goose and tablecloth. Does he live happily ever after? Sort of, until word of his good fortune gets out and he is besieged by friends wanting to share his riches. So he has to take off his hat once again and let the wee folk drive away the noisy crowd. As with most folktales, this one also features the social system's concern with values, ethics, and morals.

Classroom Applications

What lessons does this tale teach? Do your students understand the consequences of greed, stealing, and boasting, as well as the importance of paying attention to directions? Bring in a green party hat and invite the class to dramatize this lighthearted story.

Italy

Italy is located in the western Mediterranean between the Ionian and Adriatic Seas to the west, the Tyrrhenian Sea to the east, and Switzerland to the north.

 Cazzola, Gus. *The Bells of Santa Lucia.* illustrated by Pierr Morgan. Philomel, 1991. 32 pp. (ISBN 0-399-21804). Fiction, E-M.

Story Review Chart

Setting	Plot/Events	Characters	Theme
	•	•	

Cultural Paradigm Reference Classification Chart

Geographic Location	Economic System	Social System	Political System
	•	•	

In Santa Lucia, an Italian hill town of tan stone walls and red tile roofs, lives Lucinda, her mother, and her grandmother. Lucinda loves the bells of Santa Lucia: the goat bells, dog bells, cat bells, mouse bells, and the big Grandmother Bell in the village square. She especially loves her grandmother Rosa, who rings a hand bell from her sickbed. But after her grandmother dies, Lucinda hates all the bells and covers her head to hide from their sound. When the schoolmaster hears of this behavior, he coaxes Lucinda from her house by showing her three little lambs, each with its bell. Lucinda loves the littlest one, Clarissa, but rips off its bell.

One day, the wind blows over a candle, setting the lamb's stall on fire, and Lucinda is forced to ring the huge Grandmother Bell in the town square to alert the people, who save the school and the lambs. Morgan's gouache paintings, inspired by a trip to the hill towns of Italy, bring the story to life with scenes of lively turn-of-the-century village life. The social system, with its interdependence, and the economic system, showing communication by bells, are featured here.

Classroom Applications

Have your students bring in a variety of bells and set up a way to communicate with them. Or have everyone bring in a glass and spoon and fill each glass partway with water; tapping the glasses with the spoons will make bell sounds. If you regulate the amount of water in the glasses, students can create a musical scale and play a simple tune.

Fischetto, Laura. *Michael the Angel*. illustrated by Letizia Galli. Doubleday, 1993. 32 pp. (ISBN 0-385-30844-2). Biography, M-L.

Story Review Chart

Setting	Plot/Events	Characters	Theme
•		•	

Cultural Paradigm Reference Classification Chart

Geographic Location	Economic System	Social System	Political System
	•	•	

This lighthearted child's biography of Michelangelo features the stubborn and mischievous side of the great artist from his childhood in Florence, where he wanders the streets instead of going to school and gets into fights with the other art apprentices. When the ruling prince of Florence, Lorenzo de Medici, becomes his patron, he finally gets to study sculpting, his true passion. The statues he eventually carves from the lovely Carrara marble still astound and delight the world. But some Florentine critics think the nose is too long on his gigantic statue of David. Up he obligingly climbs to the great nose, makes some noise with his scalpel, and throws marble dust down on the onlookers. Now they are all satisfied, although he hasn't changed a thing! Galli's tumultuous watercolor illustrations fill two-page spreads, adding a touch of humor to life in Renaissance Florence.

Classroom Applications

What of the social system of the time? Can your students tell from the detailed illustrations how people got along with one another or how they responded to artists? Would they like to try their own hand at modeling from plaster of paris? It is a satisfying art activity; otherwise, try clay or Plasticine modeling.

 Clement, Claude. *The Voice of the Wood*. illustrated by Frederic Clement, and translated by Lenny Hort. Puffin Books, 1993. 32 pp. (ISBN 0-14-054594-8). Fiction, M-L.

Story Review Chart

Setting	Plot/Events	Characters	Theme
•	•		

Cultural Paradigm Reference Classification Chart

Geographic Location	Economic System	Social System	Political System
		•	

This strange, haunting tale of Venice is a showcase for the artist's surrealistic paintings in pink, gray, and black of the canals of Venice, soaring gondolas, carnival goers in costumes and masks, and a violin maker creating magic with his woodworking. Have your students look carefully at the cover illustration. Do they notice that the masked cello player seems to flow into the ground as he sits under one of Venice's canal bridges? Or that the underside of the bridge resembles the bark of a tree? Or that a bird's nest with eggs rests on the scrolled end of the cello's neck? What does it all mean?

It is the story of a wonderful craftsman and the tree in his garden that he loves so well. From its swaying branches, he hears a symphony of birdsong, leaves fluttering, and gondolas gliding by. Then one hard winter, the tree dies, and the craftsman is forced to cut it down. He stores the lumber in his attic until one day he decides to build a masterpiece cello in tune with the music of nature as the tree has been. After a long year of shaping and polishing, the cello is finally finished on the day of the Grand Carnival.

A famous musician in wig and mask strides into the studio to purchase the cello. But the craftsman warns him of the instrument's magic, saying only a heart in tune with the voice of the wood can play it. The angry musician snatches up the cello and begins. But only grating noises like crocodiles clawing across the stone floor issue forth. The musician tears off his mask and wig and begins a nightlong struggle to conquer the instrument. In the morning, the craftsman hears exquisite music coming from his garden. There sits the musician on the stump of the old tree, playing the cello from which leafy branches have sprouted and on which singing birds have landed.

None of the characters is named, not even the magical wood from which the musical voice emerges. Simply written with the briefest text, the story is a sophisticated one told in its illustrations.

Classroom Applications

See whether your students recognize the one social scene in which the cellist's friends desert him because he is not successful at first. Be sure to involve them also in cello music from audiotapes, videotapes, or a live player. Perhaps they can attend a concert or listen to a student cello player who visits the class.

Netherlands

The Netherlands is bounded on the west and north by the North Sea, on the east by Germany, and on the south by Belgium.

 Oppenheim, Shulamith Levey. *The Lily Cupboard*. illustrated by Ronald Himler. HarperCollins, 1992. 32 pp. (ISBN 0-06-024669-3). Historical Fiction, E–M.

Story Review Chart			
Setting	Plot/Events	Characters	Theme
•	•	•	

Cultural Paradigm Reference Classification Chart

Geographic Location	Economic System	Social System	Political System
		•	•

Set in Holland during the days of World War II, this story is about a Jewish city family who send their little daughter, Miriam, into the country for safety to live with a Dutch farm family until the danger is past. Miriam is befriended by the family's young son, Nello, who gives her a rabbit she names Hendrik, for her father. She is determined to keep the rabbit safe even if the German soldiers come. Come they do, and Miriam must hide with her rabbit in "the lily cupboard," a space behind a false wall with lilies painted on it. Miriam understands then that what she is doing for her rabbit, this brave family is doing for her.

Sensitive illustrations portray the despair of the Jewish family contrasted with the peaceful Dutch countryside and its cows, canals, and windmills. The soldiers are not shown, but danger penetrates the dark lily cupboard until they leave and the wall is finally opened. The interdependence of groups on one another in times of tragedy is the focus here.

Classroom Applications

To demonstrate how difficult and frightening it is to hide when danger lurks, have one child at a time hide briefly in a darkened closet. This can be a voluntary activity in case some children are too frightened. Be sure to ask the hiders if they are all right.

Norway

Norway is located in the northernmost part of Western Europe, bordered on the west by the Norwegian Sea and the North Sea, on the north by the Arctic Ocean, on the northeast by Russia and Finland, and on the east by Sweden.

 Emberley, Michael. *Welcome Back Sun.* Little, Brown, 1993. 32 pp. (ISBN 0-316-23647-0). Fiction, E-M.

Story Review Chart

Setting	Plot/Events	Characters	Theme
•	•		

Cultural Paradigm Reference Classification Chart

Geographic Location	Economic System	Social System	Political System
•			

A young Norwegian girl narrates this story about what it is like for herself and her family during *murketiden*, the murky time between September and March when the sun disappears behind the mountains of her little village and doesn't come out again until spring; how her mother gets cranky and the girl herself begins to feel the hunger—for sunshine; how they finally decide to make their annual climb up Mount Gausta to welcome the sun, a difficult climb in the dark with dozens of other villagers; but at the top the sun is shining gloriously on everyone. Papa carries the tired girl back down to the village, and the sun follows them back.

Classroom Applications

Can your students imagine what it would be like for them if the sun did not shine at all during the winter? Give them some black construction paper and colored chalk to illustrate their own imaginings. This story featuring geographic location gives students a chance to look at a globe and to use a flashlight as the sun to determine where else the sun does not shine in winter.

Spain

Spain is located at the southwestern edge of Western Europe, bordered on the west by the Atlantic Ocean and Portugal; on the south by the Atlantic Ocean, Gibraltar, and the Mediterranean Sea; on the east by the Mediterranean Sea; and on the north by the Bay of Biscay and France.

 Zamorano, Ana. *Let's Eat!* illustrated by Julie Vivas. Scholastic, 1996. 32 pp. (ISBN 0-590-13444-2). Contemporary Fiction, P-E.

Story Review Chart

Setting	Plot/Events	Characters	Theme
•	•	•	

Cultural Paradigm Reference Classification Chart

Geographic Location	Economic System	Social System	Political System
	•	•	

Seven people are in Antonio's family, soon to be eight. Antonio is smallest and Mama is biggest, with the new baby expected any day. Mama is happiest when everyone can assemble at the big wooden table at two o'clock to eat together. Everyone talks at once in Julie Vivas's happy mealtime scenes. On Monday, they have chickpea soup, but Papa is too busy in his carpenter's shop to come. "Ay, *que pena!* What a pity," sighs Mama in a phrase repeated every time someone is missing.

On Tuesday, they have *empanadas,* but Alicia cannot come because she is learning to dance the *sevillanas.* On Wednesday, they have *sardinas,* but Salvador cannot come because he is playing hide-and-seek with his friends. On Thursday, they have *gazpacho,* but Granny cannot come because she is busy picking tomatoes. On Friday, they have roast *pollo*, but Grandpa cannot come because he is telling a story to his friends in the *cafeteria*. On Saturday, Antonio is the one to sigh, "*Ay, que pena!*" because Mama cannot come. She is in the hospital giving birth to a baby girl. But the next Sunday, Mama comes home with little Rosa, and everyone gathers around, including the new baby, for prawns, crab, squid, mussels, and saffron rice for the *paella*. "*Que maravilla!*" sighs Mama, "How wonderful!"

Vivas's orange, blue, and green illustrations show this lively family from every perspective as they eat, talk, play, and laugh together.

Classroom Applications

Your students will soon be repeating the Spanish phrases and wanting to know what the various foods taste like. This calls for a Spanish cooking experience. What will you make together?

Sweden

Sweden is located in the northernmost part of Western Europe, bordered on the east and south by the Baltic Sea, on the east by the Gulf of Bothnia, on the west by Norway, and on the northeast by Finland.

 Schwartz, David M. *Supergrandpa*. illustrated by Bert Dodson. Lothrop, Lee & Shepard Books, 1991. 32 pp. (ISBN 0-688-09899-1). Biography, E-L.

Story Review Chart

Setting	Plot/Events	Characters	Theme
•	•	•	•

Cultural Paradigm Reference Classification Chart

Geographic Location	Economic System	Social System	Political System
•		•	•

In 1951, when Gustaf Hakansson was 66 years old, he rode in the 1,000-mile Tour of Sweden bicycle race—and came in first! This is not to say he won the race; officials would not let him enter it officially because of his age. Nevertheless, he did not feel old and did not act old, so he rode his bike from beginning to end, peddling through the night when the other racers were sleeping. Gustaf took catnaps of 3 hours or so along the way whenever he felt the need.

He was the first rider to enter the little town of Lulea on the third morning, and one of the cheering villagers called him "Supergrandpa." The name stuck, the newspapers carried his picture, and everyone along the way gave him snacks of lingonberries, rye bread, fruit juice, tea, and cake.

The reader is caught up in the excitement of the race as words and illustrations show Gustaf, with hair "white as snow" and beard "like a great white bush," coming in a hair's breadth in front of the other riders. Even the king of Sweden gives him a big hug and invites him to the palace.

Classroom Applications

Have your students watched bicycle races? Now is the time to talk about winning and losing, as well as the purpose for racing. Does this race across Sweden bring the Swedish people together? What other reasons can the class think of for racing? Have them invent a race in which everyone wins.

Switzerland

Switzerland is located in the central part of Western Europe, landlocked by Germany, France, Italy, Liechtenstein, and Austria.

 Stone, Marti. *The Singing Fir Tree.* illustrated by Barry Root. Putnam, 1992. 32 pp. (ISBN 0-399-22207-3). Folktale, E-M.

Story Review Chart

Setting	Plot/Events	Characters	Theme
•	•	•	

Cultural Paradigm Reference Classification Chart

Geographic Location	Economic System	Social System	Political System
	•	•	

Pierre the woodcarver comes to a little Swiss village in the mountains to carve his masterpiece, an ornate tower for the town's clock, but he must first find the right wood. Cedric, the baker's son, hums a tune as he watches Pierre do other carvings. When Pierre hears the same song coming from the forest above the town, he tries unsuccessfully to find its source. Cedric shows him. It is a gnarled old fir tree that sings when the wind is right. Now Pierre knows that this is the wood he must have for the clock tower. Cedric is horrified and so is the village, for the tree is a part of the village and has sung to its inhabitants for ages past.

Illustrations of determined Swiss villagers in peasant costumes are framed in wood as the story progresses. Pierre tries to cut down the tree at night, but its sticky pitch prevents him. He uses his horse to try pulling it down, but the horse stops to listen to the music. A few branches are all that Pierre secures. Then he hears the voices of the village children echoing back the song of the tree and realizes that he cannot cut down their tree. From the branches he carves a wooden bird for each of the children. Once again, as the wind rises, the wooden birds begin to sing and the old fir tree sings back.

The social system, with its focus on social groups, and the economic system, with its focus on preserving natural resources, are featured here.

Classroom Applications

Can you bring in a Swiss cuckoo clock to demonstrate this type of woodcarving? Field trips to trees are also motivated by this story. Do any trees in the vicinity need to be protected? Students can choose a tree of their own and keep a journal of its changes during the seasons.

SUMMARY

What a wide range of genres the 35 books reviewed from Western Europe display. Fiction and folktales top the list at 8 books each, with historical fiction and biography featured in 4 books each. The six additional genres are represented, but only by 1 to 3 books each.

Characters are conspicuous in 29 books; setting and plot/events, in 22 and 23, respectively. Only 5 books, however, contain a discernible theme.

Who are the characters in Western European books? Of all the books reviewed here, 19 present adult and child characters appearing together, and 12 have adult characters appearing alone. Only 1 book, by comparison, has children characters appearing alone—a very interesting finding when one considers the large number of American children's books featuring children characters acting out plots on their own. If literature reflects life, can we infer that Western European children are being encouraged to depend on adults and not act independently? It is something to consider. Let's hold judgment, however, until we have reviewed the books from the countries that follow.

The element of the cultural paradigm most frequently apparent is by far the social; reference to economic issues occurs far less frequently. Clear mention of geography or political subjects occurs in less than one third of the books.

Which books will you choose for your bookshelf? Although one book cannot represent an entire country's output, it is possible to select a representative sampling from the many countries of Western Europe to give your students an overview of this cultural area.

REFERENCES CITED
▼▼

Avery, G. (1984). Two patterns of childhood: American and English. *Horn Book Magazine.* 60(6), 794-807.

SUGGESTED REFERENCES

▼▼▼

Blake, M. E., & Breedlove, W. G. (1993). Internationalism in Danish children's literature. *Reading Teacher*, 47(3), 271-272. (Denmark)

Blockeel, F. (1996). Colonial and postcolonial Portuguese children's literature. *Bookbird*, 34(4), 12-17. (Portugal)

Borberg, K. (1996). Santa Claus's special gift to the spirit. *Bookbird*, 34(1), 13-16. (Netherlands)

Castle, K. (1996). *Britannia's children: Reading colonialism through children's books and magazines, studies in imperialism*. Manchester, UK: Manchester University Press. (United Kingdom)

Coghlan, V., & Kennan, C. (Eds.). (1996). *The big guide to Irish children's books*. Dublin: Irish Children's Book Trust. (Ireland)

Erwin, B., Hines, C., & Curtis, C. (1992). Thematic units: A Scottish approach to literature-based education. *Reading Horizons*, 33(2), 108-120. (Scotland)

Filmer, D. K. (1996). *Fantasy fiction and Welsh myth: Tales of belonging*. London: Macmillan. (Wales)

Fisher, P. J. L., & Ayres, G. (1990). A comparison of the reading interests of children in England and the United States. *Reading Improvement*, 27(2), 111-115. (England)

Garrett, J. (1993). Far-away wisdom: Three nominees for the 1992 Andersen prize. *Reading Teacher*, 46(4), 310-314.

Hill, V. R. (1996). Travels: In Munich. *Bookbird*, 34(4), 66-68. (Germany)

Khorana, M. (Ed.). (1996). *British children's writers, 1800–1880* (Dictionary of literary biography, No. 163). Detroit: Gale Research. (England)

Knowles, M., & Malmkjaer, K. (1996). *Language and control in children's literature*. London: Routledge. (United Kingdom)

Kuivasmaki, R. (1984, Winter). Children's books in Finland. *Top of the News*, 201-204. (Finland)

Lindley, M., et al. (Eds.). (1994). *Children's books of the year*. London: Young Book Trust. (United Kingdom)

Lynch-Brown, C. (1989). A profile of Annie M. G. Schmidt, 1988 Hans Christian Andersen medalist. *Early Childhood Development and Care*, 48, 19-27.

Maissen, L. (1995). Telling the tale in Groningen. *Bookbird*, 33(2), 37-38. (Netherlands)

Oittinen, R. (1989). On translating for children: A Finnish point of view. *Early Child Development and Care*, 48, 29-37. (Finland)

Parmegiani, C. (1994). The new "mise en scene": Text illustration in France today. *Bookbird*, 32(4), 18-22. (France)

Phillips, Z. F. (1995). German children's literature in exile, 1933-1950. *Bookbird*, 33(3-4), 91-93. (Germany)

Psarski, V. (1997). Illustration and text: Common department, different routes. *Bookbird*, 35(1), 31-32. (Greece)

Rochman, H. (1998). Bearing witness to the Holocaust. *Booklinks*, 7(3), 8-14. (Germany)

Rudvin, M. (1994). Translation and myth: Norwegian children's literature and English. 1994 *Perspectives: Studies in Translatology*, 2(2), 199-211. (Norway)

Sidorsky, P. G. (1990). Along the German fairy-tale road. *Childhood Education*. 66(3), 151-154. (Germany)

Sollat, K. (1997). The boundaries of fantasy in German children's literature. *Bookbird*, 35(4), 6-11. (Germany)

Thompson, J. R., & Thompson, R. A. (1994). A literature treasure house: The Internationale Jugendbibliothek in Munich. *Journal of Reading*, 37(5), 386-388. (General)

Turin, J. (1996). Country survey: France (II). *Bookbird*, 34(4), 42-47. (France)

Turin, J., & Perrot, J. (1996). Country survey: France (I). *Bookbird*, 34(1), 38-43. (France)

Urooland-Lob, T. (1997). From picture book to cuddly toy. *Bookbird*, 35(1), 12-17. (Netherlands)

vanLierop-Debrauwer, H. (1996). Still preparing smart girls for their futures: A report from the Netherlands. *Bookbird*, 34(1), 22-24. (Netherlands)

Zipes, J. (1988). Walter Benjamin, children's literature, and the children's public sphere: An introduction to new trends in West and East Germany. *Germanic Review*, 63(1), 2-5. (Germany)

CHILDREN'S BOOKS CITED

▼▼

Akerman, K. (1990). *The banshee*. New York: Philomel. (Ireland)

Aliki. (1994). *The gods and goddesses of Olympus*. New York: HarperCollins. (Greece)

Anderson, H. C. (1993). *The snow queen*. New York: Workman. (Denmark)

Anholt, L. (1994). *Camille and the sunflowers: A story about Vincent Van Gogh*. Hauppauge, NY: Barron's. (France)

Axworthy, A. (1994). *Anni's diary of France*. Dallas, TX: Whispering Coyote Press. (France)

Berenzy, A. (1995). *Rapunzel*. New York: Henry Holt. (Germany)

Carle, E. (1995). *Walter the baker*. New York: Simon & Schuster. (Germany)

Cazzola, G. (1991). *The bells of Santa Lucia*. New York: Philomel. (Italy)

Chelepi, C. (1994). *Growing up in Ancient Greece*. New York: Troll. (Greece)

Clement, C. (1993). *The voice of the wood* (L. Hort, Trans.). New York: Puffin Books. (Italy)

De Maupassant, G., & Halperin, W. A. (1996). *When chickens grow teeth*. New York: Orchard Books. (France)

Dunrea, O. (1996). *The tale of Hilda Louise*. New York: Farrar, Straus & Giroux. (France)

Emberley, M. (1993). *Welcome back sun*. Boston: Little, Brown. (Norway)

Fisher, L. E. (1993). *Gutenberg*. New York: Macmillan. (Germany)

Fischetto, L. (1993). *Michael the angel*. New York: Doubleday. (Italy)

French, V. (1995). *Lazy Jack*. Cambridge, MA: Candlewick Press. (England)

Heuck, S. (1994) *A ghost in the castle*. Toronto: Annick Press. (Germany)

Hollinshead, M. (1994). *The nine days wonder*. New York: Philomel. (England)

Hodges, M. (1997). *Saint Patrick and the peddler*. New York: Orchard Books. (Ireland)

Le Tord, B. (1995). *A blue butterfly: A story about Claude Monet*. New York: Doubleday. (France)

Lewis, K. (1992). *Floss*. Cambridge, MA: Candlewick Press. (England)

Marshall, L. (1992). *The girl who changed her fate*. New York: Atheneum. (Greece)

McDermott, G. (1990). *Tim O'Toole and the wee folk*. New York: Puffin Books. (Ireland)

McMillan, B. (1995). *Nights of the pufflings*. Boston: Houghton Mifflin. (Iceland)

Munro, R. (1996). *The inside-outside book of London*. New York: E. P. Dutton. (England)

Nichol, B. (1993). *Beethoven lives upstairs*. New York: Orchard Books. (Austria)

Oppenheim, S. L. (1992). *The lily cupboard*. New York: HarperCollins. (Netherlands)

Pastucshiv, O. (1997). *Minas and the fish*. Boston: Houghton Mifflin. (Greece)

Pyle, H., & Borgenicht, D. (1996). *The legend of King Arthur*. Philadelphia: Running Press. (England)

Schwartz, D. M. (1991). *Supergrandpa*. New York: Lothrop, Lee & Shepard Books. (Sweden)

Stone, M. (1992). *The singing fir tree*. New York: Putnam. (Switzerland)

Varvasovszky, L. (1990). *Henry in shadowland*. Boston: David Godine. (Austria)

Yolan. J. (1991). *Wings*. San Diego: Harcourt Brace. (Greece)

Zamorano, A. (1996). *Let's eat!* New York: Scholastic. (Spain)

Zolotow, C. (1993). *The moon was the best*. New York: Greenwillow Books. (France)

SUGGESTED CHILDREN'S BOOKS

▼▼

Alcorn, J. (1991). *Rembrandt's beret*. New York: Tambourine Books. (Italy)

Araujo, F. P. (1993). *Nekane: The lamina and the bear*. Windsor, Canada: Rayve Productions. (Basque, Spain)

Behan, B. (1997). *The king of Ireland's son*. New York: Orchard Books. (Ireland)

Brett, J. (1992). *Trouble with trolls*. New York: Putnam. (Norway)

Climo, S. (1995). *Atalanta's race*. New York: Clarion Books. (Greece)

Climo, S. (1996). *The Irish Cinderlad*. New York: HarperCollins. (Ireland)

Collodi, C., & Mattotti, L. (1993). *Pinocchio*. New York: Lothrop, Lee & Shepard Books. (Italy)

Corbishley, M. (1994). *Growing up in Ancient Rome*. New York: Troll. (Italy)

Delamare, D. (1993). *Cinderella*. New York: Green Tiger Press. (Italy)

DePaola, T. (1991). *Bonjour, Mr. Satie*. New York: Putnam. (France)

DePaola, T. (1997). *Days of the blackbird*. New York: Putnam. (Italy)

Erlbruch, W. (1995). *Mrs. Meyer the bird*. New York: Orchard Books. (Germany)

Forest, H. (1990). *The woman who flummoxed the fairies*. San Diego: Harcourt Brace. (Scotland)

Gervais, B. (1992). *The tightrope walker*. New York: Lothrop, Lee & Shepard Books. (Belgium)

Herriot, J. (1990). *Oscar: Cat-about-town*. New York: St. Martin's Press. (England)

Heyer, M. (1995). *The girl the fish and the crown*. New York: Viking. (Spain)

Huck, C. (1996). *Toads and diamonds*. New York: Greenwillow Books. (France)

Isadora, R. (1996). *The steadfast tin soldier*. New York: Putnam. (Italy)

Kleven, E. (1996). *Hooray, a piñata!* New York: Penguin. (Spain)

Kreye, W. (1991). *The strongman and the dragon*. New York: North-South Books. (Switzerland)

Lattimore, D. (1994). *Frida Maria*. San Diego: Harcourt Brace. (Spain)

Lemieux, M. (1993). *The pied piper of Hamelin*. New York: Morrow. (Germany)

Lewis, K. (1990). *The shepherd boy*. New York: Macmillan. (England)

Lindgren, A. (1993). *The day Adam got mad*. New York: R & S Books. (Sweden)

Littlesugar, A. (1996). *Marie in the fourth position*. New York: Philomel. (France)

Litzinger, R. (1997). *The old woman and her pig: An old English tale*. San Diego: Harcourt Brace. (England)

MacDonald, M. R. (1997). *Slop!* Golden, CO: Fulcrum. (Wales)

Manna, A. L., & Mitakidou, C. (1997). *Mr. Semolina-Semolinus: A Greek folktale*. New York: Anne Schwartz/Atheneum. (Greece)

Martin, B. (1990). *Olaf the ship's cat*. New York: Checkerboard Press. (Sweden)

Moore, H. (1992). *Annie's dancing day*. New York: North-South Books. (Germany)

Munro, R. (1992). *The inside-outside book of Paris*. New York: E. P. Dutton. (France)

Ness, E. (1997). *Tom Tit Tot: An English folktale*. New York: Simon & Schuster Children's Publishing. (England)

Parkison, J. (1997). *Inger's promise*. Kansas City, MO: MarshMedia. (Norway)

Reynolds, J. (1992). *Far north: Vanishing cultures*. San Diego: Harcourt Brace. (Finland)

Ringgold, F. (1996). *Bonjour, Lonnie*. New York: Hyperion. (France)

Scheffler, U. (1994). *The stranger*. New York: North-South Books. (Switzerland)

Service, P. F. (1990). *Wizard of wind and rock*. New York: Atheneum. (England)

Sis, P. (1996). *Starry messenger*. New York: Farrar, Straus & Giroux. (Italy)

Spyri, J., & Krupinski, L. (1996). *Heidi*. New York: HarperCollins. (Switzerland)

Stanley, D., & Vennema, P. (1990). *Good Queen Bess: The story of Elizabeth I of England*. New York: Macmillan. (England)

Talley, L. (1997). *Bea's own good*. Kansas City, MO: MarshMedia. (France)

Valens, A. (1993). *Danilo the fruit man*. New York: Dial Books for Young Readers. (Sicily, Italy)

Zelinsky, P. O. (1997). *Rapunzel*. New York: Dutton Children's Books. (Italy)

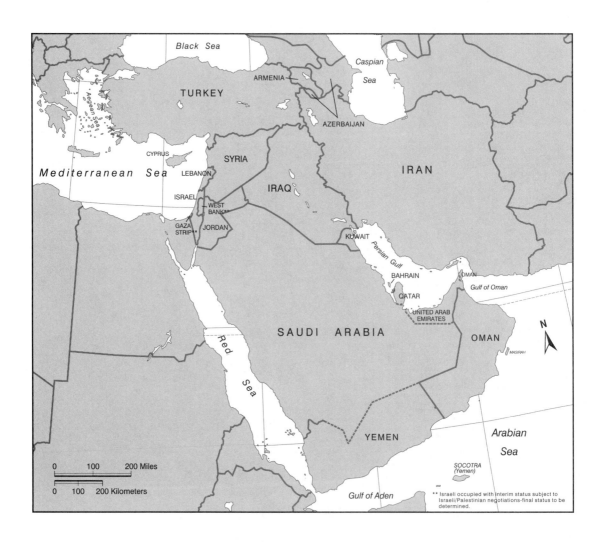

Black Sea

Caspian
Sea

ARMENIA

TURKEY

AZERBAIJAN

Aegean Sea

CYPRUS

SYRIA

IRAN

Mediterranean Sea

LEBANON

ISRAEL

IRAQ

WEST
BANK**

GAZA
STRIP**

JORDAN

KUWAIT

Persian Gulf

BAHRAIN

OMAN

Gulf of Oman

QATAR

UNITED ARAB
EMIRATES

Red

Sea

SAUDI ARABIA

OMAN

MASIRAH

N

YEMEN

Arabian
Sea

SOCOTRA
(Yemen)

0   100   200 Miles

0   100   200 Kilometers

Gulf of Aden

** Israeli occupied with interim status subject to
Israeli/Palestinian negotiations-final status to be
determined.

CHAPTER

9

Children's Books About the Middle East

THE MIDDLE EAST

The Middle East is located northeast of Africa. It is bordered on the west by the Mediterranean Sea, Egypt, and the Red Sea; on the north by the Black Sea, Georgia, Russia, and the Caspian Sea; on the east by Afghanistan, Pakistan, the Persian Gulf, and the Arabian Sea; and on the south by the Arabian Sea and the Gulf of Aden.

Countries

Armenia, Azerbaijan, Bahrain, Gaza Strip, Iran, Iraq, Israel, Jordan, Kuwait, Lebanon, Oman, Qatar, Saudi Arabia, Syria, Turkey, United Arab Emirates, West Bank, Yemen

EXAMINING THE CULTURAL REGION OF THE MIDDLE EAST AND THE PATTERNS OF CHILDREN'S BOOKS

The countries of the Middle East may be quite different from one another in many respects, but their people are all, with the exception of Israelis and Kurds, tied together by the common bond of being of Arab descent and speaking Arabic. Stories of heroes, magical feats, and great leaders have always been a part of their culture, with the old caliphs employing storytellers in their courts. But the ancient tales have taken on a new look today, appearing in written form in children's storybooks, as contemporary people are expected to become literate through reading.

Picture books featuring the Middle East available in the U.S. today are not much different from those available in the home countries. Most are folktales whose settings could be any of the countries mentioned because the Arab culture crosses so many borders. Note that 10 of 14 books reviewed here are folktales, mostly from the Arabian Nights, whose stories range from China and India to Greece and Morocco. Even Hebrew tales like *Esther's Story* cross borders into ancient Babylon, today's Syria and Iraq.

Only a few of the Middle Eastern countries listed have picture books reviewed here because so few are available, especially contemporary fiction. This is unfortunate when one realizes that today's children need to form images of children like themselves from every part of the world, especially the volatile parts, if the world is to have lasting peace. The Middle East has suffered a particularly vicious kind of stereotyping when Arabs are portrayed in the media mainly as terrorists (Kissen, 1991). We hope that books like *Sitti's Secrets* will help children who read it revise this view.

More than 70% of the books published in the Arab world itself are published in just two countries: Lebanon and Egypt. Lebanon, in fact, is home to 250 publishing houses—and this despite 16 years of bloody civil war (Hamade, 1994). Contemporary stories like *Sami and the Time of the Troubles* capture images of these difficult years like a time capsule. But not all contemporary stories reflect such reality in Lebanon. In a country where 18% of the female population is employed outside the home, children's books in Arabic still portray females most frequently as mothers in the home, followed by little girls, princesses, wives, adolescent girls, working women, and witches (Nasr, 1996). Even as a princess, the female is still dependent on a male in most of these stories. As you examine the books reviewed in this chapter, look especially for gender stereotyping. How does it compare with such stereotyping in American children's books?

COUNTRIES AND CHILDREN'S BOOKS REVIEWED

Iran

Iran is bordered on the north by Armenia, Azerbaijan, the Caspian Sea, and Turkmenistan. To the east lie Afghanistan and Pakistan; to the south, the Gulf of Oman and the Persian Gulf. Iraq and Turkey border on the west.

Wolkstein, Diane. *Esther's Story.* illustrated by Juan Wijngaard. Morrow Junior Books, 1996. 40 pp. (ISBN 0-688-12127-6). Folklore, M-L.[1]

Story Review Chart

Setting	Plot/Events	Characters	Theme
•	•	•	

Cultural Paradigm Reference Classification Chart

Geographic Location	Economic System	Social System	Political System
		•	•

Taken from the Old Testament Book of Esther, as well as oral legends, this tale tells of the time when the prime minister of Persia (Iran) decides to destroy all the Jews in the kingdom and no one can stop him but a young girl. Esther tells her own story to her diary in a first-person narrative as it is happening. Her uncle, one of the king's judges, changes her name to protect her, from the Jewish Hadassah to Esther, a Jewish and Persian name like the girl herself. In Persian, *Esther* is *Ishtar*, the goddess of love and war, first star to appear at night.

When Esther is 12 years old, a friend of her uncle who is also a judge at the King's Gate comes for dinner, sees the beautiful young girl, and calls her a queen. The next day, a guard takes her to the palace, where girls from many countries wait for one of them to be chosen as queen. After 4 years, Esther is brought before the king. She teases him and he laughs. He picks up a crown from the table and tells her she shall be queen.

Esther's uncle overhears a plot to poison the king and tells Esther to warn him; the plotters are caught. Her uncle's name is recorded in the king's *Book of Records*. Then a new prime minister is chosen who treats everyone harshly. When he finds out that Esther's uncle, who refuses to bow to him, is Jewish, he decides to kill all the Jews. Esther's uncle tells her to reveal who she is to the king and beg for his help.

As Esther fasts and prays for help, she hears a loud cry rising up from the Earth. To give her strength, thousands of ram's horns are being blown by the Jewish priests her uncle has contacted. Esther gathers her courage and walks uninvited into the throne room, an action that could bring about her death. Instead, the king lets her speak, and she invites him and the prime minister to a banquet in her room.

Afterward, the king cannot sleep and sends for the *Book of Records* to be read to him until he falls asleep. The next day, Esther looks out to see a royal parade with thousands of troops passing her window. At the head rides her uncle on the king's white horse led by the embarrassed prime minister.

But not until the next night, at the second banquet that Esther provides for the king and prime minister, does she reveal who she is and ask to have her people

---

[1]A = all ages, P = preschool, E = early elementary, M = middle elementary, L = late elementary

Cover from Esther's Story *by Diane Wolkstein, illustrated by Juan Wijngaard, 1996. New York: Morrow Junior Books, a division of William Morrow & Co., Inc. Printed with permission of William Morrow and Company, Inc.*

spared. Otherwise, she, too, will be killed. The king is furious when he finds all this to be the prime minister's doing, and the minister is put to death. Esther's uncle becomes prime minister and issues a decree that allows Jews to defend themselves against anyone who attacks them. Thus, they are able to rise up and defeat the prime minister's forces still at large.

Afterward, letters are sent to all the Jews in the land, urging them to remember this miracle that has saved them, and the holiday of Purim is established. This gripping first-person story pulls the reader into the very time and place the tale occurs. Wijngaard's detailed gouache-on-paper illustrations add to the authenticity as they appear on every other page in frames of marbleized gold.

Classroom Applications

Because letters play such an important role in this story, your students can pretend to be Esther or her uncle and write letters to one another about the situation or send letters to the people, telling them to defend themselves and later to celebrate their victory. Diary writing as Esther did can be practiced as well. Note how important the political system is in stories like this. Is this a true story? The historical facts are the basis for Jewish religious beliefs.

 Stanley, Diane. *Fortune.* Morrow Junior Books, 1990. 32 pp. (ISBN 0-688-07210-0). Folktale, M-L.

Story Review Chart

Setting	Plot/Events	Characters	Theme
	•	•	•

Cultural Paradigm Reference Classification Chart

Geographic Location	Economic System	Social System	Political System
	•	•	

Omar, a poor Persian farmer's son, has been betrothed to a neighboring farmer's daughter, Sunny, since they were young. When Omar comes of age, he has no idea how to seek his fortune, so he asks Sunny. She tells him to go to a place where people gather to do business and to keep his eyes open.

She is right. Once in a market town, he is approached by an old woman who has a tiger that will dance when someone plays a tune on a pipe. Against his will, she persuades him to buy the tiger with the little money his father has given him and to take the tiger from town to town where he will dance for money.

She is right. He is showered with so much money that he names the tiger Fortune. Within a year, he is back in his village with enough money to build a fine house. But now that he is a rich man, he thinks Sunny, a farmer's daughter, is not good enough for him. So off he goes on the tiger's back to find a princess for a wife.

The tiger takes him to a splendid city with streets of inlaid precious stones and a great palace at its center occupied by a weeping princess. When Omar hears that the princess is weeping because she lost her beloved prince just before they were to be married, he is determined to make her his bride. He rides into the palace and up to the princess's chamber without being stopped by a single guard.

The princess is afraid of the tiger until Omar soothes her by saying that the beast will carry her to her prince. With that, she embraces the tiger and—voila!—the tiger transforms into the missing prince who had been placed under a spell. Although Omar loses his bride, he is once again rewarded by being made a nobleman with house, land, and wealth.

This time, he returns to his village and asks Sunny to be his wife. She considers him carefully before answering, using the same words Omar did when he left her, but ending with her acceptance.

Classroom Applications

Folktales like this are teaching-tales with a moral to the story. Ask your students what behavior this tale is teaching: to follow good advice? to remain loyal to those who have helped you? not to let wealth blind you from missing out on love? This is another story your students may want to dramatize: with hand puppets made of papier-mâché, or as a shadow play with cutout cardboard figures behind a backlighted sheet, or as a readers' theater performance. Stanley's "jewel-like" illustrations and playful dialogue can help students create their own characters.

 DePaola, Tomie. *The Legend of the Persian Carpet.* illustrated by Claire Ewart. Putnam, 1993. 32 pp. (ISBN 0-399-22415-7). Folktale, M-L.

Story Review Chart

Setting	Plot/Events	Characters	Theme
•	•	•	

Cultural Paradigm Reference Classification Chart

Geographic Location	Economic System	Social System	Political System
	•		•

DePaola retells this Persian legend that he acquired from a friend and for the first time asks another artist to illustrate one of his books. The combination is a delightful success, with Ewart's flowing watercolor illustrations of beloved King Balash's world that is ruined when a thief steals his most precious possession: a huge diamond that had filled his palace with a million rainbows and was free for all to see.

As the thief gallops across the rocky plain, his horse stumbles, tumbling the diamond to the ground, where it shatters into a million fragments. Now King Balash's palace is filled with shadows and gloom, so he calls his people together to announce this calamity and to ask them to help him recover the diamond. A small boy, Payam, a weaver's apprentice, discovers the pieces of shattered diamond and hurries back to bring the king to the spot.

Now the king sits down to contemplate the carpet of diamonds at his feet, reflecting a million rainbows on the ground. He tells Payam that he will never return to the gloomy palace again. The boy and the people are horrified to find that they have lost their beloved ruler, thus opening them to attack by any robber-king from the desert. So Payam organizes the other young apprentices, the master weavers, and dyers of silk to make the king a glorious carpet as miraculous as the one the king stares at on the rocky plain. He also persuades the king to return to the throne for a year and a day, by which time his palace would once again be filled with color and light or he would be free to return to the shattered diamond on the ground.

Thus was born the first Persian carpet, which Payam and the weavers completed in a year and a day. Placed in the great hall where the diamond had once rested on a pedestal, the carpet filled the palace with all the colors of the rainbow and made King Balash happy once again.

Classroom Applications

This story surely calls for a weaving activity by your students. Individual looms can be simply made from cardboard squares with lines of thumbtacks at the top and bottom strung up and down with string. Strips of colored paper or yarn can then be woven in and out. Plastic yarn needles are safe and easy to handle. Or have someone bring in a small Persian carpet for the students to experience. Does it fill the classroom with colors?

Iraq

Iraq is a land-bound country in the Middle East except for a finger of land between Kuwait and Iran that stretches down to the Persian Gulf. It is bordered on the east by Syria, a part of Jordan, and Saudi Arabia; on the south by Saudi Arabia and Kuwait; on the north by Turkey; and on the west by Iran.

 Shepard, Aaron. *The Enchanted Storks.* illustrated by Alisher Dianov. Clarion Books, 1995. 32 pp. (ISBN 0-395-65377-0). Folktale, M-L.

Story Review Chart

Setting	Plot/Events	Characters	Theme
•	•	•	

Cultural Paradigm Reference Classification Chart

Geographic Location	Economic System	Social System	Political System
	•		•

At a time long ago when Baghdad is the richest city in the world, it is ruled by a much-beloved caliph who seems to know everything about everyone. People say, "The caliph has a thousand eyes," and look for spies. But in truth the caliph and his trusted vizier spend part of every day roaming through the great bazaars, disguised as merchants, asking questions, and listening to the gossip of the day.

One day in the marketplace, a peddler sells the caliph a lovely snuffbox inlaid with jewels. When he opens it, he finds it filled with snuff powder but also containing a note that reads: "A sniff of snuff for wings to soar. *Casalavair* for hands once more." Realizing it is magic snuff, the caliph and the vizier excitedly sniff a pinch of it to see what will happen to make them fly. They turn into two white storks with red and gray turbans and can communicate with one another but no one else.

After a glorious afternoon soaring above the streets, bazaars, and courtyards of the city, they fly back to the palace to say the magic word *casalavair*. But nothing happens. No matter how much they hop and flap and cry out the word, they remain as storks. Finally, they realize that an enemy has enchanted them.

The caliph's wicked brother, Omar, has coveted his throne and now claims it after a frantic and futile search for the caliph has concluded. Meanwhile, the caliph and the vizier, who fly to the forest, meet an enchanted woodpecker who was once a princess. She tells them how an evil sorcerer has put a spell on her that cannot be broken until a man asks her to marry him. The woodpecker takes them to the sorcerer's circle, and they recognize the sorcerer as the peddler who sold them the snuffbox.

While they watch in the shadows, Omar rides up to reward the sorcerer with a pouch of gold for getting rid of the caliph and the vizier. He learns how the sorcerer not only provided the pair with magic snuff but also scrambled the word of disenchantment to *casalavair* instead of *calasavair*.

After driving off the sorcerer with his sharp stork bill, the caliph says the correct word, turns back into himself, and then asks the woodpecker/princess to marry him. She quickly returns to her true self as well and accepts his offer. They borrow horses at a nearby village and ride into Bagdad to reclaim the throne. Omar is banished to the farthest ends of the Earth and forced to eat toads and snails as the caliph/stork did.

This typical Middle Eastern tale of magic and enchantment is based on tales told by Muslim storytellers and collected by folklorists. It bursts to life with the exotic illustrations of Russian artist Dianov: lavish and intricate with designs in red, gold, purple, and green that twine like vines around minarets and marketplaces while turbaned storks soar above the Tigris River and pompous Omar reins in his white steed at the sorcerer's fire.

Classroom Applications

What magic spells can your students invent? How would they use the spells if they were caliphs to rule such a great city as Bagdad? Written or dictated stories of the students' own making or a dramatization of this folktale can bring to life this era of fabulous riches, bustling bazaars, and autocratic rulers.

 Wade, Gini. *The Wonderful Bag.* Bedrick/Blackie, 1993. 28 pp. (ISBN 0-87226-508-0). Folktale, M-L.

Story Review Chart

Setting	Plot/Events	Characters	Theme
•	•	•	

Cultural Paradigm Reference Classification Chart

Geographic Location	Economic System	Social System	Political System
	•		•

In this tale from *The Thousand and One Nights*, Ali the Persian is sitting in his shop when Hamid the big mountain man walks by and snatches up a small damask bag. The surprised merchant chases after Hamid, trying to recover either the bag or the money to pay for it. But Hamid refuses, telling him that the bag and everything in it belong to him. Ali tries to rally the merchants to help him, but they rush him and Hamid off to the wise and all-seeing Kadi at the Hall of Judgment. Kadi asks Hamid to prove the bag is his by listing its contents.

Hamid tells him it contains 2 crystal flasks, a lamp with a djinn, fine Persian carpets, a cat with 6 kittens, 3 camels, 2 needles, a silver pin, and 50 mountain men who will swear that the bag is his. The astonished merchant calls Hamid a liar and then lists the contents of his bag as a large dog kennel, a peacock, 2 spotted leopards, some fellows playing dice, Prince Khrusraw riding his white stallion, a brigand's lair, a fishing net, a herd of gazelles, the entire city of Baghdad, and 1,000 merchants who will swear that the bag is his.

This answer brings Hamid to tears, while Ali continues with an impossibly long list of his bag's contents, ending with "a shroud and a coffin for the Kadi if he does not say this bag is mine." The angry Kadi opens the bag himself and turns it upside-down to see which of the two has been telling the truth. Out drops a shriveled orange peel and some olive pits.

Ali quickly saves himself by telling the furious Kadi that he was mistaken and that it wasn't his bag after all, leaving poor Hamid to face the wrath of the Kadi.

Full-page illustrations reflect the humor of the tale in the faces of the principal characters and the gathering of merchants but contain traditional Arabian Nights art, with each page framed in intricate designs against a marbleized golden background. Flying carpets, warriors on horseback, waterpipes, and a magic lamp with a blue genie drift through the pages as the two men vie for possession of the wonderful bag.

Classroom Applications

Your students may want to play their own version of the-wonderful-bag-game, passing a handbag from person to person, with each one naming one item that's inside and the next person having to repeat all of the items each time before naming his or hers, until someone stumbles and has to drop out. The last person remaining gets to keep the bag. The fun and humor of this story overshadows the seriousness of how theft and judgment were handled in old Baghdad. Be sure to have your students discuss these issues.

Israel

Israel is located at the eastern end of the Mediterranean Sea, bounded on the west by the Mediterranean Sea, the Gaza Strip, and Egypt; on the north by Lebanon; and on the east by Syria, the West Bank, and Jordan. The land comes to a point on the south, where its tip touches the Gulf of Aqaba.

 Edwards, Michelle. *Chicken Man.* Lothrop, Lee & Shepard Books, 1991. 32 pp. (ISBN 0-688-0908-1). Contemporary Fiction, E-M.

Story Review Chart

Setting	Plot/Events	Characters	Theme
•	•	•	•

Cultural Paradigm Reference Classification Chart

Geographic Location	Economic System	Social System	Political System
	•	•	

Chicken Man lives in Kibbutz Hanan, a farming commune in Israel's Jezreel Valley. He gets his name during the summer he works in the kibbutz chicken coop because the hens lay more eggs and the roosters strut more happily than ever before while he is there. But Bracha from the kitchen bakery asks for his job when a new work list is posted, and Chicken Man is moved to the laundry. There he sings so loudly that Dov from the dairy asks for the laundry job when the next work shift is announced, and Chicken Man becomes the gardener. Aviva from the pot washroom sees him happily watering the roses and trimming the lemon tree and wants that job next. So Chicken Man is shifted to the Baal-a-gan, the wildest children's house in the kibbutz.

But by then, the chickens have stopped laying, and both Chicken Man and the work committee realize how much they need him there. Quickly, they switch him to the chicken coop permanently, and by the next morning every hen has laid an extra egg.

Delightful full-page illustrations of kibbutzniks and their work, with a paragraph or so of text tucked in, help the reader visualize clearly what life in a kibbutz is all about.

Classroom Applications

A map shows each location and everyone's house. Can the reader detect anything about the climate from this story? Have your students make maps of their own neighborhoods. What do they think made Chicken Man so successful in each of his jobs that other people wanted them too? How would your students carry out those jobs themselves?

 Haskins, Jim. *Count Your Way Through Israel*. illustrated by Rick Hanson. Carolrhoda Books, 1990. 24 pp. (ISBN 0-87614-558-6). Nonfiction, M-L.

Story Review Chart

Setting	Plot/Events	Characters	Theme
•			

Cultural Paradigm Reference Classification Chart

Geographic Location	Economic System	Social System	Political System
	•	•	

An excellent introduction to the country of Israel, this book contains one number on each two-page spread, with the letter that represents it embedded in the top border of the art. In Hebrew, the first 10 letters of the alphabet are used for the numerals 1 to 10. Page 1 shows a map of Israel, along with its location on a map of Africa. Number 2 has two men—David and Goliath from the biblical story. Number 3 shows temples from the three religions—Christianity, Islam, and Judaism. Each of the other numbers represents a particular number of products, people, or religious beliefs, such as 4 for the four questions asked by children at the Passover meal and 8 for the eight native animals now found in Israel that have been reintroduced in recent times.

Classroom Applications

Have your students learn to pronounce these 10 numbers and then use them to count. Have them illustrate the numbers 1 to 10 with familiar objects.

 Shulevitz, Uri. *The Secret Room.* Farrar, Straus & Giroux, 1993. 32 pp. (ISBN 0–374–46596–7). Folktale, M–L.

Story Review Chart

Setting	Plot/Events	Characters	Theme
•	•	•	•

Cultural Paradigm Reference Classification Chart

Geographic Location	Economic System	Social System	Political System
		•	•

One day, a king is traveling through the desert on a camel; this is shown in wonderfully stylized two-page spreads. Four retainers follow, one behind the other, in colorful cassock-like robes against a white background. Their haughty expressions lead the experienced reader of folktales to guess that they are in for some sort of surprise. Sure enough, they meet an old man walking across the sand, whom the king stops to ask: Why is your head gray and your beard black? The man answers: Because my head is older than my beard. The king is so pleased with the man's clever reply that he commands him not to tell this to anyone else until he has seen the king's face 99 times.

Back at the palace, the king asks his chief counselor the same question: Why does a man's hair turn gray before his beard? The chief counselor is not clever enough to answer, but he is shrewd enough to ask one of the retainers where they had traveled. Soon he is on his way across the desert on a donkey to find the old man, which he does. But when the old man refuses to give him the answer, the king's chief counselor threatens him with prison if he does not but offers him 1,000 gold coins if he does. The old man asks for 99 copper coins instead and then gives him the answer.

When the chief counselor finally answers the king correctly, the king quickly summons the man and accuses him of disobedience. Then the man points out that he followed the king's orders to the letter and did not tell the answer until he had seen the king's face 99 times—on the 99 copper coins! This response so impresses the king that he makes the man his treasurer, rewarding him handsomely.

But the chief counselor is not pleased with the man's influence and decides to get rid of him. He accuses the man of stealing gold from the treasury and hiding it in his house. When the king hears this, he goes to the man's house with his retainers to search it high and low. They discover a locked door and a secret room. When the king orders the door unlocked, he is astonished to find an empty room. Then the man explains: He is so grateful for all the honors and riches bestowed on him that he comes to this room every day to remind himself he is still the same man with the gray head and black beard that the king once met in the desert. When the king realizes that the man is not only clever but wise, he dismisses the chief counselor and appoints the man in his place.

Classroom Applications

Can your students tell the difference between being clever and being wise? Make up some examples of actions they are familiar with. Which are wise and which are clever? Have them make up their own examples. What would they keep in a secret room to teach them a lesson? Have them write stories about it.

Lebanon

Lebanon is located at the eastern end of the Mediterranean Sea, north of Israel. It is bordered on the north and east by Syria, on the west by the Mediterranean Sea, and on the south by Israel.

 Heide, Florence Parry, and Gilliland, Judith Heide. *Sami and the Time of the Troubles.* illustrated by Ted Lewin. Clarion Books, 1992. 40 pp. (ISBN 0-395-72085-0). Contemporary Fiction, M-L.

Story Review Chart			
Setting	Plot/Events	Characters	Theme
•	•	•	

Cultural Paradigm Reference Classification Chart			
Geographic Location	Economic System	Social System	Political System
		•	•

War affects children severely. The 10-year-old Palestinian boy Sami has experienced war his entire life: a life of guns and bombs. When shooting occurs in the streets of Beirut, Sami and his family live in the basement of his uncle's house. When the shooting stops, they move back upstairs, and Sami is able to go to school again. When they have quiet days, his grandfather takes Sami, his sister Leila, and his mother to the beach for a picnic.

Now it is a bad day again, and they retreat to the basement, where Sami's uncle tells funny stories to make them laugh. Sami's mother has covered the floor and hung the basement walls with colorful Persian carpets and cushions, as well as the big brass vase that was a wedding present. Sami's father has been killed by a bomb in the marketplace. A bomb shakes the building. The grandfather tells them to remember the beautiful sunsets they have seen. He asks them to remember the "day of the children," but Sami cannot. But he does remember his father's beautiful peach orchards. They huddle around the radio, listening for the all-clear.

Now it is safe to go outside. Sami takes a broom to help clean the streets. Vendors and restaurant chairs fill the streets. A wedding party parades past. Sami's grandfather tells him to go and play. He finds his friend Amir, and they play pretend war with toy guns. Amir hopes they will have real guns when they are older. Will the fighting never stop? Then Sami remembers the day of the children. It was a clear day like today. Without warning, children flocked into the streets. Hundreds and hundreds of children started to march and shout with signs saying "Stop the fighting." Everyone cheered and laughed and cried.

Now they are back in the basement. Sami tells his grandfather that he remembers the day of the children; that maybe they can have another day of the children; and that the fighters will finally listen to the children and stop.

This gripping story is brought to life in two-page illustrations of the seated family highlighted against the black and red shadows of their basement hideaway or abroad in the daylight, carrying on street life amid bomb rubble.

Classroom Applications

This is a story without an ending. The last two-page spread shows a bombed-out street. Your students should find out what is happening in Lebanon today. Can children play safely in the streets once more? Do bombs sometimes fall? What would they do if they lived in Lebanon? Sami tells this story in a first-person narrative. Have your students relate their own first-person stories as if they, too, lived in Lebanon during the time of the troubles.

Saudi Arabia

Saudi Arabia is a large desert country bounded on the west by the Gulf of Aqaba and the Red Sea; on the north by Jordan and Iraq; on the east by Kuwait, the Persian Gulf, and the United Arab Emirates; and on the south by Yemen and Oman.

 Haskins, Jim. *Count Your Way Through the Arab World*. illustrated by Dana Gustafson. Carolrhoda Books, 1991. 24 pp. (ISBN 0-87614-487-3). Nonfiction, M-L.

Story Review Chart			
Setting	Plot/Events	Characters	Theme
•			

Cultural Paradigm Reference Classification Chart

Geographic Location	Economic System	Social System	Political System
	•	•	

Here is an excellent introductory book to the people who speak Arabic. They live in many countries in the Middle East, North Africa, and the Arabian Peninsula, where Saudi Arabia is located. Each two-page spread features a number from 1 to 10, illustrated by a scene from the Arab world representing that number. Two shows a Bedouin tent with two rooms, one for men and one for women. Five shows Muslims kneeling on prayer carpets to pray five times a day to Allah (God). Eight shows the eight ways to say "cousin" in Arabic, depending on whether the cousins are male or female and which side of the family they come from.

Classroom Applications

Have your students introduce one of their cousins by using the proper form. Make a comparison of counting from 1 to 10 in Arabic and Hebrew.

 Kimmel, Eric A. *The Three Princes*. illustrated by Leonard Everett Fisher. Holiday House, 1994. 32 pp. (ISBN 0-8234-1115-X). Folktale, M-L.

Story Review Chart

Setting	Plot/Events	Characters	Theme
	•	•	

Cultural Paradigm Reference Classification Chart

Geographic Location	Economic System	Social System	Political System
	•	•	

A tale of the desert sands, star-filled night skies, camels, and magic carpets, *The Three Princes* is told in various versions throughout Saudi Arabia, Iraq, Egypt, and Morocco. It concerns a beautiful but wise princess who is loved by three cousins: Prince Fahad, Prince Muhammed, and Prince Mohsen. Fahad and Muhammed have wealth and position, but Mohsen has only his handsome face, his cloak, and his camel. This is the cousin the princess loves best and is determined to marry.

When the *wazir*, her chief minister, disagrees with her choice because Mohsen has nothing to give her, she summons the three princes and tells them to go out into the world for a year and to bring back the rarest thing they can find. She promises to marry the prince who returns with the most wonderful thing.

After a year, the three princes meet in the desert where they had first separated and share their wonders with one another. Muhammed has a crystal ball in which a person can see anything that is happening anywhere in the world. Fahad has a magic carpet that can carry him anywhere he wants to go. Mohsen shows the others the magic orange he has found that can cure any illness, even of a dying person.

Then they begin to think about the princess whom they have not seen for a year. They peer into Muhammed's crystal ball and see her lying on a sick bed, with attending doctors saying she will not live to see the sunrise. The three princes leap on Fahad's magic carpet and are transported to the palace in the blink of an eye. Mohsen feeds his magic orange to the princess, and she is restored to health. She declares that she will marry the prince who was most responsible for saving her.

The doctors, courtiers, and wazir argue and argue about which of the three princes was most responsible. But they cannot agree. The princess admits they were all responsible, but she chooses Prince Mohsen because, as she tells them, Fahad still has his crystal ball, Muhammed still has his magic carpet, but Mohsen has used his magic orange to save the princess's life. The other two can use their magic to find other princesses, but Mohsen has given up his only possession. Therefore, she will give him in return something of equal value—herself as his bride.

Equally as fascinating as this traditional story is Fisher's art. Large two-page paintings of the three princes in their robes of red, yellow, and green against a dark blue star-studded sky dominate the work. He prepared by covering illustration boards with black and then drawing designs on them in white chalk; finally, he covered over everything with acrylic colors.

Classroom Applications

The story lends itself well to oral storytelling for your students because its plot is easy to remember. Its use of three's throughout, as well as its traditional folktale quest and test, help storytellers easily relate what comes next:

1. Description of the three princes who want to marry the princess
2. The quest for something wonderful
3. The use of each item by the princes
4. The test of which item is most responsible for saving the princess
5. Marrying of the third prince and the princess

Tell the story orally yourself as a model for your students to follow. Then challenge them to be storytellers themselves just as in the ancient Arabian Nights entertainment for the caliph. Students may want to put on robes and turbans or to sit on colorful carpets to lend an authentic atmosphere to their oral tales.

Syria

Syria is located at the eastern end of the Mediterranean Sea. It is bounded on the west by Israel, Lebanon, the Mediterranean Sea, and Turkey; on the north by Turkey; on the east by Iraq; and on the south by Jordan.

Lattimore, Deborah Nourse. *Arabian Nights: Three Tales.* HarperCollins, 1995. 64 pp. (ISBN 0-06-024585-9). Folktales, M-L.

Story Review Chart

Setting	Plot/Events	Characters	Theme
•	•	•	•

Cultural Paradigm Reference Classification Chart

Geographic Location	Economic System	Social System	Political System
		•	•

This book contains three stories from the thousand-and-one-tales of the Arabian Nights: *Aladdin,* a boy who lives in ancient Cathay, China; *The Queen of the Serpents,* about Hasib the son of a wise man from Greece; and *Ubar, the Lost City of* Brass, about a caliph from ancient Damascus, Syria. This last tale is the one reviewed here.

The caliph of Damascus loves to gather his court around him to hear stories from Talib the storyteller. One story is told about Solomon, who puts all the evil *Jinn* ("genies") in copper bottles stoppered with melted lead and sealed with his ring and throws them into the sea. Some are found by fishermen who, when they open them, find Jinn who cry, "I repent! Never again shall I ever do a wicked deed!" and fly away. On hearing this tale, the caliph is determined to see one of those bottles and to hold it in his hand. Talib tells him that the lost City of Brass would have to be found first, and the sea beyond it, where Solomon threw the bottles.

Thus begins a long and complex tale of a caravan trek through an endless desert led by Talib the storyteller; Emir Musa, the caliph's cousin; and the shakir, Emir Musa's wise man. Full-page illustrations dramatize the gruesome black stone castle they come upon, the horseman of brass who points the way, the pillar of stone with a terrible Jinn buried up to his chest, the wall of blackness with its towers of brass, and finally the City of Brass itself with its citizens frozen in time and its marketplace overflowing with silks, brocades, carpets, and vessels of ivory and gold. The seekers are nearly swallowed by an earthquake when one of their soldiers tries to take the forbidden jewels, but they finally discover the seashore where they do find a brass bottle stoppered with lead—which they take to the caliph. He pulls out the stopper and releases the Jinn who calls out his repentance and flies away across the sands to be gone forever.

This is a teaching tale with its warning tablets along the way exhorting all comers to do only good deeds and to think only good thoughts, for it was greed and evil deeds that brought down the City of Brass. In recent years, Ubar the City of Brass, which was thought to be completely fictitious, has actually been discovered through a satellite photograph and partially excavated. It makes lovers of folklore wonder what other aspects of this enchanting tale are true.

Classroom Applications

As with many of the Arabian Nights tales, this one can be converted easily to a readers' theater presentation by separating out the dialogue for each character as in a play, choosing characters and a narrator, and having the players practice reading their parts aloud until they become truly dramatic. Students enjoy presenting dramas as readers' theater because they do not have to memorize parts. Teachers favor this approach because stories can be dramatized repeatedly with different students for characters, thus giving everyone a chance to practice oral reading.

 Moore, Christopher. *Ishtar and Tammuz: A Babylonian Myth of the Seasons*. illustrated by Christina Balit. Kingfisher, 1996. 28 pp. (ISBN 0-7534-5012-7). Myth, M-L.

Story Review Chart

Setting	Plot/Events	Characters	Theme
•	•	•	•

Cultural Paradigm Reference Classification Chart

Geographic Location	Economic System	Social System	Political System
•		•	

Four thousand years ago in ancient Babylon (Syria and Iraq), the goddess of all creation, Ishtar, is worshipped by the people. She is the most beautiful, powerful, and

Cover of Ishtar and Tammuz: A Babylonian Myth of the Seasons *by Christopher Moore, illustrated by Christina Balit. 1996. Used by permission of Frances Lincoln, London, England.*

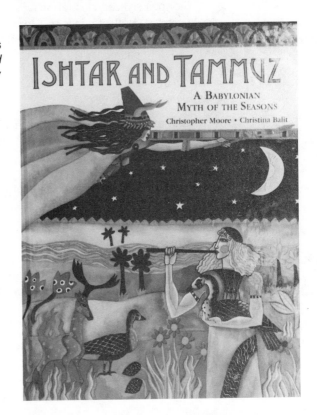

terrible being in all the heavens. Ishtar sends her son, Tammuz, to live on Earth, making it green with growing things and joyful with the sound of his flute. The people of Earth come to love and worship Tammuz; this makes Ishtar jealous. She sends her warriors down to kill Tammuz, who afterward descends into the dark underworld ruled by Ishtar's sister, Allatu.

Earth becomes barren and cold. All growing things die, rivers dry up, and birds fall silent. The desperate people pray to Ishtar to allow Tammuz to walk again on Earth, returning it to greenness and life. She finally agrees, knowing that she herself will have to descend to the underworld and confront her terrible sister, Allatu.

After being stripped of her crown, her jewels, and her powers at each of seven gates, Ishtar enters the underworld and sees her son, Tammuz, in a daze at the feet of Allatu. She falls on her knees, begging her sister to release Tammuz, but Allatu only laughs. Ishtar asks for permission at least to touch her son, and then, before Allatu can stop her, she springs to the foot of the throne, embracing Tammuz with tears streaming down her face.

Ishtar's warm tears are the waters of life to Tammuz. He awakens and clings to his mother until Allatu allows him to go—but only for 6 months. Ishtar and Tammuz have to agree that Tammuz will return to the underworld for 6 months of every year.

Now there is joy on Earth as warmth and new life spring forth. But when Tammuz returns to the underworld for 6 winter months, everything turns barren and cold. Thus it has been ever since.

Glorious stylized illustrations grace every page with bearded Babylonian men in profile making burnt offerings to Ishtar, Ishtar stripped of her regal robes approaching the jeweled throne of Allatu, and green Tammuz blessing the fruitful Earth with vineyards and date palms.

Classroom Applications

Have your students look closely at these lavish but unconventional illustrations. Do they realize the pictures represent art from ancient Babylonian pottery and tombs? Put out geometric pieces and strips of colored paper along with light and dark backing paper for making collages to represent fruitful Earth in the summer, barren Earth in the winter, and the dark underworld of Allatu.

West Bank

The West Bank is bounded by Israel on the north, west, and south and by Jordan and the Dead Sea on the east.

 Nye, Naomi Shihab. *Sitti's Secrets*. illustrated by Nancy Carpenter. Four Winds Press, 1994. 32 pp. (ISBN 0-02-768460-1). Contemporary Fiction, E-L.

Story Review Chart

Setting	Plot/Events	Characters	Theme
•		•	•

Cultural Paradigm Reference Classification Chart

Geographic Location	Economic System	Social System	Political System
	•	•	

Mona's Palestinian grandmother, her *sitti*, lives on the other side of the world, but Mona remembers her every night when she is going to sleep because she knows that the sun is just peeking through Sitti's window "brushing the bright lemons on her lemon tree." Mona remembers because she has visited Sitti and talked with her, at first through her father, who speaks Arabic. Sitti calls Mona H*abibi*, meaning "darling," and her voice "giggled and whooshed like wind going around corners," in Mona's wonderfully poetic prose.

Cover reprinted with the permission of Simon & Schuster Books for Young Readers, an imprint of Simon & Schuster Children's Publishing Division from SITTI'S SECRETS by Naomi Shihab Nye, illustrated by Nancy Carpenter. Illustrations copyright © 1994 Nancy Carpenter.

But soon they invent their own language of points and claps and hums. They use whistles and claps to thank the cow that gives Sitti a teapot of milk. Mona plays marbles with her cousins Fowzi, Sami, Hani, and Hendia without needing words. One day, Sitti takes off her scarf and allows Mona to brush out her long hair. It is striped dark and white, just as Mona has guessed. When she covers it with her scarf again, Mona feels as if she knows one of Sitti's secrets.

When Mona returns to the United States, she writes a letter to the president. She tells him about her grandmother in the West Bank who has a lemon tree in her yard that whispers secrets, who can read dreams and tea leaves and good luck on Mona's forehead. She tells him that she is worried when she watches the news on television, that if the people in the United States could meet Sitti, they would like her. She wishes the president luck and says that she votes for peace; her grandmother votes with her.

This precious story ends with Mona and her grandmother floating amid the stars while Mona thinks about the world as a huge body tumbling in space, "all curled up like a child sleeping," with people far apart but connected. And she wonders: "Does the world have a forehead?"

Classroom Applications

Illustrations help make this story extra special. Have your students comment on the first picture, with Sitti in her bed and the sun projecting through the window with an image of the globe over everything; then Sitti swinging with waves, fish, and a city in the branches of the tree; and deserts reflected on the laundry and Palestinian people in the leaves. What other unusual images can they discover?

What would your students write to the president if they were Mona? Suggest that they learn about the West Bank and the problems it is facing. Can they pretend to be a child who visits the West Bank and then writes such a letter? What else might they do to help promote peace in this troubled area? How does this story compare with *Sami and the Time of the Troubles* in Lebanon?

SUMMARY

Folktales dominate the types of children's books reviewed about the Middle East. Yet how can folktales represent the contemporary life of people in these countries? How can American children learn about the Middle East from seemingly out-of-date tales? We may wish that more contemporary fiction were available, but basic truths about a culture can still be extracted from folktales.

The story elements of setting, plot/events, and characters are equally dominant in nearly all but 2 or 3 of the 14 books reviewed, but distinct theme is important in less than half .

The social element of the cultural paradigm is most frequently featured in these books. Social and political references come in a close second and third, respectively. Geographic location serves a clear purpose in only one book. It is perhaps of interest to note that most of the folktales highlight the issue of political leadership, given the obvious roles played by some caliph, prince, or sheik. But what relevance do such rulers have, one may ask, in the modern Middle East? In attempting to answer this question, let's not forget that folktales from ages past are often an important indication of the values and beliefs held by a people. Thus, some Middle Eastern countries are still governed by men who rule much like the caliphs of old. It is less surprising, then, that many Middle Eastern folktales that are still told through contemporary books emphasize political issues.

Other folktales, such as *Fortune*, have served many generations as so-called teaching tales. Because they continue to teach important values still held by modern Middle Eastern cultures, they have been preserved well into modern times. As you place books about the Middle East on your bookshelves and share them with your students, keep in mind the words of Jeffrey Garrett (1993), the U.S. representative on the Hans Christian Andersen Award Jury:

> What we in the U.S. need in order to *understand* and *learn* from children's books from other countries . . . is a faith that there is something there waiting to be unlocked, something that just might illuminate some aspect of our own or our children's lives. (pp. 313–314)

REFERENCES CITED

Garrett, J. (1993). Far-away wisdom: Three nominees for the 1992 Andersen prize. *Reading Teacher*, 46(4), 310-314.

Hamade, S. N. (1994). Characteristics of the literature used by Arab authors in library and information science: A bibliometric study. *International Information & Library Review*, 26, 139-150.

Kissen, R. M. (1991). The children of Hagar and Sarah. *Children's Literature in Education*, 22(2), 111-119.

Nasr, J. A. (1996). Sex role images in Arabic children's literature. *Bookbird*, 34(1), 25.

SUGGESTED REFERENCES

Abdan, A. A. (1991). An exploratory study of teaching English in the Saudi elementary public schools. *System*, 19(3), 253-266. (Saudi Arabia)

Alsafi, A. T. (1994). Psychological reality and the role of the teacher in early-education sharing time. *International Review of Education*, 40(1), 59-69. (Saudi Arabia)

Baruch, M. (1994). Israel (II). *Bookbird*, 32(3), 79-81. (Israel)

Cooper, I. (1997, May). The dead sea scrolls. *Booklinks*. (Middle East)

Dudley-Marling, C. (1997). "I'm not from Pakistan": Multicultural literature and the problem of representation. *New Advocate*, 10(2), 123. (Pakistan)

Field, S. L., Burlbaw, L. M., & Davis, O. L., Jr. (1994). "I think there was a storm in the desert": Using narrative to assess children's historical understanding of the Gulf War. *Social Studies*, 85(6), 256-261. (General)

Ghazi, T. K. (1997). Islamic literature for children adopts the English language. *Bookbird*, 35(3), 6-10. (General)

Iskander, S. (1997). Portrayals of Arabs in contemporary American picture books. *Bookbird*, 35(3), 11-16. (Saudi Arabia)

Mehran, G. (1991). The creation of the new Muslim woman: Female education in the Islamic Republic of Iran. *Convergence*, 24(4), 42-52. (Iran)

Mehran, G. (1992). Social implications of literacy in Iran. *Comparative Education Review,* 36(2), 194-211. (Iran)

Rai, M. (1997). The Iranian revolution and the flowering of children's literature. *Bookbird*, 35(3), 31-33. (Iran)

Staples, S. F. (1997). Writing about the Islamic world: An American author's thoughts on authenticity. *Bookbird*, 35(3), 17-20. (General)

Zaldman, L. M. (1997). Books for Salaam, Shalom, Peace. *Bookbird*, 35(2), 42-45. (General)

CHILDREN'S BOOKS CITED
▼▼▼

DePaola, T. (1993). *The legend of the Persian carpet.* New York: Putnam. (Iran)

Edwards, M. (1991). *Chicken Man.* New York: Lothrop, Lee & Shepard Books. (Israel)

Haskins, J. (1990). *Count your way through Israel.* Minneapolis, MN: Carolrhoda Books. (Israel)

Haskins, J. (1991). *Count your way through the Arab world.* Minneapolis, MN: Carolrhoda Books. (Saudi Arabia)

Heide, F. P., & Gilliland, J. H. (1992). *Sami and the time of the troubles.* New York: Clarion Books. (Lebanon)

Kimmel, E. A. (1994). *The three princes.* New York: Holiday House. (Saudi Arabia)

Lattimore, D. N. (1995). *Arabian nights: Three tales.* New York: HarperCollins. (Syria)

Moore, C. (1996). *Ishtar and Tammuz: A Babylonian myth of the seasons.* New York: Kingfisher. (Syria)

Nye, N. S. (1994). *Sitti's secrets.* New York: Four Winds Press. (West Bank)

Shepard, A. (1995). *The enchanted storks.* New York: Clarion Books. (Iraq)

Shulevitz, U. (1993). *The secret room.* New York: Farrar, Straus & Giroux. (Israel)

Stanley, D. (1990). *Fortune.* New York: Morrow Junior Books. (Iran)

Wade, G. (1993). *The wonderful bag.* New York: Bedrick/Blackie. (Iraq)

Wolkstein, D. (1996). *Esther's story.* New York: Morrow Junior Books. (Iran)

SUGGESTED CHILDREN'S BOOKS
▼▼▼

Ben-Ezer, E. (1997). *Hosni the dreamer: An Arabian tale.* New York: Farrar, Straus & Giroux. (Saudi Arabia)

Morris, A. (1990). *When will the fighting stop? A child's view of Jerusalem.* New York: Atheneum. (Israel)

Wildsmith, B. (1997). *Joseph.* Grand Rapids, MI: Eerdmans. (Israel)

Zeman, L. (1993). *The revenge of Ishtar.* Montreal: Tundra. (Syria)

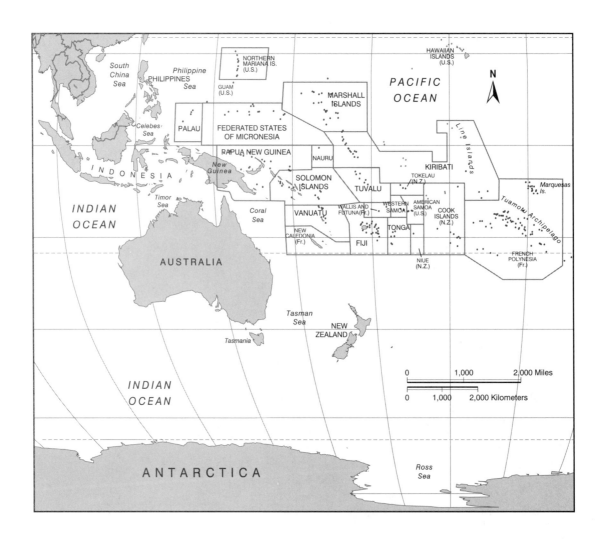

10

Children's Books About the Pacific, Australia, New Zealand, and Antarctica

THE PACIFIC, AUSTRALIA, NEW ZEALAND, AND ANTARCTICA

The Pacific, Australia, New Zealand, and Antarctica occupy the largest area of the globe, with the Bering Sea to the north, North America, Central America, and South America on the east; Asia, the South China Sea, and the Indian Ocean on the west; and Antarctica itself to the south.

Countries

Antarctica, Australia, Brunei, Cook Islands, Federated States of Micronesia, Fiji, Indonesia, Kiribati, Marshall Islands, Nauru, New Caledonia, New Zealand, Niue, Northern Marianas Islands, Palau, Papua New Guinea, Philippines, Solomon Islands, Tokelau, Tonga, Tuamotu Archipelago, Tuvalu, Vanuatu, Wallis & Tununa, Western Samoa

EXAMINING THE CULTURAL REGION OF THE PACIFIC, AUSTRALIA, NEW ZEALAND, AND ANTARCTICA AND THE PATTERNS OF CHILDREN'S BOOKS

Most countries of the Pacific are islands, from the largest, the island continent of Australia, to the tiny coral atolls, part of larger island nations. Formerly, most smaller Pacific islands were divided by geographers into the three groups of Micronesia, Polynesia, and Melanesia, depending on the types of people who settled them. Today, most of these islands have either banded together into loose confederations or become independent countries. Some are still territories of the European nations that claimed them in earlier days of exploration and settlement.

The U.S. territories of Guam and American Samoa, as well as the state of Hawaii, are not treated in this text as they are not independent countries. Icy Antarctica, at the South Pole, is considered a continental region, rather than a settled country, its only human inhabitants being transient people from various nations who have established scientific bases on its coasts. Children's books about Antarctica are reviewed in this chapter.

With the exception of Australia, few island nations have children's picture books (other than nonfiction) available in the United States. Thus, this chapter reviews mainly Australian books, more of which are becoming available for readers in the United States with every passing year. A strong interest in Australia has surfaced within the past decade as sporting events such as the America's Cup yacht race and the Olympics take center stage in American television. Motion pictures produced in Australia but available at the corner video store in the United States have also created an interested audience. As elementary students have access to Australian storybooks, this interest continues to intensify.

One study of 200 U.S. students ages 9 to 11 asked them what they would like to know about children in Australia. Responses were categorized into nine questions:

1. What kinds of foods do you eat?
2. What kinds of clothes do you wear?
3. What are your houses like?
4. What kinds of pets or animals do you have?
5. What are your schools like?
6. What is your weather like?
7. Do you have any brothers or sisters?
8. Do you have many friends?
9. Do you ever get lonesome? (Monson, Howe, & Greenlee, 1989)

As you read through the reviews of books in this chapter, keep these questions in mind to determine which books might best help your students answer such questions for Australia and any of the other countries mentioned.

COUNTRIES AND CHILDREN'S BOOKS REVIEWED

Antarctica

Antarctica is located at the southern polar region of the Earth, south of Australia and New Zealand.

 Cowcher, Helen. *Antarctica*. Farrar, Straus & Giroux, 1990. 36 pp. (ISBN 0-374-40371-6). Nonfiction, P-E.[1]

Story Review Chart

Setting	Plot/Events	Characters	Theme
•	•		

Cultural Paradigm Reference Classification Chart

Geographic Location	Economic System	Social System	Political System
•			

This visually stunning look at the southern polar region shows dazzling two-page paintings of male emperor penguins huddling together in a brooding circle against freezing storms of the dark winter; female emperor penguins feeding underwater; the hatching of their chicks before the coming of spring; Adelie penguins in their nesting colony; and then a new arrival: a terrible whirring helicopter, frightening the Adelies from their nests as skuas swoop in to eat their eggs. A base camp has been established nearby. Will the new arrivals be friends or foes?

The simple text of a sentence or two embedded in each two-page illustration is enough to portray the plight of the creatures native to this beautiful but harsh environment. It is an excellent introduction to Antarctica for younger children, focusing on geographic location.

Classroom Applications

Your students may want to create an Antarctic diorama in a cut-down cardboard carton; making plaster of paris or Styrofoam mountains, snowbanks, and icebergs; and contrasting the dazzling white background with watery blue and green paint.

 Williams, Geoffrey T. *The Last Frontier: Antarctica*. illustrated by Neesa Becker. Price Stern Sloan, 1992. 32 pp. (ISBN 0-8431-3378-3). Fictional Travel, M-L.

---

[1]A = all ages, P = preschool, E = early elementary, M = middle elementary, L = late elementary

Story Review Chart

Setting	Plot/Events	Characters	Theme
•	•		

Cultural Paradigm Reference Classification Chart

Geographic Location	Economic System	Social System	Political System
•			

This story of young Jon Michaels, who travels with his marine biologist mother to Antarctica, is reminiscent of *Anni's Diary of France*, with diary entries as Jon travels by ship, plane, and the underwater vehicle MURV. He feels seasick during a storm through the Drake Passage; watches crabeater seals hunt for krill; sees chinstrap penguins dive off an iceberg; swims in 100°F (!) water heated by a volcano at Fumarole Bay; gets dive-bombed by skuas; dives with his mother and Captain Thorn in the underwater vehicle MURV; and flies through a whiteout to the South Pole.

The text—a dialogue among Jon, his mother, and Captain Thorn—tells an exciting story of the history, scientific achievements, weather extremes, and natural life of Antarctica, interspersed with realistic illustrations and Jon's diary entries. Geographic location is the cultural paradigm featured.

Classroom Applications

Have your students pretend to be friends of Jon who go along with him and experience the same adventures. Have them, too, keep diaries of their daily happenings. Provide other nonfiction books about Antarctica, as well as videotapes or CD-ROMs (see Appendix B).

 Geraghty, Paul. *Solo.* Crown, 1995. 32 pp. (ISBN 0-517-70908-2). Fiction, P-E.

Story Review Chart

Setting	Plot/Events	Characters	Theme
•	•		

Cultural Paradigm Reference Classification Chart

Geographic Location	Economic System	Social System	Political System
•			

Floe, the mother penguin, returns from her months at sea to her mate, Fin, and a joyous celebration. When Floe lays an egg, Fin takes on the task of brooding it between his legs for 3 months until out hatches little baby Solo. Meanwhile, Floe is off swimming and diving underwater, filling up with squid for her new baby. Now it is Fin's turn to take to the sea. When he does not return, Floe must leave her baby behind to hunt for food for both of them or else they will die. Solo dodges the pecks of other penguins and hobbles away toward the sea. A dark skua swoops down to attack Solo, when suddenly a large shape emerges from the sea. It is Fin, back at last, dragging a fisherman's net that has entangled him, just in time to save his baby.

Dramatic full-page illustrations painted by this renowned wildlife artist and author make this book a fine companion volume to the previous *Antarctica*.

Classroom Applications

If your students have created an Antarctic diorama, now they can fill it with cutout emperor penguins. Fasten tabs to their backs so that they will stand up, and be sure to make a special Floe, Fin, and little Solo.

Australia

Australia is an island continent located in the southern Pacific Ocean north of Antarctica, south of New Guinea, west of New Zealand, and bordered by the Indian Ocean on the west.

 Reynold, Jan. *Down Under: Vanishing Cultures*. Harcourt Brace, 1992. 32 pp. (ISBN 0-15-224183-3). Nonfiction, E-L.

Story Review Chart			
Setting	Plot/Events	Characters	Theme
•	•		

Cultural Paradigm Reference Classification Chart			
Geographic Location	Economic System	Social System	Political System
	•	•	

Aprenula, an aboriginal Tiwi girl, joins her family to go on a walkabout through the Australian bush in this dramatically illustrated photo story. She dances the dance her grandfather gave her when she was born, collects string bark to be woven into carrying baskets for the walkabout, and catches a bandicoot that her grandmother scares out of a hollow log. Her grandmother's adopted son, Tipalipimuri, catches a huge carpet snake in a second hollow log, adding another ingredient to their meal. Meeting other Tiwi families at the beach, the children run and splash in the water together, always watchful for crocodiles. The family carves and paints a spirit pole to honor a relative who has died. Then they dance their Dreaming to send her spirit on its way.

Close-up photographs, two or three to a two-page spread, with a brief text between, realistically portray this very different way of life. It is almost as if the reader is there with the author, who lived with the Tiwi long enough to capture this vanishing culture on film. The Tiwi social system, with its time-honored customs, and the economic system, with its dependence on the natural environment to provide basic needs, set the stage for the walkabout described here.

Classroom Applications

Bring in an audiotape of Australian aborigine music for your students to dance to. Can they imagine becoming a part of the land as Aprenula does? Here also is the opportunity for another diary activity with your students as they pretend to go along with Aprenula on her walkabout.

 Oodgeroo. *Dreamtime: Aboriginal Stories*. illustrated by Bronwyn Bancroft. Lothrop, Lee & Shepard Books, 1994. 96 pp. (ISBN 0-688-13296-0). Autobiography and Folklore, M-L.

Story Review Chart			
Setting	Plot/Events	Characters	Theme
•		•	

Cultural Paradigm Reference Classification Chart			
Geographic Location	Economic System	Social System	Political System
	•	•	

The first half of this gloriously illustrated book contains true stories from the author's life on every two pages. The last half contains aboriginal folktales, mostly one to a page, with colorful illustrations in contemporary aboriginal style on every other page throughout. The author, an Aborigine from Stradbroke Island, Queensland, devoted her life to her people as a political activist, poet, and writer. Her aboriginal name, Oodgeroo, means "paperbark," given to her by the Nunukul tribe to represent her writing tools: bark from the paperbark tree and charcoal from its coals to write with. The artist, a descendent of the Bundjalung people, uses spirals, lines, and dots of blue, green, lavender, yellow, and orange to bring the reader a touch of the Dreamtime, the world of Australia's indigenous people.

The story "Kill to Eat," told in first person, shows a young Oodgeroo with her brothers and sisters out hunting birds with slingshots to supplement the meager diet of White man's rations her father earns working on a road-building crew. They know the rules about using weapons only for the gathering of food and never for the sake of killing. But when her brother misses a sure shot at a "bluey" and his sisters roar with laughter, even a nearby kookaburra joins in with its raucous chuckling. This is too much for the brother, and he fires his slingshot wildly into the tree. Down falls the kookaburra. The stricken children know they have broken two rules: (a) Kill only to eat and (b) never kill a kookaburra because its laughter brings happiness to everyone. Their father happens upon the scene just then, and they are punished in a way they would not soon forget: No more hunting for 3 months, and eating only the White man's hated rations.

Cover from Dreamtime: Aboriginal Stories *by Oodgeroo, illustrated by Bronwyn Bancroft, 1994. New York: Lothrop, Lee & Shepard Books, a division of William Morrow & Co., Inc. Printed by permission of William Morrow & Company, Inc.*

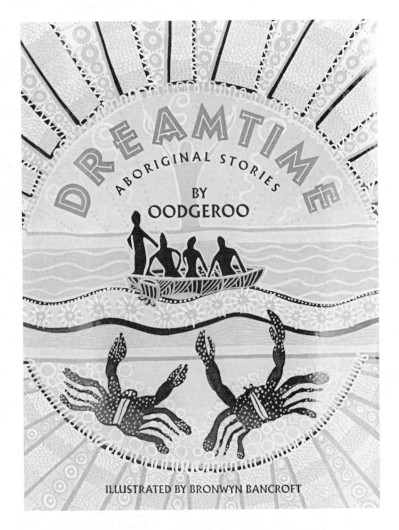

Growing up as an Aborigine in a White person's world is the theme of these first stories, whereas "Stories From the Old and New Dreamtime" relate creation myths of Rainbow Serpent and "why" tales of how trees, birds, and even stars come to be the way they are.

The social system is featured here, with its values, morals, and interpersonal relations, whereas the economic system describes natural resources in a hunting-gathering society.

Classroom Applications

Your students may want to try their hand at telling stories from their own families and illustrating them aboriginal-style. Or they can pretend to be aboriginal boys or girls and make up stories of their own based on one from this book.

Meeks, Arone Raymond. *Enora and the Black Crane*. Scholastic, 1991. 32 pp. (ISBN 0-590-46375-6). Folktale, E-L.

Story Review Chart

Setting	Plot/Events	Characters	Theme
•	•		

Cultural Paradigm Reference Classification Chart

Geographic Location	Economic System	Social System	Political System
•		•	

Enora is a young Aborigine man who lives with his people in a rain forest at the beginning of time before the birds and other animals had colors. One day, he follows a shimmering glow of colors through the trees to a clearing where birds of every kind are gathered: emus, cassowaries, scrub hens, lyrebirds, parrots, and cranes, all in their black, white, and gray feathers. As he watches, colors descend on the birds and tint their feathers every hue of the rainbow. When Enora rushes back to tell his people, they do not believe him, so he sets off once again to prove it. This time, as he watches the colors descend on the birds, he kills the bird closest to him, a crane, and takes it back to show his people. The colors, however, drain off the dead bird, leaving it black. When Enora awakens the next day, he finds himself covered with black feathers and knows he must return to the clearing as a black crane.

Full-page illustrations by the author, an award-winning aboriginal artist, bring pages to life almost as if they are red rock cliffs covered with ancient petroglyphs of people and animals.

Once again, the story features the values of the social system, but this time also the flora and fauna of a particular geographic location.

Classroom Applications

Students can try making their own paints as the artist did—perhaps by grinding up a brick and mixing it with water; or dipping pieces of brick in water; or by drawing figures on flat stones with colored chalk. Large type and short text make this a useful book for the youngest children.

 Adams, Jeanie. *Going for Oysters*. Albert Whitman, 1994. 32 pp. (ISBN 0-8075-2978-8). Fiction, E-L.

Story Review Chart

Setting	Plot/Events	Characters	Theme
•	•	•	

Cultural Paradigm Reference Classification Chart

Geographic Location	Economic System	Social System	Political System
	•	•	

The author-artist, who lived among the aboriginal people at Aurukun, Cape York Peninsula, Queensland, tells a contemporary story in text and stamped paintings of a large aboriginal family and one blond school chum who go by boat on an outing to the Love River to gather oysters. Told in the words of an excited daughter, the story carries Grandad's warning about old Yaatamay the Carpet Snake in the eastern swamp. Soon everyone is on the beach, fishing for catfish and grunter to eat while Mum makes tea and johnnycakes.

Then they're off in the boat for oysters clinging to the stilt roots of mangrove trees up in the mangrove swamp. Another feast ensues when they return with the oysters. But soon the children are off again into the swamp without heeding Grandad's warning. A noise like thunder in the ground brings the girls to a halt, and they gather up their brothers to scurry back to camp without waiting to see whether it was old Yaatamay.

Realistic illustrations on every page bring this adventure to life for the reader while the text describes family ties so close that even the frightened girls cannot desert their brothers who may be lost in the swamp. The social system, with its family structure and relationships, is featured, along with the economic system's flora and fauna, hunting and gathering.

Classroom Applications

Your students may want to write or tell stories about their own family picnics or outdoor adventures. What about oysters? Can you obtain some and bring them to class for the children to open? Why not turn this into a cooking experience and make oyster stew? Canned oysters will do just as well if raw ones are not available.

 Cowan, James. *Kun-Man-Gur the Rainbow Serpent*. illustrated by Bronwyn Bancroft. Barefoot Books, 1994. 32 pp. (ISBN 1-56957-906-7). Folktale, E-L.

Story Review Chart

Setting	Plot/Events	Characters	Theme
•	•	•	

Cultural Paradigm Reference Classification Chart

Geographic Location	Economic System	Social System	Political System
•			

Rainbow Serpent, principal cultural hero of northern Australia's Aborigines, sleeps on the bank of the river until awakened by Warlet and Ninji, flying foxes that have been insulted by the bat Kumbul. After helping them in their fight against the bat, Kun-Man-

Gur teaches them to eat the flowers of the gum trees and paper barks. Bancroft's striking illustrations done aboriginal-style are once again, as in *Dreamtime*, exotic reminders of the uniqueness of this culture's traditions.

Creation myths like this one often feature geographic location, telling of the birth of the flora and fauna of a place.

Classroom Applications

Talk with your students about people's feelings regarding snakes and how the aboriginal culture reveres such a snake as the rainbow. Have the class create their own Rainbow Serpents with finger paints, clay, or papier-mâché.

 Sheehan, Patty. *Kylie's Concert*. illustrated by Itoko Maeno. MarshMedia, 1993. 32 pp. (ISBN 1-55942-046-4). Fiction, P-E.

Story Review Chart

Setting	Plot/Events	Characters	Theme
•		•	

Cultural Paradigm Reference Classification Chart

Geographic Location	Economic System	Social System	Political System
	•		

Kylie is a talking, singing koala in this animal fantasy for younger children. One night, she leaves her eucalyptus tree and scuffles off through the forest, meeting a frightened echidna, a climbing tree kangaroo, and a tawny frogmouth bird, all warning her of a terrible danger to come. The next day, she sees for herself the mechanical monsters who tear up the ground and cut down the trees. Then she meets children who come with camcorders to film a television show about taking care of the forest and who happily discover Kylie. Kylie sings them her forest song, and all the creatures join in the concert.

Maeno's large, bright, and realistic watercolors of the animals of the eucalyptus forest are an education in themselves. The end pages also describe and illustrate 14 birds and mammals of Australia. The economic system with its flora and fauna is featured here.

Classroom Applications

Young children like to pretend. Here they can pretend to be Kylie scuffling through the forest and meeting each of the creatures (other children) mentioned in the story. For a more realistic Kylie, cut out the illustration of the koala from the dust jacket, mount it on cardboard with a tongue-depressor stick for a handle, and have the child character hold it in front of her or his face.

Wiseman, Bernard. *Little New Kangaroo.* illustrated by Theresa Burns. Clarion Books, 1993. 32 pp. (ISBN 0-395-65362-2). Fiction, P-E.

Story Review Chart

Setting	Plot/Events	Characters	Theme
•		•	

Cultural Paradigm Reference Classification Chart

Geographic Location	Economic System	Social System	Political System
•			

A baby kangaroo invites various animals to ride with him in his mother's pouch. A koala, a bandicoot, a wombat, and finally a platypus nearly overload mother kangaroo in this talking-animal story for the youngest children. Illustrations fill all the pages, with a sentence or two of rhyming text in large type tucked in. It is a lighthearted romp through the bush with all of the animals talking and playing together.

Classroom Applications

Have a follow-the-leader chain of children snake through the classroom, picking up a new animal (child) as they go. They can wear headbands with animal ears to designate what they are.

 Wheatley, Nadia. *My Place.* illustrated by Donna Rawlins. Kane-Miller, 1994. 48 pp. (ISBN 0–916291–54–5). Historical Fiction, M-L.

Story Review Chart

Setting	Plot/Events	Characters	Theme
•		•	

Cultural Paradigm Reference Classification Chart

Geographic Location	Economic System	Social System	Political System
•	•		

A series of children from ages 7 to 12 narrate 200 years of history on the same spot, decade by decade, on each two-page spread by calling their location "My Place" and telling briefly about themselves and what's happening where they live in that particular year. Starting with the year 1988, Laura, who has just turned 10, tells about coming to the city with her parents who are looking for work, going to the McDonald's restaurant on the corner for her birthday, and sitting out under the Big Tree to eat, which made it feel just like home. Each two-page spread has a "child-drawn" map showing the street, house, and always the Big Tree.

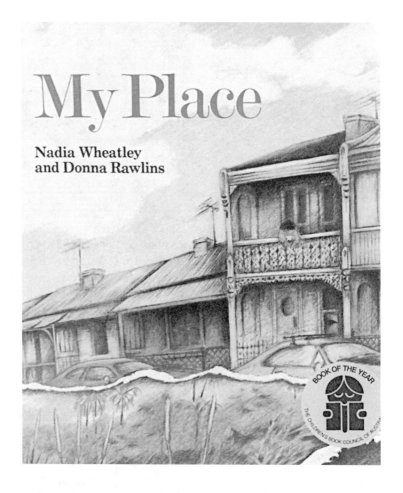

The 1978 child is 7-year-old Mike, who lives with his parents and Auntie Sofie. The 1968 child is Sofie, whose father has just painted their house blue because many houses in his Greek island homeland were that color. Her brother Michaelis is a soldier in Vietnam. Have your students look at the map to find the Big Tree on each map and then compare the neighborhood with each of the others to see how things are changing.

This is definitely a one-story-at-a-time book as your students go carefully back through Australia's history until 1788, when the child occupant of "My Place" is Barangaroo, an Aborigine who loves to climb into the big fig tree at the top of the hill. The principal focus here is the economic system.

Classroom Applications

See how many fascinating details your students can extract from each decade. Some may want to start from the end and work forward through history, the usual way of proceeding. Others may want to create their own "My Place" history. How far back can they go in their own neighborhoods year by year? They may want to create a time line for the children described in this story or make up a time line for their own neighborhood.

 Norman, Lilith. *The Paddock: A Story in Praise of the Earth.* illustrated by Robert Roennfeldt. Knopf, 1993. 32 pp. (ISBN 0-679-83887-20). Nonfiction, M-L.

Story Review Chart

Setting	Plot/Events	Characters	Theme
•	•		•

Cultural Paradigm Reference Classification Chart

Geographic Location	Economic System	Social System	Political System
•	•		

The first picture book by one of Australia's best-loved writers tells the story of a patch of land, a *paddock* in Australian jargon, from its birth from within the boiling core of the Earth; to its formation from wind and storm and rain; to its first life of algae and mosses and ferns as big as trees; to dinosaurs; to wombats as big as cows and flightless birds taller than two men; to the first Aborigines; to the European explorers who drove off the first people and chained the paddocks with fences; to the first village that grew into a town and then a city, covering the paddock with concrete and asphalt; and finally to a time in the future when the cars, people, and houses would be gone and vegetation would break through the asphalt to cover the paddock once again.

Robert Roennfeldt spent more than 800 hours on the illustrations, which cover three quarters of each two-page spread. Browns and greens dominate as the paddock turns from brown to green and back again. Norman's simple but lyrical text occupies the left-hand corner of each spread.

Classroom Applications

Can your students illustrate a story about their own "paddock" where they live, from its beginning up to modern times and into the future? Make it an exciting project for them to discover the prehistory and history of the place, including plants, animals, and people. They may want to paint a wall mural on newsprint, showing all of the plants, animals, and people who occupied and will occupy the land.

 Fox, Mem. *Possum Magic.* illustrated by Julie Vivas. Harcourt Brace, 1990. 32 pp. (ISBN 0-15-200572-2). Fiction, P-E.

Story Review Chart

Setting	Plot/Events	Characters	Theme
•	•	•	

Cultural Paradigm Reference Classification Chart

Geographic Location	Economic System	Social System	Political System
	•		

One of Australia's most popular writers for young children, especially when she teams up with artist Julie Vivas, Mem Fox is almost as well known in the United States, *Possum Magic* being a favorite of all who read it. Deep in the Australian bush live two possums—little Hush and Grandma Poss, who knows how to make bush magic. She turns wombats blue and kookaburras pink. But her best magic of all is making Hush invisible. Now she can slide down kangaroos and escape being eaten by snakes.

But one day, Hush decides that she wants to be visible again, so Grandma Poss starts them off on a long search to find out how. It has something to do with people food, she remembers, so off they peddle on Grandma Poss's bicycle to visit the cities and find out what. They try Anzac biscuits in Adelaide, mornay and minties in Melbourne, and pumpkin scones in Brisbane—to no avail. Finally, in the far north, Hush eats a Vegemite sandwich and her tail appears. On a beach in Perth, she eats a piece of pavlova and her legs and body become visible. Then in the kitchen of a casino in Hobart, she nibbles half a lamington and her head appears. She can be seen from head to tail!

Delightful illustrations of animals, food, and people trace the journey around Australia, with a map at the end to mark the route and a glossary of food names to describe these delicacies for non-Australians. The focus in this book is the economic system, with flora and fauna, as well as food and its consumption.

Classroom Applications

Would your students like to participate in an "Australia Day," preparing and eating some of the food described here?

 Maddern, Eric. *Rainbow Bird*. illustrated by Adrienne Kennaway. Little, Brown, 1993. 28 pp. (ISBN 0-316-54314-4). Folktale, P-M.

Story Review Chart

Setting	Plot/Events	Characters	Theme
	•	•	

Cultural Paradigm Reference Classification Chart

Geographic Location	Economic System	Social System	Political System
	•		

In this creation tale from the Time of Dreams, a rough, tough Crocodile Man controls fire. When other animals beg him for fire, he snaps at them and growls, "I'm boss for Fire!" Gray little Bird Woman is one of the animals who wants Fire to keep her warm and cook her food, but Crocodile Man will not share it. Bird Woman never stops watching him, waiting for her chance. It comes one day when Crocodile Man gives a huge yawn and Bird Woman zooms down and snatches his firesticks. She flies triumphantly through the forest, putting fire into the heart of every tree so that wood can be used to make fire, and then puts it into her own tail, transforming herself into Rainbow Bird.

Kennaway's realistic illustrations show a huge, sly-looking crocodile terrifying the kangaroos with its snapping jaws and then giving the biggest yawn in the world. Once again, the economic system, with its basic needs plus flora and fauna, are featured.

Classroom Applications

What birds or other animals do your students know? Can they make up tales like this about how certain animals they know came to be? Or they may want to act out this simple folktale, making and wearing headbands to represent the animal characters.

 Graham, Bob. *Spirit of Hope*. Lothian, 1993. 32 pp. (ISBN 0-05091-672-0). Fiction, E-M.

Story Review Chart

Setting	Plot/Events	Characters	Theme
•	•	•	•

Cultural Paradigm Reference Classification Chart

Geographic Location	Economic System	Social System	Political System
	•	•	

Dad and Mum Fairweather love their six children, dog, two rabbits, turtle, and especially their little house tucked between factories and a noisy highway. For 6 days, Dad works at the factory but comes home every night to romp with the children and animals, playing "captain of the ship" on the kitchen table. On the 7th day, they always have a picnic on the docks with plum jam sandwiches, ginger beer, and fruit cake. They enjoy talking with the sailors and find that the name of one ship is *Spirit of Hope*. Then one day, representatives from the factory knock on the family's door and tell them they must move—and soon—to make room for a new factory. All week long, they search for a new place to live, without any luck. Then just as excavators start digging a hole next to their house, Mum gets a bright idea from Mary's little toy house on wheels. They and their friends quickly put together a large raftlike platform on top of tied-together oil drums, raise the house onto the platform, the whole thing onto a flatbed truck, and haul it out to the docks. There they float their house at the end of the dock with the sign "Spirit of Hope" painted on the roof. And little Mary gets to be "captain of the ship."

Graham's cartoon-like illustrations portray the joys and problems of life in a modern Australian city, its moral being, Never give up hope. The economic system, with its factories and shipyards, is featured, but the social system, with its interdependence on family members and friends, shines through.

Classroom Applications

A field trip to a factory, ship, or dock would be in order here if any are nearby. Otherwise, your students might like to construct a little house in a shoebox, mount it on a board, and glue spools or film containers to the bottom. They can reenact the story, pulling their house across the room and floating it in a sink or water table.

 Bruce, Jill B. *Whose Chick Is That?* illustrated by Jan Wade. Kangaroo Press, 1995. 48 pp. (ISBN 0-86417-576-0). Nonfiction, M-L.

Story Review Chart

Setting	Plot/Events	Characters	Theme
•		•	

Cultural Paradigm Reference Classification Chart

Geographic Location	Economic System	Social System	Political System
•			

Gorgeous illustrations of Australia's unusual birds invite the reader to guess who the parent birds are of each of 11 baby birds shown on two-page spreads along with their nests. By turning the page, the reader can find the answer on another two-page spread with full-size paintings of the parent birds and factual text. Described here are black swans, boobook owls, brolgas cranes, budgerigar parakeets, eastern rosella parrots, emus, kookaburras, lyrebirds, magpies, sulphur-crested cockatoos, and wedge-tailed eagles.

Classroom Applications

Photocopies or tracings can be made of each bird for your students to color in and learn about. Then they can play their own quiz game of "Whose Chick Is That?"

 Kroll, Jeri. *You Be the Witch.* illustrated by Zoe Eastwood. Lothian, 1994. 32 pp. (ISBN 0-85091-564-3). Fiction, E-M.

Story Review Chart

Setting	Plot/Events	Characters	Theme
	•	•	

Cultural Paradigm Reference Classification Chart

Geographic Location	Economic System	Social System	Political System
		•	

The end papers in black and white show an ordinary stucco house being battered by rain, but the first two-page spread of the story lets the reader know this is the tropics. The end of a huge drainpipe pours water next to a fat-leaf green and red tropical plant with snails, spiders, and worms slithering about. "It was a shivery, shuddery Saturday" begins the tale before the reader turns the page to a full-color duplicate of the end pages, with a small boy's face peering from a window.

The story itself features Timothy, visiting his aunt for the weekend and bored because there is no one to play with—until he finds his aunt in the basement, and then "You be the witch," persuades Timothy. His aunt puts on dark glasses, speaks in a crackly voice, and chases him all over the house, trying to catch him to fatten him up with various foodstuffs for dinner. When the clock strikes noon, Timothy suddenly becomes a hungry boy and decides that he will let the witch fatten him up with chicken and gherkin and a chocolate biscuit first.

Classroom Applications

Your students should experience a contemporary Australian story like this with a setting and characters perhaps not too different from their own experience. Can they look closely at the realistic illustrations and identify items that might also be found in their own homes and ones that would not? They can then make up their own stories about being fattened up by a pretend witch.

Borneo

Borneo is located in Indonesia, an island nation in the western Pacific Ocean south of the Philippines and north of Australia.

 Climo, Shirley. *The Match Between the Winds*. illustrated by Roni Shepherd. Macmillan, 1991. 32 pp. (ISBN 0-02-719035-8). Folktale, E-M.

Story Review Chart

Setting	Plot/Events	Characters	Theme
•	•		

Cultural Paradigm Reference Classification Chart

Geographic Location	Economic System	Social System	Political System
•			

In this very blue and green island tale, the East Wind and the West Wind have a contest to see which can blow Kodok the tree frog out of his coconut palm. Bats and octopuses, fish and branches, surge across a two-page spread in a great tangle when West Wind roars. But the little green tree frog sits smiling on his palm frond. West Wind takes a bigger breath, flattens people's rice paddies and lifts the roof off their longhouse, but Kodok doesn't move. Even the West Wind's howling typhoon fails to budge the frog. But East Wind's gentle breezes make Kodok so drowsy that he slips from his leaf and plops into the mud below for a snooze. This is why the grandfathers say that the East Wind is called *Rajah Angin*, Lord of the Winds.

Classroom Applications

Do your students know how tree frogs hold their positions in a tree? This is a story they can easily dramatize. They can have their own blowing contest if you place a cutout tree frog on a branch. Have them tell which wind they represent.

New Zealand

New Zealand is located in the southern Pacific Ocean, north of Antarctica and east of Australia.

 Bishop, Gavin. *Maui and the Sun: A Maori Tale*. North-South Books, 1996. 32 pp. (ISBN 1-55858-577-X). Folktale, M-L.

Story Review Chart

Setting	Plot/Events	Characters	Theme
•	•	•	

Cultural Paradigm Reference Classification Chart

Geographic Location	Economic System	Social System	Political System
•		•	

Maui is both a trickster and a hero in many Polynesian tales. This story, told on the North Island of New Zealand, is a creation myth about a time when the days are too short to suit Maui, who likes to spend long daylight hours out fishing. He decides to catch the sun to stop him from racing across the sky so fast. First, he teaches the people of his village how to make flax into strong rope. Maui and his brothers then carry large bundles of rope to the east, where the sun rises. When they reach the edge of the pit where the sun sleeps, they make a huge net from the ropes and put it across the opening as a trap.

As the sun rises with shudders and hisses, the rope net tightens about him. He screams and heaves at the ropes, trying to bite through them, but they hold tight. Then Maui beats on the sun with his secret weapon, a hand ax made from his grandmother's jawbone. The sun begs for mercy, asking why Maui is trying to hurt Tama nui te Ra, the Great Son of the Day. When Maui hears the sun's secret name, he is able to command him to move more slowly across the sky. So Maui and his brothers loosen the ropes and let the sun proceed.

But the sun moves so slowly that he doesn't return to his pit for many months, causing people to suffer from the heat and constant daylight. Even Maui, who holds up his hand to block out the sunlight, gets burned by the fierce rays. When he rushes to the sea to cool the pain, the sun suddenly decides to trick Maui by setting.

This trick makes Maui so angry that once more he throws a rope around the sun and drags him back into the sky. He ties the other end of the rope to the moon so that when the sun next sets, he pulls the moon out of the sea, giving Maui both day and night.

Bishop illustrates his tale with clever line drawings of Maui and his brothers against dark or light backgrounds and the fiery red of the sun. Some of Bishop's ancestors come from the North Island of New Zealand, where variants of this tale are told.

Classroom Applications

Have your students illustrate one scene from this tale. Use a new medium, such as collage or colored chalk, for a change; students can be more creative than usual in a new medium.

 Lattimore, Deborah Nourse. *Punga: The Goddess of Ugly.* Harcourt Brace, 1993. 32 pp. (ISBN 0-15-292862-6). Folktale, M-L.

Story Review Chart

Setting	Plot/Events	Characters	Theme
•	•	•	•

Cultural Paradigm Reference Classification Chart

Geographic Location	Economic System	Social System	Political System
•		•	

Kiri and Maraweia are twin Maori girls living with their grandmother who is teaching them Maori ways. She hopes they will earn a fine *moko*, or chin tattoo, to show they have learned well and come of age, but they need to spend more time practicing the *haka* dance. When Maraweia sticks out her tongue to dance, she gets silly and is scolded by her grandmother for not being fierce and powerful, but rather ugly like the lizard and mudfish. Maraweia runs off through the forest, still acting silly, with Kiri chasing after her.

Kiri finally finds Maraweia with her tongue stuck out, attached to the roof pole of the great lodge of Punga, goddess of ugly. Kiri dances the haka in the moonlight to show Punga how beautiful it is and to retrieve her sister at last. When the girls finally return to their grandmother's, both have beautiful mokos on their chins.

Pages of this tale overflow with green fronds, twisted trunks, and scrolled Maori wood carvings of gods with green eyes and long tongues, contrasted with the girls in their red Maori outfits.

Classroom Applications

Let your students try their hand at reproducing the fascinating Maori images presented throughout the book. Consult other books on Maori culture and art for additional ideas and themes that could be rendered in paint, paper, clay, or other media.

Philippines

The Philippines is located in the western Pacific Ocean, south of Taiwan and north of Malaysia and Indonesia. It is bounded on the east by the Philippine Sea; on the south by the Sulu Sea, the Celebes Sea, Malaysia, and Borneo; and on the west by the South China Sea. It comprises 7,107 islands, of which 1,000 are inhabited.

 Aruego, Jose, and Dewey, Ariane. *Rockabye Crocodile: A Folktale From the Philippines.* Mulberry Books, 1993. 32 pp. (ISBN 0-688-12333-3). Folktale, P-E.

Story Review Chart			
Setting	Plot/Events	Characters	Theme
•	•	•	•

Cultural Paradigm Reference Classification Chart			
Geographic Location	Economic System	Social System	Political System
	•	•	

In this talking-animal tale, two boars live next door to one another. Amabel is cheerful and kind, whereas Nettie is mean and selfish. When Amabel goes out looking for food, she is kind to everything she meets, including a bamboo tree. It drops two little fish into her food basket, and when she says "thank you," it drops a whole shower of minnows. When she stumbles over a crocodile, she excuses herself. The crocodile tells her he will catch fish for her dinner if she will rock her baby to sleep.

Amabel goes into the dark, muddy crocodile cave and calms the howling baby, rocking him to sleep. The crocodile returns with a basketful of eels, crabs, and very large fish. She invites Amabel to return whenever she wants more fish.

When Nettie hears this story and sees the fish, she is determined to get her share. She takes her large, empty basket to the bamboo tree and tries to shake fish out of its branches. When nothing happens, she butts the tree, and it snaps back, throwing her into a prickle bush. Then she demands fish from the crocodile and hands her the basket to fill. But when Nettie tries to rock the baby crocodile to sleep, he only cries harder. The mother crocodile returns with a full basket covered tight. She tells Nettie not to open the basket until she returns home and locks all her doors and windows so that no fish will escape.

Nettie complies, but when she opens the basket, out come spiders, scorpions, bats, and rats. Amabel hears the noise and rushes over but has to break down the door to get in. Out pour the houseful of creatures, and out comes poor Nettie, saying what a fool she has been.

Delightful, whimsical illustrations are typical of Aruego and Dewey's well-established art style done with watercolors, gouache paints, and black line.

Classroom Applications

Do your students know what lesson this folktale is trying to teach its readers? Have them choose a lesson in behavior that they would like to teach and make up their own animal stories about it based on *Rockabye Crocodile*.

Polynesian Islands

The Polynesian Islands are located in the south central part of the South Pacific, with the exception of Hawaii, which is north of the equator. They include such islands as Easter Island, Cook Islands, Tonga, French Polynesia (Tahiti), New Zealand, Western Samoa, and American Samoa.

 Schields, Gretchen. *The Water Shell*. Harcourt Brace, 1995. 32 pp. (ISBN 0-15-20040-1). Folktale, M-L.

Story Review Chart

Setting	Plot/Events	Characters	Theme
•	•	•	

Cultural Paradigm Reference Classification Chart

Geographic Location	Economic System	Social System	Political System
•		•	•

On the magic island of Kua-i-Helani, people live in a changeless paradise full of bright flowers and sweet fruits where children surf on the breaking waves and sing songs into the night. They are protected by a magic egg deep in the ocean that they call the Water Shell.

Beyond this perfect world lies a world of darkness and danger ruled by the Fire Queen. One day, she sends her bird warriors beneath the waves of Kua-i-Helani to find the magic egg. They emerge in a terrible waterspout, with the Water Shell in their claws. The people of Kua-i-Helani shriek in terror as typhoons and earthquakes suddenly wrack their paradise and a giant wall of water sweeps the little girl Keiki under the sea.

There she meets a giant shark that gives her one of his teeth shaped like a fish-hook and tells her she must go to the Fire Queen and get back the Water Shell to protect her island from destruction. When Keiki finally comes to the surface, she finds her island drastically changed, with all the people gone and a huge smoking lava cone sending rivers of lava coursing across the land. Only a little yellow spider is left that spins Keiki a length of silken web for a necklace from which to hang the shark's tooth. The spider tells Keiki that the Fire Queen has the Water Shell up on her mountaintop and that Keiki must trust what she loves as she proceeds on her quest for the shell.

A rainbow appears at Keiki's feet, and she dances her way on it up to a misty cloud-filled land where she meets the Maidens of the Mist, who give her a snowy cape to protect her from the Fire Queen's flames. Next, she meets the tattooed Wind Children, with their large palm-thatched fans, who give her a magic kite shaped like a hawk to carry her high into the sky. Finally, she comes to Earth at the mouth of the Fire Queen's volcano and challenges her to appear.

When the Fire Queen does appear, Keiki sees that the Water Shell has become the Fire Queen's heart. To retrieve it, Keiki casts her spider web necklace with its magic fishhook in a perfect toss, ensnaring the Water Shell. Then she flees on the Wind Children's kite, soaring above the volcano into which she drops her snowy cape. Instantly, the volcano is frozen with ice and snow, trapping the Fire Queen within.

Returning to the island, Keiki finds only charred and smoking tree stumps. What magic is left in the Water Shell? she wonders. She cuts away her long, flowing hair and weaves it into a nest for the egg. Suddenly, it begins to crack open, and out flow water, flowers, trees bearing fruit—another island paradise. When Keiki sees her own face reflected in the water, she realizes that she, too, has changed from a child into a young woman—ready to greet the sailing canoes of people now approaching the island.

Classroom Applications

Dramatic watercolor illustrations bring the story to life, but your students can add their own brushstrokes in a class mural showing each aspect of the changing scenes from the original island paradise, to the Fire Queen's attack, to Keiki's retaliation with her various helpers along the way, to the final restoration of paradise.

SUMMARY

The 22 children's books reviewed about countries in the southern Pacific region and including Antarctica are predominantly folktales and fiction, with historical fiction, fictional travel, and nonfiction represented by relatively few books.

A setting of some sort is manifest in nearly all but 2 of the 22 books, whereas plot/events and characters are featured in 17 and 15 books, respectively. A clear theme emerges in only 4 books.

The outstanding distinction of the books about the southern Pacific region, including Australia, New Zealand, and Antarctica, is the prominence played by the geographic component of the cultural paradigm. The countries in this region all have distinctive topographies, climates, flora, and fauna. Economic and social issues surface in 10 books each, whereas some political issues are apparent only in 1 book.

What of the nine questions asked by children at the beginning of this chapter? Can your students find the answers by reading these books? You may have noted that foods, clothing, houses, pets, animals, weather, brothers and sisters, and friends are discussed or illustrated in one or more of the books reviewed for this chapter. References to schools are missing, but then so are stories set indoors. Only one story takes place entirely inside a house, but ostensibly because it is storming outside; another shows some indoor scenes. Could the abundance of stories set in the out-of-doors reflect a preference Australians and Pacific islanders have for immersing themselves in their remarkable natural environments?

Be aware, however, that many films and videos perpetuate narrow stereotypes of outback adventures and cuddly koalas (Galda & Tobin, 1992). The truth is that most Australians live in urban areas along the southeastern coast of the country. When choosing books about Australia and the Pacific cultural region for your bookshelf, be sure to include urban stories to give your students a more nearly complete picture of this fascinating region.

REFERENCES CITED
▼▼

Galda, L., & Tobin, B. (1992). Dreamtime down under: Exploring Australian books. *Reading Teacher*, 46(2), 146-156.

Monson, D. L., Howe, K., & Greenlee, A. (1989). Helping children develop cross-cultural understanding with children's books. *Early Childhood Development and Care*, 48, 3-8.

SUGGESTED REFERENCES
▼▼

Aaron, I. E., & Hutchinson, S. M. (1993). Best books for children from four countries. *Reading Teacher*, 47(3), 212-221. (General)

Almario, V., et al. (Eds.). (1994). *Bumasa at Lumaya: A sourcebook on children's literature in the Philippines*. Manila: Philippine Board on Books for Young People. (Philippines)

Barley, J. C. (1995). *Winter in July: Visits with children's authors down under*. Metuchen, NJ: Scarecrow Press. (Australia)

Bunanto, M. (1995). The comics invasion in Indonesia. *Bookbird*, 33(2). (Indonesia)

Bunanto, M. (1996). Raising the profile of Indonesian children's literature. *Bookbird*, 34(4), 29-31. (Indonesia)

Fischer, J. (1997). Children, culture, and creativity: Indonesian children's art. *Bookbird*, 35(1), 24-27. (Indonesia)

Kelly, F. (1993). Down under Australiana: Against the odds. *Emergency Librarian*, 20(4), 16-17. (Australia)

Kelly, F. (1995). Down under Australiana: "Seven little Australians"—A hundred years down the old bush track. *Emergency Librarian*, 22(4), 19-20. (Australia)

Larson, J. (1987, September). An Australian celebration. *School Library Journal*, 131-133. (Australia)

Liew, E. M. (1997). Brunei Darussalam (I). *Bookbird*, 35(3), 40-45. (Brunei)

Liew, E. M. (1997). Brunei Darussalam (II). *Bookbird*, 35(4), 50-54. (Brunei)

Mahy, M. (1996). The writer in New Zealand: Building bridges through children's books. *Bookbird*, 34(4), 6-11. (New Zealand)

Nimon, M. (1992). *Children's reading: A research report.* Paper presented at the annual conference of the International Association of School Librarianship, Belfast, Northern Ireland. (General)

Phillips, J. (1992). *Social issues in Australian children's literature.* Paper presented at the annual conference of the International Association of School Librarianship, Belfast, Northern Ireland. (Australia)

Romana-Cruz, N. (1995). Asserting themselves: Children's book publishers in the Philippines. *Bookbird*, 33(2), 18-22. (Philippines)

Saxby, M. (1995). Changing perspectives: The implied reader in Australian children's literature, 1841–1994. *Children's Literature in Education*, 26(1), 25-38. (Australia)

Simkin, J., & Dunkle, M. (1996). *Picture books for young Australians.* Melbourne: D. W. Thorpe. (Australia)

Smith, K. P. (1996). Seeking the high road: Two perspectives on growing up in Australia. *Bookbird*, 34(4), 18-23. (Australia)

Van Kraayenoord, C. E., & Paris, S. G. (1994). Literacy instruction in Australian primary schools. *Reading Teacher*, 48(3), 218-228. (Australia)

CHILDREN'S BOOKS CITED

▼▼▼

Adams, J. (1994). *Going for oysters.* Morton Grove, IL: Albert Whitman. (Australia)

Aruego, J., & Dewey, A. (1993). *Rockabye crocodile: A folktale from the Philippines.* New York: Mulberry Books. (Philippines)

Bishop, G. (1996). *Maui and the sun: A Maori tale.* New York: North-South Books. (New Zealand)

Bruce, J. B. (1995). *Whose chick is that?* Kenthurst, New South Wales: Kangaroo Press. (Australia)

Climo, S. (1991). *The match between the winds.* New York: Macmillan. (Borneo, Indonesia)

Cowan, J. (1994). *Kun-Man-Gur the rainbow serpent.* Boston: Barefoot Books. (Australia)

Cowcher, H. (1990). *Antarctica.* New York: Farrar, Straus & Giroux. (Antarctica)

Fox, M. (1990). *Possum magic.* San Diego: Harcourt Brace. (Australia)

Geraghty, P. (1995). *Solo.* New York: Crown. (Antarctica)

Graham, B. (1993). *Spirit of hope.* Port Melbourne, Victoria: Lothian. (Australia)

Kroll, J. (1994). *You be the witch.* Port Melbourne, Victoria: Lothian. (Australia)

Lattimore, D. N. (1993). *Punga: The goddess of ugly.* San Diego: Harcourt Brace. (New Zealand)

Maddern, E. (1993). *Rainbow bird.* Boston: Little, Brown. (Australia)

Meeks, A. R. (1991). *Enora and the black crane.* New York: Scholastic. (Australia)

Norman, L. (1993). *The paddock: A story in praise of the Earth.* New York: Knopf. (Australia)

Oodgeroo. (1994). *Dreamtime: Aboriginal stories.* New York: Lothrop, Lee & Shepard Books. (Australia)

Reynold, J. (1992). *Down under: Vanishing cultures.* San Diego: Harcourt Brace. (Australia)

Schields, G. (1995). *The water shell.* San Diego: Harcourt Brace. (Polynesian Islands)

Sheehan, P. (1993). *Kylie's concert.* Kansas City, MO: MarshMedia. (Australia)

Wheatley, N. (1994). *My place.* Brooklyn, NY: Kane-Miller. (Australia)

Williams, G. T. (1992). *The last frontier: Antarctica.* Los Angeles: Price Stern Sloan. (Antarctica)

Wiseman, B. (1993). *Little new kangaroo.* New York: Clarion Books. (Australia)

SUGGESTED CHILDREN'S BOOKS

▼▼▼

Aardema, V. (1997). *This for that.* New York: Dial Books for Young Readers. (Tonga)

Allen, P. (1991). *Mr. Archimedes' bath.* New York: HarperCollins. (Australia)

Allen, P. (1991). *My cat Maisie.* New York: Viking. (Australia)

Allen, P. (1994). *Clippity-clop.* New York: Viking. (Australia)

Argent, K. (1990). *Wombat and Bandicoot: Best of friends.* Boston: Little, Brown. (Australia)

Argent, K. (1991). *Happy birthday Wombat!* Boston: Little, Brown. (Australia)

Base, G. (1990). *My grandma lived in Gooligulch.* New York: Abrams. (Australia)

Berndt, C. (1994). *Pheasant and Kingfisher.* Greenvale, NY: Mondo. (Australia)

Dumbleton, M. (1991). *Dial-a-croc.* New York: Orchard Books. (Australia)

Fox, M. (1995). *Wombat devine.* San Diego: Harcourt Brace. (Australia)

Gilbert, K. (1994). *Me and Mary Kangaroo.* New York: Viking. (Australia)

Graham, B. (1994). *Zoltan the magnificent.* Port Melbourne, Victoria: Lothian. (Australia)

Hill, A. (1994). *The burnt stick.* New York: Viking. (Australia)

Lester, A. (1991). *Tessa snaps snakes.* Boston: Houghton Mifflin. (Australia)

McMillan, B. (1993). *Penguins at home: Gentoos of the Antarctic.* Boston: Houghton Mifflin. (Antarctic)

Niland, K. (1991). *A bellbird in a flame tree.* New York: Tambourine Books. (Australia)

Ottley, M. (1996). *What Faust saw.* New York: Dutton Children's Books. (New Zealand)

Paterson, A. B. (1991). *Waltzing Matilda.* New York: HarperCollins. (Australia)

Roth, S. L. (1996). *The biggest frog in Australia.* New York: Simon & Schuster Books for Young Readers. (Australia)

Seibert, P. (1996). *Toad overload: A true tale of nature knocked off balance in Australia.* Brookfield, CT: Millbrook. (Australia)

Winch, J. (1997). *The old woman who loved to read.* New York: Holiday House. (Australia)

C H A P T E R 11

Transcultural Children's Literature in the Changing Classroom

CONCLUSIONS ABOUT TRANSCULTURAL CHILDREN'S LITERATURE

Despite limited availability of books from certain cultural regions, we believe that the 241 books reviewed in the previous chapters provide a qualitative sampling of children's transcultural picture books available in the United States today. Such a collection provides the basis for framing questions for further study.

Distribution of Books Over Time

One question we can ask about transcultural children's literature is, Of the books we reviewed, how has the number of books published yearly changed over time? As Figure 11.1 shows, the number of books published yearly from 1990 to 1994 more than doubled, from 22 to 56, with 1994 the peak year between 1990 and 1997. The small number (11) of books published in 1997 is a consequence of only reviewing books that were available through early 1997.

Closer analysis of the peak publication year of 1994 reveals that much of the increase over previous years can be attributed to books about two countries—China

Region	1990	1991	1992	1993	1994	1995	1996	1997	TOTALS
Africa	1	3	7	5	10	8	2	1	37
Asia	3	5	5	2	10	4	4	2	35
Canada	3	2	3	7	2	3	3	2	25
Caribbean	2	1	5	4	5	4	2	1	24
Central Amer., Mexico, and South Amer.	3	2	1	5	6	2	3	3	25
Eastern Europe	3	2	3	1	10	1	4	0	24
Western Europe	3	3	4	7	6	5	5	2	35
Middle East	2	2	1	3	2	2	2	0	14
Pacific, Australia, Antarctica	2	2	2	7	5	3	1	0	22
TOTALS	22	22	31	41	56	32	26	11	241

Figure 11.1
Distribution of reviewed books among major geographic regions and years of publication from 1990 to 1997.

and Russia. The historic political, economic, and social changes that began unfolding in these two countries in the late 1980s and early 1990s stimulated considerable public attention in the United States and elsewhere. This interest in China and Russia conceivably could have stimulated a spate of children's books about each of these countries. One might hypothesize that the public's perceived interest level in another country is a barometer for deciding whether to write and publish children's books about a specific country. The possible relationship between major world events and personalities and the publication of transcultural children's books warrants further study. If such a relationship truly exists, then one should ask what specific factors affect it. For example, what role, if any, does instant worldwide communication play in the decision to publish children's books about other countries?

Distribution of Books by Grade Level

Another question to consider is, For which age levels are specific transcultural books primarily intended? Although we question the practice of designating age levels to children's books because of the many interacting factors that influence what children read and how, we do believe that it is important to do so in this case for two reasons. The first is to help us survey more systematically the transcultural books available. Second, age designations, despite their limitations, can assist teachers in providing a range of books that is needed in all classrooms. Initial answers to the original question about age levels begin to emerge by examining Figure 11.2. The data indicate that nearly every region has at least a few books appropriate for each of four age categories: preschool (ages 3–4), early elementary (ages 5–7), middle elementary (ages

8–9), and late elementary (ages 10–11). The one exception is the Middle East. Books about countries in this region tend to be most suited for children in the late elementary grades. The relatively small number of books (14) reviewed about Middle Eastern countries, however, may account for the absence of books for younger readers. Books associated with the African, Asian, Caribbean, and Eastern European countries are generally suited for children in the early grades. Books about Canada, Mexico, various Central and South American countries, Western European countries, and Australia are most suited for children in the middle grades. Further research should be done to determine whether these patterns hold for transcultural children's books generally. It would also be useful to determine whether the recommended age range of the readers of a book varies significantly, depending on which country that book is about and the genre. It might be the case, for example, that the more similar the culture depicted in a book is to that of the reader, the easier it would be to read and understand that book. Such books, therefore, would tend to be suitable for younger readers.

Numbers of Books About Specific Countries

When we consider what particular countries children's books are most likely to be about, two factors emerge that might influence how many books about a particular country are published: (a) historic events or well-known people associated with another country and (b) the rate of emigration from a particular country to the United States.

In the case of Africa, a relatively large number of books were published between 1990 and 1997, inclusively, about South Africa (Figure 11.3). In the early 1990s, South

Region	P-E	P-M	E-M	E-L	M-L	All	Totals
Africa	10	7	10	5	1	4	37
Asia	1	8	12	11	1	2	35
Canada	5	3	0	6	10	1	25
Caribbean	5	2	15	2	0	0	24
Central Amer., Mexico, and South Amer.	2	4	7	6	6	0	25
Eastern Europe	2	2	17	0	2	1	24
Western Europe	5	1	9	5	14	1	35
Middle East	0	0	1	1	12	0	14
Pacific, Australia, Antarctica	6	1	3	4	8	0	22
TOTALS	36	28	74	40	54	9	241

Figure 11.2
Distribution of reviewed books among major geographic regions and appropriate reading groups (P = preschool, E = early elementary, M = middle elementary, L = late elementary, and ALL = P through L).

Africa undertook a major historic political and social transformation. White South Africans' exclusive control of the government and the apartheid social system were replaced through democratic elections by Black South African majority rule and constitutionally protected equal rights. Similarly, China, Russia, and Iraq are associated in the public's eye with significant recent historic events and various well-known personalities. It seems reasonable to surmise, then, that writers, editors, and publishers make decisions that are influenced by significant events outside the United States that have attracted the public's attention.

Immigration also may play a role in determining how many books are published about another country. For example, the large numbers of books about Puerto Rico and Mexico published relative to the total numbers associated with their respective cultural regions may be attributed, at least in part, to the numbers of Hispanic and Mexican Americans in the U.S. population. It is reasonable, then, to expect that a significant

Regions and Countries	Country	Total Books for All Countries	Largest No. Books
Africa	14	37	
• Nigeria			5
• S. Africa			5
Asia	9	35	
• China			11
Canada	1	25	25
Caribbean	10	24	
• Puerto Rico			6
Central Amer., Mexico, and So. Amer.	11	25	
• Mexico			8
Eastern Europe	5	24	
• Russia			15
Western Europe	14	35	
• France			6
Middle East	6	14	
• Iran			3
Pacific, Australia, Antarctica	2	22	
• Australia			14
TOTALS	72*	241	100 (41%)

Figure 11.3
Largest number of reviewed books about specific countries in major geographic regions.

number of books have been, and will continue to be, published about the regions and countries from which relatively large numbers of people emigrated to the United States.

Whether the two aforementioned factors or others actually influence decisions about which transcultural books to publish at this point remains speculative. What have been offered are possible hypotheses to test and verify or reject. It would be instructive to study, for example, the criteria and decision-making process that editors and publishers use in selecting which books about other countries to publish. Also, we need to look at why teachers and students select particular books. A clearer understanding of the selection process might help authors, editors, publishers, and educators address the paucity of children's books about many countries. Of the 197 nations currently officially recognized, less than half (72) are represented among the 241 reviewed books. In fact, just 9 countries account for 41% of these books (Figure 11.3). Consequently, few, if any, children's books about many countries are available in the U.S. market.

Genres of Transcultural Books

To what genres do transcultural books belong? Of all the books reviewed in the previous chapters, 30% are contemporary fiction, 29% are folktales, and 12% are fiction (Figure 11.4). The remaining 30% are distributed more or less evenly among 12 other genres. Contemporary fiction is the dominant genre among books about Africa, Canada, the Caribbean, and Central/South America and Mexico; folktales is the dominant genre among books about Asia, Western and Eastern Europe, the Middle East, and the South Pacific.

Traditionally, folktales have been the major avenue open to children who have read and learned about the peoples and cultures of other countries. The relatively recent increase in contemporary fiction has provided another way for children to explore other countries. Factors responsible for the shift from the near exclusivity of folktales to a growing balance with contemporary fiction are not obvious. Perhaps the growing and pervasive power of the mass media to show real people living real lives in different countries has raised awareness and expectations. Thus, although folktales, fairy tales, and the like will always have a place, the rise in contemporary fiction and other genres signals a growing maturity of transcultural children's literature. It will be interesting to track the rise and fall in the various other genres of transcultural literature and to elucidate what variables are responsible for those changes.

Story Elements in Transcultural Books

Which aspects of a book are emphasized in transcultural literature? Tentative answers are suggested by the reviewed books (Figure 11.5). With one exception, the characters are more important in most books reviewed (221). The setting and plot/event are clearly set forth in somewhat fewer books (187 and 170, respectively), and the story's theme is important in far less than half of the books reviewed (91). This pattern holds in all regions except the South Pacific/Australia/New Zealand/Antarctica. There the setting and plot/events are important in more books (20 and 17, respectively) than characters (15), and theme remains a distant fourth. It remains unclear why this pattern in

REGION	Contemporary Fiction	Fiction	Folktales	Fairy Tales	Historical Fiction	Historical NonFiction	Legend	Informational
Africa	18	0	12	0	1	1	0	2
Asia	3	3	15	2	1	1	0	5
Canada	16	1	4	0	1	0	0	1
Caribbean	15	0	4	0	1	0	0	0
Central Amer., Mexico and South Amer.	12	0	6	0	1	0	0	3
Eastern Europe	2	9	4	6	0	0	1	1
Western Europe	3	8	8	0	4	1	3	1
Middle East	3	0	8	0	0	0	0	2
Pacific, Australia, Antarctica	0	7	9	0	1	0	0	4
TOTALS	72(30%)	28(12%)	70(29%)	8(3%)	10(4%)	3(1%)	4(2%)	19(8%)

REGION	Myth	Poetry	Counting	Alphabet	Biography	Nonfiction Travel	Fiction Travel	TOTALS
Africa	0	1	0	0	1	0	1	37
Asia	0	3	0	2	0	0	0	35
Canada	0	1	1	0	0	0	0	25
Caribbean	0	3	1	0	0	0	0	24
Central Amer., Mexico and South Amer.	0	1	0	1	1	0	0	25
Eastern Europe	0	1	0	0	0	0	0	24
Western Europe	0	0	0	0	4	2	1	35
Middle East	1	0	0	0	0	0	0	14
Pacific, Australia, Antarctica	0	0	0	0	0	0	1	22
TOTALS	1(<1%)	10(4%)	2(<1%)	3(1%)	6(4%)	2(<1%)	3(1%)	241

Figure 11.4
Distribution of reviewed books among geographic region and genre.

Region	Setting	Plot/Events	Characters	Theme	Number of Books
Africa	30 (81%)	13 (35%)	37 (100%)	7 (19%)	37
Asia	29 (83%)	18 (51%)	35 (100%)	14 (40%)	35
Canada	15 (60%)	23 (92%)	23 (92%)	4 (16%)	25
Caribbean	20 (80%)	20 (80%)	24 (96%)	16 (64%)	24
Central Amer., Mexico and South Amer.	17 (68%)	21 (84%)	22 (88%)	12 (48%)	25
Eastern Europe	22 (63%)	24 (96%)	24 (96%)	23 (92%)	24
Western Europe	22 (63%)	23 (66%)	29 (83%)	5 (14%)	35
Middle East	12 (86%)	11 (79%)	12 (86%)	6 (43%)	14
Pacific, Australia, Antarctica	20 (91%)	17 (77%)	15 (68%)	4 (18%)	22
TOTALS	187	170	221	91	241

Figure 11.5
Breakdown by geographic region of the numbers of reviewed books that feature any of four key story elements.

basic story elements consistently crosses regional boundaries. Is strong character development a traditional prerequisite for publication? It would be enlightening to compare the story elements of books published within the region/country in which the book is set with those published in the United States.

Cultural Paradigms in Transcultural Books

Which aspects of the transcultural paradigm are highlighted in children's books? A tentative answer to this question is provided in Figure 11.6, which shows how many reviewed books contain conspicuous references to geographic, economic, social, or political subjects. The social component is clearly expressed in 199 of the 241 books reviewed. This pattern holds in all regions except the Pacific/Australia/New Zealand/Antarctica, where the geographic component is featured in more books. The significance of the social component in transcultural children's books should not be too surprising, given the prominence afforded the characters in these books. One should also consider which components of the transcultural paradigm tend to be lacking in some of the books reviewed. Geography, for example, is evident in far less than half of the books about Central and South America/Mexico, Western Europe, and the Middle East. Similarly, the political component is relatively insignificant in a book except when the book is about an African or Asian country. It is intriguing that all four components of the transcultural paradigm play important roles in 75% to 100% of the books about African or Asian countries. Reasons for the apparent underrepresentation of geographic and political issues in books about countries in other regions remain to be elucidated.

Region	Geographic	Economic	Social	Political	Number of Books
Africa	30 (81%)	31 (84%)	37 (100%)	28 (76%)	37
Asia	29 (83%)	26 (74%)	34 (97%)	27 (77%)	35
Canada	12 (48%)	13 (52%)	14 (56%)	0 (0%)	25
Caribbean	20 (83%)	11 (46%)	24 (100%)	1 (4%)	24
Central Amer., Mexico and South Amer.	8 (32%)	14 (56%)	19 (76%)	6 (24%)	25
Eastern Europe	22 (92%)	15 (63%)	24 (100%)	8 (32%)	24
Western Europe	9 (26%)	15 (43%)	26 (74%)	10 (29%)	35
Middle East	1 (7%)	9 (64%)	11 (79%)	7 (50%)	14
Pacific, Australia, Antarctica	13 (59%)	10 (45%)	10 (45%)	1 (5%)	22
TOTALS	144	144	199	88	241

Figure 11.6
Breakdown by geographic region of the numbers of reviewed books that feature any of four cultural paradigm elements.

General Conclusions

Based on the books reviewed, some general conclusions can be reached concerning genres, story elements, and cultural components. Most books reviewed consist of either contemporary fiction or folktales in all geographic regions. Most books, regardless of geographic region, also contain one or two strongly developed characters and a distinct, engaging plot. Clear themes are relatively uncommon in the books reviewed, but when they are present, they range widely. The most frequently occurring theme is that of the hero who undertakes a quest leading to personal change, growth, and enlightenment. Another common theme centers on a realistic journey through a country during which the reader learns something about the people living there and their culture. The social component is consistently the most prominent of the four that comprise the cultural paradigm. Books about Africa, the Caribbean, and the Pacific/Australia/New Zealand/Antarctica region, however, also tend to highlight the physical setting and related geographic characteristics (e.g., plants, animals). In contrast, references to economic and political issues appear relatively less frequently.

ASSESSING CHILDREN'S TRANSCULTURAL AWARENESS AND RESPONSES TO THEIR READINGS

Transcultural children's literature offers several potential areas to study. In addition to the many research questions posed earlier in this chapter, we need to examine more closely some practical concerns regarding children's responses to books about other cultural regions. The following practical suggestions provide a way to approach assessing children's reactions to transcultural children's literature. After reflecting on tentative inferences drawn from the transcultural children's books reviewed for this text, it would seem reasonable to assess in particular the impact, if any, such books have on students' perceptions and understanding of the peoples and cultures of other countries.

Assessing Prior Knowledge

Students come to school with various perceptions and varying degrees of knowledge about other cultural regions and the peoples who live there. We as teachers can begin to assess the nature and extent of what our students believe and know about the peoples and cultures in other countries by asking them a series of preassessment questions. Figure 11.7 provides a list of suggested questions from which the teacher or the student can choose and discuss beliefs, attitudes, and understanding of other peoples and cultures. The number of questions selected and the questioning format employed depend on several variables, such as why students decided to read about other countries.

By discussing with students some of the questions on the preassessment questionnaire, we can find out their concepts and experiences regarding other peoples from around the world. The kinds of local, national, or international experiences that students have in one classroom will vary considerably. All travel experiences, whether around the world or to the local mall, need to be appreciated by everyone in class. This general acceptance can help create an environment where everyone feels encouraged to communicate openly and frequently. By giving students the preassessment questionnaire, we may discover how students have previously learned about other cultural regions and with which cultural regions they identify, to what extent, and why. For instance, we may discover whether our students acquired what they believe and know of other cultural regions from one or more of the following sources: reading and being read to, watching television, talking with people, having lived or traveled abroad, and having relatives (past or present) from other countries.

Assessing Awareness of a Cultural Region

To determine the overall impact that reading transcultural children's literature may have on students, asking questions from the Preassessment Questionnaire of Students' Transcultural Awareness of a Specific Culture and Cultural Region (Figure 11.8) and the Postassessment Questionnaire of Students' Transcultural Awareness of a Specific Culture and Cultural Region (Figure 11.9) may prove informative to students as well as to teachers.

By comparing the pre- and postresponses, we can discern patterns of changes in how students view other countries, peoples, and cultures generally and specifically and whether students' perceptions of themselves and their own culture have been modified and in what ways. Ideally, with continued systematic exposure to transcultural children's literature, students will begin noticing and trusting their acquired changes to cultural awareness, as well as their own development as readers.

Directions

Ask students to select and respond to some or all of the following questions either orally or in writing and either individually or in small groups.

1. Have you ever taken a trip or traveled?
2. Where did you go?
3. What do you remember most about where you went?
4. What did you like the most about your trip?
5. Was anything about the place you visited different from where you live now?
6. Was anything about the place you visited the same or similar to where you live now?
7. Did you meet any new people in the place you visited or did you see people whom you already knew?
8. Did you do anything special with the people you visited?
9. If you could take a trip to any place in the world, where would you like to go? Why do you want to go there?
10. How did you learn about this place in the world?
11. What would you need to know before you travel to this place?
12. What would you take with you on this trip?
13. How would you travel to this country?
14. What would you want to see and do when you visit this place?
15. What would you like to do with the people you visit?
16. Would you buy any souvenirs? If so, what?
17. After you return home, what might the people whom you visited tell their friends about your visit to their country?
18. After you return home, what would you tell your friends about your trip?
19. Have you ever met people from other countries who were visiting or living here in the United States? What do you remember most about them? Were you able to do anything special with them? If so, what?
20. If you could invite people from anywhere in the world to come to the United States and visit you, from which country would those people come? Why did you select that country?
21. Is there someplace special near your home or school where you would like to take these visitors? Why would you want to take them there?
22. What would you like to do with these people when they visit you?
23. If these people do not speak or understand your language, what would you do?
24. What other special place in the United States would you tell these people to visit?
25. If you could introduce these visitors to anyone in the United States, whom would that be? Why?
26. After these visitors return to their country, what might they tell their friends about you and their visit to the United States? Why do you think they will tell their friends about those things?
27. How would you keep in contact with one another?
28. Have you ever watched television, seen a movie, read a book, or visited a Web site about another country and the people who live there? Describe that country. Describe the people who live there.
29. What do you like most about your country?
30. How could you make your country a better place in which to live?

Figure 11.7
Preassessment Questionnaire of Students' General Transcultural Awareness.

Directions

Before reading selected books on a given cultural region, ask students to respond to some or all of the questions either orally or in writing and either individually or in small groups.

1. You are going to read some stories about *(name of country or cultural region)*. What can you tell me about that country?
2. What can you tell me about the people who live there?
3. If you could visit *(name of country or cultural region)*, where would you like to go and what would you like to do?

Figure 11.8
Preassessment Questionnaire of Students' Transcultural Awareness of a Specific Culture and Cultural Region.

To determine whether our students have gained a deeper and broader understanding of other cultural regions as a result of using transcultural children's literature, we can compare the results from Figures 11.8 and 11.9 and complete Figure 11.10, Analysis Summary of Pre- and Posttranscultural Awareness of Specific Cultures and Cultural Regions.

Directions

After reading selected books on a given cultural region, ask students to respond to some or all of the questions either orally or in writing and either individually or in small groups.

1. You just read some stories about *(name of the country or cultural region)*. What can you tell me about that country?
2. By reading these stories, what new information did you learn about the people who live there?
3. Where would you like to visit in *(name of the country or cultural region)*, and what would you like to do there?

Figure 11.9
Postassessment Questionnaire of Students' Transcultural Awareness of a Specific Culture and Cultural Region.

Name of Student: _____

Date: _____

Names of Books Read:

_____

_____

_____

_____

_____

_____

Content of Material

1. What new information did the student provide about the country on the basis of the book(s) read?
2. On which literary elements (e.g., setting, characters) did the student focus in her or his discussions?
3. Did the student generalize on the basis of prior knowledge or combine existing ideas with new information?
4. On which aspect (e.g., social, economic, geographic, political) of the country did the student focus?
5. What new knowledge did the student offer about the people residing in the country?
6. Did the student provide detailed information about the characters in the book?
7. Which particular genre or topic did the student emphasize or favor?
8. Did a discernible change in the student's beliefs, attitudes, and opinions toward the country and its people occur?

Figure 11.10
Analysis Summary of Pre- and Posttranscultural Awareness of Specific Cultures and Cultural Regions.

Our World and Our Future

Although the children's books associated with the nine geographic locations considered here exhibit differences, such differences can be viewed as relatively superficial. At a deeper level, the books reviewed are quite similar, indicating a commonalty of human experiences and needs. This reflects the growing realization that despite the obvious differences among the peoples and cultures of the world, some remarkable similarities also transcend both place and time and remind us of the global community to which we all belong. We hope that, when children read books about peoples and cultures from around the world, a deeper appreciation of, and commitment to, the global community will spread and flourish.

Topical Children's Book Index

ADVENTURES

Anni's Diary of France
Arabian Nights: Three Tales
Clouds on the Mountain
Dreamtime: Aboriginal Stories
Going for Oysters
My Mama's Little Ranch on the Pampas

ALPHABET

Amazon Alphabet
A to Zen: A Book of Japanese Culture
Gathering the Sun: An Alphabet in
    Spanish and English
I Is for India

ANIMALS

Amazon Alphabet
Amazon Boy
Antarctica
Baby Baboon
The Bells of Santa Lucia
Bitter Bananas
Borreguita and the Coyote
Clouds on the Mountains
Danger on the Arctic Ice
Don't Dig So Deep, Nicholas!
Down Under: Vanishing Cultures
Dreamtime: Aboriginal Stories
In the Eyes of the Cat: Japanese Poetry
    for All Seasons
The Fish Skin
Floss
The Flying Tortoise: An Igbo Tale
Fortune
Gittel's Hands
Going for Oysters
The Good Night Story
Grandfather's Dream
The Great Kapok Tree: A Tale of the
    Amazon Rain Forest
How the Ostrich Got Its Long Neck
How the Ox Star Fell From Heaven
Hush! A Thai Lullaby
If You Should Hear a Honey Guide

In the Village of the Elephants
Kashtanka
The King and the Tortoise
Knock, Knock, Terenok: A Traditional
    Russian Tale
Kun-Man-Gur: The Rainbow Serpent
Kylie's Concert
The Last Frontier: Antarctica
Little Elephant's Walk
Little New Kangaroo
The Loyal Cat
Magic Dogs of the Volcanoes
The Match Between the Winds
Mcheshi Goes to the Game Park
Minas and the Fish
The Moles and the Mireuk: A Korean
    Folktale
Moon Rope
Mucky Moose
My Arctic, 1, 2, 3
My Mama's Little Ranch on the Pampas
Nanabosho: How the Turtle Got Its Shell
Newf
Okino and the Whales
One Night: A Story From the Desert
One Small Square: African Savanna
Pequeña the Burro
The Polar Bear Son
Possum Magic
Pulling the Lion's Tail
The Rabbit's Judgment
Rhinos for Lunch and Elephants for
    Supper!
Rockabye Crocodile: A Folktale From the
    Philippines
Solo
Som See and the Magic Elephant
Tano and Binti: Two Chimpanzees Return
    to the Wild
The Turnip
Waira's First Journey
Where Are You Going, Manyoni?
Wolf Island
Zomo the Rabbit: A Trickster Tale From
    West Africa

ARTS AND CRAFTS

Abuela's Weave
Anni's Diary of France
A Blue Butterfly: A Story About Claude
    Monet
Camille and the Sunflowers: A Story
    About Vincent Van Gogh
Carnivalia! African-Brazilian Folklore and
    Crafts
Diego
Down Under: Vanishing Cultures
The Enchanted Tapestry
Enora and the Black Crane
Flowers on the Wall
Henry in Shadowland
The Hummingbirds' Gift
The Legend of the Persian Carpet
Life Around the Lake
The Little Painter of Sabana Grande
Michael the Angel
Moon Rope
Nina's Treasures
Paper Boats
The Singing Fir Tree
Vejigante Masquerader
The Voice of the Wood
Wings
A Young Painter: The Life and Paintings of
    Wang Yani, China's Extraordinary
    Young Artist

BELLS

The Bells of Santa Lucia
The Nine Days Wonder

BIOGRAPHY

Beethoven Lives Upstairs
A Blue Butterfly: A Story About Claude
    Monet
Camille and the Sunflowers: A Story
    About Vincent Van Gogh
Diego
Gutenberg

Mandela: From the Life of the South
    African Statesman
Michael the Angel
A Young Painter: The Life and Paintings of
    Wang Yani, China's Extraordinary
    Young Artist

BIRDS

Amazon Alphabet
Antarctica
The Crane's Gift
The Enchanted Storks
Enora and the Black Crane
Firebird
The Flying Tortoise: An Igbo Tale
A Ghost in the Castle
Grandfather's Dream
The Great Kapok Tree: A Tale of the
    Amazon Rain Forest
Honkers
How the Ostrich Got Its Long Neck
The Hummingbirds' Gift
If You Should Hear a Honey Guide
The Last Frontier: Antarctica
Nights of the Pufflings
Nina's Treasures
Prince Ivan and the Firebird
Rainbow Bird
The Seventh Sister: A Chinese Legend
Solo
The Tale of the Mandarin Ducks
When Chickens Grow Teeth
Whose Chick Is That?
Wings

BOATS

Amazon Boy
Going for Oysters
The Last Frontier: Antarctica
Paper Boats
Salt: A Russian Folktale
Spirit of Hope

BUS RIDE
Abuela's Weave
Gregory Cool
The Inside-Outside Book of London
Tap-Tap

BUTTERFLIES
Butterfly Boy

CELEBRATIONS
Baseball Bats for Christmas
The Bravest Flute
Carnivalia! African-Brazilian Folklore and
    Crafts
The Christmas Drum
Christmas Surprise for Chabelita
The Day Gogo Went to Vote
Diego
The Gift of a Traveler
The Golden Slipper: A Vietnam Legend
Growing Up in Ancient China
Growing Up in Ancient Greece
The Hummingbirds' Gift
I Is for India
An Island Christmas
Life Around the Lake
Magic Dogs of the Volcanoes
My Two Worlds
Not a Copper Penny in Me House
Pequeña the Burro
The Pumpkin Blanket
The Seventh Sister: A Chinese Legend
Two Pairs of Shoes
Vejigante Masquerader
The Voice of the Wood

CHILDREN RESOLVING PROBLEMS
Abuela's Weave
Amazon Boy
Baseball Bats for Christmas
The Boxing Champion
The Bravest Flute
Butterfly Boy

Clouds on the Mountain
Dreamtime: Aboriginal Stories
In the Garden
The Girl Who Changed Her Fate
Jen and the Great One
Kylie's Concert
The Legend of the Persian Carpet
The Little Painter of Sabana Grande
My Mama's Little Ranch on the Pampas
Min-Yo and the Moon Dragon
Nights of the Pufflings
One Grain of Rice: A Mathematical
    Folktale
One Night: A Story From the Desert
Pedrito's Day
Pulling the Lion's Tail
Punga: The Goddess of Ugly
The Rajah's Rice: A Mathematical Folktale
    From India
Sami and the Time of the Troubles
Sitti's Secrets
The Snow Queen
The Stonehook Schooner
The Streets Are Free
Waira's First Journey
The Water Shell
Where Is Gah-Ning?

CIRCUS
Annie . . . Anya: A Month in Moscow
A Ghost in the Castle
Kashtanka

CITY, CITY LIFE
Annie . . . Anya: A Month in Moscow
Anni's Diary of France
Beethoven Lives Upstairs
Carnivalia! African-Brazilian Folklore and
    Crafts
The Day of Ahmed's Secret
The Enchanted Storks
In the Garden
Grandpa's Visit
Growing Up in Ancient Greece

The Inside-Outside Book of London
Isla
Journey Through China
Kanu of Kathmandu: A Journey in Nepal
The Moon Was the Best
My Place
Pequeña the Burro
Sami and the Time of the Troubles
Somewhere in Africa
The Streets Are Free
The Tale of Hilda Louise
The Three Golden Keys

CLOTHING
Abuela's Weave
The Bravest Flute
Carnivalia! African-Brazilian Folklore and
    Crafts
A Christmas Surprise for Chabelita
The Empress and the Silkworm
The Golden Slipper: A Vietnam Legend
Growing Up in Ancient Egypt
I Is for India
Ishtar and Tammuz: A Babylonian Myth of
    the Seasons
The Secret Room
The Seventh Sister: A Chinese Legend
Two Pairs of Shoes
Vejigante Masquerader

COURAGE
Abuela's Weave
Ali: Child of the Desert
The Boxing Champion
The Bravest Flute
Encounter
Flowers on the Wall
I Dream of Peace: Images of War by
    Children of Former Yugoslavia
The Lily Cupboard
Min-Yo and the Moon Dragon
Newf
One Night: A Story From the Desert
Pulling the Lion's Tail

Punga: The Goddess of Ugly
The Stonehook Schooner
The Streets Are Free
The Water Shell
Zomo the Rabbit: A Trickster Tale From
    West Africa

COWBOYS
Anni's Diary of France
My Mama's Little Ranch on the Pampas

DAILY LIFE
Growing Up in Ancient China
Growing Up in Ancient Egypt
Growing Up in Ancient Greece
I Is for India
Kanu of Kathmandu: A Journey in Nepal
Let's Eat!
Masai and I
My Mama's Little Ranch on the Pampas
Not a Copper Penny in Me House

DANCING
Carnivalia! African-Brazilian Folklore and
    Crafts
Down Under: Vanishing Cultures
Fortune
I Is for India
An Island Christmas
My Kokum Called Today
The Nine Days Wonder
The Pumpkin Blanket
Punga: The Goddess of Ugly
Waira's First Journey

DANGEROUS SITUATIONS
Clouds on the Mountain
Danger on the Arctic Ice
The Fish Skin
Flowers on the Wall
Going for Oysters
Golem
I Dream of Peace: Images of War by
    Children of Former Yugoslavia

The Lily Cupboard
Magic Dogs of the Volcanoes
Newf
Pequeña the Burro
The Polar Bear Son
Sami and the Time of the Troubles
The Snow Queen
Solo
The Stonehook Schooner
The Tale of Tsar Saltan
The Water Shell

DEATH, SEPARATION
Ali: Child of the Desert
Baba Yaga and Vasilisa the Brave
The Bells of Santa Lucia
The Golden Slipper: A Vietnam Legend
Golem
The Green Frogs: A Korean Folktale
The Long Silk Strand
The New King: A Madagascan Legend
Prince Ivan and the Firebird
Som See and the Magic Elephant
The Tangerine Tree
Wings

DESERT
Ali: Child of the Desert
Arabian Nights: Three Tales
The Legend of the Persian Carpet
One Night: A Story From the Desert
The Secret Room
The Three Princes

ECOLOGY
Amazon Boy
Antarctica
Chung Lee Loves Lobsters
Danger on the Arctic Ice
Down Under: Vanishing Cultures
Grandfather's Dream
The Great Kapok Tree: A Tale of the
    Amazon Rain Forest
Jen and the Great One

Kylie's Concert
The Last Frontier: Antarctica
Life Around the Lake
Mcheshi Goes to the Game Park
Nights of the Pufflings
The Singing Fir Tree
Solo
The Paddock: A Story in Praise of the
    Earth
Tano and Binti: Two Chimpanzees Return
    to the Wild
In the Village of the Elephants
The Water Shell
Wolf Island

ENVIRONMENT
Ali: Child of the Desert
Antarctica
Baseball Bats for Christmas
Down Under: Vanishing Cultures
In the Eyes of the Cat: Japanese Poetry
    for All Seasons
Grandfather's Dream
If You Should Hear a Honey Guide
If You're Not From the Prairie . . .
In the Garden
Jen and the Great One
Kylie's Concert
The Last Frontier: Antarctica
Little Elephant's Walk
One Round Moon and a Star for Me
One Small Square: African Savanna
The Paddock: A Story in Praise of the
    Earth
Solo
Welcome Back Sun
Where Are You Going, Manyoni?
Wolf Island

ETHICS, MORAL PROBLEMS
The Empty Pot
The Market Lady and the Mango Tree
Pedrito's Day
The Polar Bear Son

Rapunzel
The Secret Room
The Snow Queen
The Stone Lion
Tim O'Toole and the Wee Folk
The Wonderful Bag

EVERYDAY LIFE

A to Zen: A Book of Japanese Culture
Coconut Kind of Day: Island Poems
At the Crossroads
The Day of Ahmed's Secret
The Distant Talking Drum
Gittel's Hands
Growing Up in Ancient China
Growing Up in Ancient Egypt
Growing Up in Ancient Greece
Journey Through China
Life Around the Lake
My Two Worlds
One Smiling Grandma
Running the Road to ABC
Russian Girl: Life in an Old Russian Town

FAMILY

African Brothers and Sisters
Ali: Child of the Desert
Amazon Boy
Annie . . . Anya: A Month in Moscow
Bearhead: A Russian Folktale
Beethoven Lives Upstairs
Big Boy
Butterfly Boy
Chinye: A West African Folk Tale
A Christmas Surprise for Chabelita
Clouds on the Mountain
The Day of Ahmed's Secret
Diego
Down Under: Vanishing Cultures
Dreamtime: Aboriginal Stories
The Enchanted Tapestry
Flowers on the Wall

Gathering the Sun: An Alphabet in
   Spanish and English
The Gods and Goddesses of Olympus
Going for Oysters
The Golden Slipper: A Vietnam Legend
Grandpa's Visit
Gregory Cool
Growing Up in Ancient China
Honkers
Hue Boy
The Hummingbirds' Gift
In the Garden
Ishtar and Tammuz: A Babylonian Myth of
   the Seasons
Isla
An Island Christmas
It Takes a Village
Let's Eat!
The Lily Cupboard
The Little Painter of Sabana Grande
The Long Silk Strand
My Kokum Called Today
My Mama's Little Ranch on the Pampas
My Two Worlds
One Night: A Story From the Desert
One Round Moon and a Star for Me
Over the Green Hills
Pedrito's Day
Pulling the Lion's Tail
The Pumpkin Blanket
Russian Girl: Life in Old Russian Town
Sami and the Time of the Troubles
Sitti's Secrets
Spirit of Hope
The Stonehook Schooner
The Streets Are Free
The Tale of Hilda Louise
The Tangerine Tree
Two Pairs of Shoes
Waira's First Journey
Where Is Gah-Ning?
You Be the Witch
A Young Painter: The Life and Paintings of
   Wang Yani, China's Extraordinary
   Young Artist

FARMS, FARMING, RANCHES

Borreguita and the Coyote
Chicken Man
Floss
Gathering the Sun: An Alphabet in
    Spanish and English
Honkers
The Hummingbirds' Gift
If You're Not From the Prairie . . .
The Lily Cupboard
My Mama's Little Ranch on the Pampas
The Pumpkin Blanket
Saint Patrick and the Peddler
The Turnip
When Chickens Grow Teeth

FATHER

Abuelita's Paradise
African Brothers and Sisters
Ali: Child of the Desert
The Christmas Drum
At the Crossroads
Gittel's Hands
Hue Boy
The New King: A Madagascan Legend
One Night: A Story From the Desert
One Round Moon and a Star for Me
Prince Ivan and the Firebird
Salt: A Russian Folktale
The Stonehook Schooner
The Tale of Tsar Saltan
The Tangerine Tree
Where Is Gah-Ning?
Wings

FEARS

Abuela's Weave
The Bravest Flute
The Christmas Drum
Going for Oysters
Golem
The Hummingbirds' Gift
The Lily Cupboard
Moon Rope

My Mama's Little Ranch on the Pampas
Pequeña the Burro
Rhinos for Lunch and Elephants for
    Supper!

FISH, FISHING

Amazon Boy
Coconut Kind of Day: Island Poems
The Fish Skin
Going for Oysters
Gregory Cool
Minas and the Fish
My Grandpa and the Sea
Nanabosho: How the Turtle Got Its Shell
The Polar Bear Son
Rockabye Crocodile: A Folktale From the
    Philippines
The Water Shell
Zomo the Rabbit: A Trickster Tale From
    West Africa

FLOWERS

A Blue Butterfly: A Story About Claude
    Monet
Camille and the Sunflowers: A Story
    About Vincent Van Gogh
The Empty Pot
Flowers on the Wall
The Golden Flower: A Taino Myth From
    Puerto Rico
The Hummingbirds' Gift
The Little Painter of Sabana Grande
Nina's Treasures
The Snow Queen

FOLKTALES

Agassu: Legend of the Leopard King
Arabian Nights: Three Tales
Baba Yaga and Vasilisa the Brave
Baby Baboon
Bearhead: A Russian Folktale
Borreguita and the Coyote
Chinye: A West African Folk Tale
The Crane's Gift

Dreamtime: Aboriginal Stories
The Empress and the Silkworm
The Empty Pot
Enora and the Black Crane
The Enchanted Storks
The Enchanted Tapestry
Firebird
The Fish Skin
The Flying Tortoise: An Igbo Tale
Fortune
The Girl Who Changed Her Fate
Gittel's Hands
The Golden Flower: A Taino Myth From
    Puerto Rico
The Golden Slipper: A Vietnam Legend
Golem
The Green Frogs: A Korean Folktale
How Music Came to the World
How the Ostrich Got Its Long Neck
How the Ox Star Fell From Heaven
The Hummingbirds' Gift
The Iroko-man: A Yoruba Folktale
Ishtar and Tammuz: A Babylonian Myth of
    the Seasons
Judge Rabbit and the Tree Spirit: A
    Folktale From Cambodia
The Junior Thunder Lord
The King and the Tortoise
Knock, Knock, Terenok: A Traditional
    Russian Tale
Kun-Man-Gur: The Rainbow Serpent
Lazy Jack
The Legend of King Arthur
The Legend of the Persian Carpet
The Loyal Cat
Magic Dogs of the Volcanoes
The Magic Purse
The Match Between the Winds
Maui and the Sun: A Maori Tale
Minas and the Fish
Min-Yo and the Moon Dragon
The Moles and the Mireuk: A Korean
    Folktale
Moon Rope
Nanabosho: How the Turtle Got Its Shell

Nina's Treasures
One Grain of Rice: A Mathematical
    Folktale
The Orphan Boy
Peboan and Seegwun
Prince Ivan and the Firebird
Pulling the Lion's Tail
Punga: The Goddess of Ugly
The Rabbit's Judgment
Rainbow Bird
The Raja's Rice: A Mathematical Folktale
    From India
Rapunzel
Rhinos for Lunch and Elephants for
    Supper!
Rockabye Crocodile: A Folktale From the
    Philippines
Saint Patrick and the Peddler
Salt: A Russian Folktale
The Secret Room
The Seventh Sister: A Chinese Legend
The Snow Queen
Song of the Chirimia: A Guatemalan
    Folktale
The Stone Lion
The Tale of the Mandarin Ducks
The Tale of Tsar Saltan
The Three Princes
Tim O'Toole and the Wee Folk
Too Much Talk
Tukama Tootles the Flute: A Tale From
    the Antilles
The Turnip
The Water Shell
Wings
The Wonderful Bag
Zomo the Rabbit: A Trickster Tale From
    West Africa

FOOD, FOOD PREPARATION

Bitter Bananas
Chung Lee Loves Lobsters
Clouds on the Mountain
Down Under: Vanishing Cultures

Dreamtime: Aboriginal Stories
In the Garden
Gathering the Sun: An Alphabet in
    Spanish and English
Going for Oysters
Growing Up in Ancient China
Growing Up in Ancient Egypt
Growing Up in Ancient Greece
How the Ox Star Fell From Heaven
I Is for India
An Island Christmas
Jasmine's Parlour Day
Let's Eat!
The Market Lady and the Mango Tree
Masai and I
My Kokum Called Today
Nina's Treasures
Over the Green Hills
The Polar Bear Son
Possum Magic
Rockabye Crocodile: A Folktale From the
    Philippines
Russian Girl: Life in an Old Russian Town
Salt: A Russian Folktale
Saturday Sancocho
The Tangerine Tree
Walter the Baker
You Be the Witch

FRIENDS, FRIENDSHIPS
Annie . . . Anya: A Month in Moscow
The Faithful Friend
Isabela's Ribbons
The Red Comb
The Yesterday Stone

FUTURE
The Fortune-Tellers
The Paddock: A Story in Praise of the
    Earth

GAMES
African Brothers and Sisters
Baseball Bats for Christmas

The Boxing Champion
Grandpa's Visit
Isabela's Ribbons
The Streets Are Free
You Be the Witch

GODS AND GODDESSES
Agassu: Legend of the Leopard King
The Fish Skin
The Gods and Goddesses of Olympus
How Music Came to the World
The Iroko-man: A Yoruba Folktale
Ishtar and Tammuz: A Babylonian Myth of
    the Seasons
The Magic Purse
Maui and the Sun: A Maori Tale
Punga: The Goddess of Ugly
The Snow Queen
Wings
Zomo the Rabbit: A Trickster Tale From
    West Africa

GRANDPARENTS
Abuela's Weave
Abuelita's Paradise
Babushka Baba Yaga
Babushka's Doll
The Bells of Santa Lucia
Butterfly Boy
The Cherry Tree
A Christmas Surprise for Chabelita
The Day Gogo Went to Vote
Down Under: Vanishing Cultures
In the Garden
The Gift of a Traveler
The Good Night Story
Grandfather's Dream
Grandpa's Visit
Gregory Cool
Honkers
Hue Boy
Isabela's Ribbons
Isla
The Long Silk Strand

Matreshka
My Grandpa and the Sea
My Kokum Called Today
My Two Worlds
Nanabosho: How the Turtle Got Its Shell
One Night: A Story From the Desert
One Smiling Grandma
Over the Green Hills
Possum Magic
Pulling the Lion's Tail
Punga: The Goddess of Ugly
Saturday Sancocho
Sitti's Secrets
Tukama Tootles the Flute: A Tale From
  the Antilles
Two Pairs of Shoes
The Yesterday Stone

HEALTH, GROWING

The Cherry Tree
Hue Boy

HELPING OTHERS

Abuela's Weave
Ali: Child of the Desert
The Bells of Santa Lucia
Butterfly Boy
Chung Lee Loves Lobsters
Clouds on the Mountain
The Crane's Gift
The Face in the Window
The Fish Skin
In the Garden
Gittel's Hands
The Hummingbirds' Gift
It Takes a Village
The Junior Thunder Lord
The Lily Cupboard
The Little Painter of Sabana Grande
The Loyal Cat
Newf
Nights of the Pufflings
One Grain of Rice: A Mathematical
  Folktale

Over the Green Hills
The Polar Bear Son
The Rabbit's Judgment
The Red Comb
Rockabye Crocodile: A Folktale From the
  Philippines
The Stonehook Schooner
The Streets Are Free
The Tale of Hilda Louise
The Turnip

HIKING

Anni's Diary of France
Clouds on the Mountain
Down Under: Vanishing Cultures
The Last Frontier: Antarctica
Waira's First Journey

HISTORY

Carnivalia! African-Brazilian Folklore and
  Crafts
Count Your Way Through Israel
Encounter
Esther's Story
The Gods and Goddesses of Olympus
Growing Up in Ancient China
Growing Up in Ancient Egypt
Growing Up in Ancient Greece
Gutenberg
The Last Frontier: Antarctica
The Lily Cupboard
My Place
The Paddock: A Story in Praise of the Earth
The Red Comb
Russian Girl: Life in an Old Russian Town
Waira's First Journey

HONESTY

The Empty Pot
The Face in the Window
One Grain of Rice: A Mathematical Folktale
Pedrito's Day
The Secret Room
The Stone Lion

HOLOCAUST AND ANTI-SEMITISM

Esther's Story
Flowers on the Wall
Golem
Let the Celebrations Begin!
The Lily Cupboard

HOUSES

Anni's Diary of France
Baba Yaga and Vasilisa the Brave
The Banshee
Beethoven Lives Upstairs
The Bells of Santa Lucia
A Ghost in the Castle
The Good Night Story
Grandpa's Visit
Gregory Cool
Growing Up in Ancient Egypt
Growing Up in Ancient Greece
Gutenberg
The House That Jack Built
Isla
Knock, Knock, Terenok: A Traditional
    Russian Tale
Let's Eat!
The Little Painter of Sabana Grande
The Match Between the Winds
Matreshka
My Place
The Pumpkin Blanket
Punga: The Goddess of Ugly
Saint Patrick and the Peddler
The Singing Fir Tree
The Snow Queen
Spirit of Hope
The Streets Are Free
The Three Golden Keys
You Be the Witch

HUMOR

Chicken Man
Don't Dig So Deep, Nicholas!
The Good Night Story
How the Ostrich Got Its Long Neck

Knock, Knock, Terenok: A Traditional
    Russian Tale
Lazy Jack
Mucky Moose
The Secret Room
Too Much Talk
When Chickens Grow Teeth
Where Is Gah-Ning?
The Wonderful Bag

IMAGINATION, IMAGINARY HAPPENINGS, MAGIC

Arabian Nights: Three Tales
Baba Yaga and Vasilisa the Brave
Babushka's Doll
The Banshee
Big Boy
Don't Dig So Deep, Nicholas!
The Enchanted Storks
The Enchanted Tapestry
The Faithful Friend
Firebird
Fortune
Henry in Shadowland
Isabela's Ribbons
Isla
The Knot in the Tracks
The Loyal Cat
Magic Dogs of the Volcanoes
The Magic Purse
Matreshka
Minas and the Fish
Possum Magic
Punga: The Goddess of Ugly
Rata, Pata, Scata, Fata: A Caribbean Story
The Seventh Sister: A Chinese Legend
The Snow Queen
Som See and the Magic Elephant
The Stone Lion
The Tale of Hilda Louise
The Tale of Tsar Saltan
The Three Princes
Tim O'Toole and the Wee Folk
Too Much Talk
The Water Shell

IMPAIRMENTS
Abuela's Weave
Butterfly Boy
Two Pairs of Shoes

INDIANS
Baseball Bats for Christmas
The Bravest Flute
The Fish Skin
In the Garden
How Music Came to the World
The Hummingbirds' Gift
Jen and the Great One
Life Around the Lake
My Kokum Called Today
Nanabosho: How the Turtle Got Its Shell
Peboan and Seegwun
The Polar Bear Son
Song of the Chirimia: A Guatemalan
    Folktale
Two Pairs of Shoes
Waira's First Journey
The Yesterday Stone

JUDGMENT
Agassu: Legend of the Leopard King
Esther's Story
Judge Rabbit and the Tree Spirit: A
    Folktale From Cambodia
The Wonderful Bag

KINGS, QUEENS, CALIPHS, LORDS, EMPERORS, PHARAOHS, RAJAS, TSARS
Agassu: Legend of the Leopard King
Arabian Nights: Three Tales
The Empress and the Silkworm
The Empty Pot
The Enchanted Storks
Esther's Story
The Flying Tortoise: An Igbo Tale
Fortune
Growing Up in Ancient Egypt
How the Ox Star Fell From Heaven

The King and the Tortoise
The Legend of King Arthur
The Legend of the Persian Carpet
Min-Yo and the Moon Dragon
The New King: A Madagascan Legend
One Grain of Rice: A Mathematical Folktale
Prince Ivan and the Firebird
The Rajah's Rice: A Mathematical Folktale
    From India
Rapunzel
Salt: A Russian Folktale
The Secret Room
The Snow Queen
Song of the Chirimia: A Guatemalan Folktale
The Tale of the Mandarin Ducks
The Tale of Tsar Saltan
The Three Golden Keys
Too Much Talk
The Water Shell
Wings

LABOR, LABOR PROBLEMS, OCCUPATIONS
Chicken Man
At the Crossroads
The Day of Ahmed's Secret
Diego
The Fortune-Tellers
In the Garden
Gathering the Sun: An Alphabet in
    Spanish and English
Gutenberg
The Knot in the Tracks
Lazy Jack
The Legend of the Persian Carpet
Minas and the Fish
My Grandpa and the Sea
The Singing Fir Tree
The Stonehook Schooner
In the Village of the Elephants
Walter the Baker

LIBRARY
Somewhere in Africa
The Three Golden Keys

Where Is Gah-Ning?

LOVE

The Crane's Gift
The Enchanted Tapestry
The Faithful Friend
Firebird
Fortune
The Golden Slippers: A Vietnam Legend
Prince Ivan and the Firebird
Rapunzel
The Seventh Sister: A Chinese Legend
The Tale of the Mandarin Ducks

LOYALTY

Bearhead: A Russian Folktale
The Faithful Friend
Fortune
Kashtanka
The Loyal Cat
The Polar Bear Son

MARRIAGE, DIVORCE, REMARRIAGE

Prince Ivan and the Firebird
Pulling the Lion's Tail
Salt: A Russian Folktale
The Tale of Tsar Saltan

MARKETS, MARKETING

Abuela's Weave
Amazon Boy
A Christmas Surprise for Chabelita
Fortune
Isla
It Takes a Village
Jasmine's Parlour Day
The Market Lady and the Mango Tree
Pedrito's Day
Saturday Sancocho
Tap-Tap
Waira's First Journey
The Wonderful Bag

MESSAGES

Esther's Story
Paper Boats

MONEY, EARNING

Abuela's Weave
Amazon Boy
The Day of Ahmed's Secret
Flowers on the Wall
Fortune
The Fortune-Tellers
The Hummingbirds' Gift
Jasmine's Parlour Day
Lazy Jack
The Loyal Cat
The Magic Purse
The Market Lady and the Mango Tree
My Grandpa and the Sea
Pedrito's Day
Saint Patrick and the Peddler
Salt: A Russian Folktale
The Stone Lion
The Tangerine Tree
Tap-Tap
Vejigante Masquerader

MOON, STARS

In the Eyes of the Cat: Japanese Poetry
    for All Seasons
How the Ox Star Fell From Heaven
Maui and the Sun: A Maori Tale
Min-Yo and the Moon Dragon
Moon Rope
One Round Moon and a Star for Me
The Orphan Boy
The Pumpkin Blanket
The Seventh Sister: A Chinese Legend

MOTHER

Big Boy
A Christmas Surprise for Chabelita
Clouds on the Mountain
The Enchanted Tapestry
The Green Frogs: A Korean Folktale

Hue Boy
Hush! A Thai Lullaby
Jasmine's Parlour Day
My Mama's Little Ranch on the Pampas
The Moon Was the Best
Okino and the Whales
Over the Green Hills
Pedrito's Day
Pulling the Lion's Tail
Rata, Pata, Scata, Fata: A Caribbean Story
Tap-Tap

MUSIC

Beethoven Lives Upstairs
The Bravest Flute
Carnivalia! African-Brazilian Folklore and
    Crafts
The Christmas Drum
How Music Came to the World
Island Christmas
The Singing Fir Tree
Song of the Chirimia: A Guatemalan
    Folktale
Tukama Tootles the Flute: A Tale From
    the Antilles
The Voice of the Wood

NUMBERS

Count Your Way Through Israel
Count Your Way Through the Arab World
Lóng Is a Dragon: Chinese Writing for
    Children
My Arctic, 1, 2, 3
One Grain of Rice: A Mathematical
    Folktale
One Smiling Grandma
The Raja's Rice: A Mathematical Folktale
    From India

PERFORMANCES

Beethoven Lives Upstairs
Carnivalia! African-Brazilian Folklore and
    Crafts
The Christmas Drum

A Christmas Surprise for Chabelita
Kashtanka

PLANTS, PLANTING

Abuelita's Paradise
Bitter Bananas
The Cherry Tree
The Empty Pot
In the Garden
Gathering the Sun: An Alphabet in
    Spanish and English
The Golden Flower: A Taino Myth From
    Puerto Rico
Jen and the Great One
Kylie's Concert
The Market Lady and the Mango Tree
Nina's Treasures
One Small Square: African Savanna
The Pumpkin Blanket
The Turnip

POEMS

A Christmas Surprise for Chabelita
Coconut Kind of Day: Island Poems
The Distant Talking Drum
In the Eyes of the Cat: Japanese Poetry
    for All Seasons
Gathering the Sun: An Alphabet in
    Spanish and English
The House That Jack Built
I Dream of Peace: Images of War by
    Children of Former Yugoslavia
If You're Not From the Prairie . . .
Not a Copper Penny in Me House
Paper Boats

POLITICAL CONCERNS

Agassu: Legend of the Leopard King
Carnivalia! African-Brazilian Folklore and
    Crafts
The Day Gogo Went to Vote
Diego
Flowers on the Wall

Gathering the Sun: An Alphabet in
Spanish and English
I Dream of Peace: Images of War by
Children of Former Yugoslavia
Let the Celebrations Begin!
The Lily Cupboard
Mandela: From the Life of the South
African Statesman
Sami and the Time of the Troubles
Sitti's Secrets
The Streets Are Free

PROMISES

The Crane's Gift
Fortune
One Grain of Rice: A Mathematical
Folktale
The Rabbit's Judgment
Song of the Chirimia: A Guatemalan
Folktale

RACES, CONTESTS, TOURNAMENTS

Bearhead: A Russian Folktale
The Legend of King Arthur
The Match Between the Winds
The Nine Days Wonder
Supergrandpa

RAIN, DROUGHT

The Clouds on the Mountains
The Face in the Window
Grandfather's Dream
The Hummingbirds' Gift
Ishtar and Tammuz: A Babylonian Myth of
the Seasons
The Junior Thunder Lord
You Be the Witch

RAIN FOREST

Amazon Alphabet
Amazon Boy
Bitter Bananas
Enora and the Black Crane

The Great Kapok Tree: A Tale of the
Amazon Rain Forest
Som See and the Magic Elephant

RELIGION

Esther's Story
Golem
I Is for India
The Loyal Cat
The Magic Purse
Russian Girl: Life in an Old Russian Town
Som See and the Magic Elephant

SCHOOL

Anni's Diary of France
Butterfly Boy
A Christmas Surprise for Chabelita
Coconut Kind of Day: Island Poems
At the Crossroads
Diego
Growing Up in Ancient Greece
The Little Painter of Sabana Grande
Running the Road to ABC
Russian Girl: Life in an Old Russian Town
Where Are You Going, Manyoni?
The Yesterday Stone

SEASONS

Antarctica
The Boxing Champion
The Cherry Tree
Danger on the Arctic Ice
In the Eyes of the Cat: Japanese Poetry
for All Seasons
Honkers
If You're Not From the Prairie . . .
Ishtar and Tammuz: A Babylonian Myth of
the Seasons
Nina's Treasures
One Small Square: African Savanna
Peboan and Seegwun
The Polar Bear Son
The Pumpkin Blanket
The Snow Queen

The Three Golden Keys
Welcome Back Sun
Wolf Island

SIBLING RIVALRY
The Enchanted Storks
The Enchanted Tapestry
The Golden Slipper: A Vietnam Legend
Ishtar and Tammuz: A Babylonian Myth of
   the Seasons
Minas and the Fish
Prince Ivan and the Firebird
Rockabye Crocodile: A Folktale From the
   Philippines
Salt: A Russian Folktale
The Stone Lion
The Tale of Tsar Saltan
The Three Princes

SLAVERY
Agassu: Legend of the Leopard King
The Red Comb

SPORTS, SWIMMING
Baseball Bats for Christmas
The Boxing Champion
Floss
Gregory Cool
Minas and the Fish
Pedrito's Day
The Streets Are Free
Supergrandpa
Where Is Gah-Ning?

STORYTELLING
Abuelita's Paradise
Arabian Nights: Three Tales
Babushka Baba Yaga
Diego
Dreamtime: Aboriginal Stories
The Gift of a Traveler
The Good Night Story
Henry in Shadowland
Nanabosho: How the Turtle Got Its Shell

The Polar Bear Son
Saint Patrick and the Peddler
Sami and the Time of the Troubles
The Three Princes
The Yesterday Stone

SOUNDS
Ali: Child of the Desert
The Bells of Santa Lucia
Coconut Kind of Day: Island Poems
The Day of Ahmed's Secret
Honkers
If You Should Hear a Honey Guide
Rhinos for Lunch and Elephants for
   Supper!
Song of the Chirimia: A Guatemalan
   Folktale

SUPERSTITION
The Face in the Window

TALKING
The Day of Ahmed's Secret
The Fortune-Tellers
Too Much Talk
Where Is Gah-Ning?

THEFT
The Secret Room
Tim O'Toole and the Wee Folk
The Wonderful Bag

TOURS, TRAVEL, TRAVELING
Ali: Child of the Desert
Annie . . . Anya: A Month in Moscow
Anni's Diary of France
Diego
Gregory Cool
The Inside-Outside Book of London
Journey Through China
Kanu of Kathmandu: A Journey in Nepal
The Last Frontier: Antarctica
The Magic Purse
Mcheshi Goes to the Game Park

The Moon Was the Best
My Two Worlds
Over the Green Hills
Salt: A Russian Folktale
The Tangerine Tree
Waira's First Journey
Where Is Gah-Ning?

TRAIN, TRAIN RIDE

Honkers
The Inside-Outside Book of London
The Knot in the Tracks

TREES

Baseball Bats for Christmas
Bitter Bananas
The Cherry Tree
The Gift of a Traveler
The Great Kapok Tree: A Tale of the
    Amazon Rain Forest
If You Should Hear a Honey Guide
Jasmine's Parlour Day
Jen and the Great One
Kylie's Concert
The Market Lady and the Mango Tree
The Red Comb
The Singing Fir Tree
The Tangerine Tree
In the Village of the Elephants
The Voice of the Wood
Where Are You Going, Manyoni?

VILLAGE

Abuela's Weave
Babushka Baba Yaga
The Banshee
The Bells of Santa Lucia
Gittel's Hands
Grandfather's Dream
The Hummingbirds' Gift
It Takes a Village
Kanu of Kathmandu: A Journey to Nepal
The Little Painter of Sabana Grande
The Magic Purse

The Market Lady and the Mango Tree
Nina's Treasures
Not a Copper Penny in Me House
Polar Bear Son
Running the Road to ABC
In the Village of the Elephants
When Chicken Grow Teeth

VOTING

The Day Gogo Went to Vote
Sitti's Secrets

WAR, FIGHTING, PERSECUTION

Diego
Esther's Story
Flowers on the Wall
Golem
I Dream of Peace: Images of War by
    Children of Former Yugoslavia
Ishtar and Tammuz: A Babylonian Myth of
    the Seasons
Let the Celebrations Begin!
The Lily Cupboard
Magic Dogs of the Volcanoes
Sami and the Time of the Troubles
The Tale of Tsar Saltan

WEATHER

Clouds on the Mountain
In the Eyes of the Cat: Japanese Poetry
    for All Seasons
How Music Came to the World
The Junior Thunder Lord
The Last Frontier: Antarctica
The Match Between the Winds
The Pumpkin Blanket
The Stonehook Schooner
The Water Shell

WINTER

Antarctica
Baseball Bats for Christmas
Gittel's Hands

Ishtar and Tammuz: A Babylonian Myth of
   the Seasons
Kashtanka
The Knot in the Tracks
Matreshka
Peboan and Seegwun
The Polar Bear Son
Russian Girl: Life in an Old Russian Town
The Snow Queen
Welcome Back Sun
Wolf Island

WRITING, PRINTING, READING

Anni's Diary of France
Beethoven Lives Upstairs

Butterfly Boy
The Day Gogo Went to Vote
The Day of Ahmed's Secret
Dreamtime: Aboriginal Stories
Esther's Story
Gutenberg
I Dream of Peace: Images of War by
   Children of Former Yugoslavia
The Last Frontier: Antarctica
Lóng Is a Dragon: Chinese Writing for
   Children
Running the Road to ABC
Russian Girl: Life in an Old Russian Town
Sitti's Secrets
The Tangerine Tree

B

Video, CD-ROM, Audiobook, and Internet Resources

Video and CD-ROM resources marked with a bullet (·) are available from Library Video Company, P.O. Box 580, Wynnewood, PA, 19096 (800) 843–3620. Those marked with an asterisk (*) are available from Discovery Channel Video, P.O. Box 4055, Santa Monica, CA 90411. Write for both catalogs. Unmarked resources are available from addresses listed.

CHAPTER 2: CHILDREN'S BOOKS ABOUT AFRICA

Videos

- African Art: An African Perspective DA0619
- African Story Magic DK5961-B
- Afro-Classic Folk Tales DD2101
- American Cultures for Children Series
    African-American Heritage DK6651
    Arab-American Heritage DK6652

"Anansi and the Talking Melon" T6-220-4696
    Delta Education: MEDIA TREASURES, P.O. Box 3000, Nashua, NH 03061-3000

- Animals in Nature Series
    African Animals DN1401
    A First Look at African Animals DN1412

"At the Crossroads" 0-02-686762-1
    SRA/McGraw Hill, 220 East Danieldale Road, DeSoto, TX 75115-2490

- The Celebration of Kwanzaa: Echoes of Africa DD4601
- Children of the Earth Series
    Africa Close-Up: Egypt and Tanzania DK 1493
- * The Great Egyptians
- Doug Jones Travelog Series
    Egypt: Gift of the Nile DT9801
- * Flight Over the Equator
- Hello! From Around the World Series
    Egypt DK3255
    Ghana DK3256
- Multicultural People of North America Series
    African Americans DD6671-K
    Arab Americans DD6673-K
- National Geographic: Really Wild Animal Series
    Swinging Safari DK437
- The National Geographic Series
    African Wildlife DN4017
    Creatures of the Namib Desert DN4023

    Gorilla DN4014
    Jane Goodall: My Life With Chimpanzees DN0433
- Nature (PBS) Series
    Echo of Elephants DN6091
    Secrets of an African Jungle (NS) DN6027
    Cheetahs in the Land of Lions DN6009
    Horse Tigers DN6038
    Jane Goodall's Wild Chimpanzees DN6048
- Nature's Newborn Series
    Lion, Wildebeest, Zebra: Vol. 1 DK1411
    Giraffe, Elephant, Animals of Africa: Vol. 2 DK1412
    White Rhino, Jackal, Monkey: Vol. 3 DK1413
    Warthog, Kudu, Waterbuck: Vol. 4 DK1414
    Elephant, Rock Hyrax, Baby Animals: Vol. 5 DK1415
    Ostrich, Camel, Tortoise: Vol. 6 DK1416
    Crocodile, Leopard, Ground Squirrel: Vol. 7 DK1417
- New Explorers: Great Mysteries Series
    Maasai: Secrets of an Ancient Culture DN0564
- * Mandela's Fight for Freedom
- * Nile: River of Gods
- Nova: Creatures of the Earth Series
    Can the Elephant Be Saved? DN4189
- Rand-McNally Video Traveler World Collection
    Egypt (RMW) DT3517
- Super Cities Series
    Cairo DT2455
- Video Expeditions Series
    Southern Africa Safari DT3561
- Video Visits Africa Series
    Morocco: A Bridge Across Time DT3665
    South Africa: A Journey of Discovery DT3654

Zimbabwe: Africa's Wildlife
Sanctuary DT3663
Kenya Safari: Essence of Africa
DT3712
- Video Visits the Middle East Series
Egypt: Land of Ancient Wonders
DT3620
- Where in the World Series
Kids Explore Kenya DK3503
* Wild India

CD-ROMs

- Africa Trail (WIN/MAC) DR 1531
Ancient Egypt (*Laser disc, CAV Level 1*)
Forest Technologies, 514 Market Loop, Suite
103, *West Dundee, IL* 60118
Magic Tales: Stories That Magically Come
to Life; Imo and the King: An African
Folktale (WIN/MAC) CMDAV2804
HACH, P.O. *Box* 11754, *Winston-Salem,*
NC 27116
- Mammals of Africa (WIN95/MAC) DR2213
- Safari (WIN95) DR1376
- Wild Africa: Okavango, Chobe,
Makgadikgadi (WIN95/MAC) DR2414
- Zurk's Science Collection
Zurk's Learning Safari (WIN/MAC)
DR1562

Internet Sites

http://www.library.uiuc.edu/arx/african.htm
(*General*)
http://www.state.gov/www/regions/nea/country-
information.html (*Middle East and North*
Africa) (*Cross Reference*)
http://www-sul.stanford.edu/depts/ssrg/
Africa/ed.html (*General*)
http://www.yahoo.com/Regional/countries/South
_Africa/Education/ (*South Africa*)

http://www.africaonline.com (*at "Rainbow" link*)
(*General*)

CHAPTER 3: CHILDREN'S BOOKS ABOUT ASIA

Videos

- American Cultures for Children Series
Chinese-American Heritage DK6654
Japanese-American Heritage DK6656
Korean-American Heritage DK6658
Vietnamese-American Heritage
DK6662
- Children of the Earth Series
Asia Close-Up: Japan and Cambodia
DK1213
* China: A Century of Revolution
- China and the Forbidden City DT1701
- Chinese New Year DK6602 C
- Exploring the World Series
Exploring the Himalayas, Nepal and
Kashmir DT1901
Touring Korea DT1901
- Families of the World Series
Families of India DK4921
Families of Thailand DK4923
- Fodor's Videos Series
Singapore DT3590
- Hello! From Around the World Series
Japan (HFW) DK3257
* In the Shadow of Angkor Wat
* Mustang: The Hidden Kingdom (*Tibet*)
- Multicultural People of North America
Series
Japanese Americans DD6680-K
Korean Americans DD6682-K
- My Sesame Street Series
Big Bird in China DK2553
Big Bird in Japan DK2568
- National Geographic: Really Wild
Animals Series
Adventures in Asia DK0439
- National Geographic Series

Living Treasures of Japan DN4041
  Tigers of the Snow DN4130
- Nature (PBS) Series
  The Elephant Men DN6021
  Lords of Hokkaido DN6025
- Raising the Bamboo Curtain Series
  DD1735
    Awakening Vietnam
    Emerging Burma and Cambodia
- Rand-McNally Video Traveler World
  Collection
    Hong Kong and Macau DT3630
    Japan (RMW) DT3507
    Mysterious Orient DT3519
    Singapore: Crossroads of Asia DT3653
    The Exotic Far East DT3715
- Super Cities Series
    Bangkok DT2451
    Hong Kong DT2457
- The Search for the Most Secret
  Animals Series
    The Search for India's Most Secret
    Animals DK4843
- Wall Street Journal's Emerging Powers
  Series
    China DD7872
    India DD7873
- Video Visits Asia Series
    China: Ancient Rhythms and
    Modern Currents DT3686
    India: Land of Spirit and Mystique
    DT3632
    Japan: The Island Empire DT3635
    Mystical Malaysia: Land of Harmony
    DT3639
    South Korea: Land of the Morning
    Calm DT3689
    Thailand: The Golden Kingdom
    DT3660
    Vietnam: Land of the Ascending
    Dragon DT3660

CD-ROMs

- China! The Grand Tour (WIN) DR1396

- Discover the Magic of India (WIN)
  DR2442
- Exotic Japan (WIN/MAC) DR1399
The Little Samurai: A Japanese Folk Tale
  (WIN/MAC) CMDAV2805
  HACH, P.O. Box 11754, *Winston-Salem*,
  NC 27116
- Magic Tales Series
    "The Little Samurai" (WIN95/MAC)
    DR1657
- The Multicultural Experience Series
    The Asian-American Experience
    (WIN/MAC) DR2254
- "The Story of Ganesha" (WIN/MAC)
  DR1884

Internet Sites

http://www.cudenver.edu/psrp/asia.html (*General*)
http://www.state.gov/www/regions/eap/eapcountry
  /html (*Asian Pacific*) (*General*)
http://asiatravel.net/thailand.html (*Thailand*)
http://www.admall.com.sg/ctryinfo.htm
  (*Cambodia/China*)

CHAPTER 4: CHILDREN'S BOOKS ABOUT CANADA
Videos

- AAA Travel Video Series
    Alberta, British Columbia, Manitoba,
    Saskatchewan DT8301
    Ontario DT8317
    Quebec and the Atlantic Provinces
    DT8319
- America's Scenic Rail Journeys
    The Canadian Rockies DT1023
- Bunch of Munsch Series
    "50 Below Zero" DK4518
- Doug Jones' Travelog Series
    The Great Canadian Train Ride
    DT9812
- Fly Away Home DK0453
- Great Canadian Parks

Kluane National Park Reserve/Saguenay-St. Lawrence Marine Park DT1033
Ts'il-os Provincial Park/Parks of Fundy DT1031
Waterton Lakes National Park/Cypress Hills Interprovencial Park DT1032
Waterfalls and Wildlife DT1001
- Indians of North America Collection
  The Huron (Ouedat; SE *Canada*) DD6690-K
  The Iroquois (Ogwea:weh; NE U.S. & *Canada*) DD6656-K
- The National Geographic: Really Wild Animals Series
  Polar Prowl DK0353
- The National Geographic Series
  Polar Bear Alert DN4025
- The Nature Connection Series
  Carnanah/Grasslands: Vol. 5 (*Alberta*) DK1575
- Nature's Newborn Series
  Elk, Moose, Deer, Vol. 9 DN1403
- On Top of the World With Anne Martin Series
  Nova Scotia DT2105
- Rand-McNally Video Traveler North America
  Canada (RNA) DT3523
- The Search for the Most Secret Animals Series
  The Search for Canada's Most Secret Animals DK4843
- Touring Canada's National Parks DT1939
- Video Visits North America Series
  Discovering Canada DT3613
- The Wolves Collection
  The Snow Wolves DN1967
- World Geography Series
  Canada (WGS) DD8908

CD-ROMs

- *Yukon Trail* (WIN/MAC) DR1374

Internet Site

http://www.state.gov/www/regions/eur/cntryinfo. html (Canada/Europe) (Cross Reference)

CHAPTER 5: CHILDREN'S BOOKS ABOUT THE CARIBBEAN

Videos

- AAA Travel Video Series
  Antigua/Barbuda DT8303
  Windward Islands DT8323
- American Culture for Children Series
  Puerto Rican Heritage DK6661
- Caribbean Collection 2 DT3704
  The Caribbean
  Holiday in the Bahamas
- The Discovery Channel Video Library
  Splendors of the Sea: The Caribbean's Secret World DN2411
- Going Places Series
  The Caribbean DT2092
- Multicultural Peoples of North America Series
  Puerto Ricans DD6685K
- National Geographic Series
  Jewels of the Caribbean DN4097
- Nova: Creatures of the Earth Series
  City of Coral DN4070
- On Top of the World With Anne Martin Series
  Cuba DT2102
  Dominican Republic DT2103
- Rand-McNally Video Traveler World Collection
  Caribbean Islands DT3714
- Underwater World Series
  Stingrays: A Caribbean Gathering DN1459
- Video Visits Islands Series
  Cuba: Island of Dreams DT3679
  Holiday in the Bahamas DT3606
  Islands of the Caribbean DT3614

Jamaica: Land of Wood and Water
DT3634
- Video Visits North America Series
Discovering Puerto Rico and the
U.S. Virgin Islands DT3670

CD-ROMs

- Ocean Life Series
Ocean Life: The Caribbean
(WIN/MAC) DR2030

Internet Sites

http://www.newtown.demon.co.uk/caribbean.html
(*General*)
http://www.ifs.univie.ac.at/~uncjin/country/html
(*Bahamas*)

CHAPTER 6: CHILDREN'S BOOKS ABOUT CENTRAL AMERICA, MEXICO, AND SOUTH AMERICA

Videos

- AAA Travel Video Series
Mexico Central DT8309
Mexico Yucatan DT8310
- American Cultures for Children
Mexican-American Heritage DK6659
- Ancient Mysteries Series
Secrets of the Aztec Empire
DD7938
- The Best of the Bill Burrud Nature
Collection
Creatures of the Amazon DH1801
- Bug City Video Series
Butterflies and Moths DK6675
- Channel 1000 Travel Series
Mexico City
Mexico
- Children of the Earth Series
South America Close-Up: Peru and
Brazil DK1494

- The Earth at Risk Environmental Video
Series
The Rain Forest (EAR) DN6629K
- Explore Series
Explore Bolivia: Orphans of the
Sun/Magic Healing, Magic Death
DD8102
- Exploring the World Series
Touring Mexico DY1910
- Eyewitness Living Earth Series
Butterfly and Moth DK9643
- Families of the World Series
Families of Mexico DK4922

"The Great Kapok" 0-02-686763-X
SRA/McGraw Hill, 220 East Danieldale
Road, DeSoto, TX 75115-2490
- Hello! From Around the World Series
Mexico and Central America DK3258
Venezuela DK3261
- Indians of North America Video
Collections
The Aztec DD6652-K
The Maya DD6657-K

Mexican Folk Art 87-005395
SRA/McGraw Hill, 220 East Danieldale
Road, DeSoto, TX 75115-2490
- Multicultural People of North America
Series
Central Americans DD6674-K
Mexican Americans DD6683-K
- National Geographic: Really Wild
Animal Series
Totally Tropical Rain Forest DK0441
- National Geographic Series
Amazon: Land of the Flooded
Forest DN0403
Tropical Kingdom of Belize DN4028
- The Nature Connection Series
Buying a Rain Forest (*Costa Rica*)
DK1571
- New Explorers: Great Mysteries Series
The Mystery of Machu Picchu (*Incas*)
DN0597
Voices in the Stones (*Maya*) DN0587
- Nova: Creatures of the Earth Series
Shadow of the Condor DN5786

- Nova: Scientific Journeys Series
    Panama: A Man, A Plan, A Canal
    DN5753
- Panama: Exploring the Panama Canal
    DD1214
- The People and Places of Mexico
    DT1002
- "Pequeña the Burro" DK8232
- Rain Forest for Children Video Series
    (*Costa Rica*)
    Animals of the Rain Forest DK6646
    People of the Rain Forest DK6647
    Plants of the Rain Forest DK6648
* Spirits of the Rain Forest
- Super Cities Series
    Mexico City DT2461
    Rio de Janeiro DT3783
- Trailside: Making Your Own Adventure
    Series
    Jungle Hiking in Costa Rica DT8022
- Video Visits South and Central America
    Series
    Argentina: Land of Natural Wonder
    DT3603
    Brazil: Heart of South America
    DT3610
    Costa Rica: Land of the Pure Life
    DT3617
    Mexico: Journey to the Sun DT3640
    Peru: A Golden Treasure DT 3645
- Wall Street Journal's Emerging Powers
    Series
    Brazil DD7871
    Mexico DD7874
- Where in the World Series
    Kids Explore Mexico DK3504

CD-ROMs

- The Amazon Trail (WIN/MAC) DR1304
- The Amazon Trail II (WIN95/MAC)
    DR2097
- Exploring the Lost Maya (WIN95/MAC)
    DR1719

- Imagination Express Series
    Destination Rain Forest (WIN/MAC)
    DR496
- Lyric Language Series
    Lyric Language Spanish
    (WIN95/MAC) DR1953
- The Magic School Bus Series
    The Magic School Bus Explores the
    Rain Forest (WIN95) DR2238
- Mayaquest (WIN95/MAC) DR1570
- Rain Forest Explorer (WIN/MAC)
    DR2122A
- Zurk's Science Collection
    Zurk's Rain Forest Lab (WIN/MAC)
    DR1373

Internet Sites

http://www.belizenet.com/ (Belize)
http://ib.nmsu.edu/subject/bord/ (*Latin America*) (*General*)
http://www.keele.ac.uk/depts/po/area/latinam.html (*General*)
http://ucsub.colorado.edu/~nunez/country.htm (*General*)

CHAPTER 7: CHILDREN'S BOOKS ABOUT EASTERN EUROPE

Videos

- Ancient Mysteries Series
    Secrets of the Romanovs DD7808
- Doug Jones' Travelog Series
    Great Cities of Europe DT9803
* Empire of the Red Bear
- Fodor's Video Series
    Hungary DT3857
- Great Railway Journeys Series
    St. Petersburg to Tashkent DD0956
- Hello! From Around the World Series
The Hermitage: A Russian Odyssey

*Home Vision, 5547 N. Ravenswood Ave.,
Chicago, IL 60640-1199*
Central Europe DK3253
* Holocaust: In Memory of Millions
• How to Be a Ballerina DK1604
• Multicultural Peoples of North America
Series
Jewish Americans DD6680-K
Polish Americans DD6684-K
"The Little Snow Girl" 87-002683
*SRA/McGraw Hill, 220 Danieldale Road,
DeSoto, TX 75115-2490*
• Musical Tales
"The Nutcracker"/"Petrushka" DK5221
• National Geographic Series
Russia's Last Tsar DN4131
The Soviet Circus DN4081
• Nursery Rhymes
"The Nutcracker" (Kiev Ballet)
DK3941
• "Peter and the Wolf" DK1319
• Rabbit Ears Collection
"The Fool and the Flying Ship"
DK5082
• Rand-McNally Video Traveler
Poland DT3520
• The Secret of Anastasia DK1942
• Super Cities Series
Budapest DT2454
Prague DT2463
St. Petersburg, Russia DT3784
• The Traveloguer Collection
Russian Journey DT8006
• Video Visits Eastern Europe Series
Baltic States: Lithuania, Latvia,
Estonia DT3608
Czechoslovakia: Triumph and
Tradition DT3618
Discovering Russia DT3677
Poland: A Proud Heritage DT3646
Ukraine: Ancient Crossroads,
Modern Dreams DT3674
Moscow and Leningrad DT3511
• Wild Discovery Series
The Great Siberian Grizzly DN2492

CD-ROMs

• Magic Tales Series
"Baba Yaga and the Magic Geese"
(WIN95/MAC) DR1659

Internet Sites

http://www.fe.doe.gov/internation/e-eur.html
(General)
*http://www.cudenver.edu/psrp/eure.html (Eastern
and Central Europe)*
http://www.ushmm.org/ (the Holocaust)
*http://www.icc.ru/baikal/railway.htm (the
Circumbaikal Railway)*

CHAPTER 8: CHILDREN'S BOOKS ABOUT WESTERN EUROPE

Videos

• American Cultures for Children
Irish-American Heritage DK6655
* The Back Roads of Europe
* The Beauty of Ireland
• "Beethoven Lives Upstairs" DK1031
• Berlin: Journey of a City DD8701
* British Rail Journeys III
• The Brothers Grimm Series
"Rapunzel" D*k*3419
• Channel 1000 Travel Series
France Collection (Paris/France)
DT3705
German Collection (Berlin/Bavaria)
DT3706
Ireland Collection DT3708
Italy Collection (Italy/Rome) DT3709
• England's Historic Treasures
A Celebration of Old Roses DD1086
The Spirit of England DD1087
Treasures of the Trust DD1088
• Exploring the World Series
Touring Austria DT1905

Touring England DT1907
Touring France DT1924
Touring Ireland DT1916
Touring Italy DT1922
Touring London, Paris, Rome DT1921
Touring Scotland DT1912
- Fodor's Video Series
  France DT3583
  Germany DT3584
  Great Britain DT3585
  Greece DT3593
  Hungary DT3587
  Italy DT3588
  Spain DT3591
  Switzerland DT3594
- Great Cities of the Ancient World Series
  Athens and Ancient Greece DD1906
  Rome and Pompeii DD1905
* Great Lakes of Europe
- The Greeks
  Athena's City/Greek Pottery DK0596
  Women and Children/Greek Schools
  DK0597
* Ireland
- A Kid in King Arthur's Court DK1151
- King Arthur and His Country DM3069
- Knights and Armor DD7679
- Michelangelo: Artist and Man DD7709-A
* The Power of the Past: Florence
- Multicultural Peoples of North America
  Series
  German Americans DD6676-K
  Greek Americans DD6677-K
  Irish Americans DD6678-K
  Italian Americans DD6679-K
- Saint Patrick: The Man, the Myth DD7787
- "The Snow Queen" DK5298
* Scotland: Beauty & Majesty
- Super Cities Series
  Amsterdam DT3576
  Barcelona DT3577
  Berlin DT2452
  Bern and Lucerne DT2453
  Florence DT2456
  Lisbon DT3579

London DT3780
Madrid DT2459
Munich DT2462
Paris DT3782
Rome DT2464
Stockholm DT2465
Venice DT3785
Vienna DT2466
* A Touch of Ireland
- The Traveloguer Collection
  Bonjour France DT8004
  Charm of Holland DT8017
  Eternal Greece DT8011
  Glory of England DT8014
  Romantic Germany DT8016
  Sí, Spain DT8008
  Song of Ireland DT8015
  Treasures of Italy DT8009
  Wonders of Norway DT8013
- Van Gogh: A Museum for Vincent DA2608

CD-ROMs

- "Beethoven Lives Upstairs" CD-ROM
  DR1545
- Imagination Express Series
  Destination: Castle (WIN/MAC) DR1494
- Leonardo the Inventor (WIN/MAC)
  DR1298
The Louvre (*Laserdisc, CAV Level 3*)
  *Forest Technologies, 514 Market Loop, Suite
  103, West Dundee, IL 60118*
Myths of Ancient Greece (WIN/MAC)
  QCD2087 (*Queue vol. 71*)
  *Queue, Inc., 338 Commerce Drive, Fairfield,
  CT 06432*
- Recess in Greece (WIN/MAC) DR1358
  & DR1358A
Vienna: The Spirit of a City (*Laserdisc, CAV
  Level 1*)
  *Forest Technologies, 514 Market Loop, Suite
  103, West Dundee, IL 60118*
- Vincent Van Gogh Revisited (WIN95)
  DR1813

Internet Site

http://weber.u.washington.edu/~hollyr/www.html
(*Central Europe*)

CHAPTER 9: CHILDREN'S BOOKS ABOUT THE MIDDLE EAST

Videos

- American Cultures for Children Series
    Arab-American Heritage DK6652
    Jewish-American Heritage DK6657
- Ancient Mysteries Series
    Legends of the Arabian Nights
    DD7937
- Animal Adventures with Jack Hanna
  Series
    Arabian Nights DK7506
- Animated Family Classics Series
    "Ali Baba" DK3984
    "Sinbad" DK3996
- Explore Series
    Explore Saudi Arabia: Kaaba, Center
    of the Universe/Bandits, Pirates,
    Flying Carpets DD8110
- Greatest Adventure Stories From the
  Bible Series
    Queen Esther DK4722
- Jerusalem: City of Heaven DD0993
- Jewish Tradition Series
    Passover: Traditions of Freedom
    DD9399
- Journey Through the Holy Land DD1202
- Multicultural Peoples of North America
  Series
    Arab Americans DD6672-K
    Jewish Americans DD6681-K
- The National Geographic Series
    Arabia: Land, Sea, and Sky DN4125
    Jerusalem: Within These Walls
    DN4032
- Nature's Newborn Series

    Ostrich, Camel, Tortoise: Vol. 6 DK1416
- Nova: Scientific Journeys Series
    Lost City of Arabia DN5808
- Splendors of the Ottoman Sultans
    The Complete Tour DD5721
- The Story of Islam DD1638
- Super Cities Series
    Istanbul DT3578
- Video Visits the Middle East Series
    Israel: A Land for Everyone DT3687
    Jerusalem: 3000 Years of Miracles
    DT3688
    Jordan: The Desert Kingdom DT3678
    Journey Through the Bible Lands
    DT3609

CD-ROMs

- Jerusalem: An Interactive Pilgrimage to
  the Holy City (WIN/MAC) DR1604
- Pathways Through Jerusalem
  (WIN95/MAC) DR1600
- Zoo Guide Series
    Life in the Desert (WIN95/MAC)
    DR2212

Internet Sites

http://www.state.gov/www/regions/nea/country-information.html (*Middle East and North
Africa*) (*Cross Reference*)

CHAPTER 10: CHILDREN'S BOOKS ABOUT THE PACIFIC, AUSTRALIA, NEW ZEALAND, AND ANTARCTICA

Videos

- Animals in Nature Series
    Great Barrier Reef DN1413
    Kangaroo/Desert Hopping Mouse
    DN1415
    Penguins/The Otters DN1417

- Antarctica: The Last Great Wilderness on Earth
- The Big Wet
    An Imax Film DN1003
- The Discovery Channel Video Library
    Emperors of Antarctica: The Emperor Penguins DN2494
    The Ends of the Earth: Enter the Dreamtime of Western Australia DN2412
    Island of the Dragons: The Exotic Creatures of Indonesia DN2409
- Exploring the World Series
    Touring Australia DT1904
    Touring New Zealand DT1911
- Fodor's Video Series
    Australia DT3581
- Going Places Series
    Sydney DT2090
- Great Train Journeys of Australia
    The Indian Pacific DT9302
- Hello! From Around the World Series
    Australia DK3251
    Bali DK3252
    New Zealand and the South Pacific Islands DK3259
- Kangaroos: Faces in the Mob DN1068
- "Kylie's Concert" DK8227
- "Koi and the Koala Nuts" DK5071
- National Geographic Series
    Antarctic Wildlife Adventure DN0431
    Australia's Aborigines DN4087
    Australia's Improbable Animals DN4037
- Nova: Creatures of the Earth Series
    Treasures of the Great Barrier Reef DN5789
- Rand-McNally Video Traveler World Collection
    Australia DT3713
- Smithsonian Fire, Ice, and Sea Series
    Penguin World DN5403
- Video Expedition Series
    Exploring Antarctica DT3568
- Video Visits Asia Series
    Indonesia: The Jeweled Archipelago DT3539

The Philippines: Pearls of the Pacific DT3681
- Video Visits Islands Series
    South Pacific: Islands of the South Pacific DT3655
- Video Visits the Outback Series
    Australia: Secrets of the Land Down Under DT3604
    New Zealand: Islands of Adventure DT3643
- World Geography Series
    Australia/New Zealand DD8906

CD-ROMs

- Antarctica: The Last Continent (WIN) DR1390
- Ocean Life Series
    Ocean Life: The Great Barrier Reef (WIN/MAC) DR1294
    Ocean Life: Micronesia (WIN/MAC) DR1292
- World Walker: Destination Australia (WIN/MAC) DR2010

Internet Sites

http://www.keele.ac.uk/depts/po/area/austral.htm (Australia)
http://www.state.gov/www/regions/eap/eapcountry /html (Asian Pacific)
http://www.worldwide.edu/resources/austriaplan. html (Australia)

CHAPTER 11: TRANSCULTURAL CHILDREN'S LITERATURE IN THE CHANGING CLASSROOM

Videos

- Sesame Street Series
    Around the World DK2613

CD-ROMs

- 3-D Atlas (WIN/MAC) DR1388 & DR1388A
- Encarta Virtual Globe 98 (WIN95) DR1622
- Global Explorer (WIN) DR1168
- The Great World Passport (WIN95/MAC) DR1973 & DR1973A
- Multimedia World Factbook (WIN) DR1351
- My First Amazing World Explorer (WIN/MAC) DR1671
- Picture Atlas of the World (WIN/MAC) DR1054A
- Rand-McNally World Atlas (WIN/MAC) DR1961

Tales From Long Ago and Far Away I (WIN/MAC) QCD2063 (*Queue vol. 71*) *Queue, Inc., 338 Commerce Drive, Fairfield,* CT 06432

Tales From Long Ago and Far Away II (WIN/MAC) QCD2064 (*Queue vol. 72*)

Queue, Inc., 338 Commerce Drive, Fairfield, CT 06432
- World Atlas and Almanac (WIN/MAC) DR1112 & DR1112B
- World Geography: Nigel's World Adventures (DOS/MAC) DR1231
- World Tour (WIN95/MAC) DR2166

Internet Sites

http://www.yahoo.com/Regional/countries
http://www.nmun.org/ (National Model UN)
http://www.un.org/Docs/sc.htm (UN Security Council)
http://www.state.gov/www/background_notes/index. html (Background Notes on Countries— U.S. Dept. of State)
http://www.fis.utoronto.ca/people/faculty/easun/ tcscl.htm (Toronto Centre for the Study of Children's Literature)

C

Publishers' Address List

Harry N. Abrams, Inc., 100 Fifth Ave., New York, NY 10011

Africa World Press, 11 Princess Rd., Suites D, E, & F, Lawrenceville, NJ 08648

Annick Press Ltd., P.O. Box 1338, Ellicott Station, Buffalo, NY 14205

Atheneum Publishers, 1230 Avenue of the Americas, New York, NY 10020

Barefoot Press, P.O. Box 28514, Raleigh, NC 27611

Barron's Educational Services, Inc., 250 Wireless Blvd., Hauppauge, NY 11788-3917

Peter Bedrick Books, Inc., 2112 Broadway, Suite 318, New York, NY 10023

Boyds Mills Press, 815 Church St., Honesdale, PA 18431

Bradbury Press, 1230 Avenue of the Americas, New York, NY 10020

BridgeWater Press, 100 Whitethorne Dr., Moraga, CA 94556

Candlewick Press, 2067 Massachusetts Ave., Cambridge, MA 02140

Caroline House, 815 Church St., Honesdale, PA 18431

Carolrhoda Books, Inc., 241 First Ave., N, Minneapolis, MN 55401

Checkerboard Press, 164 Lincoln Hwy., No. 103, Fairless Hills, PA 19030-1000

Children's Book Press, 246 First St., Suite 101, San Francisco, CA 94105

Chronicle Books, 85 Second St., San Francisco, CA 94103

Clarion Books, 215 Park Ave. S., New York, NY 10003

Crown Publishing Group, 201 E. 50th St., New York, NY 10022

Dial Books for Young Readers, 375 Hudson St., New York, NY 10014-3657

Doubleday (and Doubleday Books for Young Readers), 1540 Broadway, New York, NY 10036-4094

Dutton (and Dutton Children's Books), 375 Hudson St., New York, NY 10014

Wm. B. Eerdmans Publishing Co., 255 Jefferson Ave., SE, Grand Rapids, MI 49503-4554

Enslow Publishers, Inc., P.O. Box 699, Springfield, NJ 07081-0699

Farrar, Straus & Giroux, Inc., 19 Union Sq., W, New York, NY 10003

Four Winds Press, 1230 Avenue of the Americas, New York, NY 10020

W. H. Freeman, 41 Madison Ave., E 26th, 35th Flr., New York, NY 10010

David R. Godine Publisher, Inc., P.O. Box 9103, Lincoln, MA 01773

Green Tiger Press, 1230 Avenue of the Americas, New York, NY 10020

Greenwillow Books, 1350 Avenue of the Americas, New York, NY 10019

Groundwood-Douglas and McIntyre CN, Dist. by Firefly Books Ltd., P.O. Box 1338, Ellicott Sta., Buffalo, NY 14205

Gulliver Books, 525 B. St., Suite 1900, San Diego, CA 92101-4495

Harcourt Brace & Co., 525 B. St., Suite 1900, San Diego, CA 92101-4495

HarperCollins Publishers, 10 E. 53rd St., New York, NY 10022-5299

Highsmith Press, P.O. Box 800, Hwy. 106 E., Fort Atkinson, WI 53538-0800

Holiday House, Inc., 425 Madison Ave., New York, NY 10017

Henry Holt & Co., Inc., 115 W. 18th St., New York, NY 10011

Houghton Mifflin Co., 222 Berkeley St., Boston, MA 02116

Hyperion, 114 Fifth Ave., New York, NY 10011

Kane-Miller Book Publishers, Box 310529, Brooklyn, NY 11231-0529

Key Porter (Toronto), Dist. by Firefly Books Ltd., P.O. Box 1338, Ellicott Sta., Buffalo, NY 14205

Kingfisher, 2150 N. Tenaya Way, No. 1052, Las Vegas, NV 89128

Kingfisher, LKC, 95 Madison Ave., New York, NY 10016

Alfred A. Knopf, Inc., 201 E. 50th St., New York, NY 10022

Larousse Kingfisher Chambers, Inc., 95 Madison Ave., 12th Floor, New York, NY 10016

Lee & Low Books, Inc., 95 Madison Ave., Room 606, New York, NY 10016

Little, Brown and Company, Inc., 34 Beacon St., Boston, MA 02108

Lodestar Books, 375 Hudson St., New York, NY 10014-3657

Lothian Publishers, AT, Dist. by Seven Hills Books, 49 Central Ave., Cincinnati, OH 45202

Lothrop, Lee & Shepard Books, 1350 Avenue of the Americas, New York, NY 10019

Macmillan, 201 W. 103 St., Indianapolis, IN 46290

Marshmedia, 5901 Main St., Kansas City, MO 64113-1432

Margaret K. McElderry Books, 1230 Avenue of the Americas, New York, NY 10020

Millbrook Press, Inc., 2 Old New Milford Rd., Brookfield, CT 06804

Mondo Publishing, 1 Plaza Rd., Greenvale, NY 11548

William Morrow & Co. (and Morrow Junior Books), 1350 Avenue of the Americas, New York, NY 10019

Mulberry Paperback Books, 1350 Avenue of the Americas, New York, NY 10019

North-South Books, Inc., 1123 Broadway, Suite 800, New York, NY 10010

Orchard Books, 95 Madison Ave., 7th Flr., New York, NY 10016

Oxford University Press, Inc., 98 Madison Ave., New York, NY 10016

Philomel, 200 Madison Ave., New York, NY 10016

Price Stern Sloan, Inc., 11835 Olympic Blvd., 5th Flr., Los Angeles, CA 90064

Puffin Books, 375 Hudson St., New York, NY 10014-3657

Putnam Publishing Group, 200 Madison Ave., New York, NY 10016

R&S Books, Dist. by FS&G, 19 Union Sq., W., New York, NY 10003

Raincoast Books CN, Dist. by Orca Book Publishers, P.O. Box 468, Custer, WA 98240-0468

Random House, Inc., 201 E. 50th St., New York, NY 10022

Rayve Productions, Inc., Box 726, Winsor, CA 95492

Read Advent; Varsity Read Servs, P.O. Box 261431, Columbus, OH 43226-1431

Rizzoli International Publications, Inc., 300 Park Ave., S, New York, NY 10010

Running Press Book Publishers, 125 S. 22nd St., Philadelphia, PA 19103-4399

Sand River Press, 1319 14th St., Los Osos, CA 93402

Scholastic, Inc., 555 Broadway, New York, NY 10012-3999

Scientific American Books for Young Readers, 41 Madison Ave., E. 26th, 35th Flr., New York, NY 10010

Charles Scribner's Sons, 1230 Avenue of the Americas, New York, NY 10020

Second Story Press, Dist. by LPC InBook, 1436 W. Randolph St., Chicago, IL 60607

Silver Press, P.O. Box 480, Parsipanny, NJ 07054

Simon & Schuster, 1230 Avenue of the Americas, New York, NY 10020

St. Martin's Press, Inc., 175 Fifth Ave., Rm. 1715, New York, NY 10010

Tambourine Books, 1350 Avenue of the Americas, New York, NY 10019

Thomson Learning, 115 Fifth Ave., New York, NY 10003

Troll Communications, 100 Corporate Dr., Mahwah, NJ 07430

Tundra Books, Box 1030, Plattsburgh, NY 12901

Viking Penguin, 375 Hudson St., New York, NY 10014-3657

Walker & Co., 435 Hudson St., New York, NY 10014-3941

Western Publishing, 850 Third Ave., 7th Flr., New York, NY 10022

Whispering Coyote Press, 300 Crescent Ct., Suite 1150, Dallas, TX 75201

Albert Whitman & Co., 6340 Oakton St., Morton Grove, IL 60053-2723

Workman Publishing Co., 708 Broadway, New York, NY 10003-9555

A P P E N D I X

D

Activities for Preservice and Inservice Educators

A set of activities based on the reviewed books is presented here to help the professional prepare to use transcultural children's literature in an elementary classroom.

GENERAL

1. Research a specific cultural region (country) of the world. Describe how that region reflects the geographic, social, economic, and political elements of the cultural paradigm.

2. Describe how you might introduce transcultural children's literature to students. Identify and justify key decisions that you make.

3. Identify connections between books about a particular region of the world and the student's home culture. For example, have students find out whether any of their family members immigrated from another country or region to the United States.

4. Apply the guidelines enumerated in Figure 1.7 as a self-assessment tool. What did you discover about yourself concerning your knowledge and understanding of other cultures? Which sections did you answer most easily? Which did you find to be most difficult? Which answers did you feel most confident about and why?

5. To respond more confidently to the questions in Figure 1.7, note which ones raised the greatest doubts in your mind. On the basis of this list of questions, scan through the references at the end of a particular chapter or consult Appendix B for materials that appear to provide the background information you need.

6. Compare the artistic techniques, styles, and visual motifs in the illustrations of various books across different cultures.

ELEMENTS OF THE TRANSCULTURAL PARADIGM
Geographic

1. Research the main climates, topographies, and natural resources of a given geographic region.

2. What major environmental issues and problems were raised in the reviewed books? How do the characters in those books deal with those issues and problems?

3. Compile lists of the major plants and/or animals mentioned in books set in each geographic region.

Economic

1. The marketplace is important in many cultures. Characterize the ways marketplaces are similar and different from one cultural region to another.

2. Compile a list of the sundry ways the people in the reviewed books obtain the resources, including money, to support themselves and their families.

3. Describe the various ways children contribute to the economic well-being of their families.

4. Compare characters who are honest with respect to financial matters with those who are dishonest. Similarly, compare the poor with the wealthy, and the hardworking with the indolent. Extend these comparisons across cultural regions to see whether any patterns emerge.

Social

1. How do younger members of a family perceive and treat grandparents and one another? Do these family interactions vary with cultures? If so, describe the pattern you find.

2. Compare the folktales and fairy tales of different cultures in terms of moral values, ethical conduct, and good and evil.

3. Contrast the ways books set in different cultural regions depict family life. Associate family structure and dynamics with social and economic standing.

4. Examine how a book portrays misdeeds (violations of moral tenets) and crimes (violations of law). Similarly, how does a book present the criminal, and how are judgment and punishment decided and rendered? Extend this analysis across cultures and look for similarities and differences.

5. Compare parents and parenting from one cultural region to another. Determine whether gender-specific parenting roles exist. If so, characterize them as a function of cultural region.

Political

1. Find out which countries in the various cultural regions are democracies. What other forms of government exist in these regions?

2. Choosing leaders is an important decision in most societies. In those books with a discernible political dimension, ascertain how leaders are chosen and what their leadership attributes are.

3. Describe how injustices are shown, endured by the victim, and eventually ended. Is the notion of injustice universal, or does it manifest itself in ways that are culturally distinct?

MAJOR STORY ELEMENTS
Setting

1. Research the history of a specific country or geographic region. Focus on key political, economic, and social changes, particularly recent ones.

2. Select several books with strong setting components. For each, describe the setting's interplay with the plot and characters.

3. Identify and describe specific instances when the physical environment plays a crucial role in determining the outcome of a story.

4. Contrast the rural and urban ways of life within the same cultural region and among different cultural regions.

Plot/Events

1. The stories reviewed encompass numerous plots and events. Some are similar, many are different. Compare similar plots and sequences of events in books from at least two cultural regions.

2. List those books that have plots and events that closely imitate everyday experiences of your students.

3. Compare across cultures those events that can be identified as fun, humorous, sad, scary, painful, surprising, embarrassing, inspiring. Do any clear culture-related patterns emerge as to what books portray as fun, humorous, and the like?

Characters

1. Compare the female and male characters in terms of their personal attributes, behaviors, and attitudes toward themselves and others. Applying this analysis to books set in different cultural regions, ascertain whether clear differences or similarities exist and, if so, describe them.

2. Animal characters appear in many of the reviewed books. In what ways and to what extent are they shown to have humanlike characteristics?

3. The ways people dress are often hallmarks of their respective cultural regions. Compile descriptions, including drawings and photographs, of the dress—formal and informal, traditional and contemporary—of people living in different cultural regions.

4. Compare the emotions of characters appearing in a sampling of books from different cultural regions. For example, how do characters living in Africa, Asia, and other cultural regions show courage and fear, joy and sorrow, love and hate?

Theme

1. Compare the hero-quest theme across cultural regions.

2. How does the portrait of the trickster vary from culture to culture? Give specific examples.

3. How is the eternal and universal conflict between good and evil dealt with? Do different cultures resolve this struggle in distinct ways, or in ways that transcend cultural differences?

4. Characterize how large social gatherings (e.g., festivals, celebrations, parties) influence the themes of various books. Apply this analysis across cultures. What do you discover?

5. Identify some moral, ethical, or legal dilemmas raised. Are these dilemmas resolved in ways that seem to be culturally specific, or do the solutions cross cultural boundaries?

6. How is love expressed between siblings, parent and child, grandparent and grandchild, man and woman? Are certain manifestations of love culturally specific, or are they more universal in nature? Provide a few specific examples.

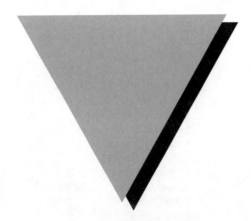

Author/Title/Illustrator Index

A to Zen: A Book of Japanese Culture, 84
Aardema, Verna, 33, 178–179
Abuela, 3
Abuela's Weave, 170–171
Abuelita's Paradise, 146–147
Ada, Alma Flor, 182–184
Adams, Jeanie, 312–313
African Brothers and Sisters, 51–52
Agassu: Legend of the Leopard King, 31–32
Akerman, Karen, 265–266
Aladdin, 296–297
Alexander, Lloyd, 24–26
Ali: Child of the Desert, 8, 38–39
Aliki, 261
Allen, Jonathan, 120
Amazon Alphabet, 190
Amazon Boy, 190–191
Anderson, Hans Christian, 245–246
Anholt, Laurence, 252–254
Anni's Diary of France, 251–252
Annie . . . Anya: A Month in Moscow, 213–214
Antarctica, 307

Arabian Nights, 282
Arabian Nights: Three Tales, 296–297
Argueta, Manlio, 169–170
Arnold, Katya, 223
Aruego, Jose, 324–325
At the Crossroads, 43–44
Axworthy, Anni, 251–252
Ayres, Becky Hickox, 225–226
Ayto, Russell, 248–249

Baba Yaga and Vasilisa the Brave, 214–216
Babushka Baba Yaga, 216–217
Babushka's Doll, 217–218
Baby Baboon, 52–53
Baker, Leslie, 117–118
Balit, Christina, 297–298
Bancroft, Bronwyn, 310–311, 313–314
Banks, J. A., 2
Banshee, The, 265–266
Barry, David, 82–83
Baseball Bats for Christmas, 110–111
Bearhead: A Russian Folktale, 218–219

Beaty, J. B., 195
Becker, Neesa, 307–308
Beethoven Lives Upstairs, 242–244
Bells of Santa Lucia, The, 268
Berenzy, Alix, 258–259
Beyer, David, 126–127
Biddle, Megumi, 84–85
Biddle, Steve, 84–85
Bieger, E. M., 6
Big Boy, 50
Binch, Caroline, 5, 154–156, 159–161
Bishop, Gavin, 322–323
Bishop, R. S., 4, 16
Bitter Bananas, 39–40
Blankley, Kathy, 26–27
Blue Butterfly, A: A Story About Claude Monet, 252
Bochak, Grayce, 80–81, 86–87
Bond, Ruskin, 77–78
Boni, Simone, 249–250
Book Links, 5
Bookbird, 5
Borgenicht, David, 249–250
Borreguita and the Coyote, 178–179

Bouchard, David, 118
Boxing Champion, The, 111–112
Bravest Flute, The, 171–172
Brown, Marcia, 33
Bruce, Jill B., 320
Brusca, Maria Cristina, 188–189
Brynjolson, Rhian, 119–120, 122,
    128–129
Burns, Theresa, 315
Butterfly Boy, 179–181

Cameron, Scott, 242–244
Camille and the Sunflowers: A Story
    About Vincent Van Gogh,
    252–254
Camm, Martin, 71–72
Carle, Eric, 259–260
Carnavalia! African-Brazilian Folklore
    and Crafts, 191–192
Carpenter, Nancy, 34–35
Carpenter, Naomi, 298–300
Carrier, Roch, 111–112
Casilla, Robert, 177–178
Castaneda, Omar S., 170–171
Cazzola, Gus, 268
Chang, Cindy, 75–76
Chekov, Anton, 221–223
Chelepi, Chris, 262
Cherry Tree, The, 77–78
Cherry, Lynn, 192–193
Chi, M. M-Y., 64
Chicken Man, 289–290
Chinye: A West African Folk Tale,
    40–41
Christmas Drum, The, 208–210
Christmas Surprise for Chabelita, A,
    176–177
Chung Lee Loves Lobsters, 112–113,
    129
Clancy, Frances, 116–117
Clement, Claude, 269–270
Clement, Frederic, 269–270
Clement, Gary, 114
Climo, Shirley, 321–322
Clouds on the Mountain, 172–173
Coconut Kind of Day: Island Poems,
    153–154
Cohen, Sheldon, 111–112
Cooper, Floyd, 29–30, 46–47

Cooper, Martha, 137–138
Count Your Way Through Israel,
    290–291
Count Your Way Through the Arab
    World, 293–294
Cowan, James, 313–314
Cowcher, Helen, 307
Cowen-Fletcher, Jane, 22–23
Craft, Kinuko Y., 214–216
Crane's Gift, The, 84–85
Czernecki, Stefan, 185–186,
    233–234

D'Ottavi, Francesca, 249–250
Da Volls, Andy, 30–31
Da Volls, Linda, 30–31
Dabcovich, Lydia, 124
Dalgliesh, Alice, 232–233
Daly, Niki, 36–37, 48–49
Danger on Arctic Ice, 113
Das, Prodeepta, 78–79
David, Rosalie, 28–29
Day Gogo Went to Vote, The, 11, 44–46
Day of Ahmed's Secret, The, 8, 27–28
De Maupassant, Guy, 255–256
Delacre, Lulu, 151–152
Demi, 67–68, 79–80, 85–86, 227
DePaola, Tomie, 286–287
Desputeaux, Helene, 127–128
Dewey, Ariane, 324–325
Dianov, Alisher, 287–288
Diego, 181–182
Dillon, Leo and Diane, 91–92
Distant Talking Drum, The, 41
Dodson, Bert, 273–274
Don't Dig So Deep, Nicholas!, 114
Doney, Todd L. W., 98–100
Dorros, Arthur C., 3, 149–150
Dowd, F. S., 64
Down Under: Vanishing Cultures,
    309–310
Dreamtime: Aboriginal Stories,
    310–311
Dudly-Marling, C., 6, 15
Dunrea, Olivier, 255
Dupré, Rick, 31–32

Eastwood, Zoe, 320–321
Edwards, Michelle, 289–290

Ehlert, Lois, 194–195
Eitzen, Allan, 77–78
Elleman, B., 22
Emberley, Michael, 271–272
Empress and the Silkworm, The, 66–67
Empty Pot, The, 67–68
Enchanted Storks, The, 287–288
Enchanted Tapestry, The, 68–69
Encounter, 136–137
Engelbreit, Mary, 245–246
Enora and the Black Crane, 312
Esterl, Arnica, 90–91
Esther's Story, 282, 283–285
Ettl, Dianne, 54
Ewart, Claire, 286–287
Eyvindson, Peter, 119–120,
    128–129

Face in the Window, The, 141–142
Faithful Friend, The, 144–146
Federov, Mikhail, 224–225
Firebird, 219–221, 227
Firebird: A Russian Folktale, 227
Fischetto, Laura, 269
Fischman, Sheila, 111–112
Fish Skin, The, 114–115
Fisher, Leonard Everett, 257–258,
    294–295
Floss, 246–247
Flowers on the Wall, 206–207
Flying Tortoise, The: An Igbo Tale, 42,
    50
Fortune, 285–286, 301
Fortune-Tellers, The, 24–26
Fox, Mem, 317–318
French, Vanessa, 51–52
French, Vivian, 248–249

Gál, László, 68–69
Galante, Luigi, 249–250
Galda, L., 327
Galli, Letizia, 269
Garay, Luis, 174–176
Garrett, Jeffrey, 301
Gathering the Sun: An Alphabet in
    Spanish and English, 182–184
Geraghty, Paul, 308–309
Gershator, Phyllis, 42–43, 134–136,
    158–159

Ghost in the Castle, A, 256–257
Gift of a Traveler, The, 210–211
Gilchrist, Cherry, 226–228
Gilliland, J. A., 8
Gilliland, Judith Heide, 27–28, 292–293
Girl Who Changed Her Fate, The, 260–261
Gittel's Hands, 211–213
Godine, David R., 244–245
Godkin, Celia, 128
Gods and Goddesses of Olympus, The, 261
Going for Oysters, 312–313
Golden Flower, The: A Taino Myth From Puerto Rico, 147–148
Golden Slipper, The: A Vietnam Legend, 100–101
Goldstein, Peggy, 73–74
Golem, 202–204
Good Night Story, The, 115–116
Gordon, Ginger, 136–137
Graham, Bob, 319–320
Grandfather's Dream, 101–102
Grandpa's Visit, 116–117
Grant, C. A., 2, 3
Great Kapok Tree, The: A Tale of the Amazon Rain Forest, 192–193
Green Frogs, The: A Korean Folktale, 92–93
Greenlee, A., 306
Gregory Cool, 5, 154–156
Greve, Andreas, 115–116
Grifalconi, Ann, 157–158, 171–172
Grimm, J. and K., 43
Growing Up in Ancient China, 69–70
Growing Up in Ancient Egypt, 28–29
Growing Up in Ancient Greece, 262
Gunning, Monica, 142–143
Gustafson, Dana, 293–294
Gutenberg, 257–258

Hadithi, Mwenye, 52–53
Halperin, Wendy Anderson, 255–256
Hamade, S. N., 282
Han, Suzanne Crowder, 94–95
Hanley, Anne, 118–119

Hanson, Regina, 141–142, 143–144
Hanson, Rick, 290–291
Harris, V. J., 3, 6
Harrison, Troon, 114
Haskins, Jim, 290–291, 293–294
Heide, Florence Parry, 8, 27–28, 292–293
Henderson, D., 22
Henry in Shadowland, 244–245
Heo, Yumi, 92–93, 94–95
Heuck, Sigrid, 256–257
Hillman, Elizabeth, 74–75, 76
Himler, Ronald, 270–271
Ho, Minfong, 97
Hoban, Tana, 254–255
Hodges, Margaret, 266–267
Hollinshead, Marilyn, 250–251
Holmes, Olivia, 224–225
Hom, Nancy, 64–65
Hong, Lily Toy, 66–67, 70–71, 76
Honkers, 117–118
Hook, Richard, 69–70
Hooper, Maureen Brett, 208–210
Hort, Lenny, 269–270
House That Jack Built, The, 161–162
How Music Came to the World, 184–185
How the Ostrich Got Its Long Neck, 33
How the Ox Star Fell From Heaven, 70–71
Howe, K., 306
Huang, Tze-si, 85–86
Hubbard, Woodleigh, 94
Hue Boy, 11, 159–161
Hummingbirds' Gift, The, 185–186
Hush! A Thai Lullaby, 97

I Dream of Peace: Images of War by Children of Former Yugoslavia, 234–235
I is for India, 78–79
Ichikawa, Satomi, 148–149
If You Should Hear a Honey Guide, 34
If You're Not From the Prairie . . . , 118
In the Eyes of the Cat: Japanese Poetry for All Seasons, 85–86
In the Garden, 118–119
In the Village of the Elephants, 83

Inside-Outside Book of London, The, 247–248
Iroko-Man, The: A Yoruba Folktale, 42–43
Isabela's Ribbons, 148–149
Isadora, Rachel, 43–44, 47–48, 219–221, 227
Ishtar and Tammuz: A Babylonian Myth of the Seasons, 297–298
Isla, 149–150
Island Christmas, An, 156–157
It Takes a Village, 22–23

Jacaranda Designs, 35–36
Jaffe, Nina, 147–148
Jasmine's Parlour Day, 157–158
Jen and the Great One, 119–120
Jobe, R. A., 110
Johnson, Paul Brett, 266–267
Jordan, Martin, 190
Jordan, Tanis, 190
Joseph, Lynn, 156–157, 157–158
Journey Through China, 71–72
Judge Rabbit and the Tree Spirit: A Folktale From Cambodia, 64–65
Junior Thunder Lord, The, 72–73

Kanu of Kathmandu: A Journey in Nepal, 96
Kashtanka, 221–223
Keens-Douglas, Richardo, 116–117
Keller, Holly, 101–102
Kelly, Jo'Anne, 97–98
Kendall, Russ, 228
Kennaway, Adrienne, 52–53, 318–319
Kessler, Cristina, 49
Killilea, Marie, 110, 122–123
Kim, Holly C., 42–43
Kimmel, Eric A., 218–219, 294–295
King and the Tortoise, The, 26–27, 50
Kissen, R. M., 282
Kleven, Elisa, 149–150
Knock, Knock, Ternock: A Traditional Russian Tale, 223
Knot in the Tracks, The, 224–225
Korean Cinderella, Yen Shen, The: A Cinderella From China, 101
Kroll, Jeri, 320–321

Kroll, Virginia, 34–35, 51–52, 179–181
Krykorka, Vladyana, 110–111
Krykorka, Vladyanna, 120–121
Kun-Mar-Gur the Rainbow Serpent, 313–314
Kurtz, Jane, 29–30
Kurusa, 9, 196–197
Kusugak, Michael Arvaarluk, 110–111, 120–121
Kwon, Holly H, 94
Kylie's Concert, 314

Lang, J., 42
Langton, Jane, 228–230
Larry, Charles, 123–124
Last Frontier, The: Antarctica, 307–308
Lattimore, Deborah Nourse, 296–297, 323–324
Lauture, Denize, 138–139
Lazy Jack, 248–249
Le Tord, Bijou, 252
Leahy, A., 4
Lee, J., 76
Legend of King Arthur, The, 249–250
Legend of the Persian Carpet, The, 286–287
Lessac, Frané, 41, 142–143
Let the Celebrations Begin!, 11, 207–208
Let's Eat!, 272–273
Lewin, Ted, 27–28, 38–39, 190–191, 292–293
Lewis, E. B., 50
Lewis, Kim, 246–247
Life Around the Lake, 186–187
Lily Cupboard, The, 270–271
Little Elephant's Walk, 52–53
Little New Kangaroo, 315
Little Painter of Sabana Grande, The, 177–178
Lo, D. E., 4
Lodge, B., 227
Loewen, Iris, 121–122
Lohstoeter, Lori, 176–177
London, Jonathan, 8, 38–39
Lóng Is a Dragon: Chinese Writing for Children, 73–74

Long Silk Strand, The: A Grandmother's Legacy to her Granddaughter, 86–87
Louie, Y-Y. B., 64
Low, Alice, 76–77
Loyal Cat, The, 87–88
Lum, Darrell, 100–101
Lynn, Joseph, 153–154

Macaulay, Kitty, 115–116
MacDonald, Hugh, 112–113
Maddern, Eric, 318–319
Maeno, Itoko, 187–188, 314
Magic Days of the Volcanoes, 169–170
Magic Purse, The, 88–90
Manchur, Carolyn Marie, 118–119
Mandela: From the Life of the South African Statesman, 46–47
Mao Wall, Lina, 64–65
Marchetti, B., 64
Margolies, Barbara A., 96
Market Lady and the Mango Tree, The, 10, 23–24
Markun, Patricia Maloney, 177–178
Marshall, Laura, 260–261
Masai and I, 34–35
Match Between the Winds, The, 321–322
Mathers, Petra, 178–179
Matreshka, 225–226
Matthews, Wendy, 210–211
Maui and the Sun: A Maori Tale, 322–323
Mayer, Marianna, 214–216
McBride, Angus, 28–29
McDermott, Gerald, 56–57, 267–268
Mcheshi Goes to the Game Park, 35–36
McLellan, Joe, 122
McMillan, Bruce, 264–265
Meade, Holly, 97, 158–159
Medearis, Angela Shelf, 32–33
Meeks, Arone Raymond, 312
Mennen, Ingrid, 36–37, 48–49
Meyer, Ronald, 221–223
Michael the Angel, 269
Mikolaycak, Charles, 218–219
Milhous, Katherine, 232–233
Miller, Gloria, 121–122

Mills, Judith Christine, 125–126
Min-Yo and the Moon Dragon, 74–75
Minas and the Fish, 262–263
Mitchell, Rita Phillips, 11, 159–161
Molan, Chris, 262
Moles and the Mireuk: A Korean Folktale, 94
Mollel, Tolowa M., 26–27, 42, 54–56
Mollol, Tolowa M., 50
Monson, D. L., 306
Moon Rope, 194–195
Moon Was the Best, The, 254–255
Moore, Christopher, 297–298
Morgan, Pierr, 232–233, 250–251, 268
Morin, Paul, 54–55
Morrisseau, Brent, 114–115
Mucky Moose, 120
Munro, Roxie, 247–248
Munsch, Robert, 110, 127–128
My Arctic, 120–121
My Grandpa and the Sea, 152–153
My Kokum Called Today, 121–122
My Mama's Little Ranch on the Pampas, 188–189
My Place, 315–317
My Two Worlds, 137–138

Nagano, Makiko, 100–101
Namioka, Lensey, 87–88
Nanabosho: How the Turtle Got Its Shell, 122
Narahashi, Keiko, 88–90
Nasr, J. A., 282
Nerlove, Miriam, 206–207
New Advocate, The, 5
New King, The: A Madagascan Legend, 37–38
Newf, 122–123
Nichol, Barbara, 242–244
Nights of the Pufflings, 264–265
Nina's Treasures, 233–234
Nine Days of Wonder, The, 250–251
Nodar, Carmen Santiago, 146–147
Nolan, Dennis, 263–264
Norman, Lilith, 317
Not a Copper Penny in Me House, 142–143

Nourse Lattimore, Deborah, 211–213
Nye, Naomi Shihab, 298–300

Ober, Carol, 184–185
Ober, Hal, 184–185
Oberdieck, Bernard, 256–257
Okino and the Whales, 90–91
Olaleye, Isaac, 39–40, 41
Oliviero, James, 114–115
Oliviero, Jamie, 97–98
One Grain of Rice: A Mathematical Folktale, 79–80
One Night: A Story From the Desert, 49
One Round Moon and a Star for Me, 36–37
One Small Square: African Savanna, 54
Onyefulu, Obi, 40–41
Oodgeroo, 310–311
Oppenheim, Shulamith Levey, 270–271
Ordóñez, Maria Antonia, 150–151
Orphan Boy, The, 50, 54–55
Orr, Katherine, 152–153
Osa, O., 22
Over the Green Hills, 47–48

Paddock, The: A Story in Praise of the Earth, 317
Palacios, Argentina, 176–177
Papa, Liza, 191–192
Paper Boats, 80–81
Parkison, Jami, 187–188
Pastuchiv, Olga, 262–263
Paterson, Diane, 146–147, 208–210
Paterson, Katherine, 91–92
Peboan and Seegwun, 123–124
Pedrito's Day, 174–176
Pequeña the Burro, 187–188
Perrone, Donna, 82–83
Picó, Fernando, 150–151
Pike, K., 64
Pinkey, Brian, 144–146
Piumini, Roberto, 224–225
Plume, Ilse, 228–230
Polacco, Patricia, 216–217, 217–218

Polar Bear Son, The, 124
Possum Magic, 317–318
Presilla, Maricel E., 186–187
Priestley, Alice, 172–173
Prince Ivan and the Firebird, 226–228
Prince, Amy, 181–182
Pulling the Lion's Tail, 29–30
Pumpkin Blanket, The, 124–125
Punga: The Goddess of Ugly, 323–324
Pushkin, Alexander, 230–231
Pyle, Howard, 249–250

Queen of the Serpents, The, 296–297

Rabbit's Judgment, The, 94–95
Rainbow Bird, 318–319
Rajah's Rice, The: A Mathematical Folktale from India, 82–83
Ramsey, P. G., 168, 197
Rappaport, Doreen, 37–38
Rapunzel, 258–259
Rata, Pata, Scata, Fata: A Caribbean Story, 158–159
Rawlins, Donna, 315–317
Ray, David, 265–266
Reading Teacher, The, 5
Reasoner, Charles, 75–76
Red Comb, The, 150–151
Reynold, Jan, 309–310
Rhinos for Lunch and Elephants for Supper!, 50, 55–56
Rhodes, Timothy, 185–186, 233–234
Ripplinger, Henry, 118
Rockabye Crocodile: A Folktale From the Philippines, 324–325
Roennfeldt, Robert, 317
Roffe, Mike, 71–72
Root, Barry, 274–275
Ruffins, Reynod, 138–139
Rumplestiltskin, 43
Running the Road to ABC, 138–139
Russian Girl: Life in an Old Russian Town, 228

Sackett, Elisabeth, 113
Safarewicz, Evie, 40–41
Saint James, Synthia, 134–136
Saint Patrick and the Peddler, 266–267

Salt: A Russian Folktale, 228–230
Sami and the Time of the Troubles, 282, 292–293
San Souci, Robert D., 68–69, 144–146
Sanchez, Enrique O., 170–171
Sánchez, Enrique O., 147–148
Sanderson, Esther, 126–127
Saport, Linda, 141–142
Saturday Sancocho, 193–194
Sayre, April Pulley, 34
Schart Hyman, Trina, 24–26
Schatschneider, Lori Ann, 173–174
Schields, Gretchen, 325–326
Schindler, S. D., 34
Schmidt, Jeremy, 83
Schoenherr, Ian, 122–123
Schoenherr, Jan, 49
Schroeder, Alan, 98–100
Schwartz, David M., 273–274
Secret Room, The, 291–292
Seventh Sister, The: A Chinese Legend, 75–76
Shannon, David, 136–137
Sheehan, Patty, 314
Shepard, Aaron, 287–288
Shepherd, Roni, 321–322
Shulevitz, Uri, 291–292
Silva, Juan Hilario, 185–186
Silva, Reyes de, 185–186
Silva, Simón, 182–184
Silver, Donald M., 54
Silverman, Erica, 211–213
Simmons, Elly, 169–170
Singing Fir Tree, The, 274–275
Sis, Peter, 205–206
Sisulu, Elinor Batezat, 11, 44–46
Sitti's Secrets, 282, 298–300
Smith-Ayala, Emilie, 172–173
Snow Queen, The, 245–246
Sogabe, Aki, 87–88
Solo, 308–309
Som See and the Magic Elephant, 97–98
Somewhere in Africa, 48–49
Song of the Chirimia: A Guatemalan Folktale, 173–174
Soto, Gloria, 186–187
Spagnoli, Cathy, 64–65

Speidel, Sandra, 153–154
Spirin, Gennady, 221–223, 230–231
Spirit of Hope, 319–320
Spurll, Barbara, 42, 55–56
Stanley, Dian, 285–286
Steele, Philip, 71–72
Stevenson, Harvey, 143–144
Stock, Catherine, 51, 139–141, 156–157
Stone Lion, The, 98–100
Stone, Marti, 274–275
Stonehook Schooner, The, 125–126
Stow, Jenny, 161–162
Streets Are Free, The, 9, 196–197
Supergrandpa, 273–274
Suzán, Gerardo, 179–181

Tagore, Rabindranath, 80–81
Tale of Hilda Louise, The, 255
Tale of the Mandarin Ducks, The, 91–92
Tale of Tsar Saltan, The, 230–231
Tangerine Tree, The, 143–144
Tano and Binti: Two Chimpanzees Return to the Wild, 30–31
Tap-Tap, 139–141
Teague, Ken, 69–70
Thompson, Ian, 71–72
Thousand and One Nights, The, 288, 296–297
Three Golden Keys, The, 205–206
Three Princes, The, 294–295
Tim O'Toole and the Wee Folk, 267–268
Tobin, B., 327
Too Much Talk, 32–33
Topooco, Eusebio, 189–190

Torres, Leyla, 193–194
Tortoise and the Hare, 42
Trivas, Irene, 213–214
Troshkov, Andrei, 226–228
Tukama Tootles the Flute: A Tale From the Antilles, 134–136
Turnip, The, 232–233
Two Pairs of Shoes, 126–127

Ubar, the Lost City of Brass, 296–297
Uchida, Yoshiko, 88–90
UNICEF, 233–234

Van Nutt, Robert, 72–73, 210–211
Varvasovszky, Lasio, 244–245
Vejigante Masquerader, 151–152
Vitale, Stefano, 32–33
Vivas, Julie, 207–208, 272–273, 317–318
Voice of the Wood, The, 269–270
Volkmer, Jane Anne, 173–174

Wade, Gini, 288–289
Wade, Jan, 320
Waira's First Journey, 189–190
Wales, Anthony, 112–113
Wallner, John, 74–75
Walter the Baker, 259–260
Water Shell, The, 325–326
Watson, Mary, 23–24
Watson, Pete, 10, 23–24
Welcome Back Sun, 271–272
Wells, Ruth, 84
Wheatley, Nadia, 315–317
When Chickens Grow Teeth, 255–256
Where Are You Going, Manyoni?, 51
Where is Gah-Ning, 127–128
Whose Chick Is That?, 320

Wijngaard, Juan, 283–285
Wild, Margaret, 11, 207–208
Williams, Geoffrey T., 307–308
Williams, Karen Lynn, 139–141
Williams, Laura E., 86–87
Wilson, Sharon, 44–46
Wings, 263–264
Winter, Jeanette, 181–182
Winter, Jonah, 181–182
Wiseman, Bernard, 315
Wisniewski, David, 202–204
Wolf Island, 128
Wolkstein, Diane, 283–285
Wonderful Bag, The, 288–289
Wood, Ted, 83
Wynne, Patricia J., 54

Yep, Laurence, 72–73
Yesterday Stone, The, 128–129
Yolen, Jane, 117–118, 136–137, 263–264
Yoshi, 84
You Be the Witch, 320–321
Young Painter, A: The Life and Paintings of Wang Yani— China's Extraordinary Young Artist, 76–77
Young, Ed, 39–40

Zagwyn, Deborah Turney, 124–125
Zamorano, Ana, 272–273
Zawadzki, Mark, 90–91
Zhensun, Zheng, 76–77
Zola, Meguido, 118–119
Zolotow, Charlotte, 254–255
Zomo the Rabbit: A Trickster Tale From West Africa, 56–57
Zubizarreta, Rosa, 182–184

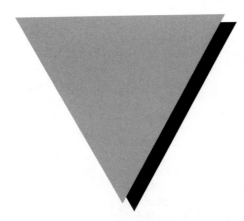

Subject Index

Aborigines, Australian, 309–310
  rainbow snakes and, 313–314
Acting. See Dramatization, story
Adulthood, passage to, 49
Adventure stories, 344
Advertising, market simulation and, 139–141
Advice
  following good, 285–286
  seeking, 64–65
Africa, 20–60
  Benin, 22–24
  Cameroon, 24–27
  Egypt, 27–29
  Ethiopia, 29–30
  Gambia, 30–31
  Ghana, 31–33
  Kenya, 33–36
  Lesotho, 36–37
  Madagascar, 37–38
  Morocco, 38–39
  Nigeria, 39–43
  South Africa, 43–49
  studying authors writing about, 50

Sudan, 49
Tanzania, 50
Zimbabwe, 51
Agriculture versus aquaculture, 152–153
Alphabet(s)
  books, 344
  comparing, 27–28
  Cyrillic, 213–214
  developing own book of, 78–79, 190
  in Spanish and English, 182–184
Analysis summary of Pre- and Posttranscultural Awareness of Specific Cultures and Cultural Regions, 341–342
Animals
  African, 52–53
  of Arctic region, 124
  Australian, 313–314, 315, 317–319
  Australian versus Canadian, 114
  books about, 344
  comparing captive/wild habitats of, 30–31

explanatory stories about, 114–115
fabric made from, 66–67
fears of, 187–188
Filipino, 324–325
food chain and, 128
Fox and Mole stories, 194–195
habitats, African wildlife, 35–36
interdependency of plants, humans and, 34
loyalty to master, 221–223
treatment of, 256–257
tree frogs, 321–322
Antarctica, 304–306, 307–309
Antilles, 134–136
Anti-Semitism. See Holocaust
Apologizing to others, 141–142
Aquaculture, 152–153
Aquariums, classroom, 262–263
Arabic culture, 282
Arabic language, 282
  counting using, 293–294
Arctic region
  animals of, 124
  making dioramas of, 113

Argentina, 188–189
Art
    Chinese *versus* U.S., 69–70
    Monet's, 252
    Van Gogh's, 252–254
Artists, social system and, 269
Art projects. *See also* Collage;
        Dioramas; Map(s); Mask-
        making
    animal headbands, 315,
        318–319
    Arctic life mural, 124
    building replicas of Jack's
        house, 161–162
    cardboard box homes, 262
    carnival crafts, 191–192
    carnivals, Caribbean and other,
        151–152
    coloring, 320
    crafts to celebrate Christmas-
        like events, 210–211
    cut paper, forest or wooded
        area, 39–40
    egg painting, Ukrainian,
        233–234
    flowers in vase, 252–254
    folk art, 43
    helping others through,
        185–186
    house on wheels, 319–320
    life themes murals, 181–182
    making paint for, 312
    Maori cultural themes, 323–324
    modeling, 269
    Monet's colors, use of, 252
    natural environments and, 118
    nature study mural, 54
    neighborhood life mural, 317
    nested dolls, Russian, 225–226
    ocean profile, 90–91
    painting animals, 76–77
    painting with natural materials,
        177–178
    paper cutouts, special
        moments, 86–87
    passports, making, 213–214
    props and costumes, 94
    protest banners/signs, 196–197
    puppet-making, 283–285

    Rainbow Serpents, 313–314
    sacrifice for others, illustrating,
        202–204
    sculpting, 269
    seasons, 297–298
    shadowboxes, 244–245
    Tarascan people, 186–187
    tree frogs, 321–322
    turtle backs, 122
    volcanoes, 169–170
    water color mural of islands,
        325–326
Arts and crafts books, 345
Asia, 62–106
    Cambodia, 64–65
    China (People's Republic of),
        65–77
    India, 77–83
    Japan, 84–92
    Korea, 92–95
    Nepal, 95
    Thailand, 96–98
    Tibet, 98–100
    Vietnam, 100–102
Australia, 304–306, 309–321
    aborigines in, 309–314
    animals of, 314–315
    birds of, 312, 320
    bush country, 317–318
    folktales of, 318–319
    geographical history of,
        315–317
    homes in, *versus* U.S. homes,
        320–321
    illustrating life in, 114
    life in, 319–321
    stereotyping of people from, 327
Austria, 242–245
Author studies, 50
Aztec myths, 184–185

Baba Yaga stories, variations in,
        216–217, 225–226
Babylonian pottery and tombs,
        297–298
Bahamas, 136–137
Ballet, learning about, 219–221
Bananas, taste of, 39–40
Banishment, 259–260

Banshee spirit, 264–265
Beading activity, 126–127
Bedtime stories, 97
Beethoven, Ludwig van, 242–244
Behavior, lessons in, 324–325
Beliefs
    personal, standing up for,
        170–171
    societal, 43
Bells, activities with, 251–252, 268
Benin, 22–24
Bicycle races, 273–274
Biographies, 345
Birds
    in Australia, 312, 320
    books about, 345
    emperor penguins, 308–309
    migratory, 101–102
    puffin rescue, night-time,
        263–264
    symbolic, 84–85
Boat books, 345
Bolivia, 189–190
Book bonding, 3, 6
    transcultural children's
        literature, children and, 5
Book production/assembly
    alphabet, 78–79, 190
    cookbooks, 79–80
    counting-books, 162, 290–291
    creation myths, 184–185
    desktop publishing, 257–258
    family stories, 146–147
    games and friendship, 148–149
    miscommunications, 70–71
    research results, 84, 136–137
    Russian dictionary, 213–214
    sayings, country, 70–71
    science scrapbook, 190
    special moment, 86–87
Borneo, 321–322
Brazil, 190–193
Buses, riding, 139–141
    book about, 346
Business practices, market
        simulation and, 139–141
Butterfly project, 179–181

Caliphs, books about, 355

Calligraphy, 73–74
Cambodia, 64–65
Cameroon, 24–27
Canada, 108–131
    Arctic Circle region, 110–111,
        113, 120–121, 124
    Canadian geese, 117–118
    Chinese in, 127–128
    Cree Indians of, 114–115,
        121–122, 126–127
    French, 124–125
    Gaspe Peninsula region, 122–123
    Indians of, 119–120, 128–129
    Inuits of, 124
    Lake Ontario port region,
        125–126
    Metis Indians of, 118–119
    moose of, 120
    Ojibway Indian stories, 122,
        123–124
    Ontario, northern region of, 128
    prairie land of, 118
    Prince Edward Island, 112–113
    provinces and territories, 108
    Quebec, 111–112
Caribbean, 132–164
    Antilles, 134–136
    Bahamas, 136–137
    cultural region of, 134
    Dominican Republic, 137–138
    Haiti, 138–141
    Jamaica, 141–144
    Martinique, 144–146
    Puerto Rico, 146–152
    St. Lucia, 152–153
    Trinidad and Tobago, 153–158
    U.S. Virgin Islands, 158–159
Carnival(s), 151–152
    Brazil, 191–192
Carpets, Persian, 286–287
Cats, 87–88
Cattle ranching, Argentine versus
    U.S., 188–189
Celebrations, books about, 346.
    See also Christmas; Holiday
    celebrations
Cello playing, 269–270
Central America, 165–188,
    197–199

El Salvador, 169–170
    Guatemala, 170–174
    Mexico, 178–188
    Nicaragua, 174–176
    Panama, 176–178
Challenge, personal, 43
Change(s)
    agent of, 4, 196–197
    character transformation,
        64–65
    coping with, 29–30
    drastic versus incremental,
        262–263
Children
    abduction of, 244–245
    resolving problems, books
        about, 346
Children's literature in changing
        world, 1–18
    book bonding and, 6
    ensuring authentic portrayal of
        cultures in, 6
    making connections in, 6–12
    selecting transcultural, 12–16
    transcultural, 1–6
    world connections, 12–17
China (People's Republic of),
        65–77
    ancient China, 66–70, 74–75
    language of, writing, 73–74
    legends of, 75–76
    modern, 71–72, 76–77
Choices, making, 233–234
Christmas. See also Holiday
        celebrations
    celebrations, other countries',
        210–211
    in Central and South America,
        176–177
    music, other countries',
        208–210
    at Repulse Bay, Canada,
        110–111
Cinderella stories
    Korean, 100–101
    Nigerian, 40–41
    Russian, 214–216
Circus, 256–257
    books about, 346

Russian, 221–223
Cities
    books about, 346–347
    great, 254–255
Citizenship, cultural paradigm and,
        11
City life
    books about, 346–347
    versus country life, 48–49, 96
Civil rights movement, U.S.,
        206–207
Cleverness versus wisdom, 291–292
Climate
    clothing and, 26–27
    cultural paradigm and, 7
    housing and, 161–162
    Israeli, 289–290
Clocks, Swiss cuckoo, 274–275
Clothing. See also Weaving
    books about, 347
    China versus U.S., 69–70
    royal, of African rulers, 26–27
Clowns, Russian versus U.S.,
        221–223
Cobwebs, 74–75
Coconut water, tasting, 154–156
Co-cultures, U.S., 134
Collage
    animal, 194–195
    of seasons, 297–298
    story, 127–128
Colombia, 193–194
Communication
    email, students in other
        countries and, 137–138
    and miscommunication, 70–71
    with rest of world, 12–17,
        80–82
Communities. See also
        Neighborhood(s)
    in Africa, 22–23
    individual contribution to,
        27–28
Compassion, lack of, 68–69
Concentration camps, 206–208
Condors, learning about, 189–190
Confidence, gaining, 208–210
Conquering peoples,
        consequences of, 136–137

Contests, books about, 358
Controversy, researching, 83
Cookbooks, 79–80
Cooking activity, 121–122. See also
    Food
    Australian food, 317–318
    baking pretzels, 260
    books about, 351–352
    making stew, 193–194
    oysters, 312–313
    Spanish foods, 272–273
Costumes, oral storytelling and,
    294–295
Counting-books, 357
    activity involving, 120–121
    making, 162, 290–291
    two-language, 293–294
Country life/setting
    animal life in, 53
    versus city life, 48–49, 96
Courage, books about, 347
Cowboys, books about, 347
Crafts. See Art projects
Cranes, white, of Japan, 84–85
Creation myths. See also Folktale(s)
    Australian, 318–319
    Aztec music, 184–185
    Chinese, 74–75
    Puerto Rican, 147–148
    Scandinavian, 245–246
Criticism, self-, 233–234
Cuckoo clocks, Swiss, 274–275
Cultural paradigm, 6–12
    economic system, 8–10
    geography, 7–8
    political system, 11–12
    reference classification chart,
        17
    social system, 10–11
Cultural regions/neighborhoods, 6
Culture(s)
    African, 52
    differences of, 112–113
    ensuring authentic portrayal of,
        6
    personal problem solving and,
        159–161
Cyrillic alphabet, 213–214
Czech Republic, 201–206

Daily life, books about, 347
Dance
    books about, 347
    The Firebird Suite and, 219–221
    Indian Round, 121–122
    morris, 250–251
Dangerous situations, books
    about, 347–348
Dark, fear of, 264–265
    learning to cope with, 270–271
Death
    books about, 348
    coping with, 29–30
    of father, the king, 37–38
Debate, group, 94–95
Decisions, moral, 46–47
Democracy, participatory, 44–46,
    196–197
Denmark, 245–246
Deserts
    books about, 348
    learning about, 38–39
    life in, 49
Desktop publishing, 257–258
Diamonds, creation of, 74–75
Diaries, keeping, 251–252,
    283–285, 307–308, 309–310
Dictating stories. See also Making-
    up stories; Stories; Telling
    stories; Writing
    animal tales, 122–123
    bedtime lullabies, 97
    about Caribbean travel,
        149–150
    contemporary Cinderella,
        100–101
    about enchanted favorite toys,
        217–218
    nested dolls stories, 225–226
    about pets, 122–123
    about special talents/interests,
        76–77
Difference. See also Gender roles
    among people, 218–219
    cultural, 112–113
Digging, pretend backyard holes,
    114
Dioramas. See also Art projects
    Antarctic, 307, 308–309

Central America, volcanoes
    and, 169–170
    icy sea, 113
    of the seasons, 123–124
Discovery, concept of, 66–67
Discussion groups
    comparing Jack's houses
        variations, 161–162
    love, nature of, 219–221
    personal problem solving and,
        159–161
Divorce, coping with, 29–30
    books about, 355
Dock, field trip to, 319–320
Dogs, skills of, 246–247
Dolphins versus sharks, 154–156
Dominican Republic, 137–138
Doubling, power of, 79–80, 82–83
Doubt, self-, 208–210
Dragon myths, 74–75
Dramatization, story. See also
    Readers' theater
    presentation
    Arabian Nights: Three Tales,
        296–297
    Baby Baboon, 53
    Borreguita and the Coyote,
        178–179
    The Bravest Flute, 171–172
    The Enchanted Storks, 287–288
    The Fish Skin, 114–115
    The Flying Tortoise, 42
    The Goodnight Story, 115–116
    The Great Kapok Tree, 192–193
    Kylie's Concert, 314
    The Legend of King Arthur,
        249–250
    The Match Between the Winds,
        321–322
    The Moles and the Mireuk, 94
    Mucky Moose, 120
    The Pumpkin Blanket, 124–125
    Rapunzel, 258–259
    Rata, Pata, Scata, Fata: A
        Caribbean Story, 158–159
    The Snow Queen, 245–246
    Spirit of Hope, 319–320
    Tim O'Toole and the Wee Folk,
        267–268

Too Much Talk, 32–33
Where is Gah-Ning?, 127–128
Drawing. *See* Illustrations, drawing
Dreams. *See also* Wishes
actualizing, 101–102
drawing perfect, 68–69
Drought, books about, 358
Drums, making, 121–122
Ducks, mandarin, 91–92

Eastern Europe, 200–238
Czech Republic, 201–206
Poland, 206–208
Romania, 208–213
Russian Federation, 213–233
Ukraine, 233–234
Yugoslavia, former, 234–235
Ecology, books about, 348
Economic systems
African types of, 52
chart of, 9
cultural paradigm and, 8–10
imaginary worlds, 230–231
market simulation and,
139–141, 157–158
medieval, 257–258
relationship with social systems
and, 44
resource conservation and, 83
Ecosystem, concept of, 54
Egg incubating activity, 117–118,
255–256
Egg painting, Ukrainian, 233–234
Egypt, 27–29, 282
Elections, mock, 46
Ellis Island National Park, 143–144
El Salvador, 169–170
Email
Congressional representatives
and, 46
games in different countries
and, 148–149
Net pals and, 144–146
students in other countries
and, 137–138
world connections and, 80–81
Emperors, books about, 355
Empress, as discoverer, 66–67
Endangered species, 190–191

in rain forests, 192–193
England, 246–251
Environment(s)
books about, 348
elements of, 118
endangered species, 190–191,
192–193
follow-the-leader activity and,
120–121
learning about, 119–120
preserving beauty in nature
and, 186–187
Ethics, 245–246
books about, 348–349
Ethiopia, 29–30
Europe. *See* Eastern Europe;
Western Europe
Everyday life, books about,
348–349
Expectations, peer *versus* parental
versus self, 141–142
Experience, belief that comes with,
32–33
Explanatory stories. *See also*
Creation myths
Canadian, 114–115
good *versus* evil, 245–246
Korean, 92–93
personal environment, 184–185

Fabric construction, 66–67
Factory, field trip to, 319–320
Families. *See also* Heritage,
ancestral
books about, 349
celebratory events of, 208–210
child's place in, 36
displaced, 136–137, 143–144
entertainment in, 116–117
extended, in Africa, 22–23,
47–48
individual contribution to,
27–28
interdependence of, 319–320
picnics/outdoor adventures of,
312–313
similarities of, across cultures,
35
single-parent, 244–245

Farms/farming, books about, 350
Fate
changing one's, 260–261
group debate about, 94–95
Father, books about, 350
Favorite places, 204–206
Favorite toys, enchanted, 217–218
Fear, coping with, 55–56, 142–143
books about, 350
danger and, 270–271
darkness and, 264–265
important roles and, 187–188
of others, 218–219
Feelings, discussing, 67–68
Festivals, 75–76
Firebird stories, 226–228
Firebird Suite, The, 219–221
Fish/fishing, 190–191
books about, 350
Flying, 255
paper airplanes, 263–264
Folktale(s). *See also* Creation myths;
Explanatory stories;
Trickster tales
animals with magical abilities,
91–92
Australian, 318–319
books, 350–351
Cambodian, 64–65
coyote or wolf, 178–179
discovering similar, 69
Japanese, 88–90, 91–92
Korean, 92–93, 94
mathematical, from India,
79–80, 82–83
Middle Eastern, 282, 300
Milky Way, 75–76
Russian Federation, 214–221,
226–231
West African, 40–41
from Yoruba, 42–43
Follow-the-leader activity, 120–121
baby kangaroo's friends, 315
Guatemalan mountains,
172–173
Food. *See also* Cooking activity
Australian, 317–318
books about, 351–352
Caribbean, 134–136

Food. *See also* Cooking activity, *continued*
chain, of animals and plants, 128
Chinese *versus* U.S., 69–70
holiday meals, 142–143, 156–157
oysters, 312–313
Spanish foods, 272–273
staples, rice as, 79–80
sweet *versus* bitter, 39–40
variety in, 112–113
Forests. *See* Rain forests
Fox and Mole stories, 194–195
France, 251–256
French, learning, 111–112
Friends
books about, 352
desertion by, 269–270
letterwriting with, 143–144
making and keeping, 144–146, 148–149
Frogs, 91–92
Frustration, coping with, 259–260
Future
books about, 352
variations in prediction of, 24–26

Gambia, 30–31
Games
blowing contest, 321–322
books about, 352
buried treasure, 266–267
family, 116–117
favorite, 148–149
non-television, 154–156
question-and-answer, cultural learning and, 52
quiz, of "Whose Chick is That?", 320
rainy day, 41
Where is Gah-Ning?, 127–128
winter, 111–112
wonderful-bag, 287–288
Gardening activity, 118–119, 232–233. *See also* Plants
books about, 357
as honorable occupation, 182–184

pumpkins, 147–148
Gender roles, 211–213, 282. *See also* Difference
Geography
as African theme, 22
cultural paradigm and, 7–8
East African, 53
Himalayas, 96
swamps, worldwide, 90
Germany, 256–260
Ghana, 31–33
Giant stories, 134–136
Giving, 260–261
Globe, geography activity using, 271–272
Gods/goddesses, books about, 352
Good luck. *See* Luck
Goree Island (near Senegal, Africa), 143–144
Government. *See* Political systems
Grandparents, 179–181
books about, 352–353
Russian *versus* other countries', 217–218
Greece, 260–264
Greed, 68–69
Growing, books about, 353
Growing up, 90–91
Guatemala, 170–174
Gutenberg, Johann, 257–258

Haiti, 138–141
Halloween, mask-making and, 151–152
Hands, 260–261
Hang gliding, 255
Health, books about, 353
Hebrew
counting in, 290–291, 292–293
learning, 211–213
Helping others, 150–151
through arts and crafts, 185–186
books about, 353
risks of, 91–92
Heritage, ancestral. *See also* Families
cultural understanding and, 5, 118–119
gardening and, 118–119

versus modern day life, 244–245
neighborhood, 317
stories of, 86–87, 146–147, 310–311
Heroes, cultural, 242–244
Hiking, books about, 353
Himalayas
as geographic backdrop, 98–100
learning about, 77–78, 96
History
books about, 353
recent events, transcultural book publication quantities and, 333–335
Holiday celebrations, 142–143, 156–157, 208–210
Holocaust, 202–204, 206–208, 270–271
Homesickness, 221–223
Honesty
books about, 353
personal, 67–68
Houses
books about, 354
comparing Jack's, 161–162
Humans, interdependency of plant, animals and, 34
Humorous books, 354

Iceland, 264–265
Identity, mistaken, 55–56
Illustrations, drawing, 41, 57
animal tales, 56–57
Arctic life, 124
Australian trickster tales, 322–323
about Caribbean travel, 149–150
diaries, 251–252
enchanted favorite toys, 217–218
environment, personal, 118
food chain of plants and animals, 128
of home town, 254–255
of new environments, 154–156
painting animals, 76–77
of pets, 122–123
of plants growing, 67–68
of puffins, 264–265
tapestries, 68–69

about traveling to Caribbean, 149–150
of winter without sunshine, 271–272
Illustrations, learning about, 298–300
Imaginary happenings, books about, 354
Imaginary worlds, creating, 230–231. *See also* Making-up stories
Immigrant experiences, U.S., 143–144
Immigration, transcultural book publication quantities and, 333–335
Impact, of small and insignificant things, 66–67
Impairments, books about, 355
Importance, role of, 187–188
India, 77–83
Indians, books about, 355
Indigenous people, 136–137
    Brazil, 191–192
    Central America, South America, Mexico, 168
Inexplicable experiences, 54–55
Interests, special, 76–77
Internet
    Circumbaikal Railway and, 224–225
    connecting with world and, 80–81
    Ellis Island National Park and, 143–144
    email, Net pals and, 144–146
    Prague/Czech Republic and, 205–206
    researching other countries with, 137–138
    scientific information about Venus and, 54–55
    silk, researching, 66–67
    U.S. Holocaust Memorial Museum and, 206–208
    war, children discussing on, 234–235
Interviews, student, 137–138
    with older relatives/friends, 147–148, 205–206
Inuits, Christmas trees and, 110–111

Iran, 282–287
Iraq, 287–289
Ireland, 265–268
Israel, 289–292
    founding of, 202–204, 207–208
Italy, 268–270

Jack and the Beanstalk, and other giants, 134–136
Jack tales, 248–249
Jamaica, 141–144
Japan, 84–92
    ancestral heritage and, 86–87
    exploring culture of, 84
    folktales, 88–90, 91–92
    ocean and, 90–91
    poetry of, 85–86
    rural northern region of, 87–88
    white cranes' significance for, 84–85
Jews
    history of, 202–204, 206–207
    religious beliefs of, 283–285
    traditions of, 211–213
    during World War II in Europe, 270–271
Job, success in, 289–290
Judging others, 225–226
    before knowing them, 218–219
    unfairly, 216–217
Judgment
    books about, 355
    old Baghdad system of, 288–289

Kenya, 33–36
Kindness
    concept of, 72–73, 84–85
    extending, to someone in need, 141–142
King Arthur legend, 249–250
Kings, books about, 26–27, 28–29, 31–32, 37–38, 50, 355
Korea, 92–95

Labor/labor problems, books about, 355
Language(s), studying other, 73–74
    Arabic, 293–294
    French, 111–112

Hebrew, 211–213, 290–291, 293–294
    Russian, 213–214
    Spanish, 173–174, 188–189, 272–273
Leaders
    Baghdad caliphs, magic spells of, 287–288
    empress, as discoverer, 66–67
    kings, expectations of, 31–32
    moral decisions of, 46–47
    responsibilities of, 37–38
    world, expectations of, 32
    writing to Congressional, 46
Lebanon, 282, 292–293
Legends. *See* Folktale(s)
Lesotho, 36–37
Lessons, hard to learn, 134–136
Letters, writing, 143–144, 283–285
    to the president, 298–300
Levitation, power of, 87–88
Library
    books about, 355–356
    visit to, 48–49
Life
    country *versus* city, 48–49, 96
    cycle of, 37–38, 77–78
    learning from, 83
    ocean, 90–91
    other's control of, 46–47
    rural island, 154–156
    Russian girl's *versus* U.S. student's, 228
    simple, quiet, 87–88
Llamas, learning about, 189–190
London, England, 247–248
    versus Paris, 254–255
Lords, books about, 355
Losing *versus* winning, 273–274
Lost, coping with being, 38–39
Love, nature of, 219–221
    books about, 356
    good *versus* evil and, 245–246
Loyalty, 144–146, 285–286
    books about, 356
Luck
    bad, 260–261
    good, 97–98
    symbols of, 75–76

Lullabies, creating, 97
Lying, 67–68
    lost money and, 174–176

Madagascar, 37–38
Magic
    books about, 354
    inventing spells, 287–288
    words, wishes and, 158–159
Making-up stories. *See also*
        Dictating stories; Stories;
        Telling stories; Writing
    about creation, 318–319
    about teaching behavior,
      324–325
Mandela, Nelson, 46–47
Maori culture, 322–324
Map(s). *See also* Art projects
    Australia, 317–318
    Axis domination in Europe,
      206–207
    of Canada, making, 125–126
    global awareness and, 80–82
    imaginary worlds, 230–231
    Israeli kibbutz, 289–290
    locating places on, 315–317
    migratory bird, 101–102
    neighborhood, 289–290,
      315–317
    recording places visited on,
      80–81
    Siberia, Circumbaikal Railway,
      224–225
    student community and school,
      138–139
Mardi Gras, mask-making and,
    151–152
Markets
    in Africa, 22–23
    books about, 356
    discoveries and, 66–67
    open air *versus* shopping malls,
      139–141
    outdoor, 23–24, 157–158
    simulation of, 139–141
    in South America, 193–194
Marriage, books about, 356
Martinique, 144–146
Masai culture, 35

legend of Venus and, 55
Mask-making, 53. *See also* Art
    projects
    animals, 314
    dramatizing explanatory stories
      and, 114–115
    story reenactment and,
      115–116
    vejigante, 151–152
Mathematics, 79–80, 82–83
Maya, learning about, 172–173
Memories, sharing, 86–87
Messages
    alteration of, 70–71
    books about, 356
Mexico, 167–169, 178–188,
    197–199
Michelangelo, 269
Middle East, 280–302
    Iran, 282–287
    Iraq, 287–289
    Israel, 289–292
    Lebanon, 292–293
    Saudi Arabia, 293–295
    stereotyping of people from,
      282
    Syria, 295–298
    West Bank, 298–300
Milky Way, discovering the, 75–76
Mistaken identity, 55–56
Mobiles, painted egg, 233–234
Monet, Claude, 252
Money
    balancing principles and need
      for, 152–153
    books about earning, 356
    lost, dealing with, 174–176
    market day at school and,
      139–141
    unlimited supply of, 88–90,
      98–100
Moon, books about, 356
Moral decisions, 46–47
Moral lessons, 40–41, 43,
    258–259, 285–286
Moral problems, books about,
    348–349
Moral values, 67–68, 245–246
Morocco, 38–39

Mother, books about, 356–357
Mountains, learning about, 96
    Himalayas, 77–78
    life in, 98–100
Multicultural children's literature, 3
Multicultural education, 2–3
    book bonding and, 3
Music
    Australian aborigine, 309–310
    Aztec creation myth about,
      184–185
    Beethoven's, 242–244
    books about, 357
    Caribbean, 134–136, 153–154
    cello, 269–270
    Christmas, other countries',
      208–210
    comparisons of, 134–136
    Czechoslovakian, 204–206
    drums, construction for,
      121–122
    flute, 173–174
    Indian flute, 171–172
    lullaby writing, 97
    morris dancing and, 250–251
    poetry and, 85–86
    Russian dance, 219–221
    water-glass "bells" activity, 268
Mysterious experiences, 54–55
Myths. *See also* Creation myths;
      Explanatory stories
    Greek, 261, 263–264

Natural phenomena
    describing, 120–121
    explaining, 33, 73
    history of, 54
    recording personal environment
      of, 118
Natural resources
    conservation of, economic
      systems and, 83
    cultural paradigm and, 7
    preserving/planting trees,
      119–120
    principles about *versus*
      economic need, 152–153
Neighborhood(s)
    cultural regions and, 6

discovering own, 317
maps of, 289–290, 315–317
Nepal, 95
Nested dolls, Russian, 225–226
Netherlands, 270–271
News broadcasts, global, 80–81
News events, transcultural book
publication quantities and,
333–335
Newspaper(s)
visiting a, 257–258
writing for, 196–197
New Zealand, 304–306, 322–324
Nicaragua, 174–176
Nigeria, 39–43
Night-time puffin rescue, 263–264
Norway, 271–272
Numbers, books about, 357
Nursing home, visiting/storytelling
in, 179–181

Occupations, books about, 355
Oceans
life in, 90–91
overfishing, 152–153
Older, advantages of being, 50
Oral history, recording, 137–138,
205–206
Oral storytelling, 178–179,
248–249, 294–295
Oral traditions, learning about, 42
Orphanages, 255
Owls, white, 256–257
Oysters, learning about, 312–313

Paints, making, 312
Panama, 176–178
Parasailing, 255
Parental expectations, 141–142
Paris, France, 254–255
Peace, children promoting, 298–300
Peer expectations, 141–142
Penguins, emperor, 308–309
Performances, books about, 357
Persian carpets, 286–287
Personal experience
belief that comes with, 32–33
learning from, 83
memories, sharing, 86–87

Peru, 194–195
Pets, stories about, 122–123,
221–223, 246–247
Pharaohs, books about, 355
Philippines, 324–325
Photographs/photography
comparing special places using,
137–138
environment, personal, 118
family scrapbooks of, 86–87
ocean creatures, 90–91
versus paintings, 254–255
spelling with, 78–79
studying topic of, 78–79
Picture books, Arabic nations and,
282
Piñata parties, 187–188
Pirates, learning about, 146–147
Plants. See also Gardening activity
African, 52–53
around Jack's houses, 161–162
books about, 357
fabric made from, 66–67
food chain and, 128
growing, 67–68
interdependence of animals,
humans and, 34
life cycle of, 77–78
Poetry
books of, 357
writing, 41, 85–86, 153–154
Poland, 206–208
Polar bears, 124
Political concerns, books about,
357–358
Political systems
change in, 44
chart of, 12
cultural paradigm and, 11–12
England versus U.S., 247–248
Esther's Story, 283–285
imaginary worlds, 230–231
mistreatment by, 206–207
monarchy versus morality,
263–264
participatory democracies,
44–46, 196–197
statements about, through art,
181–182

succession controversies of,
249–250
Polling places, visiting, 46
Polynesian Islands, 325–326
Postassessment Questionnaire of
Students' Transcultural
Awareness of a Specific
Culture and Cultural Region,
339, 341
Poster displays
dreams, actualizing, 101–102
endangered species, 190–191
fabric manufacture, 66–67
frogs, research on, 92–93
about traveling to Caribbean,
149–150
Pourqoi stories, 42, 93
Preassessment Questionnaire of
Students' Transcultural
Awareness of a Specific
Culture and Cultural Region,
339, 341
Printing shops, 257–258
Problems, personal, 159–161
Problem-solving activity, 232–233
Promises
books about, 358
impossible, 211–213
Props, oral storytelling and,
294–295
Puerto Rico, 146–152
Puffins, 263–264
Pumpkin blankets, making,
124–125
Pumpkins, creative uses of,
147–148
Puppet shows, 178–179, 192–193,
217–218, 283–286

Queens, books about, 355

Rabbits, in folktales, 64–65
Racing
books about, 358
purpose of, 273–274
Radio, shortwave, 80–81
Railroads, 224–225
Rain, books about, 358
Rain forests, 146–147

books about, 358
endangerment of, 192–193
U.S. forests *versus*, 39–40
Rajas, books about, 355
Ranches
books about, 350
life on, 188–189
Readers' theater presentation,
283–285, 296–297
Religion
books about, 358
Chinese *versus* U.S. beliefs,
69–70
Remarriage, books about, 355
Repulse Bay, Canada, 110–111
Research
citation of sources for, 70–71
other countries, with Internet,
137–138
potential, transcultural
children's literature and, 5–6
rain/thunder/lightning
explanations, 72–73
results, book production/
assembly and, 136–137
scientific method and, 77–78
silk, on Internet, 66–67
Venus, on Internet, 54–55
Resource conservation. *See* Natural
resources
Respect, concept of, 72–73, 84–85
Rhyming stories, cumulative, 223
Rice, learning about, 79–80, 113
Rivera, Diego, 181–182
Romania, 208–213
Rugs, Persian, 286–287
Rulers, expectations of, 32
Rumors, dealing with, 170–171
Rural settings. *See* Country
life/setting
Russian, learning, 213–214
Russian Federation, 213–233
Baba Yaga stories, variations in,
216–217, 225–226
Cinderella stories, 214–216
circus in, 221–223
dance in, 219–221
folktales of, 214–221, 226–231
history of, 223

nested dolls, 225–226
railroads in, 224–225

Sacrifices, for others, 202–204
Safety
foolhardy risks and, 263–264
travel and, 127–128
during war, 292–293
Sahara Desert, 38–39
St. Lucia, 152–153
Salt, learning about, 228–230
Saudi Arabia, 293–295
Sayings, country, 70–71
on good luck, 97–98
School
bus rides to, 139–141
importance of, 46–47
learning at, 138–139
on the way to, 51, 138–139
Schooners, stonehook, 125–126
Science, legends and, 55, 72–73
creation myths, 74–75
Scientific method, 77–78. *See also*
Research
Sculpting, 269
Seasons, 111–112, 297–298
Secrets, sharing, 27–28
Selecting transcultural children's
literature, 12–16
complementary techniques for,
16
guidelines, 13–15
Self-criticism, 233–234
Self-doubt, 208–210
Separation, books about, 348
Shadowboxes, 244–245
Shared book collections, 40
Sharks *versus* dolphins, 154–156
Ship, field trip to, 319–320
Shoes, activities with, 126–127
Shopping malls *versus* open-air
markets, 139–141
Shortwave radio, world
connections and, 80–81
Siblings
feelings about, 98–100
rivalry among, 228–230
Silk fabric, making of, 66–67,
74–75

Singing, poetry and, 85–86
Slave(s)
Brazilian, 191–192
Central America, South
America, Mexico and, 168
versus immigrant experience,
143–144
U.S. history of, 150–151
Snakes, 313–314
Social systems
African types of, 52
artists and, 269
chart of, 10
cultural paradigm and, 10–11
helping others and, 150–151
national races (competitions)
and, 273–274
racing and, 273–274
relationship with economic
systems, 44
Sounds, personal, 27–28
South Africa, 43–49
Cape Town, 48–49
extended families in, 47–48
Mandela and, 46–47
political change in, 43–44
voting in, for black people,
44–46
South America, 167–169, 188–199
Argentina, 188–189
Bolivia, 189–190
Brazil, 190–193
Colombia, 193–194
Peru, 194–195
Venezuela, 195–197
South Pacific, 304–329
Antarctica, 307–309
Australia, 309–321
Borneo, 321–322
New Zealand, 323–324
Philippines, 324–325
Polynesian Islands, 325–326
Soviet Union, former. *See* Russian
Federation
Spain, 272–273
Spanish
learning, 173–174, 188–189,
272–273
stories in English and, 194–195

Speaking different languages, 73–74
Special moment class book, 86–87
Spider webs, 74–75
Spring, changes of, 111–112
Stars
    books about, 356
    constellations, learning about, 36–37
    Milky Way, discovering the, 75–76
Stereotyping
    of Australians, 327
    of gender roles, 282
    of Middle Easterners, 282
Stones, special, 128–129
Stories. See also Dictating stories; Making-up stories; Telling stories; Writing
    about Christmas in Central and South America, 176–177
    about favorite places, 204–206
    generational, 86–87, 146–147, 310–311
    about gods/goddesses, 261
    as legends, 249–250
    on-the-way-to school, 51, 138–139
    special stones, 128–129
    about visiting Guatemala, 172–173
Story reenactment. See Dramatization, story
Story review chart, 16
Storytelling, 42
    circle, about traveling to Caribbean, 150
    oral, 178–179, 248–249, 294–295
    wall hangings, 125
Stravinsky, Igor, 219–221
Sudan, 49
Sugar cane, learning about, 146–147
Swamps, concept of, 88–90
Sweden, 273–274
Switzerland, 274–275
Symbols, 226–228
    hands as, 260–261

Syria, 295–298

Talents, special, 76–77
Tanzania, 50
Tapestry, discovering, 68–69
Tarascan people
    environmental threats to, 186–187
    straw figures of, 185–186
Teachers, transcultural children's literature and, 5–6
Technology, modern, 257–258. See also Email; Internet
Telling stories. See also Dictating stories; Making-up stories; Stories; Writing
    about being aboriginal, 310–311
    about family, 310–311
    about family picnics/outdoor adventures, 312–313
    in the first-person, 292–293
Thailand, 96–98
Theft, old Baghdad system for, 288–289
Tibet, 98–100
Time lines, 315–317
Tobago, 153–158
Topography, cultural paradigm and, 7
Tortoises, 42. See also Turtles
Tour guides, pretending to be, 96
Tournaments, books about, 358
Transcultural awareness, 338–342
    assessing cultural region awareness, 339, 341, 342
    assessing prior knowledge, 339, 340
Transcultural children's literature, 1–6
    assessing children's responses to, 338–342
    background of, 2
    basic beliefs, 3–6
    book distribution by grade level, 332–333
    book distribution over time, 331–332
    children, book bonding and, 5

conclusions about, 331–338
cultural paradigms in, 337
definition of, 2
genres of, 335, 336
nature of, 5
rationale, 4–5
representative, from cultural and geographic regions, 16–17
research potential of, 5–6
selecting, 12–16
    about specific countries, 333–335, 336
    story elements in, 335, 337, 338
Transgenerational relationships, 146–147
Transportation
    China versus U.S., 69–70
    school bus rides, 139–141
Trans-Siberian Railroad, 224–225
Trapeze, children and, 221–223
Travel
    to Caribbean destinations, 149–150
    to cities, 213–214
    diaries, 251–252
    to London, 247–248
    to modern China, 71–72
    modes of, 127–128
    in Nepal, 96
    planning, 137–138
Treasure, buried, 266–267
Trees, learning about, 119–120, 274–275
Trickster tales, 42
    Maui and the Sun: A Maori Tale, 322–323
    Zomo the Rabbit, 57
Trinidad, 153–158
Trust, betrayal of, 54–55
Truth
    exaggerating, problems with, 211–213
    telling the, 67–68
Tsars, books about, 355
Turtles, art projects and, 42, 122

Ukraine, 233–234
Ultralight flying, 255

U.S. Holocaust Memorial Museum, 206–207
U.S. Virgin Islands, 158–159

Valentine's Day *versus* Chinese Milky Way Festival, 75–76
Values, social, 84–85, 245–246
Van Gogh, Vincent, 252–254
Vendors' specialties, in Africa, 22–24
Venezuela, 195–197
Venn diagrams
    agriculture *versus* aquaculture, 152–153
    life cycles, plants *versus* human, 77–78
    Moscow, Russia *versus* U.S. city, 213–214
    rural *versus* urban life, 96
    Russian girl's life *versus* yours, 228
    students' families *versus* other cultural regions' families, 34–35
Venus, legend *versus* facts about, 54–55
Vietnam, 100–102
Visiting relatives, process of, 47–48
Volcanoes, living near, 169–170
Voting, importance of, 46, 196–197

Walkabout, Australian aborigine, 309–310
War, children discussing, 234–235, 292–293
Wealth, handling, 88–90, 98–100
Weaving, 84–85, 170–171, 286–287
Web sites. *See* Internet
Weights, measuring using, 82–83
Welfare of others. *See also* Economic systems; Political systems; Social systems

concept of, 91–92
conditions for providing, 98–100
West Bank, 298–300
Western Europe, 240–278
    Austria, 242–245
    Denmark, 245–246
    England, 246–251
    France, 251–256
    Germany, 256–260
    Greece, 260–264
    Iceland, 264–265
    Ireland, 265–268
    Italy, 268–270
    Netherlands, 270–271
    Norway, 271–272
    Spain, 272–273
    Sweden, 273–274
    Switzerland, 274–275
Whales, 90–91
Wildlife conservation, 101–102
Wind, power of, 321–322
Winning *versus* losing, 273–274
Winter
    games, 111–112
    special clothing for, 245–246
    without sunshine, 271–272
Wisdom
    acquiring, 56–57, 64–65
    versus cleverness, 291–292
Wishes, magic words and, 158–159. *See also* Dreams
Witches, 320–321
Work, books about, 355
Writing. *See also* Dictating stories; Making-up stories; Stories; Telling stories
    about aboriginal life, 310–311
    about Africa, 50
    alternate endings, 87–88
    animal tales, 56–57, 122–123
    bedtime stories/lullabies, 97

about Caribbean travel, 149–150
Cinderella stories, 100–101, 214–216
to Congressional leaders, 46
in different languages, 73–74
about discoveries, 66–67
about enchanted favorite toys, 217–218
about family picnics/outdoor adventures, 312–313
family stories for class book, 146–147
first-person stories, 292–293
about flying, 255
about homelife, 262
letters, 143–144, 283–285, 298–300
nested dolls stories, 225–226
about new environments, 154–156
for newspapers, 196–197
about pets, 122–123
plays, 283–285
poetry, 41, 85–86
about school, on the way to, 138–139
about special talents/interests, 76–77
about teaching wisdom *versus* cleverness, 291–292

Young, advantages of being, 50
Yugoslavia, former, 234–235

Zimbabwe, 51
Zoos
    llamas in, 189–190
    preparing to visit, 35–36
    treatment of animals in, 256–257

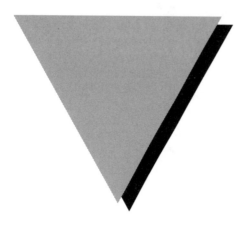

About the Authors

LINDA PRATT

Dr. Linda Pratt has directed a graduate program in reading education and has taught undergraduate and graduate courses in literacy education for over 20 years. Throughout her career she has promoted using children's literature as a core for developing literacy in children and as a vehicle for strengthening teaching proficiencies in preservice and inservice teacher educators. In addition to her on-campus teaching, Dr. Pratt has taught courses to American college students on two islands in the Bahamas, where she has lived part-time for over 17 years. These courses have been field based in elementary and secondary schools and have provided rich transcultural experiences for the American college student participants.

In addition to Dr. Pratt's island living, she has traveled extensively to various parts of the world, including Africa, Asia, Canada, the Caribbean, Eastern Europe, Western Europe, Mexico, and South America. In many of these regions, she has also presented her views on transcultural children's literature. Her ideas have been warmly received by numerous practicing teachers and university educators, who have communicated the direct applicability of Dr. Pratt's views to their own cultures and countries.

JANICE J. BEATY

Dr. Janice J. Beaty has taught children's literature and early graduate levels in the following courses: Introduction to Children's Literature; Adolescent Children's Literature; Childrens's Literature, An Issues Approach; Folktales for Children: The Oral Tradition; and Folklore of the Caribbean.

Her strong interest in the children's literature field derives from her collecting folktales on the island of Guam in the Pacific and on San Salvador Island in the Bahamas, as well as writing children's books during the 1960s: *Plants in His Pack, A Biography of Edward Palmer; Seeker of Seaways, A Biography of Matthew Fontaine Maury;* and *Nufu and the Turkeyfish.*

Dr. Beaty is a world traveler who is especially interested in early childhood and children's literature wherever she goes. She has visited Mexico, Guam, Japan, China, Hong Kong, Taiwan, Bahamas, Bermuda, Trinidad, Tobago, England, Germany, Austria, Czechoslovakia, Hungary, Russia, Poland, Italy, Greece, Lebanon, Syria, Jordan, and Egypt.

Her strong interest in bringing children and books together has prompted her to write text books, as well: *Picture Book Storytelling* and *Building Bridges with Multicultural Picture Books.*

Dr. Beaty is presently engaged as a full-time writer of early childhood textbooks, in working with the Early Childhood Professional Development Network in Columbia, South Carolina, as a guest on their distance-learning broadcasts, and as a coproducer of teacher-training videos. Her textbooks include: *Observing Development of the Young Child, fourth edition; Skills for Preschool Teachers, fifth edition; Building Bridges with Multicultural Picture Books; The Computer as a Paint Brush* (with H. Tucker); *Preschool Appropriate Practices, second edition; Converting Conflicts in Preschool;* and *Picture Book Storytelling.*